Teaching Late-Twentieth-Century Mexicana and Chicana Writers

Teaching Late-Twentieth-Century Mexicana and Chicana Writers

Edited by

Elizabeth Coonrod Martínez

Modern Language Association of America
New York 2021

Printed in the United States of America

Library of Congress Cataloging-in-Publication Data

Name: Martínez, Elizabeth Coonrod, editor.
Title: Teaching late-twentieth-century Mexicana and Chicana writers / edited by Elizabeth Coonrod Martínez.
Description: New York : The Modern Language Association of America, 2021. | Series: Options for teaching, 10792562 ; 53 | Includes bibliographical references. | Summary: "Offers pedagogical techniques for teaching Mexicana and Chicana writers of the late twentieth century in undergraduate classes. Topics include precursors and influences, testimony and chronicle, borderlands culture, gender and identity, cross-cultural connections, and indigeneity. Includes syllabus suggestions and information on editions, reference works, biographies, film adaptations, and online resources"—Provided by publisher.
Identifiers: LCCN 2020028953 (print) | LCCN 2020028954 (ebook) | ISBN 9781603295086 (hardcover) | ISBN 9781603295093 (paperback) | ISBN 9781603295109 (EPUB) | ISBN 9781603295116 (Kindle edition)
Subjects: LCSH: Mexican literature—Women authors—History and criticism. | Mexican literature—Women authors—Study and teaching (Higher). | Mexican literature—20th century—History and criticism. | Women and literature—Mexico—History—20th century. | American literature—Women authors—History and criticism. | American literature—Hispanic American authors—History and criticism. | American literature—Hispanic American authors—Study and teaching (Higher). | American literature—20th century—History and criticism. | Women and literature—United States—History—20th century.
Classification: LCC PQ7133 .T43 2021 (print) | LCC PQ7133 (ebook) | DDC 860.9/92870896872—dc23
LC record available at https://lccn.loc.gov/2020028953
LC ebook record available at https://lccn.loc.gov/2020028954

Options for Teaching 53
ISSN 1079-2562

Cover illustration: Crystal Galindo, *Corazones Cósmicas*, 2015, acrylic on wood.

Published by The Modern Language Association of America
85 Broad Street, Suite 500, New York, New York 10004-2434
www.mla.org

Para mi ahijado, Diego Aguilar, amante de la literatura

Contents

Part V: Drama and Performance

Elizabeth Coonrod Martínez

Introduction: Literary Precursors, Influences, Innovations, and Criticism

What are the similarities and differences among Mexicana writers, Chicana writers, and other Latin American women writers? A common perception is that all Latinas publishing in the late twentieth century wrote about passion and cooking, diaries and love stories, and in a style loosely dubbed magical realism. The work of the Chilean novelist Isabel Allende was marketed in this manner, as was the film created from the Mexican writer Laura Esquivel's first novel, *Como agua para chocolate* (*Like Water for Chocolate*).

Chile and Mexico are of course different nations, and their writers' accounts of life in them are not alike. Still, in the early 1990s teachers in the United States tended to couple texts created in English—such as Sandra Cisneros's *The House on Mango Street*—with English-accessible works, often simply a subtitled film (such as the one adapted from Esquivel's book), with little explanation of differences. Teachers likely adopted this approach because little background was in print, especially in English, on women's literary production. This volume in the Options for Teaching series provides that extensive background, and this introduction points out texts that are in translation. When the essays in this volume mention the titles of foreign-language works, translations are provided parenthetically as an aid to readers; however, the presence of a translated title does not mean that an English-language version of the work is available.

When readers encounter women-centered plots and feminist discourse in creative narratives by notable authors working in a similar time period in different countries, they might feel invited to categorize these authors jointly, but doing so can erase separate sociopolitical and historical experiences. Novelists in the late twentieth century innovated narrative structure, style, and language, adapting a variety of techniques to offer historical assessments and provocative, subtle, and at times defiant discourses. *The House on Mango Street* is often taught in a simplistic manner, perhaps because it is thought to be aimed at younger readers, but at the college level this approach ignores the many layers of significance found between the lines. The multiple layers of discourse in Esquivel's novel are also significant, and it is now possible to connect that novel to the two subsequent books released by the author. Classes today can be designed that feature only the work of Mexicana writers or Chicana writers.

The authors discussed in this volume share a designated literary period, from the late 1970s to the turn of the twenty-first century, and invoke resistance to patriarchal, social, and literary values while inventing new strategies in discourse. But just as each national history is different, each group of writers has distinct precursors, influences, and social interventions. This volume provides essays on primary authors from each nation, followed by essays that consider additional comparative, visual, and other teaching strategies, and finally essays that connect dramatic work to this period, loosely identified as a Latina boom.[1]

Those who teach composition and reading, literature survey courses, and other topics in English or Spanish, as well as cultural studies, Latino studies, interdisciplinary and comparative studies, humanities, and some general education courses, will procure ideas here to engage students' critical thinking and social and historical awareness, and perhaps discover new authors or ideas for their own research. For advanced-level classes, some instructors have shied from assigning novels by women from this period because of misconceptions that they are too "lite,"[2]—a term signifying "unimportant" that was used disparagingly by male critics in Mexico and by a few critics in the United States during the 1990s. Today we know it is easy to be deceived by a *light*-appearing plotline. Promotional practices in the 1990s described works by Latinas as depicting girls and exotic female characters, love affairs, and scintillating recipes. For example, a 1994 New York City magazine ad marketing new novels by Latina writers who shared the same agent used a full-page photograph that was titled "The Four Amigas" and that included Sandra Cisneros, Ana Castillo, Denise Chávez, and Julia Alvarez in smiling poses, sitting or standing together. Not one of them holds her book in the photograph, adding to the impression that the marketing approach was all about their gender and the gender of their characters.

Julia Alvarez's Dominican American experience is different from that of the Chicanas Cisneros and Castillo, who were born in Chicago, or that of Denise Chavez, born in the rural Southwest. In the middle to late twentieth century, Chicanas who grew up in California, New Mexico, Texas, and the Midwest often participated in the civil rights and student movements, as well as protests in the Southwest about land grants and rights taken from their forebears. Meanwhile, in Mexico women writers reacted to the dominant discourses propagated by a political system that upheld certain ideals of the Mexican Revolution while denying rights or access to women and marginalized communities. Mexicana writers emerged from urban or university environments and often participated in writing workshops.

There are a few points of connection between the best-known writers in each nation: Sandra Cisneros was born in 1954, the same year Elena Poniatowska (1932–) published her first book, *Lilus Kikus*, which was discounted by critics because it appeared only to be about a little girl. By the 1990s, when Poniatowska had published several more books and Cisneros's first book was to be reissued by a major press, the two writers shared the same New York literary agent, Susan Bergholz, who asked Poniatowska to prepare a Spanish translation of *The House on Mango Street*, in a promotional exchange between the United States and Mexico. Each author's first book bears a similar callout at its end: the young female character in *Lilus Kikus* resolves in the final chapter to believe in the signs that seem to signal the writer's path, and in *The House on Mango Street* the female narrator vows to seek "a house quiet as snow / a place for myself to go / clean as paper before the poem," again a nod to a life of writing (108). Among critics, there are varying opinions, some referring to *The House on Mango Street* as a novel, others as a series of vignettes or a collection of stories, and the original novella *Lilus Kikus* has been confused with its later rerelease in an edition that also includes a collection of new short stories.

While readers may identify similarities between the two books, each author's work invites greater in-depth study, a process I have occasionally described to students as dissecting the parts. Students enjoy identifying the rebellious and subversive characters in these works, their possible motivations, and how the texts are structured. These elements can lead them to identify female archetypes, uses of imagery, the purposes of recognizable artifacts—recipes, photos, letters, etc.—and from there, the ways innovations and hybrid structures process sociohistorical discourse. As noted by the Latin American literary critic Debra Castillo, "[a]t its best Latin American feminist writing is antihegemonic and challenges a monumentalizing or totalizing view of literature. It is, therefore, multiply voiced and tends to operate within a field of sinuous and shifting positionalities rather than from a single, fixed position" (xxii).

This volume offers rich opportunities for introducing conversations on intersectionalities and interfaces apt for teaching border studies, transnational studies, dissident voices, topics in race and gender, sexualities and disabilities, contemporary Mexican history or Latino history in the United States, and literary and social movements. Pedagogical strategies (coupled with critical readings) will help students examine how the creative craft takes shape, discuss possible reasons for resistance to hegemonic constructs, and approach the complexities of narrative fiction. Culturally responsive pedagogy, defined by the education theorist Gloria Ladson-Billings as "using cultural referents to impart knowledge, skills and attitudes" (17–18), provides helpful methodologies in guiding what has traditionally been labeled foreign literature. That approach is "slowly causing traditional trends to be reversed" (in terms of low grades and dropouts) and affecting educational policies and procedures in a positive manner (Lynch). The teaching strategies here seek to promote student engagement in this literary period of innovation and visibility by Mexicana and Chicana writers, calling attention to their precursors, influences, and distinct narrative productions.[3]

History, Precursors, and Production in Mexico

The late twentieth century indeed saw an escalation in books published by women, aided by the ensuing global nature of publishing, and saw expanded access to those books. The authors bursting on the scene had studied and were influenced by female predecessors and took advantage of certain openings in the social arena for discussion.

A primary influence and precursor for these authors is the prolific colonial writer and cloistered nun Sor Juana Inés de la Cruz (1651–95). A role model for Mexicanas and Chicanas due to both her extensive writing and her non-elite and low-income status (having been born as a mestiza to an unwed woman), she chose the convent for the privileges it offered of reading and writing, the life of the mind. Her numerous volumes of essays, poetry, and theater were published only because of a royal benefactor (also a woman). Mexican school texts depict her primarily as pious but also salute her for promoting Indigenous Mexican cultural and artistic practices in her texts. Several Chicana writers evoke her life and work in plays, poetry, and critical essays.[4] The earliest creative text in English about her was a drama created by a Chicana in El Paso, Estela Portillo Trambley's *Sor Juana*. In Mexico a crucial writer of the mid–twentieth century, Rosario Castellanos, speaks of Sor Juana's direct influence; Castellanos in turn was of great influence on the next generation.

Culturally in Mexico, Sor Juana has been evoked as one vertex of a cultural triangle of influence on the female gender, in which the Virgen de Guadalupe represents spirituality, and the Indigenous woman interpreter Malinche (considered a traitor) represents a role not to emulate.[5] By the late twentieth century, Mexicana writers would identify a new triad of influence that included the outstanding writers Sor Juana, Castellanos, and Elena Garro, at times substituting Poniatowska.

Chicana female symbology often resides in Indigenous figures: the *curandera* ("woman healer"); La Malinche, recreated as a symbol of decisive action; and the virgin mother Guadalupe, who is also the Aztec goddess Tonantzín: "We made Our Lady of Guadalupe into a feminist icon by taking away her passivity and turning her into a champion for women. In order to do this, we had to do research," states Martha Cotera, a librarian archivist and early political activist in the 1970s (qtd. in O'Hanlon).[6]

In Mexico the 1970s are seen as the breakthrough era for a feminist movement that began in the 1920s when a new government solidified following the 1910 Revolution. Mexicanas participated in that war as *curanderas*, *soldaderas* ("women soldiers"), and cooks serving with the men who traveled in the trains and on horseback. After victory, they sought equal citizenship and the right to vote, as their participation merited. They helped rebuild the nation's structures and participated in new cultural foundations. Various studies elucidate how Mexican women helped formulate the need for revolutionary change in the early twentieth century, mediating between elite and popular imaginings of Mexico. But when women's right to vote was raised at the convention for the 1917 Constitution, laughter was heard around the room, and the matter was dropped. Politicians made promises they would later renege on, but women continued to lobby for voting rights, which were finally ordered by presidential decree in 1953. The right for women to hold land in their own names and the right to assets upon divorce were not enacted until the 1970s.[7]

The United Nations General Assembly in 1945 enshrined the goal of gender equality in article 1 of its charter—the first international agreement to affirm principles of equality between women and men. Little changed, however, as the Cold War ensued. A major turning point came three decades later, when the UN General Assembly announced the World Conference on Women in 1975, which, after a dispute among UN member countries in which the United States advocated for a gender-neutral conference, Mexico City offered to host. Proclaimed International Women's Year, 1975 was a pivotal moment for global attention to women's status and rights. Notwithstanding other politics, this meeting led to the establishment of the UN Decade for Women, ensuing conferences, and the creation of the UN Development Fund for Women to evaluate women's needs in disenfranchised communities. Significantly, the conference in 1975 turned a spotlight on Mexico and Latin America.

The women representatives who traveled to the conference included delegates from the First World and the Third World. A Bolivian miner's wife and activist, Domitila Barrios de Chungara, was invited because of her leadership and the decade-long efforts of her seventy-member collective of miner's wives, the Housewives Committee. They had sought an increase in the miners' meager wages and attendance to the miners' medical needs. These women were often jailed, even following their peaceful, two-hundred-mile march to the capital, La Paz, in 1973. During her testimony at the conference, Barrios noted that the experiences or rights espoused by what she referred to as well-manicured, chauffeur-driven participants from First World nations contrasted starkly with the issues faced by women in her country: where men were forced to work extremely long hours in the mine for little pay, women had to find ways to earn extra money for their households, and there were prohibitions against organizing for worker rights.

Her moving speech brought attention to the intersection of race, economics, and sexism, and to the experiences of women in Latin America, whose economic status differed greatly from that of women in the First World. Barrios and her collective—soon joined by hundreds more—led a hunger strike later that year that eventually brought down the Bolivian dictatorship and opened the way to democracy. Her words were so influential that she received a request to publish her UN testimony as a book, released in 1978 as *Si me permiten hablar . . .* (*Let Me Speak!*; by Barrios and Moema Viezzer). This book and others in the 1970s, often referred to as testimonial literature, brought attention to the roles of women in disenfranchised communities.

Through local politics and the UN conference, opportunities finally opened in the 1970s: several Mexicana writers published, received awards, and attended writing workshops. It is thus important to recognize that when the first novels by Ángeles Mastretta (1949–), *Arráncame la vida*, published in English as *Tear This Heart Out*, and by Laura Esquivel (1950–), *Como agua para chocolate*, were released in 1985 and 1989 respectively—and sold like hotcakes—their success built on the awareness of the status of women that had developed in the previous decade. Later Mastretta became the first Latin American woman writer to receive the prestigious Rómulo Gallegos Prize (equivalent to the Pulitzer Prize) for her second novel, *Mal de amores* (1996), released in English as *Lovesick* (1997), while male critics complained that publishers only wanted to select women. Women writers heretofore had been invisible.

For example, Nellie Campobello (1900–86) participated in the immediate postrevolutionary literary period of the 1930s, but only male authors were feted for their novels on the social crisis of the 1910 Revolution. She was also instrumental, with her sister, in traveling to various regions to create and choreograph what would be called the Ballet Folklórico de México. Her 1931 innovative account, *Cartucho*, with short, brisk chapters and precise prose (rather like descriptive snapshots—or bullets) should be a highlighted work in the era of avant-garde fiction. By documenting the rural people of northern Mexico whose livelihoods were sacrificed, as well as the many lives lost on the battlefield that go unmentioned in official histories, she memorializes their existence. She also brings attention to Pancho Villa, the general in northern Mexico who, with Emiliano Zapata, was left out of official history when the new government took hold (both men were eliminated by two successive new regimes).

Instead of being acknowledged, Campobello was ignored and forgotten; she lived in anonymity in Mexico City. Finally, in the 1990s questions were raised, and it was discovered that she had died in 1986.[8] Two essays in this volume offer insights for teaching her work to undergraduate students: Emron Esplin evaluates Campobello's techniques in preparing revised editions of *Cartucho* and includes an accompanying table to show how editions of the work vary. In part 3 Anne McGee discusses Campobello's first text alongside Cisneros's first book. In each case, the contributors dig deep into the discourse and significance of Campobello's innovative narratives.

Elena Garro (1916–98) should be categorized as a member of the Latin American Boom literary generation for her fascinating first novel, *Los recuerdos del porvenir* (1963)—which received the prestigious Xavier Villaurrutia Award. This book was translated into English (by a scholar in the United States) rather soon after: *Recollections of Things to Come*, published in 1969 with a university press. Also, a long story that is frequently included in course anthologies and that has been translated into English is "La culpa es de los Tlaxcaltecas" ("It's the Fault of the Tlaxcaltecas"), from Garro's second book, *La semana de colores* (*The Week of Colors*), retitled *La culpa es de los Tlaxcaltecas* in new editions. Garro's subsequent novels have seen little critical attention or translation. She retreated into exile after the student protest movement of 1968, in which she was involved.

Rosario Castellanos (1925–74) published the groundbreaking novel *Balún Canán* in 1957, and it was released in English as *The Nine Guardians* (1992). In the novel, Castellanos reveals through acute social commentary the longstanding practice inherited from the colonial enterprise to disparage "Indians" who were held like slaves on haciendas. The novel's central tension revolves around the governmental edict, upon victory of the revolution, that a schoolhouse and a basic education must be provided to the workhands, which was followed by the hacienda owners' extreme objection and prejudice. The central character, a girl who is also the narrator, observes all. In his essay, David Dalton contrasts this early Mexicana novel with a first novel by the Chicana Helena María Viramontes—which also has a girl protagonist and a focus on social discourse. A subsequent novel, *Ciudad real* (*City of Kings*), garnered Castellanos the Xavier Villaurrutia Award in 1960.

Oswaldo Estrada discusses significant essays by Castellanos that help college-age readers understand the role of women writers in Mexico as well as their influences, demonstrating how Castellanos was influenced by Sor Juana. Castellanos excelled in production—leaving behind extensive poetry, essays, and novels—but it is in her essays that strategic ideas are found. Many Mexicana writers will attest to having read Castellanos's MA thesis, *Sobre cultura femenina* (*On Feminine Culture*), and to its impact on their thinking. Estrada shows how Castellanos's innate understanding of feminism imbues these critical essays. An introvert who was somewhat insecure despite her excellent writing and analytic abilities, Castellanos was not highly celebrated in her nation until after her untimely death. When her works saw English translation and critical study in the 1980s, Chicana writers quickly found affinity in them. Emily Hind's essay in this volume picks up topics in letters and poems by Castellanos and by two other Mexicana writers, to open classroom discussion on perceptions about women in popular media and about appearance and privileged positions.

While *Lilus Kikus*, the first account by Poniatowska, was treated as a children's book by critics who failed to recognize her subversive critical commentary of a patriarchal system, Poniatowska's second work of fiction, the testimonial novel *Hasta no verte, Jesús mío* (1969), which was published in English as *Here's to You, Jesusa!* (2002), drew immediate attention for its focus on the Mexican Revolution through the invisible *soldadera* as protagonist, and its strategic use of underclass language.[9] Her third creative work, *Querido Diego, te abraza Quiela* (1978), released in English as *Dear Diego* (1986), took the form of a series of letters addressed to a fictional version of the famous painter Diego Rivera from his spouse of ten years, whom he left behind in Paris; this text would gain greater attention in English translation. *Hasta no verte, Jesús mío*, however, won critical attention and made Poniatowska the first Mexicana to receive the Mazatlán Prize for Literature. She garnered additional critical attention for her account, the first to get past government censorship, about the massacre of students and other demonstrators by federal troops during the October 1968 protest in Mexico City: *La noche de Tlatelolco* (1971), released in English as *Massacre in Mexico* (1975).

This hybrid text intermingles first-person accounts (by family members of those who were missing, and by others who were jailed) with newspaper and official releases and with information pursued through research about the hundreds who were killed or missing. Poniatowska's subsequent nonfiction pursued social commentary in the form of essays about the ongoing process of squatters taking over open land out of necessity and about the 1985 earthquake, following which lives were lost because of government inaction; interviews with those jailed for years on end for labor strike activities; and the profile of a thirteen-year-old girl who was raped, tried to access an abortion (which is illegal in Mexico and accessible only by appealing to the courts), and suffered a lengthy legal process that barred her, causing further injustice. Poniatowska is known widely for her impact on *chronicle* ("nonfiction") writing, a genre described excellently by Pedro García-Caro in his essay discussing *Gaby Brimmer*, which is about the girl seeking the abortion and which provides a sense of the Mexican legal system in terms of rights to abortion; he analyzes Poniatowska's great skill in writing about disenfranchised communities.

The essay by Mark Mascia takes up issues of social justice and social stratification in Poniatowska's short stories, how to relate Poniatowska's writings to those of other Mexican writers, and how to stimulate intellectual and affective skills in younger readers. The prolific Poniatowska has released many novels, two of which are based on the lives of the cutting-edge artists Tina Modotti and Leonora Carrington, respectively. Magdalena Maíz-Peña and Luis Peña discuss these two works in the context of life writing, digital biopics, and visual discourse, creating theoretical frameworks to understand subjectivities, sexualities, gender, and performativity. Poniatowska's texts often defy literary categorization and elude critical analysis.[10]

Several other women writers appeared in the crucial 1970s, many publishing stories and essays in literary magazines and anthologies. In 1976 an important literary magazine, *Fem*, was launched in Mexico City by Alaide Foppa (a Guatemalan exile who lived in Mexico City for years and was later murdered in Guatemala) and Margarita García Flores. Poniatowska participated in this group, providing a room in her house for the editorial process. *Fem* still thrives, now online (www.revistafem.com), and supports new emerging writers.

In 1978 a first novel and delicious satire released by Margo Glantz (1930–), *Las mil y una calorías: Una novela dietética* (*The Thousand and One Calories: A Dietary Novel*), brought a positive response; her innovative fourth book, *Las genealogías* (1981), published in English as *The Family Tree: An Illustrated Novel* (1991), describes the arrival of her Jewish immigrant parents from Ukraine in Mexico City, where she was born (she was not raised with Jewish customs or religious faith). She received the prestigious Xavier Villaurrutia Award in 1984.[11] Her literary criticism is as extensive as her creative work; no essay here discusses her work, but many excellent scholarly articles are available.

María Luisa Puga (1944–2004) also released her first work of fiction, *Las posibilidades del odio* (*The Possibilities of Hatred*), in 1978. This series of six stories set in Kenya, where she lived for a year, represents its postcolonial conditions and its seventy-year struggle over historical inequalities, as well as reflecting Puga's memories of Mexico. Nine novels and four collections of short stories followed, and Puga won the Xavier Villaurrutia Prize in 1983. Despite living with a physical disability caused by rheumatoid arthritis, she led writing workshops for many years and wrote on a daily basis. Her final book, *Diario del dolor* (*Diary of Pain*), published in 2004, is a fictional diary in which the diarist converses with her antagonist, pain personified as Dolor. Beth Jörgensen offers a comparative analysis of one chapter each from *Las posibilidades del odio* and *Diario del dolor*, showing how to guide discussions on the representation of disabilities and offering suggestions for accessible secondary texts.

Silvia Molina published her first novel, *La mañana debe seguir gris*, in 1977, and it was released in English as *Grey Skies Tomorrow* in 1993. The novel garnered Molina the Xavier Villaurrutia award earlier in her career than did the works of other writers who received the award, and she was a participant in Poniatowska's writing workshop. Nathanial Gardner guides a close reading of one of Molina's stories, while also offering possible workshop influences and tips for identification of patterns of imagery, symbols, and codes. Liliana Pedroza delves into the sociopolitical ambiance of the 1970s women's movement, describes the impact Castellanos had on new women writers such as Molina, and then explicates Molina's topics of childhood, adolescence, parental authority, abortion, and emerging maturity in her early short stories, showing that they reflect ideas more than plots. Molina's historical novel, *Ascensión Tun* (1981), is a poignant account that restores a segment of Yucatán history and relates the philosophical observations of a Maya elder who reminisces on the mid-nineteenth-century caste wars.

Another participant in Poniatowska's workshop during the 1980s, the Sephardic Mexican writer Rosa Nissán (1939–), published her novels in the 1990s. The first, *Novia que te vea* (1992), broke new terrain by including extensive portions of dialogue in Ladino—an archaic form of Spanish retained by Spanish Jews who were forced to leave Spain in 1492, and the colonial heritage language spoken by people in remote areas of Latin America. The protagonist is based loosely on Nissán—born in Mexico City to immigrant parents and raised with Sephardic customs and the Jewish faith. Her second novel, *Hisho que te Nazca* (1996), continued the life of this protagonist, now a married woman with five children, and included her interactions with friends and relatives, as well as her divorce and immediate loss of economic status. The two novels were released in English translation together, as Like a Bride *and* Like a Mother (2002). Nissán's novels sold very well in Mexico, where women appeared to identify with female characters finding their way in a patriarchal system. Manuel Medina offers background history and strategies for teaching both texts, methodologies for distinguishing between fiction and autobiography, and a focus on life in Mexico City in the mid–twentieth century, especially for women. He shows that Nissán's unique cultural perspective offers strategies for considerations of other identities.

The Jewish Costa Rican film director Guita Schyfter was seeking stories that had Jewish characters and were set in Mexico when Poniatowska referred her to Nissán; Schyfter created a film released shortly after *Novia que te vea* (and with the same title) that used the main character from Nissán's novel and that inserted a second character of Ashkenazi heritage who speaks Yiddish: the two characters are friends coming of age in Mexico City. The film was popular in Mexico and saw wide circulation at foreign film festivals. The characters' youthful feminist desires include striving to secure more freedom than is traditionally granted girls and defying the rules by choosing their own husbands. Nissán's subsequent books—a collection of short stories; a hilarious novel published in 2003, *Los viajes de mi cuerpo* (*The Travels of My Body*), about the sexual adventures of two pudgy Mexicanas; and two chronicles on her travels to India and Israel—are delightful reads. Nissán currently leads her own writing workshops.

In 1982, before works by Mastretta and Esquivel garnered attention, Brianda Domecq (1942–) released a collection of stories that hit squarely on feminist issues: *Bestiario doméstico* (*Domestic Bestiary*) targets the loss of personhood in domestic life (and could be studied alongside Castellanos's scintillating short story "Cooking Lesson" ["Lección de cocina"]). In 1988 Domecq also published her thesis, *Acechando al unicornio: La virginidad en la literatura mexicana* (*Stalking the Unicorn: Virginity in Mexican Literature*). Like Puga, in the early 1970s she was kidnapped from her car on the way home and held for ransom for over a week. Domecq created a novelized version of that psychological experience, *Once días . . . y algo más* (1979), published in English as *Eleven Days* (1995). An intriguing historical novel that was the product of seventeen years of research and writing, *La insólita historia de la Santa de Cabora* (1990), released in English as *The Astonishing Story of the Saint of Cabora* (1998), was based on scant information about a real-life *curandera* in northern Mexico, a mestiza born out of wedlock to a man on whose ranch she lives; she becomes a child assistant to the kitchen cook, an older *curandera* who recognizes her abilities and teaches her about medicinal herbs. The real-life Teresa Urrea became a spiritual leader to the near-enslaved Indigenous and mestizo mine workers in her region. They protested working conditions and the constant incursions of ranch owners who were taking their lands, and their protests gained the attention of the federal government and the dictator Porfirio Díaz, who sent armies to this northern state to brutalize and remove Native Yaqui and Mayo men to faraway prisons in eastern Mexico. In a short time Teresa Urrea was arrested, put on a train with her father, and sent into exile across the border to the United States in 1892.

The *curandera* is an important figure for Mexican and Chicano culture—as both a healer and a spiritual guide—with roots in Indigenous life, and is always significant to small communities.[12] Domecq's research focused on the Yaqui Indigenous people in northwest Mexico, who have a long history of trying to prevent ranchers from taking their lands and of being rounded up for forced work in the mines. Domecq read early newspaper accounts of the conflict, and she visited sites in that region and across the border in Arizona, where Urrea had continued her work as a healer among Indigenous and local peoples. After the release of her novel, Domecq donated her extensive research documents to the Arizona Historical Society, where the Chicana Elena Díaz Björkquist consulted them after reading Domecq's novel. Díaz Björkquist created a moving historical performance about Urrea, presented Chautauqua-style through the Arizona Humanities Council in the late 1990s and afterward. Her contribution to this volume is not a scholarly study but instead a description of her preparations for that performance; she describes discovering Teresa Urrea in a brief essay when she was a college student, reading Domecq's novel later in life, and applying that experience to the creation of a dramatic presentation. Her one-woman presentation traveled throughout the Southwest, relating the story of the invisible Native Yaqui (both in the United States and in Mexico) and of the mestiza healer.

The prolific Carmen Boullosa (1954–) received the Xavier Villaurrutia Award in 1989 for her complex novel with a child narrator, *Antes*—the same year Laura Esquivel published her famous first novel. *Antes* was published in English as *Before* (2016). Boullosa participated in a year-long fellowship for new writers during which she created her novella, *Mejor desaparece* (1987), published in English as *Just Disappear* (2009). Her third book, released in 1992, *Llanto: Novelas imposibles* (*Weeping: Impossible Novels*), was a curious short novel in which the Aztec ruler Moctezuma II comes back to life in contemporary Mexico City; three women who find him in a park proceed to take him to visit national monuments as they meditate on colonial history. Rabi'a Hakima deconstructs a fragment, or story, from

Mejor desaparece (from an earlier English translation) and discusses reactions by first-year college students and how they can move from thinking an author is "crazy" to understanding the purposes and designs of complex creative writing. Jessica Burke's more in-depth essay discusses three early novels by Boullosa, analyzing her fragmented narratives and use of marginalized characters, her novels' constantly changing structure and form, and transitions in physical, metaphorical, and textual bodies. Emily Hind's contribution brings attention to one of Boullosa's essays.

Currently, Boullosa and a few other contemporary Mexicana writers—including Cristina Rivera Garza (1964–) and Valeria Luiselli (1983–)—reside in the United States; their novels and essays bring additional tangents to accounts that straddle an imposed border and chilling realities confronted by contemporary subjects.

The two novels that burst on the scene in the late 1980s—*Arráncame la vida* (1985), by Mastretta, which was released in English as *Tear This Heart Out* (1997), and *Como agua para chocolate* (1989), by Esquivel, which was published in English as *Like Water for Chocolate* (1992)—should not be dismissed: they were innovative *entradas* ("opening works") to a great diversity and profusion of authors. Critical articles and online reading guides on these key texts are accessible, as are two excellent critical collections: *The Boom Femenino in Mexico: Reading Contemporary Women's Writing*, edited by Nuala Finnegan and Jane E. Lavery, and *Laura Esquivel's Mexican Fictions*, edited by Elizabeth Willingham.

For instructors teaching Esquivel's novel, just the premise that Tita, the main character, should not marry and should instead remain with her mother is an effective tool for cultural research: is that premise truly a tradition or simply an edict by Tita's mother? Of Esquivel's subsequent novels, two connect directly to the first work, providing new reflections on that premise. Each novel by Esquivel reveals innovations and new ideas: her fourth, *Malinche: Novela* (2006), released in English as *Malinche: A Novel* (2006), is discussed briefly by Betsy Sandlin in her meticulous guide to the fluctuating meanings of the cultural icon La Malinche as revealed through visual thinking strategies. Esquivel's second novel, *La ley del amor* (1995), published in English as *The Law of Love* (1996), is set in the twenty-third century with memory flashbacks to previous eras, including the Spanish arrival in the Americas, and teaches Native philosophies and society's need to find harmony through collective analysis. The novel is not science fiction, and it exhibits excellent turns of culture-specific humor. The work was not readily understood by critics, who did not yet appreciate cinematographic qualities in written narrative, though new critical studies have now offered insights.[13]

Readers in the United States did not become aware of Mastretta as quickly—her first and second novels were released in English translation the same year—but in Mexico she was all the rage. A journalist at first, Mastretta received a fellowship from the Mexican Writers' Center in 1974, worked on a book of poetry, then spent ten years working on her first novel, which opens saucily, with sexual innuendo, then continues to surprise and delight with details on Mexican politics and party formation following the revolution. This novel earned the Mazatlán Prize for Literature for best book of the year. Ten years after that Mastretta released *Mal de amores*. The story revolves around the daughter of a pharmacist in Veracruz who travels to Mexico City and joyfully witnesses the election results for Francisco I. Madero (who was later murdered); she then participates in the 1910 Revolution, traveling by train to administer aid as a *curandera*, and later studies medicine in Texas and Chicago. As the novel ends, she is home in Veracruz, married with children, but she occasionally sees her former companion from the Revolution. Women readers in Mexico have liked and remarked on the fact that she keeps both men in her life. Although the essays in this volume do not discuss works by Mastretta, her novels deserve representation in university classes.

The following section is an overview of important conferences, anthologies, translations, and critics that have brought interpretation and understanding to significant late-twentieth-century Mexican literature and Mexicana writers. The section is followed by sections on the emergence of Chicana literature and criticism in the United States.

Translations, Anthologies, and Criticism

The three earliest texts by Mexicana writers in English translation inspired Chicanas in the academic environment in the United States, who were finding few examples of literature that was connected to Mexican culture and that was available in English. The first was Garro's remarkable novel, released as *Recollections of Things to Come* in 1969. Nearly two decades later, in 1988, two crucial translations arrived: *A Rosario Castellanos Reader* (edited and translated by Maureen Ahern), with selections from Castellanos's notable writings and a good introduction; and Campobello's two novels in one volume, *Cartucho* and *My Mother's Hands* (translated by Doris Meyer and Irene Matthews), also with an introduction. Thus the works of three major early- and mid-twentieth-century Mexicana writers were unveiled in the United States.

New translations of Castellanos's books would follow. Poniatowska was becoming known through university talks because of the release in English of her journalistic book on the 1968 student massacre, *La noche de Tlatelolco*; her novel on the Mexican Revolution, *Hasta no verte, Jesús mío* (a translation of which was released in 1988, though the 2002 translation, by Deanna Heikkinen, is better known); and in 1986 her short novel fictionalizing an early period from Diego Rivera's life, *Querido Diego, te abraza Quiela*, translated by Katherine Silver. Not until the late 1990s would other translations of Poniatowska novels be published.

A crucial scholarly text on Mexicana writers arrived in 1989, *Plotting Women: Gender and Representation in Mexico*, by Jean Franco, which studies the subtleties of Mexicana prose—beginning with the work of Sor Juana—and addresses the negative impact of the postrevolutionary period on women's efforts toward equality: "The revolution with its promise of social transformation encouraged a messianic spirit that transformed mere human beings into supermen and constituted a discourse that associated virility with social transformation in a way that marginalized women at the very moment when they were, supposedly, liberated" (102).

In 1994, a first book-length study on Poniatowska's writing style and topics, *Engaging Dialogues: The Writing of Elena Poniatowska*, was released by the scholar Beth Jörgensen. That year another new book arrived, *The New Narrative of Mexico: Sub-versions of History in Mexican Fiction*, by Kathy Taylor, which studies four contemporary Mexican writers, of which two are women; Taylor engages Poniatowska's testimonial work and Garro's "inversions of fiction." In 1998 the Canadian scholar María Elena de Valdés published *The Shattered Mirror: Representations of Women in Mexican Literature*, focalizing contested patriarchal codes in the literary representations of Castellanos, Poniatowska, Luisa Josefina Hernández, Puga, and the Chicana Cisneros.

A few anthologies released in the 1990s offer short interviews with writers and translated selections from their work and include *Contemporary Mexican Women Writers*, by Gabriella de Beer, profiling Molina, Mastretta, Domecq, Puga, and Boullosa; and *Broken Bars: New Perspectives from Mexican Women Writers*, by Kay S. García, profiling Molina, Mastretta, Poniatowska, and Domecq.[14] For a volume of short critical surveys by several critics, see *Knives and Angels: Women Writers in Latin America*, edited by Susan Bassnett.

The Scholarly Emergence of Mexicana Writers

In Mexico between the 1980s and the early 1990s, three successive conferences were highly influential in establishing that Mexicana writers were a force to be reckoned with; these conferences included perspectives on Chicana writers. A 1984 year-long seminar and workshop, launched by the flagship campus of El Colegio de México in Mexico City and its interdisciplinary women's studies program, proposed to study and restore the record of women writers in Mexico. A major conference followed a few years later at a sister campus, El Colegio de México Frontera Norte, a large research university near the border. Organizers published a book afterward as part of their project. In 1993 Chicana scholars and creative writers in the United States were invited to collaborate in a major colloquium on women writers, convened in Mexico City. Thus, despite different sociopolitical conditions in each nation, scholarship pulled the creative productions of Mexicanas and Chicanas in that era into discussion.

Critical anthologies were patiently collected and prepared for publication by the actively involved Mexicana scholars at these universities as well as at Mexico's preeminent public university, the National Autonomous University of Mexico. The first release consisted of two volumes, published in 1988 and 1990, in response to the conference held in Tijuana: *Mujer y literatura mexicana y chicana: Culturas en contacto* (*Women and Mexicana and Chicana Literature: Cultures in Contact*), edited by Aralia López González, Amelia Malagamba, and Elena Urrutia. Soon afterward editors Ana Rosa Domenella and Nora Pasternac compiled and published a book to restore the legacy of writers of the nineteenth century: *Las voces olvidadas: Antología crítica de narradoras mexicanas nacidas en el siglo XIX* (*Forgotten Voices: A Critical Anthology of Mexicana Writers Born in the Nineteenth Century*).

In 1995, López González released a follow-up volume, *Sin imágenes falsas, sin falsos espejos: Narradoras mexicanas del siglo XX* (*No False Images, No False Mirrors: Mexican Narrators of the Twentieth Century*), with an introduction by Urrutia and six hundred pages of analysis on twenty Mexicana writers, beginning with Campobello and ending with Boullosa, plus excerpts from their works. In 1996 El Colegio de México released a tome edited by Pasternac, Domenella, and Luz Elena Gutiérrez de Velasco, *Escribir la infancia: Narradoras mexicanas contemporáneas* (*Writing Childhood: Contemporary Mexicana Narrators*), with essays by Mexicana writers and key scholarly discussions on the creative process of Mexicana writers, early influences on the writers, their use of child characters, and how their works are reflected in criticism. Authors studied include Campobello, Garro, Castellanos, Glantz, Poniatowska, Puga, Molina, Boullosa, Josefina Vicens, Bárbara Jacobs, Guadalupe Dueñas, Inés Arredondo, Amparo Dávila, and Aline Pettersson. For instructors who read Spanish, this excellent overview includes biographical and bibliographic information on each writer.

A professor at the National Autonomous University of Mexico, Claire Joysmith, released an extensive book in 1996 drawn from presentations by participants in the 1993 colloquium. Titled *Las formas de nuestras voces: Chicana and Mexicana Writers in Mexico*, some chapters are in Spanish, others in English. The volume is organized in sections with short essays on some of the topics raised during the colloquium, such as "thinking differences," cognitive desires, dis-encounters, historical-literary perspectives, the border (with perspectives from either side), and differences between contemporary Mexicana and Chicana writers, and the volume includes a transcript of a dialogue between the two groups. The book's contents are evenly divided between Mexicana and Chicana scholars and writers, and the combination represents an innovative turn for new critical books of the era. There is an extensive introduction by Joysmith, followed by a newspaper essay on the colloquium by Poniatowska, who was in attendance throughout the event; in the essay she reflects on the attention to production by Chicana writers (which was being criticized by male critics):

> No Mexican woman writer has ever spoken to me of [examples of popular culture] but I have heard lengthy treatises from them about Borges. Chicanas, on the other hand, crossed the 2,000-mile border that separates us from the most powerful country in the world, carrying the Virgin of Guadalupe, La Malinche, La Llorona, and Coatlicue, and over there they gave them new value and a new identity they did not have previously. (48; my trans.)

Joysmith's introduction draws from an essay published by the Chicana scholar Tey Diana Rebolledo in 1984 to argue that "[w]riting, after all, is naming, mapping, and leading, as well as creating" (Rebolledo, "Witches" 167; qtd. in Joysmith 14), and from Ana Castillo to state that language is "the vehicle by which we not only represent ourselves but perceive ourselves in the world" (Castillo, "Massacre" 167; qtd. in Joysmith 13). While the introduction is in Spanish, Joysmith leaves quotations—and significant terms used during the conference, including the consistent use of "ourselves"—in their original language. This pays tribute to "[e]l bilinguismo como convivencia textual" ("bilingualism as textual coexistence"; 19; my trans.) in contemporary creativity, says Joysmith, who adds that "las formas de sus voces, la elección de su código linguístico" ("the forms of their voices, and choice of linguistic code"; 20; my trans.) of those attending the colloquium in Mexico City should be respected.

The colloquium had emphasized that, whether in English, Spanish, or both, women were writing their female lives and bringing presence to their communities. Nearly twenty years after the inaugural UN-declared International Women's Year, and the conference hosted in Mexico City, this scholarly colloquium in the same city represented a solid focus on creative work and criticism by women writers and on their connections to Mexican culture and heritage.

History, Precursors, and Production in the United States

In the United States during the 1980s and 1990s more women entered the academy, taking up research, as noted by Martha Cotera (qtd. in O'Hanlon), from new perspectives. They often had to convince advisors in order to pursue dissertations on ignored women writers' contributions and then became forerunners in new theory: Norma Alarcón (who founded Third Woman Press in 1987) was an early trailblazer in Chicana criticism; her dissertation was the first in English to study the work of the Mexicana Rosario Castellanos from the 1950s through the early 1970s. In Texas, from the late 1970s, Chicanas were contributing to small journals, even creating short-lived ones such as *Malintzín*, with a focus on women writers. Chicana creative writing occurred in limited form early in the century, but the most critical initiatives had roots in the activism and impact of the civil rights movement.

The civil rights struggle intensified as African Americans and Latinos returned from the Korean and Vietnam Wars, and as their veterans' benefits were repeatedly denied them. The Chicano Movement grew into the 1970s, fomented through the longstanding denial of rights and status by the United States government to Mexican American people. Protests in California by teachers and high school students, including school walkouts, as well as lawsuits for access, demonstrated the need for representation in the educational system; these actions finally led to courses in what were termed ethnic studies and Chicano studies. The agrarian component of the struggle included field workers' strikes led by Dolores Huerta and César Chávez, which gave rise to the term *Chicano*: migrant workers referred to themselves as "meshicanos," applying the Indigenous pronunciation of the *x*, or "sh," and protestors picked it up (without the first syllable). Chicano then became the term used by those entering academia: former students and activists who were producing creative work.

Academic scholarship expanded, needing platforms for the discussion of research and publishing ventures. The first step was the establishment in 1972, in San Antonio, Texas, of a national caucus of professors, students, and researchers. The founding members were social scientists who did research on Chicano issues. The caucus morphed into the National Association for Chicano Studies, expanding and hosting a national conference in a different city each year. In 1995, following a decade of pressure from within the organization, it was renamed the National Association for Chicano and Chicana Studies. Journals sprouted up in the late 1960s and 1970s in Texas; California; Albuquerque, New Mexico; and the Midwest, providing important initial outlets for production by Chicanos and Chicanas.[15] Soon centers for Chicano studies were being created at universities where books could be released. Since mostly men occupied the editorships and consulting boards, in the San Francisco Bay Area Chicana scholars developed groups to shake up scholarship and theory.

In 1982 at the University of California, Davis, the political science professor Adaljiza Sosa-Riddell established the group Mujeres en Marcha (Women on the March), which met in her office or at regional campuses to foment collaborations between academic and community women and facilitate discussions around the workplace, children, and education. This group evolved into the organization Mujeres Activas en Letras y Cambio Social (Women Active in Letters and Social Change), which published working papers, critical monographs, and then a journal. Its first conference at Davis in 1984 was Voces de la Mujer (Women's Voices), and a book published soon afterward through the Center for Mexican American Studies at the University of Texas at Austin was titled *Chicana Voices: Intersections of Class, Race, and Gender* and edited by Teresa Córdova et al. (and in 1993 was reissued by another university press because of avid interest). In 1993 Mujeres Activas en Letras y Cambio Social released a volume of essays, *Chicana Critical Issues*, edited by Alarcón and published by Third Woman Press, which has seen several reissues. Córdova was a member of the pioneering group that created a peer-reviewed journal for the organization in 1997, first called *Voces: A Journal of Chicana/Latina Studies* (now *Chicana/Latina Studies*), a strategic outlet for works by Chicanas that is now over twenty years old. Founding editor Sosa-Riddell published the journal out of her home for the first three years, and now it is hosted by a different university every five years.

As noted in the earlier section on translations, anthologies, and criticism, during the 1990s a few women academics from the United States traveled to interview Mexicana writers, then prepared books with excerpts from these writers' works, providing some of the earliest translations into English of those works.

Precursors to Chicana Literature

More than a few women took up writing and thought about Mexican American experience and culture decades prior to the civil rights movement; some were only able to publish stories in magazines, but others published books in English. The earliest of these women was likely María Amparo Ruiz de Burton (1832–95). Ruiz de Burton met a young United States military officer on the cusp of the United States war against Mexico; they were married in 1849, and homesteaded a ranch near San Diego, where he was posted, and where their children were born. While the Treaty of Guadalupe guaranteed that the property rights of Spanish colonials (referred to as "Californios" in California, and elsewhere as "Spanish" or "Mexican") who owned lands in the vast territory taken over by the United States would be honored, it is now recognized that in most cases they were not. Ruiz de Burton was early in exposing this fact in her publications in English. She accompanied her husband back east when he was recalled to participate in the Civil War. Stationed in Boston during Reconstruction, he contracted malaria and died. As a widow, she returned to her property in San Diego but found large chunks of the land sectioned out to new ranches, and squatters were living in her home.[16] Ruiz de Burton then pursued a legal remedy through the courts for years to regain her property, to no avail; she was still in court proceedings at the time of her death. The novels she published in 1872 and 1885 record this experience and her efforts to counter negative portrayals of "Mexicans" and Californios prevalent since 1848.[17]

In northern New Mexico, which retained its Spanish colonial flavor and culture long after 1848, women writers published articles, recipes, and commentary in Spanish in local newspapers. Early in the nineteenth century they began releasing books in English to preserve their traditions and customs, as politics heated up and New Mexico sought statehood.[18] Books by Nina Otero Warren (1881–1965), Cleofas Jaramillo (1878–1956), and Fabiola Cabeza de Vaca (1894–1991) offer delightful insights about life during the early generations of hyphenated experience. While no essay in this volume addresses these precursors, an excellent source is Rebolledo's critical study *Women Singing in the Snow: A Cultural Analysis of Chicana Literature*.

In Texas near the border, where families descended from late-seventeenth-century Spanish settlers lived marginalized lives (many having lost their lands due to usurpers and new state laws), it was more difficult for women writers to publish (except in newspapers in Spanish). An early and impressive writer whose works in English were only released posthumously, the schoolteacher and folklorist Jovita González (1904–83) prepared two novels between the 1930s and the 1940s. These contain gems of ranch-related practices and customs, culinary practices, and the lore and stories of a people working now as ranch hands on their forebears' lost ranches. In his essay, Marcel Brousseau assesses the posthumous editions of her novels, annotated and released by scholars in the late 1990s: he demonstrates strategies for close readings, contrapuntal readings, and archival research to help engage discussion on what Mary Louise Pratt calls contact zones, where "peoples geographically and historically separated come into contact with each other and establish ongoing relations, usually involving conditions of coercion, radical inequality, and intractable conflict" (*Imperial Eyes* 6).[19] his essay examines the practice of literary reclamation. His study highlights the importance of researching a variety of sources to fully understand literary precursors.

Another early-twentieth-century writer, Josefina Niggli (1910–83), was born in Monterrey, in northern Mexico, to parents born in the United States. Her father, born near the border, worked in northern Mexico during his entire adult life, thus she grew up in Mexico and identified as Mexican. As the 1910 Revolution grew more heated, she and her mother would head to Texas for sporadic periods (as other Mexicans did). They established a second home in San Antonio, where Niggli completed a college degree while writing poetry and participating in community theater ventures. She decided to pursue a master's degree in playwriting at the University of North Carolina, a cutting-edge new program in folk or community theater. Although fully bilingual, Niggli resolved to write in English so that the public in the United States could learn about Mexican culture through her plays and her novels. Thus her creative work bridges borders. Several of her one-act plays were staged in the late 1930s and brought peasant life into focus (a subject also pursued by the Mexican literati during the immediate postrevolutionary period). Niggli's master's thesis was an extensive three-act play featuring her homeland in northern Mexico and the Virgen de Guadalupe.

In the mid-1940s, as she moved between her family homes in San Antonio and Monterrey, Niggli published two novels, the first (*Mexican Village*) relating village life and customs through rural characters, including a *curandera*, and the second (*Step Down, Elder Brother*), set in urban Monterrey, describing the political and social changes in the immediate postrevolutionary period and including significant Indigenous cultural factors.[20] Alberto Varón situates the second novel in the pre-civil-rights era in the United States, to demonstrate fervent social change and to discuss the novel's significance for Mexican American experience and cultural symbology. In 1964 Niggli published her final novel, *A Miracle for Mexico*, notably the first account in English on the appearance of the Virgen de Guadalupe in 1531 (which includes phrases written in Nahuatl, a practice later connected to Chicano literature). An intriguing account set in the early 1500s, when colonization was underway in Mexico City, it inserts a fictional teenage boy—son of an Indigenous woman and an absent Spanish father—who serves as interpreter between the church bishop and Guadalupe's messenger, who only speaks Nahuatl. Malinche is a minor character (and the novel uses her name in Nahuatl, Malintzín).[21] Niggli's other plays and novels received numerous awards, but in 1964 this historical novel received only minor attention.

In part 5, Norma Valenzuela discusses Niggli's play *Soldadera* together with the work of two contemporary Chicana playwrights for their effectiveness in considering a transnational imaginary. Strategies applied by Valenzuela promote understanding of race and ethnicity, gender, sexualities, family relations, and community interactions, oriented through popular culture and critical readings.

The Inception of Chicana Literature

Chicana/o literature is loosely defined in terms of its inception in the 1970s Chicano Movement, whose protests sought representation and greater access to education for Chicanos and Chicanas. But more recent critical studies define a starting point of 1848 in Texas, the Southwest, and California. There is also the creative impetus of the early twentieth century. What is evident is that the generations that evolved into Chicanos after 1848, or even after the civil rights movement, lived in subaltern status within the hegemonic system. The Spanish language was prohibited in school and most public venues, therefore writers of Mexican descent wrote in English, but then they purposely sprinkled their early poetry with Spanish and Indigenous Mexican words after the Chicano Movement, as written descriptions of Chicano cultural experience emerged. Chicanas focalized symbolic representations and imagery of women to reflect their experiences, but also to assert their work, since they had been relegated to the sidelines by their Chicano cohorts.

A prime example of such an early Chicana writer is Estela Portillo Trambley (1936–98), an El Paso Community College drama teacher and activist who toiled alongside Chicanos during the protest movement and could be labeled the first Chicana novelist and playwright of the Chicano Movement era. When the early Chicano publisher Quinto Sol announced an award for new fiction, Portillo Trambley submitted her novel *Trini* in the early 1970s, following the first recipients, the Texan Tomás Rivera and the New Mexican Rudolfo Anaya, who received the first two awards for their novels, respectively, in 1971 and 1972. Portillo Trambley had to wait many years while the works of new (male) recipients of the award were published, and finally (after a legal battle between the partners who controlled Quinto Sol made possible the release of earlier unpublished works) she retrieved *Trini*, and it was published in 1986, shortly after Cisneros's first book. *Trini* was then criticized by Chicana critics for not being feminist enough.[22] In his essay, Ron Thomas discusses using her novel and the novels of other new Chicana writers of the 1980s in an interesting strategy to get students to apply visual skills and critical thinking in preparing a *PowerPoint* presentation. His other examples include works mentioned below—Ana Castillo's *Mixquiahuala Letters*, Viramontes's *Under the Feet of Jesus*, and Cisneros's *House on Mango Street*—as well as Margarita Cota-Cárdenas's complex novel *Puppet* (1985).

Students of Portillo Trambley asked her to write plays in English that they could understand and perform; she founded what was called a Hispanic company for drama in El Paso, where her plays were performed during the 1970s (the same era that Luis Valdez began creating plays in California). Portillo Trambley's *The Day of the Swallows* (which stirred controversy because of its metaphorical suggestion of lesbianism) was released in the Quinto Sol journal *El Espejo* in 1971, and in 1976 in a collection of her plays by Notre Dame University Press. In 1983 she released a second collection with the Bilingual Review Press, the title play of which was the first creative work in English on Sor Juana. Her three-act play in that collection, *Black Light*—staged at Chamizal National Theater in El Paso in 1975—won second place in the New York Shakespeare Festival's Hispanic American Playwright's competition. She also published short stories with characters who rebel against cultural and religious traditions, subtly seeking to escape from prescribed roles for women. Her works often explore Mexican Indigenous myths and cosmology (as do the works of Niggli, from a generation earlier). Portillo Trambley is deserving of greater critical attention.

A Chicana from California, Viramontes (1954–) is recognized both as a long-term scholar and for her career as a creative writer, launched in 1985 with *"The Moths" and Other Stories.* Her first novel, *Under the Feet of Jesus* (1995; dedicated to César Chávez), focused on migrant working conditions in the central California agricultural fields during the 1970s through one family.[23] Highlighting the perspective of child protagonists in first novels by Viramontes and Castellanos, David Dalton shows in his essay that difficult and emotional accounts can engage critical thinking on ideology, nationalism, and language. Sheila Marie Contreras introduces critical vocabulary suited to student readers to motivate them to examine domestic issues and resistance, using both the collection of short stories by Viramontes and a collection by the Chicana Alma Luz Villanueva (1944–), *Weeping Woman: "La Llorona" and Other Stories.*[24]

The highly celebrated first book by Cisneros, *The House on Mango Street*, released in 1984, received the Before Columbus Foundation American Book Award. Because Cisneros was unhappy with the fact that the publisher had slightly altered phrases in the final chapter of her book, she reissued the book with a major press (and her agent's help) in 1991; that version is now considered the more authentic text. Rather than expressing concern over whether the book should be labeled a coming-of-age novel or collection of loosely related stories, Shelley García advocates for an approach from the lens of genre analysis, which allows readers to transgress genre boundaries and to move beyond traditional definitions and can help them understand innovative strategies by women writers. Peter Schmidt offers teaching strategies for several of Cisneros's stories from *"Woman Hollering Creek" and Other Stories* (1991), and tools for the analysis of female archetypes such as the Virgen de Guadalupe, Tonantzín, and Malinche.

Born in Chicago like Cisneros, Ana Castillo (1954–) published her first—and most successful book critically—in 1986: *The Mixquiahuala*

Letters. Ashley Pérez provides an astute guide to this somewhat confusing text, engaging critical analysis through examination of the book's ambiguities and contradictions. Castillo's third novel, *So Far from God* (1993), reflects on northern New Mexico's colonial past, its spiritual and cultural traditions, United States involvement in Vietnam, and contemporary social activism. Leigh Johnson discusses this novel together with the first novel by the Chicana Demetria Martínez (1960–), *Mother Tongue* (1994), finding in the two authors' techniques critical commentary on oppression, racism, sexism, and the American dream. Johnson's essay applies the theories of Anzaldúa, Patricia Hill Collins, and Cherríe Moraga.

The pivotal 1980s also brought the Chicana playwright and novelist Denise Chávez (1948–) to public attention: her first novel, *The Last of the Menu Girls* (1986), is an early critical gem. Several books followed that received critical attention and were read with delight for their humor. Mary Jane Hurst tackles *Face of an Angel* (1994) as an introduction to a small town in the Southwest; the novel's main character is a diner waitress. Situating the novel in both world literature and American fiction, Hurst delineates the structure and themes of trauma, work, and family, exploring issues of gender, feminism, sexuality, work, language, and spirituality. Chávez's next novel, *Loving Pedro Infante* (2001), an over-the-top, enjoyable read, is studied by Laura Alonso-Gallo for its depiction of male and female archetypes, patriarchal ideology, ethnic pride, and popular culture. Alonso-Gallo uses critical techniques and historical background to assess similarities and differences between the mentality of the protagonist and that of her namesake, Saint Teresa of Ávila.

A somewhat less-known Chicana writer is Lucha Corpi (1945–), whose several novels can be categorized as detective fiction. Her books take place in the San Francisco Bay Area. The strategy of Carol Pearson's essay is to interrogate both the texts and the readers' own lives and views, showing how detective fiction can be both feminist and community-oriented. Corpi's first book was *Delia's Song* (1989), followed by *Eulogy for a Brown Angel* (1992), *Cactus Blood* (1995), and *Black Widow's Wardrobe* (1999); Pearson focuses primarily on a later book, *Crimson Moon* (2004), reviewing the others and noting how close readings can identify subversion, self and group identity, dreams, and the Malinche archetype. Betsy Sandlin directly engages La Malinche as both a historical and a symbolic figure, and as a figure of critical significance in literary studies, using a pedagogical approach to analysis through group work and visual thinking strategies to review the fluctuating meanings of the cultural icon.

In her essay, Margaret Cantú-Sánchez pairs a novel set in the border-town of Laredo, Texas, *Canícula: Snapshots of a Girlhood en la Frontera* (1995), by Norma Elia Cantú (1946–), who calls the work an "autoethnobiography" (xi), with the landmark book *Borderlands / La frontera: The New Mestiza* (1987), by Anzaldúa, both of which are hybrid texts that contain personal essays, criticism, creative pieces, and elements of Mexican and Chicano culture. Cantú-Sánchez relates a successful strategy of using a *mestizaje* of epistemologies (a blending of cultural experiences and formal education ideologies) to help introduce Mexican American history and literature in the classroom.

Like Portillo Trambley, Alicia Gaspar de Alba (1958–) was born in El Paso and prepared a creative work on Sor Juana, the important role model for intellectual life. Gaspar de Alba's work was an extensive historical novel: *Sor Juana's Second Dream* (1999), which provides in-depth descriptions of Sor Juana's research and writing in philosophy, science, and astronomy. An especially fascinating long scene late in the novel describes the nun-writer being subjected to an Inquisition trial in a Mexico City colonial court for daring to write and argue against the essay of an eminent priest who criticized her ideas and her writing. This work and another novel by Gaspar de Alba are discussed by Carolina Alonso, who also discusses books by Anzaldúa, Emma Pérez, Moraga, and Carla Trujillo. Alonso's essay describes the design of a course on Chicana lesbian writers. Her study plan includes blogs and discussions to evaluate constructs of family and historical discourse.

Anzaldúa and Moraga coedited an important book of essays by a variety of contributors, *This Bridge Called My Back: Writings by Radical Women of Color*, published in 1981, which set the stage for Chicana feminist criticism. In 1983 Moraga launched Kitchen Table: Women of Color Press, with Audre Lorde and Barbara Smith, where she published her first work, *Loving in the War Years: Lo que nunca pasó por sus labios* (1983, later reissued by the University of Texas Press), and the reissue of *This Bridge Called My Back*. Moraga is a highly recognized playwright whose first collection, *Giving Up the Ghost* (1986), received an American Book Award. In her essay, Susan Méndez shows how to teach gender and sexual identity in the 1960s through Moraga's play *Shadow of a Man* (1990). Set in Los Angeles, inside a family home, the play transmits attitudes from the era about gender and sexuality. Méndez defines her discussions through critical work by Eve Sedgwick and thematic analysis of ghosts, shadows, and homosocial bonding.

Two additional essays in this volume highlight the power of critical-cultural performance to encourage strategic writing. Adrianna Santos discusses how performances of *The Panza Monologues* (Grise and Mayorga) can open awareness on real-life issues of Chicana women and provide a deeper understanding of women's and queer narratives in the borderlands. William Stark's survey of Violeta Luna's creations and performances—bridging both Mexicana and Chicana cultural history—opens discussion on social justice, Native archetypes, history, and dominant society and culture. These examples of dramatic work round out the goals of Chicana writers during the late twentieth century.

Two additional important Chicana writers from the period (and not covered by the essays here) are Mary Helen Ponce (1938–), who wrote a semiautobiographical account about neighborhood life in Los Angeles in the mid–twentieth century, *Hoyt Street* (1993), and the New Mexican Chicana Erlinda Gonzales-Berry (1939–), whose short novel *Paletitas de guayaba* (1991), composed in Spanish (and recently published in English as *On a Train Called Absence* [2012]), is structured by a train ride to Mexico City, which serves symbolically and subconsciously to represent the thoughts of the main character, Mari: throughout her journey she meditates on her hybrid identity and, upon arrival in Mexico City, travels back in time to dialogue with her namesake, the historical figure whose Catholic name is Marina and who is known as Malinche. In the novel, Malinche discusses her mythical status and her meaning for Chicanas like Mari.

Critical and Theoretical Publications

Anzaldúa and Moraga's impressive anthology *This Bridge Called My Back* drew from discussion circles and critical processes active in the San Francisco Bay Area. Published through the small, feminist Persephone Press in Massachusetts, the book became a pioneering text for Chicana and Chicana lesbian studies. Chicana feminists were also looking to establish their own presses. The organization Mujeres Activas en Letras y Cambio Social worked with university centers and presses, and Alarcón—having completed her doctorate in the Midwest, where she launched *Third Woman Journal* in 1981—arrived in 1985 to teach at the University of California, Berkeley, where she soon converted her journal to a book press, working with the active feminist circles. Third Woman Press published two expanded reissues of *This Bridge Called My Back*, in 2002 and 2008 (the first of which includes Alarcón's critical essay revising the concept of Malinche

["Chicana's Feminist Literature"]). Chicana writers were also finding access to two independent presses founded in the early 1970s, Arte Público Press and Bilingual Review Press—which released *Beyond Stereotypes: The Critical Analysis of Chicana Literature* (1985), by the scholar María Herrera-Sobek.

Anzaldúa's strategic theoretical analysis in her hybrid and bilingual narrative *Borderlands / La frontera* elaborates on the state of in-betweenness or *nepantla*—and describes it as a place of consistent grating or as the reopening of a wound that is the invisible border, or borderlands experience, which is never fully defined or acknowledged. Anzaldúa's unique book opened ideas and theory on the borderlands in terms of gender and sexualities, Native philosophy and origins, experience, and the hegemonic system's constraints. Anzaldúa also devoted attention to the rich legacy of Mesoamerican philosophy and how it influences Mexican American culture and creative output. Her book has been important to the academic fields of cultural studies, anthropology, American studies, and literatures.

Anthologies of creative work were important in the 1980s and 1990s, offering additional material for critical understanding. A collection that was pioneering in its research and that required several years of preparation, *Infinite Divisions: An Anthology of Chicana Literature* (1993), by Rebolledo and Eliana Rivero, opened awareness to an extensive history and solid body of writings by Chicana women.[25] Two years later Rebolledo released her significant study, *Women Singing in the Snow*, on the themes, techniques, imagery, icons—including La Virgen de Guadalupe, the *curandera* as a healer and spiritual leader, La Malinche, La Llorona, and Sor Juana—and critical intentions in Chicana creative production.

Ana Castillo, also a member of feminist critical circles in the Bay Area, worked with Alarcón and Moraga to prepare a collection of critical essays, *The Sexuality of Latinas* (Alarcón et al.). Later she published an insightful book of essays of cultural analysis, *Massacre of the Dreamers: Essays on Xicanisma* (1994)—coining the term "Xicanisma" for Chicana feminism, differentiated from male Chicanismo—and *Goddess of the Americas: Writings on the Virgin of Guadalupe* (1996), discussing the deep structures of Indigenous conceptology and Native thought. In these books she asserts that Chicana identity can only be grasped through an understanding of Native philosophy.

Herrera-Sobek and Viramontes coedited a collection, *Chicana Creativity and Criticism: New Frontiers in American Literature* (1996), that documents the rise of the new literary genre and admonishes literary critics in the United States to resist attempting to fit texts by Chicana writers into preestablished theoretical frameworks and instead to identify the writers as standing at the intersection of gender and race. An essay in *Chicana Creativity and Criticism* by Rebolledo and Yvonne Yarbro-Bejarano explores influences between Chicana creative writers and critics, noting how they worked together in shaping the late-twentieth-century period. Theoretical foundations laid in this period by critics such as Alarcón, Anzaldúa, Rebolledo, Moraga, Yarbro-Bejarano, Herrera-Sobek, and Viramontes are excellent reading preparation for instructors who intend to teach the work of Chicana creative writers.

The innovative stories and novels by Mexicanas in the 1970s, and their bestselling novels in the late 1980s, can be related to the creative work and critical and theoretical studies by Chicana writers in the 1980s and 1990s, all of which defined what would be called a Latina boom by some critics and were neither light nor insufficient but instead highly innovative, spirited, and thoughtful and included varieties of style, structure, and language as well as important discourse. Some commonalities would surface in themes, opening new perspectives to histories, gender, and sexualities. The scant references since 1848 to women of Mexican heritage either as "[c]hile Queens, the spicy Mexican women of the saloon, or as enduring, suffering mothers," as noted in the introduction to *Infinite Divisions* (Rebolledo and Rivero 1), was countered by this rich period of Mexicana and Chicana literary production. The collaborative scholarship pursued by feminists in the Bay Area, in new conferences being convened and in publications, joined profuse creative production and efforts by women scholars in Mexico, where, at colloquiums and through joint critical studies, connections were drawn between women writers on either side of the border. It was not easy in either nation to work against the grain of established critical systems, but collaborative projects and conferences, international interventions, and translations all helped open awareness and expand readership.

Notes

1. The strategic focus here is on narratives produced in the 1980s and 1990s by Mexicanas and Chicanas, and thus not on Latina writers more generally.

2. In Mexico the term was picked up from advertising in the 1990s: Pepsi Lite, yogurt lite, etc.

3. This period was referred to as a boom by critics and literary agents for marketing purposes, similar to the 1960s boom in novels by Latin American male writers, whose aesthetic was also called "magical realism."

4. Sor Juana is the focus of a few children's books in English, including Martínez, *Sor Juana Inés de la Cruz*. An excellent early translation of a critical text of

hers, by Margaret Sayers Peden, is *A Woman of Genius: The Intellectual Autobiography of Sor Juana Inés de la Cruz*, released in bilingual format by a small press. For interesting critical and teaching ideas, the Modern Language Association volume *Approaches to Teaching the Works of Sor Juana Inés de la Cruz*, edited by Emilie L. Bergmann and Stacey Schlau, is recommended.

5. This view of Malinche treats the Native peoples of the region as part of one nation and assumes that they could have been collectively betrayed.

6. Cotera was a founding member of the Raza Unida Party in Crystal City, Texas, the Texas Women's Political Caucus, and the National Women's Political Caucus. In 1974 she established the early Chicana Research Learning Center at the University of Texas.

7. See the introduction to Mitchell and Schell (1–14). Books about and by the Mexicana Antonieta Rivas Mercado (1900–31) are also informative for their take on the early women's rights movement.

8. For those who read Spanish, Poniatowska's book of essays *Las siete cabritas* (*The Seven Sisters*; not in translation) delightfully describes and rescues from erasure the important early literary figures of Campobello, Castellanos, and Garro, as well as four female artists.

9. *Lilus Kikus* was reissued in 1967 as *Los cuentos de Lilus Kikus*; the edition includes another eight stories. *Hasta no verte, Jesús mío* is currently more frequently assigned (in English translation) in history classes than in literary studies classes, perhaps because the novel captures, and offers tribute to, colloquial (low-class) Spanish—a clever linguistic strategy—which some readers may find off-putting. (This technique of capturing spoken language may have occurred to the writer Rosa Nissán because of her participation in a workshop led by Poniatowska.)

10. Poniatowska's work remains little recognized in the United States despite the fact she is one of Mexico's great contemporary writers. Only a few of her novels and short stories have seen English translation, but more of them need to be translated; critical studies and dissertations have taken up several of her works.

11. This award went to Angelina Múñiz-Huberman in 1985 for her short story collection *Huerto cerrado, huerto sellado* (Closed Garden, Sealed Orchard); Bárbara Jacobs in 1987 for her first novel, *Las hojas muertas* (The Dead Leaves); and Carmen Boullosa in 1989 for her novel *Antes* (Before). Poniatowska was selected for the award in 1971 for *La noche de Tlatelolco*, but she refused it, declaring no one could award a prize to those murdered in 1968.

12. The *curandera*'s cultural significance is discussed by the Chicana scholar Tey Diana Rebolledo in her critical text *Women Singing in the Snow: A Cultural Analysis of Chicana Literature*.

13. See Martínez, "Cultural Identity."

14. Several other profiles were published in that decade: Pinto; Castro-Klarén et al.; Jehenson; Agosín; and Jones and Davies.

15. See the special issue of *Diálogo* edited by Elizabeth Coonrod Martínez and Gabriela Baeza Ventura (vol. 20, no. 2, Fall 2017) on the history of Chicano- and Latino-focused journals.

16. This practice was similar to that of settlers moving into Native towns and taking over properties, such as the homes of the Cherokee nation in Georgia, whose leaders, after traveling to Washington, DC, and engaging in political dialogue, returned to find squatters in their homes.

17. See Ruiz de Burton's collected letters, published by Arte Publico Press (*Conflict*). Ruiz de Burton also founded a theater in San Diego in the 1950s and wrote plays to entertain the soldiers stationed in San Diego; later she created a longer play modeled on Cervantes's *Don Quixote*.

18. New Mexico did not become a state until 1912.

19. See also Pratt, "Arts."

20. This novel was recently translated into Spanish as *Apártate, hermano* by the Mexican novelist David Toscano.

21. The publisher unfortunately wanted to market this novel as a juvenile book for a new children's literature series, and it was classified as such in the Library of Congress catalog (though book reviews at the time stated it was definitely not a children's book). See Martínez, *Josefina*, which includes examples of her plays and narratives.

22. Critics ignored the fact that *Trini* was composed fifteen years prior. See Helena María Viramontes's foreword in the rerelease of Portillo Trambley's novel (i–vi).

23. A more recent novel by Viramontes, *Their Dogs Came with Them* (2007), is complex and highly recommended. It describes those left homeless after families are pushed out of a neighborhood when a major freeway system is constructed in Southern California, and it explores how memory is being permanently erased.

24. Villanueva received numerous awards for her poetry, and in 1989 the American Book Award for her novel *The Ultraviolet Sky*.

25. This remarkable collection dug into the Bancroft Library at the University of California, Berkeley, and other old archives to promote the work of women in print since 1848. The introduction weaves history and themes to introduce the fifty-six authors and 178 short texts in the anthology, a new vision of Chicana production. The project began with a National Endowment for the Humanities grant received in 1984 and the initial goal to represent "an intellectual/critical history of Chicana literature dating from the 1960s" (Rebolledo and Rivero xix), but after visiting numerous libraries in the West and Southwest and consulting with descendants of early writers, the editors discovered that it was a much vaster project, dating further back and involving hundreds of chapbooks, journals, magazines, newspapers, and unpublished materials.

Works Cited

Agosín, Marjorie, editor. *A Dream of Light and Shadow: Portraits of Latin American Women Writers*. U of New Mexico P, 1995.

Ahern, Maureen, editor. *A Rosario Castellanos Reader*. Translated by Ahern et al., U of Texas P, 1988.

Alarcón, Norma, editor. *Chicana Critical Issues*. Third Woman Press, 1993.

———. "Chicana's Feminist Literature: A Re-vision through Malintzin; or, Malintzin Putting Flesh Back on the Object." *This Bridge Called My Back: Writings by Radical Women of Color*, edited by Gloria Anzaldúa and Cherríe Moraga, 3rd ed., Third Woman Press, 2002, pp. 182–89.

Alarcón, Norma, et al., editors. *The Sexuality of Latinas.* Third Woman Press, 1993.

Anzaldúa, Gloria. *Borderlands / La frontera: The New Mestiza.* Spinsters / Aunt Lute, 1987.

Anzaldúa, Gloria, and Cherríe Moraga, editors. *This Bridge Called My Back: Writings by Radical Women of Color.* Persephone Press, 1981.

Barrios de Chungara, Domitila, and Moema Viezzer. *Let Me Speak! Testimony of Domitila, a Woman of the Bolivian Mines.* Monthly Review Press, 1978.

Bassnett, Susan, editor. *Knives and Angels: Women Writers in Latin America.* Zed Books, 1990.

Bergmann, Emilie L., and Stacey Schlau, editors. *Approaches to Teaching the Works of Sor Juana Inés de la Cruz.* Modern Language Association of America, 2007.

Boullosa, Carmen. *Antes.* Vuelta, 1989.

———. *Llanto: Novelas imposibles.* Ediciones Era, 1992.

———. *Mejor desaparece.* Océano, 1987.

Campobello, Nellie. Cartucho *and* My Mother's Hands. Translated by Doris Meyer and Irene Matthews, U of Texas P, 1988.

Cantú, Norma E. *Canícula: Snapshots of a Girlhood en la frontera.* U of New Mexico P, 1995.

Castellanos, Rosario. 1957. *Balún Canán.* Fondo de Cultura Económica, 1990.

———. *Ciudad real.* Alfaguara, 1997.

———. "Cooking Lesson." *Another Way to Be: Selected Works of Rosario Castellanos*, Translated by Myralyn F. Allgood, U of Georgia P, 1990, pp. 104–12.

———. *Sobre cultura femenina.* Fondo de Cultura Económica, 2005.

Castillo, Ana. *Goddess of the Americas: Writings on the Virgin of Guadalupe.* Riverhead, 1996.

———. "Massacre of the Dreamers." *Critical Fictions: The Politics of Imaginative Writing*, edited by Philomena Mariana, Bay Press, 1991, pp. 161–76.

———. *Massacre of the Dreamers: Essays on Xicanisma.* U of New Mexico P, 1994.

———. *The Mixquiahuala Letters.* Bilingual Press, 1986.

———. *So Far from God.* W. W. Norton, 1993.

Castillo, Debra. *Talking Back: Toward a Latin American Feminist Literary Criticism.* Cornell UP, 1992.

Castro-Klarén, Sara, et al., editors. *Women's Writing in Latin America.* Westview Press, 1991.

Chávez, Denise. *Face of an Angel.* Farrar, Straus and Giroux, 1994.

———. *The Last of the Menu Girls.* Arte Público Press, 1986.

———. *Loving Pedro Infante.* Farrar, Straus and Giroux, 2001.

Cisneros, Sandra. *The House on Mango Street.* 1984. Vintage Books, 1991.

———. *"Woman Hollering Creek" and Other Stories.* Vintage Books, 1991.

Córdova, Teresa, et al., editors. *Chicana Voices: Intersections of Class, Race, and Gender.* 1986. U of New Mexico P, 1993.

Corpi, Lucha. *Black Widow's Wardrobe.* Arte Público Press, 1999.
———. *Cactus Blood.* Arte Público Press, 1995.
———. *Crimson Moon.* Arte Público Press, 2004.
———. *Delia's Song.* Arte Público Press, 1989.
———. *Eulogy for a Brown Angel.* Arte Público Press, 1992.
Cota-Cárdenas, Margarita. *Puppet.* Relámpago Books, 1985.
DeBeer, Gabriella. *Contemporary Mexican Women Writers: Five Voices.* U of Texas P, 1996.
Domecq, Brianda. *Acechando al unicornio: La virginidad en la literatura mexicana.* Fondo de Cultura Económica, 1988.
———. *Bestiario doméstico.* Fondo de Cultura Económica, 1982.
———. *La insólita historia de la Santa de Cabora.* Planeta, 1990.
———. *Once días . . . y algo más.* Universidad Veracruzana, 1995.
Domenella, Ana Rosa, and Nora Pasternac, editors. *Las voces olvidadas: Antología crítica de narradoras mexicanas nacidas en el siglo XIX.* El Colegio de México, 1997.
Esquivel, Laura. *Como agua para chocolate.* Anchor Books, 1989.
———. *La ley del amor.* Grijalbo, 1995.
———. *Malinche: Novela.* Atria Books, 2006.
Finnegan, Nuala, and Jane E. Lavery, editors. *The Boom Femenino in Mexico: Reading Contemporary Women's Writing.* Cambridge Scholars Publishing, 2010.
Franco, Jean. *Plotting Women: Gender and Representation in Mexico.* Verso / Columbia UP, 1989.
García, Kay S. *Broken Bars: New Perspectives from Mexican Women Writers.* U of New Mexico P, 1994.
Garro, Elena. *Recollections of Things to Come.* Translated by Ruth L. C. Simms, U of Texas P, 1969.
———. *Los recuerdos del porvenir.* Joaquín Mortiz, 1963.
———. *La semana de colores.* Porrúa, 2006.
Gaspar de Alba, Alicia. *Sor Juana's Second Dream.* U of New Mexico P, 1999.
Glantz, Margo. *Las genealogías.* Martín Casillas, 1981.
———. *Las mil y una calorías: Una novela dietética.* Premiá, 1978.
Gonzales-Berry, Erlinda. *Paletitas de guayaba.* Albuquerque: El Norte, 1991.
Grise, Virginia, and Irma Mayorga. *The Panza Monologues.* U of Texas P, 2014.
Herrera-Sobek, María. *Beyond Stereotypes: The Critical Analysis of Chicana Literature.* 1985.
Herrera-Sobek, María, and Helena María Viramontes, editors. *Chicana Creativity and Criticism: New Frontiers in American Literature.* 2nd ed., U of New Mexico P, 1996.
Jacobs, Bárbara. *Las hojas muertas.* Ediciones Era, 1987.
Jehenson, Myriam Yvonne. *Latin American Women Writers: Class, Race, and Gender.* State U of New York P, 1995.
Jones, Anny Brooksbank, and Catherine Davies. *Latin American Women's Writing: Feminist Readings in Theory and Crisis.* Oxford UP, 1996.

Jörgensen, Beth. *Engaging Dialogues: The Writing of Elena Poniatowska*. U of Texas P, 1994.
Joysmith, Claire, editor. *Las formas de nuestras voces: Chicana and Mexicana Writers in Mexico*. Universidad Nacional Autónoma Mexicana / Third Woman Press, 1995.
Ladson-Billings, Gloria. *The Dreamkeepers: Successful Teaching for African American Students*. Jossey-Bass, 1994.
López González, Aralia, editor. *Sin imágenes falsas, sin falsos espejos: Narradoras mexicanas del siglo XX*. El Colegio de México, 1995.
López González, Aralia, et al., editors. *Mujer y literatura mexicana y chicana: Culturas en contacto*. El Colegio de la Frontera Norte, 1988–90. 2 vols.
Lynch, Matthew. "What Is Culturally Responsive Pedagogy?" *Huffpost*, 14 Dec. 2011, www.huffpost.com/.
Martínez, Demetria. *Mother Tongue*. Ballantine, 1994.
Martínez, Elizabeth Coonrod. "Cultural Identity and the Cosmos: Laura Esquivel's Predictions for a New Millennium in *The Law of Love*." *Laura Esquivel's Mexican Fictions*, edited by Elizabeth Willingham, Sussex Academic Press, 2010, pp. 136–52.
———. *Josefina Niggli, Mexican American Writer: A Critical Biography*. U of New Mexico P, 2007.
———. *Sor Juana Inés de la Cruz*. Millbrook Press, 1994. Hispanic Heritage.
Mastretta, Ángeles. *Arráncame la vida*. 1985. Vintage Books, 1997.
———. *Mal de amores*. Alfaguara, 1996.
Mitchell, Stephanie, and Patience A. Schell. *The Women's Revolution in Mexico, 1910–53*. Roman and Littlefield, 2007.
Molina, Silvia. *Ascensión Tun*. Martín Casillas, 1981.
———. *La mañana debe seguir gris*. Joaquín Mortiz, 1977.
Moraga, Cherríe. *Giving Up the Ghost*. Moraga, Heroes, pp. 1–35.
———. Heroes and Saints *and Other Plays*. South End Press, 1994.
———. *Loving in the War Years: Lo que nunca pasó por sus labios*. South End Press, 1983.
———. *Shadow of a Man*. Moraga, Heroes, pp. 37–84.
Múñiz-Huberman, Angelina. *Huerto cerrado, huerto sellado*. Editorial Oasis, 1985.
Niggli, Josefina. 1945. *Mexican Village*. The U of North Carolina P, 2015.
———. *A Miracle for Mexico*. New York Graphic Society Publishers, 1964.
———. *Step Down, Elder Brother*. Rinehart, 1947.
Nissán, Rosa. *Hisho que te Nazca*. Plaza y Janés, 1996.
———. Like a Bride *and* Like a Mother. U of New Mexico P, 2002.
———. *Novia que te vea*. Planeta, 1992.
———. *Los viajes de mi cuerpo*. Planeta, 2003.
O'Hanlon, Morgan. "Feminist Martha Cotera Fights to Represent Chicanas in Academia." *The Daily Texan*, 29 Nov. 2016, thedailytexan.com/2016/11/29/feminist-martha-cotera-fights-to-represent-chicanas-in-academia.
Pasternac, Nora, et al., eds. *Escribir la infancia: Narradoras mexicanas contemporáneas*. El Colegio de México, 1996.

Pinto, Magdalena García. *Women Writers of Latin America: Intimate Histories.* U of Texas P, 1991.
Ponce, Mary Helen. *Hoyt Street.* U of New Mexico P, 1993.
Poniatowska, Elena. *Los cuentos de Lilus Kikus.* Universidad Veracruzana, 1967.
———. *Hasta no verte, Jesús mío.* Ediciones Era, 1969.
———. *Lilus Kikus.* Biblioteca Era, 1954.
———. Lilus Kikus *and Other Stories by Elena Poniatowska.* Translated by Elizabeth Coonrod Martínez. U of New Mexico P, 2005.
———. *La noche de Tlatelolco.* Ediciones Era, 1971.
———. *Querido Diego, te abraza Quiela.* Biblioteca Era, 1978.
———. *Las siete cabritas.* Ediciones Era, 2001.
Portillo Trambley, Estela. *Day of the Swallows: A Play in Three Acts. El Grito*, vol. 4, no. 3, Spring 1971, pp. 4–47.
———. Sor Juana *and Other Plays.* Bilingual Press, 1986.
———. *Trini.* 1986. Foreword by Helena María Viramontes, Feminist Press, 2005.
Pratt, Mary Louise. "Arts of the Contact Zone." *Profession*, vol. 91, 1991, pp. 33–40.
———. *Imperial Eyes: Travel Writing and Transculturation.* Routledge. 1992.
Puga, María Luisa. *Diario del dolor.* Alfaguara, 2004.
———. *Las posibilidades del odio.* Siglo XXI, 1978.
Rebolledo, Tey Diana. "Witches, Bitches and Midwives: The Shaping of Poetic Consciousness in Chicana Literature." *The Chicano Struggle: Analyses of Past and Present Efforts*, edited by John A. García and Teresa Córdova, Bilingual Press, 1984, pp. 166–77.
———. *Women Singing in the Snow: A Cultural Analysis of Chicana Literature.* U of Arizona P, 1995.
Rebolledo, Tey Diana, and Eliana S. Rivero. *Infinite Divisions: An Anthology of Chicana Literature.* U of Arizona P, 1993.
Ruiz de Burton, María Amparo. *Conflict of Interest: The Letters of María Amparo Ruiz de Burton.* Edited by Rosaura Sanchez and Beatrice Pita, Arte Público Press, 2001.
Sayers Peden, Margaret. *A Woman of Genius: The Intellectual Autobiography of Sor Juana Inés de la Cruz.* Lime Rock Press, 1982.
Taylor, Kathy. *The New Narrative of Mexico: Sub-versions of History in Mexican Fiction.* Bucknell UP, 1994.
Valdés, María Elena de. *The Shattered Mirror: Representations of Women in Mexican Literature.* U of Texas P, 1998.
Villanueva, Alma Luz. *The Ultraviolet Sky.* Bilingual Review Press, 1988.
———. *Weeping Woman: "La Llorona" and Other Stories.* Bilingual Review Press, 1994.
Viramontes, Helena María. *And Their Dogs Came with Them.* Atria Books, 2007.
———. *"The Moths" and Other Stories.* Arte Público Press, 1985.
———. *Under the Feet of Jesus.* Plume, 1995.
Willingham, Elizabeth, editor. *Laura Esquivel's Mexican Fictions.* Sussex Academic Press, 2010.

Part I

Mexicana Writers and Their Precursors

Emron Esplin

Teaching *Cartucho* and Nellie Campobello's Goal of Restoring Pancho Villa to Mexican History

Nellie Campobello's groundbreaking early-twentieth-century book *Cartucho: Relatos de la lucha en el norte de México* (*Cartucho: Tales of the Struggle in Northern Mexico*) is crucial reading for courses on the 1910 Mexican Revolution, the borderlands of Mexico and the United States, and Mexicana and Chicana literatures. Doris Meyer and Irene Matthews's translation into English makes *Cartucho* accessible to classes held in English or Spanish. However, Campobello's scintillating, short accounts of the men and women who fought for and against Campobello's historical protagonist, Francisco (Pancho) Villa, can be difficult for undergraduates to comprehend because of the specific historical context from which *Cartucho* developed, the fragmented nature of these individual accounts or *estampas*, and the discontinuous style of the entire narrative, which combines the fragments without overtly connecting them. This brief discussion of why her book should be taught includes a plan for guided instruction from three different historical angles:

Historicize the time and setting of the book: Students complete basic readings on major combatant figures of the 1910 Revolution—Venustiano Carranza, Álvaro Obregón, Emiliano

Zapata, Villa, or others—to map social factors and intricate rivalries between competing leaders of the struggle. The readings highlight individual participants and demonstrate the multifaceted nature of this complex civil war.

Clarify the author's context and motivations: The professor guides students through a selection of supplemental primary source materials to facilitate understanding of Campobello's goal to redeem Pancho Villa from a political smear campaign at the national level that started after his 1915 defeat in Celaya. *Cartucho* also demonstrates the resistance Campobello faced as a woman in a publishing culture that favored novels on the revolution written by men and the difficulties of speaking out as a *norteña* ("northern Mexican woman") when the leaders of the new government identified with Mexico City and central Mexico.

Provide a "genetic" reading of the text: To help students view the major changes that occurred between Campobello's various editions of *Cartucho* and grasp the significance of specific textual alterations, the professor should create a handout that outlines those revisions (or use this essay's appendix) and offer close readings of at least two *estampas* that underwent major changes (one that was deleted and another that doubled in length) between the 1931, 1940, and 1960 editions.

Cartucho is a significant text for courses on the revolution, the borderlands of Mexico and the United States, and Mexicana and Chicana literatures for several reasons. First, in the direct aftermath of the revolution (the 1930s and 1940s), Campobello was the sole female writer in Mexico to approach the revolution through narrative fiction. The crucial literary genre of the early twentieth century in Mexico, *la novela de la Revolución* ("the novel of the revolution"), was dominated by men. Campobello's *Cartucho* stands out because it provides a narrative that views the violence through the eyes of a child, a young girl also named Nellie. The book offers a unique, painful, and eerily clairvoyant take on the war that is lacking in better-known novels, such as Mariano Azuela's *Los de abajo* (*The Underdogs*) or Rafael F. Muñoz's *Vámonos con Pancho Villa* (*Let's Go with Pancho Villa*). For a war in which the figure of *la soldadera* has become iconic, Campobello offers one of the few narratives in this genre that takes women at face value and portrays them as real participants in the action without falling into worn-out stereotypes on one side of the other of the Eve/Mary binary.[1] Furthermore, Campobello's narrative has an avant-garde form—short and stark accounts—in contrast to the traditional form of most novels about the revolution by male writers.

Second, *Cartucho* offers a markedly regional perspective on the revolution that champions one of its defeated leaders—the infamous Pancho Villa, dubbed *el centauro del norte* ("the centaur of the north")—and casts him as a hero for the Mexican nation-state, in contrast to his portrayal in Mexico City as a bandit. During the years directly following the revolution, the political figures based in Mexico City vilified Villa and Zapata, both of whom were leading rural revolutionary figures. Campobello's almost unconditional praise for Villa both prefigured and helped to create his more positive current image in Mexican culture.

Third, the avant-garde nature of this fragmented narrative—told through the eyes of a child—influences Mexican literature, Latin American literature, Chicana literature, and world literature in both direct and indirect ways. *Cartucho*'s influence directly effects later twentieth century Mexicana and Chicana literatures as well as the greatly touted mode of magical realism. Elena Poniatowska, one of Mexico's renowned contemporary writers, names Campobello as one of the seven outstanding women of Mexico's twentieth century in her narrative *Las siete cabritas* (*The Seven Sisters*), while literary critic Jorge Aguilar Mora establishes continuity from Campobello to Juan Rulfo to Gabriel García Márquez: "*Cien años de soledad* no hubiera sido posible sin *Pedro Páramo* y *Pedro Páramo* no hubiera sido posible sin *Cartucho* de Nellie Campobello" ("*One Hundred Years of Solitude* would not have been possible without *Pedro Páramo*, and *Pedro Páramo* would not have been possible without *Cartucho*, by Nellie Campobello"; 10).[2]

In short, Campobello wrote *Cartucho* in the early twentieth century on the margins of gender, region, and genre. She has now gone from being marginalized as a woman writer, a *norteña*, and an author of an avant-garde narrative to being a precursor, at least partially, in the development of a visible magical realist narrative style. Her support of Villa has also become a national norm rather than a peripheral view.

Civil wars are not "civil." Just as the violent upheaval of the Civil War tore the United States at its seams, so too the complex civil war in Mexico at the beginning of the twentieth century, typically described in the singular as the Mexican Revolution, shook the Mexican nation-state. The revolution was, instead, many revolutions, combining a series of disparate upheavals and multiple levels of alliance and intrigue. Students can better understand *Cartucho*—a fragmentary, localized text about a multifaceted national war—when provided a clear historical context.

Assigning historical readings can help delineate the inception of the war to oust the long-term dictator Porfirio Díaz, the subsequent overthrow of the elected president Francisco I. Madero by Victoriano Huerta, and the eventual defeat of Huerta by disparate regional groups including Zapata's army in the south, Villa's in the north, and the tacitly allied forces of Venustiano Carranza and Álvaro Obregón—all in little over a decade. The assigned texts should highlight the eventual and complete falling out between Villa and the Carranza-Obregón alliance because this antagonism shapes the entire plot of *Cartucho*. Campobello's book takes place in Villa's northern Mexico in the later years of the revolution when the Villistas' primary enemies were theoretically their former allies—the followers of Carranza. This background helps students understand the rivalries in *Cartucho* that appear to pit some of Villa's followers against other Villistas.

Specific readings that demonstrate this context include the following: Martín Luis Guzmán's autobiographical novel *El águila y la serpiente* (available in an abridged English version as *The Eagle and the Serpent*), or his later and much longer *Memorias de Pancho Villa* (translated as *Memoirs of Pancho Villa*), which both clearly develop Villa, Carranza, and Obregón, but also demonstrate Villa's closest relationships with men such as Rodolfo Fierro and Tomás Urbina. Assigning selections from Guzmán's novel introduces students to the core canon of *la novela de la Revolución*, the genre in which Campobello inserts herself with *Cartucho*. Readings from the memoir can help students better understand Villa as a complex historical figure. In short, Guzmán's works prepare students to understand both the regional and personal rivalries at play in Campobello's text. Luis Aguirre Benavides's personal history of the revolution, *De Francisco I. Madero a Francisco Villa: Memorias de un revolucionario* (*From Francisco I. Madero to Francisco Villa: Memories of a Revolutionary*; unavailable in English), is another powerful text that creates a clear context for *Cartucho*. Aguirre Benavides cites letters that he and others wrote during the conflict and reprints lengthy military documents, but the most interesting parts of his book are his descriptions of the relationships between various leaders (especially Villa, Obregón, and Carranza) and their troops. Unlike many books that deal directly with Villa, including Campobello's literary corpus, Aguirre Benavides's text is not obsessed with redeeming or condemning Villa. Its stance toward Villa is both laudatory and critical and feels evenhanded.

Enlightened through selections from these readings, students will better understand *Cartucho*'s regional complexity from the start. This background prepares students for the pro-Villa and anti-Carranza sentiments visible from the first *estampa* forward, and more importantly, it clarifies certain episodes in which the Villistas appear to be battling each other. For example, the context surrounding Villa's relationship with Urbina provided by the sixth chapter of Aguirre Benavides's book (79–88), Guzmán's chapter "El sueño del compadre Urbina" ("Compadre Urbina's Drowsiness") from *El águila y la serpiente* (364–70),[3] and the twenty-fifth and twenty-sixth chapters of Edgcumb Pinchon's *Viva Villa!* (315–21, 322–25) significantly alters the reading of Campobello's *estampa* "Los hombres de Urbina" ("Urbina's Men") by detailing Villa's long-running friendship with Urbina and how it ended when Urbina abandoned Villa's cause in 1915. Without the context, this piece might look like a critique of Villa, since in it Nellie's mother laments the execution of a young follower of Urbina named Santos Ortiz, who is killed for not recognizing Villa as his leader even though the whole community does not want Ortiz to die. With the contextual apparatus in place, Ortiz's unwillingness to re-ally himself with Villa can be understood as tantamount to treason, and his execution, while still cast as tragic by Nellie, her mother, and the community, no longer reads as a critique of Villa.

Pancho Villa's current status as a revolutionary icon in Mexico hides the historical fact that in postrevolutionary Mexico the powerbrokers who created the nation's historical narrative openly maligned him. Campobello was an unabashed supporter of Villa at a time when such a view was not the norm outside of Villa and Campobello's home region of northern Mexico. To help students understand both Campobello's motives for writing *Cartucho* and the environment in which she created this book, the professor can assign Campobello's autobiographical prologue to *Mis libros* ("Prólogo"). Reading the prologue, which consists of just over thirty-six pages, allows students to have a high-quality conversation about how an author can challenge a particular political hegemony. Passages from the prologue demonstrate the ambiance of the era in which Campobello first wrote *Cartucho*: for instance, "A Francisco Villa lo consideraban peor que al propio Atila. A todos sus hombres los clasificaban de horribles bandidos y asesinos. . . . [L]o atacaban sistemáticamente con el solo propósito de desvirtuarlo y destruirle su personalidad de gran mexicano y de guerrero genial" ("They considered Francisco Villa worse than Attila himself. They classified his men as horrible bandits and killers. . . . They attacked him systematically with the sole purpose of misrepresenting him and destroying his persona as a great Mexican and a brilliant warrior"; 14), and "Me negaron el saludo gentes que se habían dicho amigos, pues no querían nada con la defensora, según ellos y sus mentiras, de bandidos" ("People that had said they were my friends refused to greet me, since they didn't want anything to do with the defender, according to them and their lies, of bandits"; 26–27).

Professors can help students notice the reference to a smear campaign against Villa's reputation, which served as an initial impetus for creating *Cartucho*, and they can follow this reference with an in-depth examination of her narrative style, her own revolutionary act. The following passage provides Campobello's call to arms, in which she invites readers to consider the "real" revolutionaries and to take back their history:

> Y por lo que hace al general Villa, ya lo he dicho una y otra vez: su leyenda negra cubría hasta el más inocente gesto de su vida diaria. ¿Por qué no lo defendieron quienes sabían que era mentira lo que de él contaban? Misterio no es: tenían miedo. . . . La verdad debe decirse. Nosotros, los hijos de los verdaderos revolucionarios, tenemos la obligación de hablar y pedir que se descorra la cortina. La historia lo pide así, pues nuestra patria no es propiedad de unos cuantos, carrancistas, obregonistas o callistas. (44)
>
> And for what this does to general Villa, I have already said it again and again: his black legend covered even the most innocent movement of his daily life. Why didn't those who knew that what was said about him was a lie defend him? This is no mystery: they were afraid. . . . The truth should be told. We, the children of the true revolutionaries, have the obligation to talk and ask that the curtain be drawn back. History asks it to be so, since our homeland is not the property of a few supporters of Carranza, Obregón, or Calles.

For advanced courses that allow for more extensive reading from Campobello's corpus, her biography of Villa, *Apuntes sobre la vida military de Francisco Villa* (*Notes on the Military Life of Francisco Villa*), also reveals her strong opinions about both Villa's image and Mexican history. One of her more laudatory comments appears in the book's introductory note: "Encuentro situado a Francisco Villa como el único genio guerrero de su tiempo, uno de los más grandes de la historia; el mejor de América y después de Gengis Kan, el más grande guerrero que ha existido" ("I find Francisco Villa situated as the only brilliant warrior of his time, one of the greatest in history; the best in America, and after Genghis Khan, the grandest guerrilla that has ever lived"; 10). In short, assigning the prologue to *Mis libros* and selections from *Apuntes* helps situate the metaphorical battlefield where Campobello fired her first *cartucho* ("cartridge") and makes her target clear: the redemption and restoration of Villa to Mexican history.

For a basic understanding of Campobello's biography, her narrative style, and the historical reasons behind some of the revisions she made in the later editions of *Cartucho*, professors can assign Jorge Aguilar Mora's "El silencio de Nellie Campobello" ("Nellie Campobello's Silence"), which serves as the introduction to Ediciones Era's 2000 republication of *Cartucho*. For classes in which students do not read Spanish, Dennis Parle's "Narrative Style and Technique in Nellie Campobello's *Cartucho*" can also be helpful before professors set up a genetic reading of the different editions of *Cartucho*. A complete genetic analysis of the textual changes Campobello performed between the first edition in 1931, the second edition in 1940, and the reissue of that second edition in her collection *Mis libros* in 1960 (the version used by the book's English translators in 1988) requires greater time and, perhaps, graduate-level study. However, some attention to Campobello's revisions can happen at the undergraduate level. The appendix below can be used as a handout or a digital document to direct students toward both moderate and significant revisions in the text.[4]

The appendix creates several points of entry for compelling discussions about the Revolution itself, Campobello's investment in it, and how her desire to portray Villa in a positive light only increased through time. In a class that can study all three editions of *Cartucho*, students will discover that the second edition includes twenty-four new vignettes, several depicting Villa directly. The first edition reveals Villa's shadow rather than his presence, while the second openly portrays him in both personal and positive ways. Also, the second edition only omits one *estampa* that appeared in the first edition—a piece titled "Villa" that can be read as an open critique of the general since it ends with Nellie's mother (the book's other connecting thread) criticizing Villa for his unwillingness to provide for the widows of his dead followers. Evaluating both editions together helps students see the political intentions of the author, her reclaiming of Villa. Finally, Campobello only revised one piece when she reissued the second edition in *Mis libros*, the vignette "Nacha Ceniceros," but the revision is substantial. In both the first and second editions, this piece ends with Nacha's death after Villa demands that she be executed for killing one of his men. The revision literally rewrites the narrative by proclaiming: "Esta fue la versión que durante mucho tiempo prevaleció en aquellas regiones del Norte. La verdad se vino a saber años después. Nacha Ceniceros vivía"

("This was the version that was told for many years in the North of Mexico. The truth came out some time later. Nacha Ceniceros was still alive"; *Cartucho* [*Mis libros*] 79; *Cartucho* [Cartucho] 21). Then the revision offers a description of Ceniceros's life after the revolution. To be sure that the audience does not miss the effect of this shift, Campobello includes the following didactic paragraph toward the end of the revision: "La red de mentiras que contra el general Villa difundieron los simuladores, los grupos de la calumnia organizada, los creadores de la leyenda negra, irá cayendo como tendrán que caer las estatuas de bronce que se han levantado con los dineros avanzados" ("The curtain of lies against General Villa, spread by organized groups of slanderers and propagators of the black legend, will fall, just as will the bronze statues that have been erected with their contributions"; 80; 21).

After historicizing *Cartucho* as a part of Mexico's complex revolution, contextualizing Campobello's motives for writing the book, and examining the revisions she offered through the book's three printings, professors can include *Cartucho* as one of the primary sources their students can examine in a final paper or other significant writing assignment. Having students conduct research on the secondary literature around *Cartucho* through a general database such as the *MLA International Bibliography*, or a more specific database like the *Hispanic American Periodicals Index*, emphasizes the text's former marginalized status. These searches demonstrate how the majority of critics have treated *Cartucho* in a less laudatory way than they have treated the other *novelas de la Revolución*, and this process allows for high-quality class discussion and compelling student writing around the important question of how a text's genre and an author's gender, region, or political affiliation affect that text's reception.

Notes

1. Azuela's *Los de abajo* provides a typical example of how the Eve/Mary dichotomy limits female agency. The novel's three primary women—Demetrio Macías's wife (the angel of the house or Mary figure), La Pintada (the *soldadera* whom the novel casts as a whore), and Camila (the young girl who becomes a fallen woman)—have no real choices within Mexico's patriarchal society. While they make distinct decisions, all three characters are abandoned (and in Camila's case, dead) by the end of the novel. For two novels written after *Cartucho* that break out of the Eve/Mary dichotomy, see Elena Garro's *Los recuerdos del porvenir* (*Recollections of Things to Come*) and Elena Poniatowska's *Hasta no verte, Jesús mío* (*Here's to You, Jesusa!*; 2002); Poniatowska's novel has also been published in English as *Until We Meet Again* (1993).

2. Translations in the essay are mine unless otherwise indicated.

3. The abridged translation of Guzmán's novel does not include this particular chapter.

4. Almost every *estampa* received minor changes in punctuation and spacing between the first and second editions of *Cartucho*, and several vignettes went through a few sentence-level changes without the meaning of those revised sentences being altered. These minor changes are not included in the appendix.

Appendix: *Cartucho* Editions

First Spanish Edition (1931)	Second Spanish Edition (1940)	English Translation (1988; from 1960 Version in *Mis libros*)	Changes between First and Second Editions
"Integrales"			Introduction; appears only in the first edition
"Inicial"			Campobello's explanatory note; appears only in the first edition
"Hombres del norte"	"Hombres del norte"	"Men of the North"	First section of the book in all editions
"Cartucho"	"Él"	"He"	
"Elías"	"Elías"	"Elías"	
"El Kirilí"	"El Kirilí"	"El 'Kirilí'"	
"Bustillos"	"El coronel Bustillos"	"Colonel Bustillos"	
"Bartolo"	"Bartolo de Santiago"	"Bartolo from Santiago"	
"Agustín García"	"Agustín García"	"Agustín García"	
"Villa"			The only *estampa* in the first edition that does not appear in the second edition
	"Las cintareadas de Antonio Silva"	"Antonio Silva's Sword Whippings"	New to the second edition
"Fusilados"	"Fusilados"	"The Executed"	Second section of the book in all editions
"4 soldados sin 30-30"	"Cuatro soldados sin 30-30"	"Four Soldiers without 30-30s"	
"El fusilado sin balas"	"El fusilado sin balas"	"Executed without Bullets"	
"Epifanio"	"Epifanio"	"Epifanio"	Final line added
"Zafiro y Zequiel"	"Zafiro y Zequiel"	"Zafiro and Zequiel"	
"José Antonio y othón"	"José Antonio tenía 13 años"	"José Antonio was Thirteen"	
"Nacha Ceniceros"	"Nacha Ceniceros"	"Nacha Ceniceros"	Significant revision between second edition and the version in *Mis libros* that doubles the piece's length
	"Los cinco de la tarde"	"Five O'clock in the Afternoon"	New to the second edition

(*continued*)

Appendix *(continued)*

First Spanish Edition (1931)	Second Spanish Edition (1940)	English Translation (1988; from 1960 Version in *Mis libros*)	Changes between First and Second Editions
"Los 30-30"	"Los 30-30"	"The 30-30s"	Brief additions
"Por un beso"	"Por un beso"	"For a Kiss"	Brief additions
"El corazón del coronel Bufanda"	"El corazón del coronel Bufanda"	"The Heart of Colonel Bufanda"	Significant revisions to the penultimate paragraph
"La sentencia de Babis"	"La sentencia de Babis"	"Babis' Sentence"	
"El muerto"	"El muerto"	"The Dead Man"	
"Mugre"	"Mugre"	"Grime"	Significant elisions and revisions
"Las tarjetas de Martín López"			Appears at the end of section 2 in the second edition
"El centinela del mesón del Águila"	"El centinela del mesón del Águila"	"The Sentinel of El Aguila Barracks"	
"El general Rueda"	"El general Rueda"	"General Rueda"	
"Las tripas del general Sabarzo"	"Las tripas del general Sabarzo"	"General Sobarzo's Guts"	
"El ahorcado"	"El ahorcado"	"The Hanged Man"	
"Desde una ventana"	"Desde una ventana"	"From a Window"	Significant but brief elision
"Los hombres de Urbina"	"Los hombres de Urbina"	"Urbina's Men"	Significant textual changes throughout
"La tristeza de 'El Peet'"	"Las tristezas de El Peet"	"El Peet's Sadness"	
"La muerte de Felipe Angeles"	"La muerte de Felipe Ángeles"	"The Death of Felipe Angeles"	
	"La muleta de Pablo López"	"Pablo López's Crutch"	New to the second edition
	"La camisa gris"	"The Gray Shirt"	New to the second edition
	"La sonrisa de José"	"José's Smile"	New to the second edition
	"Tomás Urbina"	"Tomás Urbina"	New to the second edition
	"El Jefe de las Armas los mandó fusilar"	"The Commanding Officer Ordered Them Executed"	New to the second edition
	"Las águilas verdes"	"The Green Eagles"	New to the second edition
	"Las tarjetas de Martín López"	"Martín López's Snapshots"	Appears earlier in section 2 in the first edition
"En el fuego"	"En el fuego"	"Under Fire"	Third section of the book in all editions
"El sueño de 'El Siete'"	"El sueño de El Siete"	"El Siete's Dream"	Significant textual changes throughout
"Las cartucheras de 'El Siete'"			Appears later in the second edition under the title "Sus cartucheras" with minor and major changes, including a new closing paragraph

Appendix *(continued)*

First Spanish Edition (1931)	Second Spanish Edition (1940)	English Translation (1988; from 1960 Version in *Mis libros*)	Changes between First and Second Editions
"Los heridos de Pancho Villa"	"Los heridos de Pancho Villa"	"Pancho Villa's Wounded Men"	Textual changes throughout
"Los tres meces de Gloriecita"	"Los tres meces de Gloriecita"	"Little Gloria's Three Months"	Textual changes throughout
"Mi hermano 'El Siete'"	"Mi hermano y su baraja"	"My Brother and His Deck of Cards"	The last *estampa* in the book in the first edition; significant changes in the second edition, including title change
	"Sus cartucheras"	"His Cartridge Belts"	Appears earlier in the first edition under the title "Las carchuteras de 'el siete'"
	"El cigarro de Samuel"	"Samuel's Cigarette"	New to the second edition
	"Las balas de José"	"José's Bullets"	New to the second edition
	"El milagro de Julio"	"A Miracle for Julio"	New to the second edition
	"Las sandías"	"The Watermelons"	New to the second edition
	"Las rayadas"	"The Loaves of Bread"	New to the second edition
	"La voz del General"	"The General's Voice"	New to the second edition
	"Las lágrimas del general Villa"	"General Villa's Tears"	New to the second edition
	"El sombrero"	"The Hat"	New to the second edition
	"Los vigías"	"The Lookouts"	New to the second edition
	"Los dos Pablos"	"The Two Pablos"	New to the second edition
	"Los oficiales de la Segunda del Rayo"	"The Officers of Segunda del Rayo"	New to the second edition
	"Abelardo Prieto"	"Abelardo Prieto"	New to the second edition
	"Las hojas verdes de Martín López"	"The Green Leaves of Martín López"	New to the second edition
	"Tragedia de Martín"	"The Tragedy of Martín"	New to the second edition
	"Las mujeres del norte"	"The Women of the North"	New to the second edition
	"Ismael Máynez y Martín López"	"Ismael Maynez and Martín López"	New to the second edition

Works Cited

Aguilar Mora, Jorge. "El silencio de Nellie Campobello." *Cartucho: Relatos de la lucha en el norte de México*. Ediciones Era, 2000, pp. 9–43.

Aguirre Benavides, Luis. *De Francisco I. Madero a Francisco Villa: Memorias de un revolucionario*. A. del Bosque, 1966.

Azuela, Mariano. *Los de abajo*. 1916. Fondo de Cultura Económica, 1995.

Campobello, Nellie. *Apuntes sobre la vida militar de Francisco Villa*. EDIAPSA, 1940.

———. *Cartucho*. Cartucho *and* My Mother's Hands. Translated by Doris Meyer and Irene Matthews, U of Texas P, 1988, pp. 1–90.

———. *Cartucho. Mis libros*, by Campobello, CGESA, 1960, pp. 47–181.
———. *Cartucho: Relatos de la lucha en el norte de México.* Ediciones Integrales, 1931.
———. *Cartucho: Relatos de la lucha en el norte de México.* 2nd ed., EDIAPSA, 1940.
———. "Prólogo." *Mis libros*, by Campobello, CGESA, 1960, pp. 9–45.
Garro, Elena. *Los recuerdos del porvenir.* Joaquín Mortiz, 1963.
Guzmán, Martín Luís. *El águila y la serpiente.* 1928. Editorial Anahuac, 1941.
———. *Memorias de Pancho Villa.* 3rd ed., Compania General de Ediciones, 1954.
Parle, Dennis J. "Narrative Style and Technique in Nellie Campobello's *Cartucho.*" *Kentucky Romance Quarterly*, vol. 32, no. 2, 1985, pp. 201–11.
Pinchon, Edgcumb. *Viva Villa!* Harcourt, Brace and Company, 1933.
Poniatowska, Elena. *Hasta no verte, Jesús mío.* Ediciones Era, 1969.
———. *Las siete cabritas.* Ediciones Era, 2000.

Oswaldo Estrada

Sor Juana's Legacy and Rosario Castellanos's Feminist Essays

Teaching the feminist thought of Rosario Castellanos (1925–74) in an undergraduate literature seminar helps students identify the strides toward gender equality made by earlier generations and how or why she has influenced many Mexicana and Chicana writers born since the mid–twentieth century. Through her writings on imposed female silence, self-sacrifice, and women's lack of participation in the creation of local culture, Castellanos denounces a history of female subordination, which she experienced personally in her own estrangement and ambivalent condition. She used her writing, as Elena Poniatowska points out, as a form of therapy or confession to confront male authority, to seek social and political change, and to liberate herself and other women trapped in a world made for men (*¡Ay vida* 57). A true intellectual, Castellanos situates herself in her writings as an exile on the margins, or as the author of a combative language that seeks to speak the truth to power. If organic intellectuals, according to Edward W. Said, use their ability to speak so as to articulate a particular message, or to convey a subversive attitude or dissident opinion to and for others (11), then Castellanos is certainly one of them. Her writing proves that even in the twenty-first century, although women have won many feminist battles, we must continue fighting for gender equality and for the recognition of women's intellectuality.

At the University of North Carolina, Chapel Hill, I regularly teach a first-year seminar titled Mexican Women across Borders and Genres. As an introductory literature course for first-year students, it is meant to expose undergraduates to the intellectual life of the university. It is taught in English, using primary and secondary texts in English or in English translation, to expose a wide range of students outside the Spanish major to how scholars analyze literary texts as sources of knowledge. The course explores various narratives by which Mexican women live or are expected to live. Participants read poems, letters, stories, chronicles, and short novels by Mexicanas and Chicanas of the twentieth century whose writing transgresses several genres and challenges traditional notions of gender and marginality. Taking into account the negative impact that religion, colonialism, nationalism, and modernization have had on the representation of Mexican women, the course addresses, among other themes and topics, the role of memory and discourse, the inevitable formation of otherness, identity construction, gender ambiguities, moral subversions and inversions, textual experimentation and performance, and the long-lasting effects of gender violence and its portrayal as a psychological trauma. Throughout the semester we read works by Poniatowska (*¡Ay vida* and *Soldaderas*), Sandra Cisneros, Gloria Anzaldúa (26–35), Cristina Rivera Garza, María Luisa Puga, Cherríe Moraga, Margo Glantz, and Ana Clavel, among others.

To provide undergraduates with a historical perspective on women's use of the word, we spend the first week discussing the early feminism of the colonial nun Sor Juana Inés de la Cruz as portrayed in her famous 1691 *Poet's Answer to the Most Illustrious Sister Filotea de la Cruz* (*Answer* 39–105), and some of her poems, such as her "Philosophical Satire" (156–59). After viewing María Luisa Bemberg's film *I, the Worst of All*, we spend the following week examining some of Rosario Castellanos's feminist poems—"Silence near an Ancient Stone" (*Rosario* 81), "Presence" (88), and "Self-Portrait" (100–01)—and such essays as "Once Again Sor Juana" (222–25), "Woman and Her Image" (236–44), and "Self-Sacrifice Is a Mad Virtue" (259–63). These essays, in particular, demonstrate Castellanos's controversial ideas in regard to machismo and otherness, gender inequality, historical determinism, and invisibility. Although we read other critical and theoretical works on gender throughout the semester, by Michel Foucault (1–13), Judith Butler (3–44), and Toril Moi (49–67), for example, I want students to understand from the beginning of our course not only Castellanos's pioneering feminism but also the fact that in-depth reflections as regards gender inequality were produced in Latin America starting in the colonial era, throughout the nineteenth century, and certainly during the mid-1960s and early 1970s, when Castellanos composed some of her best feminist pieces. In my experience, teaching the feminism of Castellanos at the beginning of a course on contemporary Mexicana and Chicana writers works well, as it allows students to see how she has influenced several writers who are from Mexico or of Mexican descent, who were born in the 1950s and over the following two decades, and who live on both sides of the border between Mexico and the United States. If this course were taught in Spanish, it could also be offered as a special topics course or as a senior seminar for majors.

The first essay that we discuss during our third week of classes, "Once Again Sor Juana," originally written in 1963, was included in *Summary Judgments* (1966), a collection of essays that passed largely unnoticed, even though it was composed almost a decade before Hélène Cixous and Luce Irigaray began to publish their controversial feminist manifestos (Ahern 39–40). Since students have already spent the first two weeks learning about Sor Juana's reflections on women's access to knowledge, I begin class with a five-minute warm-up where students in small groups discuss overall differences and similarities between the nun's arguments for women's intellectuality and Castellanos's in the mid–twentieth century. After students have the opportunity to share their thoughts with the entire class, we do a new, close reading of "Once Again Sor Juana," highlighting how Castellanos uses her public writing to disassemble a predetermined destiny for women by denouncing their mythologization.

Unlike Mexico's saintly mother, the Virgin of Guadalupe, or the Indigenous interpreter Malinche—dubbed a traitor by some contemporary Mexicans and the founder of a mestizo nation by others—Sor Juana is regarded as an anomaly. In "Once Again Sor Juana," Castellanos writes: "The initial stigma she poses for us is not her genius (sufficient to worry many doctors) but her femininity" (223). While in her master's thesis, *On Feminine Culture*, which she defended in 1950, Castellanos states that societies keep women at a safe distance from the production of culture, in this particular essay—published thirteen years later—she tackles head-on why Sor Juana, the Baroque intellectual, is considered a threat to society:

> Not because she chose the convent, a very commonplace deed in the New Spain of her time. Not because she wrote somewhat charming verse, because it was already a saying that in this newly founded metropolis there were more poets than fertilizer (and fertilizer was very abundant). No, it was because it was a woman who wrote those poems. Because it was a woman who had an intellectual vocation and transformed it into literary work. (224)

Analyzing this passage allows students to recognize Castellanos as a true intellectual who rejects ready-made formulas and conventional language, and who creates, instead, a dissident discourse capable of changing calcified perceptions and inherited points of view (Said 23). No less powerful and controversial is the passage where she points out that Sor Juana's work provoked the admiration of her contemporaries "not for its intrinsic qualities but because it sprang from a hand whose natural employment should have been cooking or sewing" (Castellanos 224). Armed with these arguments, Castellanos effectively revives Sor Juana's intellectual defense of women's access to knowledge, as exposed in her *Poet's Answer to the Most Illustrious Sister Filotea de la Cruz*, where the nun provides historical examples of women like Saint Gertrude or Saint Paula who greatly benefited from "studying, reading and writing" (79). Simultaneously, though, Sor Juana depicts herself in opposition to other women of her own time who limit their lives and blindly accept their oppression without seeking any transformations, new horizons, and other possibilities (Schwartz 63).

With the purpose of extending our discussion of "Once Again Sor Juana," toward the end of class we watch the three-minute book trailer of Virginia Woolf's *A Room of One's Own* (1929), found on *YouTube* and performed by the English actress Eileen Atkins. As we confirm that Woolf's renowned feminist text exposes in the early twentieth century countless moments of prejudice against women writers for their natural inclination to read and write in a world made for men, we also understand why Castellanos, more than three decades later, furiously rejects a psychoanalytic reading of Sor Juana—such as the one carried out by Ludwig Pfandl in 1963—that reduces her intellectuality to a neurotic and narcissistic impulse. The feminist lesson that Castellanos delivers in "Once Again Sor Juana" is just as persuasive as Woolf's essay, especially since she ends her argument with a rhetorical question that expands beyond the printed page: "Wouldn't it be fairer to think that Sor Juana, like any other human being, possessed a backbone, that it was her own vocation that she chose among all the different kinds available to her, the one she was most able to count on achieving?" (225).

To further analyze Castellanos's denouncement of women's misrepresentation, systematic mythologization, and distorted portrayals, we begin our next class by discussing "Woman and Her Image," the persuasive text with which she opens her feminist discussion in *A Woman Who Knows Latin* (1973). In her study of this text, Maricruz Castro Ricalde identifies the articulation of a strong feminist discourse that seeks to deconstruct, from a universalist perspective, the "feminine myth" using Castellanos's own voice and that of other female intellectuals like Simone de Beauvoir and Woolf (186–87). Castro Ricalde's observation is absolutely right. Drawing from Beauvoir and Woolf, Castellanos asserts that in the course of history, "more than a natural phenomenon, a component of society, or a human creature, woman has been myth" (236). As mythical figures, she argues, women are condemned, ab initio, to incarnate a set of predetermined principles that erase their willpower, consciousness, and spirit. With guided questions, students work in small groups to decipher the arguments with which Castellanos creates a feminist discourse. Thus, students have the opportunity to discuss among themselves the claims that women, as female deities, are stripped of their humanity; that female beauty is not only an ideal composed and imposed by men but a permanent physical and mental limitation; and that, as "the Angel[s] in the House," according to Woolf, women must be excellent models of virtue, purity, and ignorance.

By going over passages of "Woman and Her Image" where Castellanos exposes the mythologization of women and its fatal consequences, students recognize how she elaborates "an overtly feminist viewpoint with wit and clarity" (Lindstrom 66). A central topic of our discussion is her denunciation of maternity as a societal imposition that awkwardly allows women to obtain a metaphoric certificate of "genuine citizenship." Students enjoy connecting Castellanos's negative portrayal of pregnancy as "a sickness whose outcome is always catastrophic for whomever suffers it" with current debates on women and education, delayed pregnancies, gender discrimination against professional women who become pregnant, the cost of being a single mother, and so on (241). This discussion reinforces something that Castellanos defends in many of her essays and also in her poetry, novels, and plays: that a woman's identity is purely based on her sex and not on her own choices, true gender identity, diverse life experiences, intellectual capacity, goals, and personal achievements (Rivero 91).

As we move to the next essay, we reflect on contemporary societies' need to keep women away from the production and propagation of knowledge. After all, as Castellanos rightly argued over four decades ago in "Woman and Her Image," learned nuns like Sor Juana and other transgressive women who fight against a predetermined destiny of passiveness and psychological confinement still represent a threat: "Each one in her way and in her own circumstances denies the conventional, making the foundations of the establishment tremble, turning hierarchies upside down, and achieving authenticity." Castellanos's feminist lesson here is crystal clear: to become her true self, a woman must reject "those false images that false mirrors offer a woman in the enclosed gallery where her life takes place" (244).

Castellanos pursues this combative attitude against socially determined sex roles in another essay that we analyze during the same class period, "Self-Sacrifice Is a Mad Virtue," originally published in the newspaper *Excélsior* on 21 February 1971. This time Castellanos the polemicist, with her distinctive argumentative voice, affirms:

> Let us not yield to the simple sophistry of the antifeminists who proclaim an inferiority attributable to sex. Sex, as well as race, does not constitute any biological, historical, or social predetermination. It is simply a collection of conditions, a frame of concrete references within which humankind makes the effort to attain fulfillment in the development of its creative potential. (259–60)

Her words, students conclude during our open discussion, are very current—especially given the twenty-first century's heated debates on gender, gender roles, transgender subjects, the LGBTQ community in Mexico and the United States, and the ongoing discrimination against those individuals whose gender identity or expression differs from their assigned sex. "The essence of femininity does not exist," Castellanos writes, "because what is one thing in one culture is considered to be something else in another, is not considered at all, or is part of the characteristics of masculinity" (260). Her reasoning, of course, speaks volumes about diversity; different ways one can be a woman, regardless of one's capacity or desire to produce children; and women's supposedly natural inclination to self-sacrifice.

Subsequently, working in pairs, students choose one of Castellanos's statements with which she concludes her essay, read it out loud, and supplement it with contemporary interpretations and additions of their own. These statements include the following:

> "It is not just—and therefore neither is it legitimate—that one of the two persons who make up the couple gives all, yet does not expect anything in return."
>
> "It is not just—thus it is not legitimate—that one of them has the opportunity to develop intellectually, while the other has no alternative but to remain subject to ignorance." (262)
>
> "It is not just—therefore it is not legal—that one of them is master of his own body and disposes of it at will, while the other reserves her body, not to derive benefits, but to unwillingly have it acted upon." (262–63)

What students comment on, as they examine the validity of her postulates, is indeed revealing. Individually and collectively, they confirm that Castellanos, in agreement with Luce Irigaray's theorizations on women's bodies, sees women's sexuality as multiple and does not see women's bodies as passive sexual vessels or as objects that merely supplement male activity (Guerra 67). Castellanos's feminist discourse calls for action, especially when Castellanos discusses, near the end of her essay, women's need to engage in a political battle to own their true selves. "Winning the battle," concludes the public intellectual, "requires not only lucidity of mind, determination of character, and moral courage, which is a serious matter, but additional resources like astuteness and, above all, persistence" (263). Through this activity, students understand that Castellanos crafts her feminist discourses as an ethicist or moralist, drawing from personal experience, using an ironic voice, to challenge the authority of inherited notions and to create awareness in a community of women readers (O'Connell 210–15). To continue thinking about Castellanos's feminism, later in the semester students have the opportunity to rewrite one of her essays from a twenty-first-century perspective, while also reflecting on her current legacy.

Through this early introduction to the feminism of Castellanos, students are better prepared to discuss, over the course of several weeks, how she influences Mexicana and Chicana writers of the late twentieth and early twenty-first centuries. The works of some authors born in the 1960s, such as Clavel, Rosa Beltrán, Adriana González Mateos, and Rivera Garza, are marked by the overt articulation of gender, gender roles, and gender transgressions. And the work of Moraga and other Chicana writers not only reflects the legacy of Anzaldúa but also that of Castellanos, whose subversive feminist voice continues to fuel discussions on women, gender equality, gender performance, lesbianism, and dissident identities. All of these writers question the erroneous idea that power and knowledge are masculine, and, as women intellectuals, they participate through their writings in current political debates that redefine sovereignty and the use of privilege (Franco 30–38). By examining their work, students reactivate Castellanos's teachings and confirm, time and again, that self-sacrifice and self-denial are mad virtues, that indeed women must continue fighting to participate in the creation of culture, and that it is never too late to turn hierarchies upside down to achieve authenticity.

Works Cited

Ahern, Maureen. "Reading Rosario Castellanos: Contexts, Voices, and Signs." *A Rosario Castellanos Reader: An Anthology of Her Poetry, Short Fiction, Essays, and Drama*, edited by Ahern, translated by Ahern et al., U of Texas P, 1988, pp. 1–79.

Anzaldúa, Gloria. *The Gloria Anzaldúa Reader*, edited by AnaLouise Keating, Duke UP, 2009.

Bemberg, María Luisa. *I, the Worst of All.* Produced by Christopher Granier-Deferre, GEA Cinematográfica, 1990.

Butler, Judith. *Gender Trouble: Feminism and the Subversion of Identity.* Routledge, 1999.

Castellanos, Rosario. *A Rosario Castellanos Reader: An Anthology of Her Poetry, Short Fiction, Essays, and Drama.* Edited by Maureen Ahern, translated by Ahern et al., U of Texas P, 1988.

Castro Ricalde, Maricruz. "*Mujer que sabe latín*: Rosario Castellanos y el ensayo." *Rosario Castellanos: Perspectivas críticas: Ensayos inéditos*, edited by Pol Popovic Karic and Fidel Chávez Pérez, Tecnológico de Monterrey / Miguel Ángel Porrúa, 2010, pp. 169–97.

Cisneros, Sandra. *The House on Mango Street.* Vintage Books, 1993.

Clavel, Ana. *Shipwrecked Body.* Translated by Jay Miskowiec, Aliform Publishing, 2008.

Cruz, Sor Juana Inés de la. *The Answer / La respuesta.* Edited and translated by Electa Arenal and Amanda Powell, Feminist Press, 1994.

Foucault, Michel. *The History of Sexuality.* Translated by Robert Hurley, Vintage Books, 1990.

Franco, Jean. *Ensayos impertinentes.* Edited by Marta Lamas, Océano / Debate Feminista, 2013.

Glantz, Margo. *The Wake.* Translated by Andrew Hurley. Curbstone Press, 2005.

Guerra, Lucía. *Mujer y escritura: Fundamentos teóricos de la crítica feminista.* Universidad Nacional Autónoma de México, 2007.

Lindstrom, Naomi. "Rosario Castellanos: Pioneer of Feminist Criticism." *Homenaje a Rosario Castellanos*, edited by Maureen Ahern and Mary Seale Vásquez, Albatros Hispanófila, 1980, pp. 65–73.

Moi, Toril. *Sexual / Textual Politics: Feminist Literary Theory.* Routledge, 2003.

Moraga, Cherríe. "For the Color of My Mother." *This Bridge Called My Back: Writings by Radical Women of Color*, edited by Moraga and Gloria Anzaldúa. State U of New York P, 2015, pp. 10–11.

O'Connell, Joanna. *Prospero's Daughter: The Prose of Rosario Castellanos.* U of Texas P, 1995.

Poniatowska, Elena. *¡Ay vida, no me mereces!* Joaquín Mortiz, 1985.

———. *Las Soldaderas: Women of the Mexican Revolution.* Translated by David Dorado Romo, Cinco Puntos Press, 2006.

Puga, María Luisa. "Memories on the Oblique." Translated by Leland H. Chambers. *Scents of Wood and Silence: Short Stories by Latin American Women Writers*, edited by Kathleen Ross and Yvette E. Miller, Latin American Literary Review Press, 1991, pp. 164–71.

Rivera Garza, Cristina. *No One Will See Me Cry.* Translated by Andrew Hurley. Curvestone Press, 2003.

Rivero, Eliana. "Visión social y feminista en la obra poética de Rosario Castellanos." *Homenaje a Rosario Castellanos*, edited by Maureen Ahern and Mary Seale Vásquez, Albatros Hispanófila, 1980, pp. 85–97.

A Room of One's Own. YouTube, uploaded by English Agundez, 15 Oct. 2012, www.youtube.com/watch?v=LrOtIVqLKHg. Book trailer.

Said, Edward W. *Representations of the Intellectual.* Vintage Books, 1996.

Schwartz, Perla. *Rosario Castellanos: Mujer que supo latín. . . .* Editorial Katún, 1984.

Woolf, Virginia. *Killing the Angel in the House: Seven Essays.* Penguin Books, 1995.

Pedro García-Caro

Testimony and Chronicle in Elena Poniatowska's *Las mil y una . . . La herida de Paulina*

Elena Poniatowska's multifaceted work as journalist, chronicler, and creative writer, addressing a wide range of social issues and themes, has challenged and circumvented the gender roles of public intellectuals despite a profoundly patriarchal literary scene. Additionally, her prose writings creatively and playfully explore the interconnections of different genres such as the novel, short story, chronicle, and *testimonio*, the hybrid prose genre that emerged in the mid–twentieth century. Stemming from the judicial act of bearing witness, the *testimonio* narrative usually consists of the autobiographical testimony of a figure rendered invisible by society, generally written in conversation with an anthropologist or journalist who acts as witness to the testimony. The presence of a witness is an important condition of *testimonio*, as it provides a sense of authority over the authenticity of the narrative and at times, in the case of testimonial ethnographies (i.e., indigenous testimonies edited within a Western anthropological framework), leads to controversial interactions between the subject and the editor or researcher. Examples of the genre as practiced by women writers and subjects include *Si me permiten hablar: Testimonio de Domitila* (*Let Me Speak: Testimony of Domitila, a Woman of the Bolivian Mines*, 1977), by Moema Viezzer and Domitila Barrios, and *Me llamo Rigoberta Menchú y así me nació la conciencia* (*I, Rigoberta Menchú: An Indian Woman in Guatemala*), by Elizabeth Burgos and Rigoberta Menchú, which have received ample attention from literary and cultural critics; the work by Burgos and Menchú has even inspired some controversy (Arias; Stoll). Poniatowska's approach to *testimonio* narratives favored a more experimental approach in her early works *Hasta no verte, Jesús mío* (1969; *Until We Meet Again*), featuring a woman soldier, and *La noche de Tlatelolco: Testimonios de historia oral* (1971; *Massacre in Mexico*), on the horrifying 1968 student massacre by government forces. In the 1950s, a young Poniatowska assisted the (later controversial) American anthropologist Oscar Lewis when he studied poverty in Mexico City, where it is thought she gained some of her early ideas for hybrid narrative forms combining ethnography, *testimonio*, and chronicle.

With roots in texts from the era of colonization, the chronicle (from *chronos*, the Greek word for "time") is a fairly well-established journalistic genre, now associated with extended reportage and sociopolitical commentary resulting from both ample field research and a clearly defined and positioned journalistic voice. *Testimonio* seeks to open up the direct voices of those who have not been heard, and who have even been erased by official history. The distinct etymological and historical origins of both genres should allow for a clear understanding of their differences as well as their parallels: one genre is a study based on a journalist's observations, the other is a quasi-legal testimony (from *testis*, the Latin word for both "witness" and "testicle," an etymology that points to the patriarchal act of taking an oath and providing an honorable deposition), and both involve a party in a conflict who is bearing witness. There is thus a clear, organic relation between these two genres: testimonies are a necessary element for the basic compilation of a chronicle, providing a direct transcription of a life, or a set of events, a sense of immediacy, and access to the subject. The chronicle generally would combine the materials of testimonies with other important circumstantial elements. In effect, chronicle and testimony share a narrative of events from an individual's viewpoint, but they differ in the authority conferred on their authors and narrators. The chronicle narrative often assumes the objectivity of a researcher's viewpoint, while *testimonio* derives its authority from the narrator's attestation of direct participation in, agency over, and witnessing of the events at hand. This background can serve to acquaint students with the purpose of these two genres and the ways in which Poniatowska places herself as a chronicler.

Students may assume that *testimonio* narrative is autobiographical, but this assumption may not hold true in Latin American contexts: *testimonio* is the autobiography of a subject (often a survivor of trauma) who belongs only marginally to Western narrative traditions, and who perhaps provides this narrative as an oral statement to be edited and presented by others. In turn, the chronicle can be tied to a journalist's political or social agenda—for instance, to denounce patriarchal acts of oppression, as in Rosario Castellanos's series of literary chronicles and reviews for the *Excélsior* newspaper. Andrea Reyes, editor of the posthumous compilation of Castellanos's articles, describes them as "articles" and "ensayos" rather than "chronicles," demonstrating once more the fluidity and pliability of the genre (Reyes 15). *Ensayo*, or essay writing, is an even larger generic concept that encompasses most nonfiction prose. The chronicle as a genre is associated with a deep commitment to a social cause and the plight of subaltern subjects in Latin America, as noted by Mercedes Alonso: "La obligatoria solidaridad del cronista con los subalternos funciona como máxima del género desde los orígenes" ("The obligatory solidarity of a chronicler with the subaltern functions as a foundational feature of the genre since its origins"; 14).[1] Setting forth these explanations helps students understand the extensive scope of Poniatowska's narrative. They can then proceed to better grasp the assigned reading by Poniatowska, *Las mil y una . . . La herida de Paulina* (2000; *The Thousand and One . . . Paulina's Wound*).[2]

A text that effectively evokes the social changes generated by the 1994 NAFTA trade deal on a border town, Mexicali, in Baja California, *Las mil y una* is one of Poniatowska's most significant feminist chronicles, oscillating between a feminist, politically infused essay and a sociological, journalistic chronicle. Viviane Mahieux notes that the chronicle is "a flexible and malleable genre, . . . notoriously difficult to define" ("Chronicle") and describes it elsewhere as "a forum where long-lasting aesthetic influences and immediate occurrences intersect and interact." (*Urban Chroniclers* 7). *Las mil y una* goes well beyond the articles and columns in newspapers that are often described as *crónicas* in the Latin American journalistic tradition, and it superbly illustrates some of the tensions between chronicle and *testimonio* through the multiple perspectives through which its main protagonist is introduced. Students can embark on a detailed study of *Las mil y una* by tracing the historical reportage on the dreadful incident and legal aftermath experienced by Paulina Ramírez Jacinto, the central subject of the reportage.

The extended, mass-market journalistic coverage captured in Poniatowska's text—heavily illustrated in black and white with eighty-two images, including photographs and other pictures—came at the end of an eventful summer during the presidential campaign that shook Mexico, when a candidate outside the Institutional Revolutionary Party was elected on 2 July 2000. The victory of Vicente Fox ended seventy years of one-party rule. The turmoil of this election period is key context for Poniatowska's denunciation of underprivileged women's inability to exercise the constitutional right to end a pregnancy resulting from rape. In a country with deeply entrenched Catholic mores, the case of Paulina Ramírez Jacinto was particularly notorious: A thirteen-year-old who had recently migrated north with her large family from Oaxaca to Mexicali, Paulina had been raped by a heroin addict who broke into their ramshackle cabin in the early hours of 31 July 1999. The family was living in one of the large sprawling *colonias* ("shanty towns") that rapidly emerged in the wake of the *maquiladora* ("assembly plant") craze brought by NAFTA. Less than a month later, Paulina and her mother discovered that the girl had become pregnant. After securing a judicially authorized order for abortion, for two months they were unsuccessful in convincing public health medical officers and doctors in Mexicali to perform the abortion. Poniatowska's book examines in detail the role of Catholic priests, including the Baja California bishop, and agents for Catholic pro-life activists in pressuring both the medical staff in the main public hospital and the powerless mother and daughter. Coerced and deceived, Paulina's mother was led to fear for her daughter's life. Paulina herself had been shown photographs of older fetuses and given false information about the risks to her future fertility and about her possible excommunication, and pro-life activists had visited her in her hospital room even as she waited for days on end for a surgical procedure that never materialized. On 13 April 2000, Paulina became the mother, at age fourteen, of an unwanted child. Her case with the Inter-American Commission of Human Rights against the Mexican government—cited verbatim in the text—sums up her legal claim against the Mexican state.

Declaring that her human rights were violated when she was prevented by state authorities from exercising her right under Mexican law to terminate the pregnancy, she and her family attempted to sue the government. Since the Ramírez Jacinto family had to seek legal resolution outside the Mexican court system, this story became an account of global human rights, multinational free trade agreements, and women's rights. The settlement was symbolically signed on International Women's Day, 8 March 2006, with both parties acknowledging that victims of sexual violence are entitled to the recognition, enjoyment, exercise, and protection of all their human rights, including the civil, political, economic, social, and cultural rights enshrined in regional and international human rights instruments. The agreement included proposals for legislative reform through the Mexican Congress, health sector reforms through the Health Secretariat, and some training programs to be conducted upon request. Since the settlement agreement was pronounced years after Poniatowska's book was published, the book likely had an impact on public awareness and the negotiations. Poniatowska's chronicle is engaged with pressing social and political events and provides a context for the study of border culture—and in particular the impunity of those who commit sexual abuses and femicide, an escalating form of gender-based violence—surrounding the neoliberal transnational *maquiladora* economic complex, whose epicenter is in Ciudad Juárez (González Rodríguez 13–14).

Poniatowska quotes from Carlos Fuentes's metaphor of the border as a "cicatriz que no cierra" ("scar that does not close"; Poniatowska 20) in presenting her account. Changes brought by NAFTA, the first of many multinational trade agreements, open to societal discussion issues such as the transnational movement of workers and the circulation of capital and commodities by the powerful. This chronicle provides terrain for discussion of these factors. In this transnational configuration Mexico is clearly identified as a vulnerable partner; the mass migration of the period identified by Poniatowska through the story of Paulina is testimony of that weakness. Students can be encouraged to identify Poniatowska's discourse in her introduction, such as the following commentary on the surge of migrants at the border, stated in critical, sardonic, postnationalist terms: "Los mexicanos emigran porque la patria, esa señora vestida de blanco que alzaba la bandera tricolor en los libros de texto, no puede ni sabe alimentarlos" ("Mexicans migrate because their motherland, that lady dressed in white who hurled the tricolor flag in the schoolbooks, is neither able nor knowledgeable [enough] to feed them"; 19). This chronicle pursues a relentless analytical position indicating the fracture in such a promise of the secular postrevolutionary state to guarantee citizens in general, and women in particular, to protect the rights enshrined in the 1917 Constitution (and subsequent expansions of rights). The right to abortion in Mexico has had a long and complex history in both federal and state legislation since its first incorporation into the constitution in 1931. Baja California is one of thirty-one states where the termination of a pregnancy derived from a rape is legal by state law. This lawful recognition and the public prosecutor's authorization were, nonetheless, not followed in Paulina's case. Poniatowska's narrative consistently emphasizes the failure of the secular state to guarantee this teenage victim of rape the right to interrupt her unwanted pregnancy.

Throughout the text, Poniatowska discusses what she calls the dogmas of the fanatics, particularly Thomas Aquinas's more flexible account of the beginning of human life in the second and third month of pregnancy—oddly, forty days for male embryos and eighty for female embryos (78)—and she also discusses Catholic women activists who advocate for the right to decide. This discussion can be understood as an attempt to engage Catholic readers on their own terms. Her episodic uses of first-person narrative permit reflection on the experiences of motherhood; on her marriage to the scientist Guillermo Haro, who taught her that "la ciencia no tiene las certezas de la iglesia, es más humilde y parte de verdades mucho más fragmentarias" ("science does not have the certitudes of the church, it is humbler than the church, and its truths are much more fragmentary"; 158); and on her musings about whether (as many have thought) she was an unwanted child: "¿Fui una hija o un hijo deseado? A lo mejor en mi inconsciente pienso que nunca lo fui" ("Was I a wanted girl or child? Perhaps in my subconscious I think I never was"; 56). Poniatowska's trademark sense of humility, heroic unpretentiousness, and self-effacement characterizes the public persona that emerges in these uses of the first person. "Su segura servilleta" ("Your sincere serviette"; 35)—a playful alteration of the expression "su segura servidora" ("your sincere servant")—exemplifies her ear for the vernacular and capacity for humor even in the context of such a sensitive and heart-wrenching case study of patriarchal violence.

The title of the book offers another interesting angle for discussion: *Las mil y una* condenses the narrative tensions between fiction and testimony, literature and journalism, so masterfully controlled by Poniatowska: it is an abbreviated reference to the medieval Middle Eastern collection *The Thousand and One Nights*, better known to the English reader as *The Arabian Nights*. Poniatowska frontloads her impending discussion of a violent act against a young woman with allusions to the fearless dancer and storyteller who recites unfinished tales to the king in order to forestall her ultimate sacrifice. By conjuring the newly wed virgin Scheherazade, Poniatowska suggests that "Paulina's Wound" is one of hundreds of stories narrated to halt patriarchal violence on a young woman. The chronicle both relates an account and also delays and denounces male authority and violence on the female body.

Paulina has been the victim of dual traumas: First she was raped, losing her childhood, her innocence, her schooling, and her prospects of normal passage into female adulthood. Her second trauma was having to give birth to the child. Motherhood as a choice becomes the right that the feminist activists Marta Lamas and Isabel Vericat recognize and defend as they guide Poniatowska in her journalistic trip into the labyrinths of Baja California's medical, religious, and political hierarchies of male power.

The violence against a poor, migrant teenager who is raped and then denied the right to an abortion, and her and her family's struggle for justice, is narrated in a hybrid mode that uses short segments as focal points separated by journalistic headings in capital letters, numerous illustrations, and lengthy accounts from newspaper articles discussing the case. By reading a selection from Mahieux, students will learn to define the chronicle as an unstructured, hybrid literary genre that "combines literary aestheticism with the journalistic responsibility to inform." ("Chronicle"). Poniatowska's embrace of this mode testifies to the validity of Paulina's account, her testimony, even as the chronicler departs into her occasional personal mode.

The final third of Poniatowska's book cites at length at least ten newspaper articles that appeared in *La Jornada*, *The New York Times*, *Proceso*, *Reforma*, *Zeta* (Tijuana), *La voz de la frontera*, and *El sol de México*, among others. This section of the book recreates the urgency of the national and international public debate about the complicities of the Catholic church and the failed *estado laico mexicano*, the secular state, even as the political scene was striving for change. Poniatowska is thus able to reaffirm with a wide variety of voices and viewpoints the overwhelming evidence that women's reproductive rights are not universal in Mexico, that young working-class women are quite vulnerable in the shifting social landscape of neoliberal globalization, and that the Mexican judicial system has been eroded.

A film that could accompany the teaching of this text is *El crimen del padre Amaro* (2002; *The Crime of Father Amaro*), starring Mexican actor Gael García Bernal and based on the 1875 Brazilian novel by José Maria Eca de Queirós. The film openly denounces the double standards and false morality of a village priest who engages in sex with an underage, gullible girl (played by Ana Claudia Talancón), leaving her pregnant; she bleeds to death after a botched abortion. Students can conduct research on reviews to understand that for contemporary Mexican viewers this film adaptation was a clear echo of recent public debate over reproductive rights and the fraught role of the church. Following rich discussion in the classroom and even the comparing of historical eras, students can pursue papers of a historical or comparative nature on the film and Poniatowska's chronicle, for their important sociocultural and religious critical interventions, and for how the arts, including the writing genres of chronicle and *testimonio*, can assert and demand women's rights.

There's a rich bibliography on the social and cultural impacts of NAFTA on the lives and bodies of women factory workers along the Mexican border with the United States (see Mattingly and Hansen; Domínguez-Ruvalcaba and Corona). From Lourdes Portillo's 2001 documentary on the women who disappeared in Juárez, *Señorita extraviada*, to Roberto Bolaño's massive novel *2666*, the first decade of the twenty-first century saw an explosion of cultural and academic production that reflected on the transnational neoliberal border as a site for a permanent state of siege on women's bodies, with femicide emerging as a key concept to understand the gendered forms of state, gang, and structural violence along the border. Students reading about these early years of the century should be guided through Melissa Wright's "A Manifesto against Femicide" and could discuss and then write about the specific pressures exercised on women's bodies in the wake of deregulated markets, free-zone industrial complexes, and the impunity of patriarchal criminality over women's bodies in the era of free trade, *maquiladoras*, and narcotraffic. Then they would be better prepared for tackling *Las mil y una*.

Ileana Rodríguez's notion of "disempowered subjects" would be particularly interesting as a way to link the erasure of rights and social guarantees experienced by Paulina with the prevalent disappearance and torture of women along the border who have turned, in Rodríguez's words, into "perishable, disposable beings" (168). Sergio González Rodríguez has duly noted that the extremely gruesome patterns of bodily violence and utter social destruction caused by cartel and state fights were preceded by this upsurge in femicides, whose impunity prefigured the widespread lack of juridical security in Mexico in the new century (González Rodríguez 11). Paulina's story appears in hindsight as a significant early case in which the stonewalling of a patient and the lack of juridical guarantees to secure her right to end a pregnancy highlight the configuration of a patriarchal state on its way to becoming increasingly unaccountable, toxic, and even lethal.

Notes

1. Translations in this essay are mine unless otherwise indicated.

2. This work can only be done in a Spanish-language course, since no English translation of *Las mil y una* has been released.

Works Cited

Alonso, Mercedes. "Historia de una institucionalización: La crónica-testimonio modelo, 1970–2005." *Textos Híbridos*, vol. 2, no. 2, 2012, pp. 1–19.

Arias, Arturo, editor. *The Rigoberta Menchú Controversy.* U of Minnesota P, 2001.

El crimen del padre Amaro. Directed by Carlos Carrera, Instituto Mexicano de Cinematografía, 2002.

Domínguez-Ruvalcaba, Héctor, and Ignacio Corona. *Gender Violence at the U.S.-Mexico Border: Media Representation and Public Response.* U of Arizona P, 2010.

Fuentes, Carlos. *La frontera de cristal: Una novela en nueve cuentos.* Aguilar, 1995.

González Rodríguez, Sergio. *The Femicide Machine.* Translated by Michael Parker-Steinback. MIT Press, 2012.

Inter-American Commission on Human Rights. *Ramírez Jacinto v. Mexico.* Case 161/02, report no. 21/07, doc. 22, rev. 1, 2007, www.cidh.oas.org/annualrep/2007eng/Mexico161.02eng.htm.

Mahieux, Viviane. "The Chronicle." *Oxford Bibliographies*, 5 May 2017, www.oxfordbibliographies.com.

———. *Urban Chroniclers in Modern Latin America: The Shared Intimacy of Everyday Life.* U of Texas P, 2011.

Mattingly, Doreen J., and Ellen R. Hansen. *Women and Change at the U.S.-Mexico Border: Mobility, Labor, and Activism.* U of Arizona P, 2006.

Poniatowska, Elena. *Las mil y una . . . La herida de Paulina.* Plaza y Janés, 2000.

Reyes, Andrea. Introduction. *Mujer de palabras: Artículos rescatados de Rosario Castellanos*, edited by Reyes, vol. 1, Conaculta, 2004, pp. 13–30. 3 vols. Lecturas mexicanas.

Rodríguez, Ileana. *Liberalism at Its Limits: Crime and Terror in the Latin American Cultural Text.* U of Pittsburgh P, 2009.

Stoll, David. *Rigoberta Menchú and the Story of All Poor Guatemalans.* 1999. Routledge, 2007.

Wright, Melissa. "A Manifesto against Femicide." *Antipode*, vol. 33, no. 3, 2001, pp. 550–66.

Mark J. Mascia

Teaching Contemporary Mexico to General Education Students through Elena Poniatowska's Stories

Instructors in undergraduate Spanish programs may wonder whether they can successfully teach Elena Poniatowska's texts to a class composed entirely of students who are not involved in a Spanish major program primarily focused on literature and who may have little background in the subject. In my view, the answer is a resounding yes. Many students in my classroom had not heard of Poniatowska before enrolling in my upper-division classes in Spanish. In a special topics course I designed, Modern Mexican Literature, I bring focus to her early collection of short stories, *De noche vienes* (*You Come at Night*), which I have found achieves a meaningful effect in the classroom. Teaching these stories, however, requires adjusting one's learning expectations and teaching methods to meet the needs of a particular group of students. Here I will show precisely what has worked successfully with my students.

First, I must make several observations about my Spanish program. The Spanish major is the only foreign-language major in the department where I teach. Consisting of thirty-one credits, the major offers the Advanced Composition and Grammar sequence as its entry point. From there, majoring students must take at least one course in literature, one course in culture, and a number of electives (which can include other literature and culture classes, all in Spanish). Graduating seniors must complete a one-credit online portfolio for major assessment. It is not a program designed to prepare future doctoral candidates in literature. Most majors pursue careers as teachers, in K–12 education. Some have other career interests, notably in the health professions, law, nursing, or business. Some students might choose an advanced course like this as part of the Spanish minor, while others take it as a humanities core elective, and others still are native speakers and just want to hone their grammar skills.

Therefore, for many students this may be their first introduction to any formal study of literature in Spanish; in some cases, they may have come directly out of a high school Spanish curriculum where English was the primary language spoken in class. Students do not often possess the necessary writing skills to analyze literature in another language. For many, the exposure to writers like Poniatowska in the original Spanish is not unlike the exposure to Shakespeare or Jane Austen in a survey literature class in English, in that students sometimes see Poniatowska's writing as simply a requirement for a course.

Many of our students are the first in their families to attend college and may not have encouragement outside of class to read literary works; in fact, often they are expected to choose a preprofessional career track and hence view Spanish as no more than a "useful skill." For these students the course is another three credits in a larger curriculum, and Poniatowska is just another author. But what I have discovered in assigning stories from *De noche vienes* is that students enjoy them. Upon identifying and organizing a set of predetermined learning outcomes based on realistic expectations and respect for the students' backgrounds, instructors can ensure an enjoyable exploration for themselves and students alike.

To begin, one must discuss the social and cultural setting of Poniatowska's Mexico. The collection first appeared in 1979 and hence is written in fairly contemporary Spanish that does not contain the same linguistic challenges as, for example, texts from the Spanish golden age would. However, students cannot be expected to know about contemporary Mexico, as much of what they have learned about Mexico comes from the mainstream American media. Some students begin the course with preconceived notions regarding Mexico, conjured by American popular culture, which are often shaped by anti-Latino bigotry and tropes of undocumented immigration and drug cartels. As a result, it is worth discussing issues such as the social stratification that came out of the colonial era and Mexico's oligarchic system. Rich discussion can ensue about social and economic inequalities (as well as gender-based inequality) as themes observable in the stories of *De noche vienes*; however, many students may not initially be able to pinpoint why the social circumstances got that way. The instructor aids their comprehension and study by briefly addressing historical and background issues.

My class begins with a segment on Mexican society in the twentieth century, including a historical overview that begins with the 1910 Revolution or even earlier, to help open discussion and ensure that students understand the depictions they will engage in Poniatowska's text of impoverished or humble characters as well as those of the upper classes. I begin by giving a general lecture in a portion of the class, detailing the history of Mexico since the early twentieth century. I have taught Latin American civilization and use my notes on the subject, which are based on a textbook I once used, by Eugenio Chang-Rodríguez. I do not use *PowerPoint* presentations, nor do I test students on the history; my purpose is only to give a thorough background. Chang-Rodríguez's textbook may be helpful especially for faculty members who are in a generalist's position like mine, since the textbook helped me to successfully bridge my teaching of another course with my teaching of this one. In turn, I find this opening strategy helps undergraduate students better grasp basic Mexican history and approach the context and setting of Poniatowska's stories. Our discussion takes place in an open forum format, so that students feel comfortable discussing the more serious issues they will encounter.

While the language in these stories is generally easily understood by students who have reached advanced Spanish, students can be curious about the author's background. Upon reading a brief biography of Poniatowska, students are often surprised that she has a Polish surname and was born in France. Since the majority of students in my classes are often women, they are interested in reading women authors, and many students can be especially interested in Poniatowska's eye toward social injustice, visible in both her creative work and her essays. The latter could also be assigned, or her subject matter gleaned through biographies.

In terms of methodology, Modern Mexican Literature explores the twentieth century through four major writers, balancing shorter and longer texts, and more recondite plots or language alongside somewhat simpler ones. Themes focus on social inequality, gender roles, relations between Mexico and the United States, and historical memory. I like to begin with the novel *Los de abajo* (*The Underdogs*), by Mariano Azuela, exposing students to the crisis of the Mexican Revolution, then move to Juan Rulfo's novel *Pedro Páramo*, which focuses on social class and the oligarchy, and which has touches of magical realism and nonlinear narrative. These more complicated readings are followed by essays from *El laberinto de la soledad* (*The Labyrinth of Solitude*) by Octavio Paz, such as "El pachuco y otros extremos" ("The Pachuco and Other Extremes"; 143–63), "Máscaras mexicanas" ("Mexican Masks"; 164–81), "Nuestros días" ("The Present Day"; 320–40), and "México y los Estados Unidos: Posiciones y contraposiciones: Pobreza y civilización" ("Mexico and the United States: Positions and Counterpositions: Poverty and Civilization"; 445–67), which open discussion on ideas about the formation of Mexican cultural identity, contemporary issues such as poverty and power, and of course, relations with the United States. This historical background and the examples of fictional and nonfictional works help prepare students to understand the world of Poniatowska's narrative. The final three weeks of the semester are then spent with the stories in *De noche vienes*, which brings students to topics in the more contemporary era.

Although I assign the entire text, I dialogue with the class to pick which stories to discuss based on how they appeal to the students and how class discussion develops organically. As noted, language usage is not much of a problem, but I encourage students not to look up every word they do not know and instead to bring questions to class discussion. Nor do I provide translations of any kind. However, students are required to post on the discussion boards in the *Blackboard* system (posts are graded for credit), so that I can keep them on task about their readings, and to arrive at class prepared. I require a minimum of one substantive post per week, written in Spanish, but students cannot simply write that they enjoyed the stories or that they were hard to read. For every story we discuss in class, I start the discussion by asking the students for general, fact-based information (such as about the plot and characters) as a point of departure for discussing themes and topics. I have learned that the instructor always needs to lead with a little fact-based summary before discussing issues and meanings within a text. Though we do not have the time to discuss every single story in great detail, the students at least must be thorough about the stories they pick.

I feel that having depth in the course rather than breadth helps me market the course. The course themes of human dignity and social justice are a good fit for the mission of a university like mine, one that is modeled on Catholic higher education and that has a liberal arts college. Rather than assign secondary sources, I choose to advertise the course in such a way that it speaks to the relevance of Mexico in the contemporary world while not appearing intimidating or too difficult.

Compared to the earlier texts we read, Poniatowska's stories are more relatable to the students' world if the instructor provides adequate guidance. Students can engage with the characters on a personal level (a few are close to the students' ages). Also, on a broader level, the instructor might want to have students compare their society with Poniatowska's late-twentieth-century Mexico City settings. A few universal themes in the stories—with cultural and social variants—are love, emotion, and the institution of marriage. How do students feel when they see women characters trying to carve out freedom and autonomy in a society where they must seemingly accede to the whims of the men in their lives? Are there similarities and differences in current American society? Ideas of control in a relationship, feelings of abandonment, and the challenges of love and infidelity are themes for class discussion.

For "La ruptura" ("The Rupture"; Poniatowska, *De noche* 11–15), I ask about how male-female romantic relationships work, and whether there is an imbalance of power in them. This leads to discussion of the characters, then of students' feelings about life. In this story, Manuela contemplates killing Juan and treating him as a hunted trophy. In addition to possible reasons for her fury, I ask students whether this shocks them and use it as an example to start examining power and gender. Here, I ask students to think about Manuela's imagination, which renders Juan an object. Does that action invert the traditional balance of power in patriarchal marriage? As a result of these questions, students are able to examine how the author subverts social expectations of gender and to see that women are no longer the "hunted" unequals (15).

"Cine Prado" ("Prado Cinema"; 26–30) offers a version of passion and jealousy: although the male narrator is smitten by and obsessed with an actress, after relating how well she performed in earlier films, now, sitting in the movie theater, he does not like a new role she has taken on. As he becomes more incensed, he knifes her image on the screen. When the police arrive, he is raving about her behavior. I ask students whether, in this story, women have gained the upper hand. Students had no problems discussing this story, and in fact some of them found it amusing that a male character could be so weak; now it is the man who is "insane" and not the stereotyped "crazy female."

When reading "El limbo" ("Limbo"; 31–45), students viscerally react to the idea of a poor and indigenous servant having to abandon a newborn child, left for dead by the indifferent and wealthy family for whom she works. Here students are forced to consider class distinctions in Mexico in terms of poverty, ethnicity or race, and power. Many of my students, especially those who want to teach, have some professional interest in children and their well-being, and they have shared their emotional reactions to child abandonment and the callous indifference of the affluent family in the story. An angle of discussion I have not seen come up yet in class, but which is likely to occur, is how the servant became pregnant, and whether the father is a member of the family she works for.

"El inventario" ("The Inventory"; 56–65) taps into students' affective responses through its themes of mourning and grief and its exploration of the attachment humans have to objects belonging to the deceased. As students discuss the visceral, earthy topics of these stories—as seen in marital relationships, dying children, stark differences between the rich and the poor, or the grinding and utterly debilitating effects of losing a loved one—they recognize these as profoundly contemplative readings.

Students' intellectual prowess is challenged in the two stories "La felicidad" ("Happiness"; 66–70) and "Métase mi prieta, entre el durmiente y el silbatazo" ("My Dark One, Get between the Sleeper and the Whistle"; 101–20). The first is a stream of consciousness by the female character as she observes her lover, sleeping after their lovemaking, where students only begin to discern that her contemplation may express a permanent departure. They have not raised concerns about the stark sexuality in the stories or reported any question about appropriateness, but they seem a little less engaged in the stream-of-consciousness narrative, not appreciating its rhythmic flow. Perhaps the story is better suited to a course where literary techniques are discussed. On the other hand, students appear to enjoy the creativity in "Métase mi prieta," where the male protagonist, a train engineer, expresses the love he feels for his train engine as he might express his love for his wife. This play on words and ideas, while perplexing at first to some students, helps them think about how observations are made about real life. As discussion moves from confusing descriptions and how to understand them to human emotions to characters' motivations, students begin to lose apprehensions and become more comfortable participating in class discussions.

Also challenging is "Love Story" (83–92); students can be encouraged to discuss how the story is not ostensibly an account of a romance but addresses class and ethnic distinctions (and obsession again). The upper-class woman is simultaneously repelled by her maid (because she considers her inferior) and attracted to her (or at least obsessed with whether she is doing chores properly). Students can tap into the psyches and emotions of these characters, and group discussion leads to fruitful writing exercises, especially after students understand the denouement, which is both tantalizing and graphic. They can also be asked why Poniatowska created a title in English. "La casita de sololoi" ("The Little House of Sololoi"; 93–100) depicts an unfulfilling, unequal marriage for the female protagonist, again inviting discussion of male-female roles. By now, as students begin to identify common thematic threads in the stories, they are able to give greater shape to their ideas for writing a paper.

The final section of stories in the book offers rich material for discussion and comparison to the earlier stories. "El rayo verde" ("Green Lightning"; 121–27) questions whether happiness is reachable or more than ephemeral for women trapped in unfulfilling relationships. In "De Gaulle en minería" ("De Gaulle in Mining"; 128–48) students can be surprised to find an introduction to Mexican high society and its contacts with Europe. To help them understand the background, the story can be related to America's experience during World War II and the invasion of Normandy: I make references to the film *Saving Private Ryan*, which helps students understand the power of platonic love that war veterans have for their comrades in arms.

A more complex story, and certainly the longest, "De noche vienes" uses humor to consider a case where a woman is arrested for having five husbands at once (149–65). Students can be asked if bigamy is an issue in the story, as they grapple with the character's sweet testimony. To help students find angles for discussion, we concentrate on how the woman relates the different needs that her husbands have and the service that she provides (she is a nurse) to each one, while on Sundays she tends to her father. She also declares that she would never embark on a relationship without entering marriage.

After the final reading, we spend a class period workshopping ideas for student papers. Students must arrive at class prepared to discuss Poniatowska's characters and themes and potential messages: for example, gender roles, the nature of love, and Mexican social hierarchies. The preparatory work for writing the papers is also completed following the other readings; I find that devoting a portion of class time to a short workshop helps students develop ideas for their writing (they can use earlier observations posted to *Blackboard*) and helps them feel more comfortable about an important project on which they will be graded. The online discussion comments, with questions that ensue, serve in-class discussion and analysis of topics, reinforce what the students read, and keep them on task about their readings. Such technological (and group work) skills help foment both discussion and greater understanding, and even vocabulary acquisition for writing assignments. I have also noted that making use of such aids as *Blackboard* or blogs and other online platforms helps allay student fears about language study and promotes greater learning. Giving students access, and control over, these tools made readings more fun and the topics more relatable for them.

It was greatly rewarding for me to see how far students progressed in their command of the Spanish language as they pursued ideas and wrote papers. And this we know: literature was meant to be read and felt, not just analyzed. As we factor empathy into reading assignments and respect for students as consumer-creators of their own reading experience, we can promote greater awareness of such Mexican writers as Poniatowska and further the language acquisition of students who are not specifically majoring in literature.

Works Cited

Azuela, Mariano. *Los de abajo.* Edited by Marta Portal, 13th ed., Ediciones Cátedra, 1999.

Chang-Rodríguez, Eugenio. *Latinoamérica: Su civilización y su cultura.* 3rd ed., Heinle and Heinle, 2000.

Paz, Octavio. *El laberinto de la soledad.* Edited by Enrico Mario Santí, 13th ed., Ediciones Cátedra, 2007.

Poniatowska, Elena. *De noche vienes.* 10th ed., Ediciones Era, 2000.

Rulfo, Juan. *Pedro Páramo.* Edited by José Carlos González Boixo, 15th ed., Ediciones Cátedra, 2000.

Saving Private Ryan. Directed by Steven Spielberg, DreamWorks Pictures, 1998.

Beth E. Jörgensen

Illness and Disability: From Narrative Prosthesis to Life Experience in Works by María Luisa Puga

This essay brings the work of María Luisa Puga (1944–2004) into dialogue with the field of disability studies and thus views a relatively understudied writer through a unique lens. Puga was a highly regarded novelist, essayist, and *cronista* ("chronicler"), whose work frequently explored themes of the cultural outsider, and whose protagonists often experienced illness or disability in some form. Her work has not yet been translated into English, so this material is most suitable for college students taking an upper-level elective taught in Spanish.

The field of disability studies has had an important impact on literary studies since the 1980s. Monographs by Rosemarie Garland-Thomson, G. Thomas Couser (*Recovering Bodies* and *Vulnerable Subjects*), and Diane Price Herndl and edited volumes by Alan Gartner and Tom Joe and by Sharon L. Snyder and colleagues are examples of the new thinking in the humanities around the representations of disability in literature. Nevertheless, disability studies approaches to literature remain underrepresented in analyses of works by Mexicana and Chicana writers. In fact, Spanish American literature as a whole is still relatively marginalized in the field, which has been dominated since the early 1980s by British scholars and scholars in the United States who have been working primarily on English-language texts.[1]

To offer a concise, practical guide to introducing humanities-focused disability studies into courses treating Spanish American literature, I will outline a study plan for chapter 1 of Miguel Ángel Asturias's canonical novel *El Señor Presidente* (*The President*; 11–15) and, for more central focus, two excerpts from works by Puga: chapter 2 of the novel *Las posibilidades del odio* (*The Possibilities of Hate*; 25–58) and two accounts from the autobiographical *Diario del dolor* (*Diary of Pain*; 9–22 [entries 1–21], 64–84 [entries 64–88]). I keep the readings brief, so that four class periods are enough to accomplish the dual goals of exposure to Puga's writing and a consideration of the value that disability studies brings to our reading of literature.

The publication of *Las posibilidades del odio* in 1978 announced not only the entrance of Puga into the Mexican literary scene but also her return to Mexico after a decade spent in Europe and Africa. The book attracted immediate interest and high praise for offering multiple perspectives on the effects of colonialism on the colonized through a series of loosely connected narratives set in Nairobi, Kenya. After the arrival of *Las posibilidades del odio*, Puga's virtually exclusive dedication to writing throughout the rest of her life yielded a corpus of ten novels, four collections of short stories, numerous chronicles and essays, children's literature, and regular columns for the Mexican periodical *El Economista*. Puga also devoted substantial time and energy to teaching literature workshops in Michoacán, where she lived, and throughout Mexico. In her essay "The Hidden Language," quoted by George Szanto in an article from 1996, Puga remarked on the importance for everyone, not just professional writers, of putting stories into written form. "I talk to them about writing as a necessity for every person. Like a space, a possession to which we all have the right. . . . To be able to express oneself clearly . . . is the germ of our freedom" (Puga 328; qtd. in Szanto 7). The final book Puga completed during her lifetime was *Diario del dolor*, a creative diary published in fall 2004, shortly before her early death that December.[2]

Puga's work is centrally concerned with issues of identity and processes of self-understanding, especially as they pertain to the exploration and representation of female subjectivity in a patriarchal society. In an interview with Gabriella de Beer from the mid-1990s, Puga stated that she had brought to Mexican literature "a voice of the independent woman" (Puga, "María" 41). Her work lends itself to being taught in classes on Mexican literature, Spanish American prose fiction, gender studies, the Mexican Student Movement of 1968, the female bildungsroman, theories of autobiography, and history and identity in postcolonial contexts. A critical bibliography exists to inform and support these approaches.[3]

Here I suggest how to guide students to a new reading of the famous first chapter of Asturias's *El Señor Presidente*, followed by selections from Puga's work. Her texts, in particular, belong in any course on representations of disability in literature, or on identity formation that seeks to address the impact of disability on the biopsychosocial construction of the subject. In the selection from Asturias's work and the two selections from Puga's work, essential concepts for disability studies theory come into play. The first is the concept developed by David Mitchell and Sharon Snyder of illness or disability as a "narrative prosthesis" in Western literature. Their foundational insight that the representation of disabled characters frequently serves aesthetic and ideological purposes that are extrinsic to the experience of living with a disability is illustrated in both the opening chapter of *El Señor Presidente* and chapter 2 of *Las posibilidades del odio*. In contrast to these fictional representations of disability, disability studies discourse on the value of life writing can enrich our reading of *Diario del dolor*, which places the experience of living with rheumatoid arthritis at the center of its performance. The work of Couser (on disability life writing) and Henrietta Nickels Shirk (on diaries of illness) provides a theoretical underpinning to the teaching of this text.[4]

Mitchell's essay in the volume *Disability Studies: Enabling the Humanities*, published by the MLA in 2002, gives a concise explanation of narrative prosthesis, and he illustrates the concept with analyses of two familiar stories. Mitchell's thesis is that "disability pervades literary narrative, first as a stock feature of characterization and, second, as an opportunistic metaphoric device" (15). As a feature of characterization, disability serves to set one character apart and motivates the act of storytelling by attracting interest and demanding that the anomaly be explained by virtue of its difference from the norm (21). The children's story "The Steadfast Tin Soldier," by Hans Christian Andersen, is exemplary of this meaning of narrative prosthesis, or "the perpetual discursive dependency on disability" (15), given the tin soldier's missing leg.

Mitchell's "materiality of metaphor" refers to the ways in which the disabled body can signify an abstract idea and anchor it in material reality (24–25). Mitchell asserts, for example, that Oedipus's lameness and blindness "serve as a symbol for the tragedy of hubris or the limits of human knowledge" (25). In other conventional associations, obesity can be a metaphor for greed or laziness, while ulcerations signify corruption. Ultimately, Mitchell critiques the overwhelming tendency to use disability as a metaphor for "social and individual collapse" or "things gone awry" in the light of its negative impact on attitudes toward real people with disabilities (16, 24).

Asturias's *El Señor Presidente* and Puga's *Las posibilidades del odio* illustrate the use of disability as narrative prosthesis and as metaphor. Chapter 1 of *El Señor Presidente* portrays the beggars that gather at night by the Portal del Señor in harsh terms of deficiency, degradation, and disability. The intersection of poverty and disability, which will also figure importantly in chapter 2 of *Las posibilidades del odio*, is a key factor in the construction of Asturias's beggars. The beggar nicknamed Pelele, a mentally disturbed and easily agitated "idiota" ("idiot"), stands out from the anonymous mass (6). His irrational behavior sets him apart from the others and attracts the taunts of a military officer, with tragic consequences. The characterization of Pelele is a clear example of narrative prosthesis. His difference from the rest, manifested in violent outbursts triggered when the word "madre" ("mother") is spoken near him (7), motivates the narrative focus on his story. Among the other beggars there are also blind men and a deaf woman, as well as a "mulato degenerado," or "degenerate mulatto" (8), an example of the conventional association of blackness with deficiency and the intersectionality of race, disability, and poverty. Metaphorically, the description of the beggars as disabled, suspicious toward each other, criminal, violent, and consumed by hatred and fear signifies the breakdown of social ties and the alienation experienced by a population living under dictatorship. The novel is understood to represent Guatemalan society under the repressive regime of Manuel Estrada Cabrera, and Asturias's beggars serve as an "opportunistic metaphor" for the corruption of social norms of cooperation, communication, and the common good (Mitchell 15).

We see some of the same meanings of alienation and oppression attached to the disabled protagonist of chapter 2 of *Las posibilidades del odio*. However, Puga's depiction of a fictional black amputee who is a beggar in Nairobi succeeds in going beyond the primarily metaphorical function exemplified in Asturias's work, to bring to the fore the concrete effects of living in poverty with a disability. In the narrative, the beggar is twenty-six years old, and he lives on the streets, begging by day and sleeping at night in an alley under a makeshift shelter. The narrator describes his body and the precarious conditions under which he lives, and offers flashbacks to the beggar's childhood and youth, when he lived in a rural village and suffered abuse at the hands of his uncle after the death of his parents. Later he lived in the forest in association with the Mau Mau rebels, and after he suffered a gunshot wound, he was captured and arrested. His detention brought him to a prison in the city, and then to a hospital where his injured leg was amputated. The protagonist's disability can be seen as a narrative prosthesis in that it marks him as different from other poor, black Kenyans, and the fact of his missing leg arouses the reader's interest in the story behind its loss, which is revealed through the flashbacks. He is also a metaphor for postcolonial society and "social and individual collapse" due to colonial-era economic and political oppression and systemic racism (Mitchell 16). His parents lost their lives because they opposed the colonial regime, and the child remained under the control of a substitute parent. The uncle allied himself with the white regime despite being black and betrayed norms of family loyalty in his abuse of his nephew. The protagonist's violence-induced disability, his poverty, his orphanhood, and his invisibility as a poor black man signify the position of the colonized racial other in Kenya.

A careful reading of the chapter also reveals the ways in which Puga is able to go beyond her character's metaphorical function to give insights into the lived experience of disability, poverty, and imposed racial inferiority. She does this in part by having the extradiegetic narrator transfer the narrative point of view to the protagonist through the use of free indirect style. For example, descriptions of the crowds of people who pass in the street are oriented from below, so that shoes and legs are the primary images. The chapter also describes in detail how painfully the protagonist moved his body along the ground before he was given a crutch, and what the crutch means to him as his most prized possession. The many dangers that he faces from the police, dogs, drunks, and cars, and the scarcity of food, water, and adequate shelter, define a situation of extreme precarity that is commonly experienced by the disabled poor. To a degree that exceeds the depiction of Pelele in *El Señor Presidente*, Puga's beggar acquires status as an individual, because the literary devices employed by Puga effectively convey the physical, psychological, and social dimensions of his identity.

After two class periods discussing these fictions, the third and fourth class periods of the study plan treat the topic of disability life writing through a reading of Puga's *Diario del dolor*. In this brief text composed of one hundred undated entries, the diarist engages in a one-sided dialogue with "Dolor," the personification of the pain that is her constant companion. Theories of disability life writing and diaries of illness frame the discussion of the text. In his studies of autobiographies and other forms of life writing by people with disabilities, Couser defends the importance of these modes of writing as a way of giving expression to the realities of living with a disability from within that experience. Disability life writing has the potential to offer a counternarrative to conventional representations, including those that exemplify narrative prosthesis. The introduction to his 1997 monograph *Recovering Bodies: Illness, Disability, and Writing* provides a concise treatment of the history of this subgenre of autobiography in the United States, and it gives a number of insights into what is at play in Puga's autobiographical *Diario* (Couser 3–17). Primary among these is the assertion that "[b]odily dysfunction may stimulate . . . autobiographical narrative of illness or disability—by heightening one's awareness of one's mortality, threatening one's sense of identity, and disrupting the apparent plot of one's life. Whatever form it takes, bodily dysfunction tends to heighten consciousness of self and of contingency" (5). As a complement to Couser's work, Henrietta Nickels Shirk's article "Cancer Diaries" addresses the genre of the diary written by women who are living with serious illness. Some characteristics identified by Shirk and manifested in *Diario del dolor* are the tendency to refer to one's symptoms in the third person to distance the self from the bodily dysfunction; the structure of a dialogue between the conscious, suffering "I" and the dysfunctional body; and an intense awareness of the mind-body dichotomy that is "the essential distinguishing characteristic of the human condition" (Shirk 30).

In Puga's case, it is not cancer but the painful and debilitating effects of rheumatoid arthritis that threaten her sense of identity and "the apparent plot" of her life, as Couser says (*Recovering Bodies* 5). A textual analysis of the *Diario* informed by the recommended articles invites an examination of the following themes: the impact of the invasive presence of pain; the body's vulnerability to illness; the conflictive relationship between the diarist's past identity and her present, unfamiliar self; the experience of being caught between fleeting moments of well-being and lurking disability; and the traumatic loss of an assumed, and for all of us illusory, bodily integrity and stable identity. It is important to discuss how *Diario del dolor* is a hybrid text that combines features of a diary (usually read as a nonfictional account of daily life) and fictional devices such as the personification of Dolor, the absence of dates to ground the text in a specific time frame, and the text's dual status as a private and a public document. Finally, unlike many stories that show a disabled character "overcoming" disability, *Diario* portrays losses that bring no gain and brokenness that does not resolve into cure. It thus confirms the vulnerability and contingency of the human subject, which disability life writing is uniquely positioned to represent. A critical text on life writing could be assigned if the class focuses on fiction and semiautobiographical writing. This course plan could also serve classes that include exercises in translating the assigned texts.

The following is a brief outline of four classes:

For day 1, assign Mitchell and chapter 1 of Asturias, and ask students to think about two themes prior to class: the representation of the *pordioseros* ("beggars") as narrative prostheses and what they signify; and other examples of literature or film (Spanish American, American, British) that feature characters that can be understood to serve as narrative prostheses.

For day 2, assign chapter 2 of *Posibilidades del odio*. Discussion will focus on the representation of the amputee beggar as a narrative prosthesis and a metaphor, but also as a well-developed representation of disability as a lived experience of bodily impairment and a socially imposed identity.

For day 3, assign the introduction to Couser, *Recovering Bodies*; Shirk; and selections of *Diario del dolor* (entries 1–21). Focus the discussion on identifying the ideas expounded in the two essays that are most relevant to Puga's *Diario* and the dynamic of the dialogue between the diarist and her silent interlocutor, Dolor. How does she construct Dolor as an intimate enemy, whose unwanted companionship she must ultimately accept? How can we interpret the alternating references to Dolor as "tú" ("you") and "él" ("he")?

For day 4, continue with selections from *Diario del dolor* (entries 64–88). Focus the discussion on the personification of Dolor and the attribution of aggression and power to him, as well as humorous details that diminish his power over the diarist; and on the passages in the *Diario* that express nostalgia for the identity that the diarist once claimed and her dread at becoming strange and unrecognizable to herself under the stress of pain.

The selections from writings by Asturias and Puga offer concise, accessible examples of literary depictions of disability that are suitable for study in upper-level Spanish elective courses at the undergraduate level. The readings can easily be expanded for graduate students specializing in Spanish American literature. Early exposure to disability studies theory will encourage students to reconsider the representation of disability in literature and the status of disabled people in society.

Notes

1. I recommend the following pioneering works on Latin American literature from a disability studies perspective: Antebi; Minich; Janzen; and Antebi and Jörgensen.

2. Puga is not included in the well-known reference works on Spanish American writers, but biographical information and insights into her writing can be located in Puga, "María"; and in the publications by Hind (an interview); Szanto (an interview-based essay); and Domenella (an overview of Puga's corpus).

3. For examples of approaches to Puga's work in the existing scholarship, see Anderson; Domenella; Hind; López; and Valdés.

4. An alternative example of disability life writing that lends itself well to study in a college course is Gabriela Brimmer and Elena Poniatowska's multivoiced autobiography *Gaby Brimmer.* See also Jörgensen.

Works Cited

Anderson, Danny J. "Cultural Conversation and Constructions of Reality: Mexican Narrative and Literary Theories after 1968." *Siglo XX / 20th Century*, vol. 8, nos. 1–2, 1990, pp. 11–30.

Antebi, Susan. *Carnal Inscriptions: Spanish American Narratives of Corporeal Difference and Disability.* Palgrave Macmillan, 2009.

Antebi, Susan, and Beth E. Jörgensen, editors. *Libre Acceso: Latin American Literature and Film through Disability Studies.* State U of New York P, 2016.

Asturias, Miguel Ángel. *El Señor Presidente.* Losada, 1948.

Brimmer, Gabriela, and Elena Poniatowska. *Gaby Brimmer.* Editorial Grijalbo, 1979.

Couser, G. Thomas. *Recovering Bodies: Illness, Disability, and Life Writing.* U of Wisconsin P, 1997.

———. *Vulnerable Subjects: Ethics and Life Writing.* Cornell UP, 2004.

Domenella, Ana Rosa. "María Luisa Puga, del testimonio poscolonial al cuerpo del dolor: Un camino reflexivo a través de la escritura." *María Luisa Puga: La escritura que no cesa*, edited by Domenella, Tecnológico de Monterrey, 2006, pp. 25–36.

Garland-Thomson, Rosemarie. *Extraordinary Bodies: Figuring Physical Disability in American Culture and Literature.* Columbia UP, 1997.

Gartner, Alan, and Tom Joe, editors. *Images of the Disabled, Disabling Images.* Praeger, 1987.

Herndl, Diane Price. *Invalid Women: Figuring Feminine Illness in American Fiction and Culture, 1840–1940.* U of North Carolina P, 1993.

Hind, Emily. *Entrevistas con quince autoras mexicanas*. Iberoamericana, 2003.
Janzen, Rebecca. *The National Body in Mexican Literature: Collective Challenges to Biopolitical Control*. Palgrave Macmillan, 2015.
Jörgensen, Beth E. "Teaching *Gaby Brimmer*: A Disability Studies Approach." *Diálogo*, vol. 17, no. 1, Spring 2014, pp. 23–31.
López, Irma M. *Historia, escritura e identidad: La novelística de María Luisa Puga*. Peter Lang, 1996.
Minich, Julie Avril. *Accessible Citizenships: Disability, Nation, and the Cultural Politics of Greater Mexico*. Temple UP, 2014.
Mitchell, David T. "Narrative Prosthesis and the Materiality of Metaphor." *Disability Studies: Enabling the Humanities*, edited by Sharon L. Snyder et al., Modern Language Association, 2002, pp. 15–30.
Mitchell, David T., and Sharon L. Snyder. *Narrative Prosthesis: Disability and the Dependencies of Discourse*. U of Michigan P, 2001.
Puga, María Luisa. *Diario del dolor*. Alfaguara, 2004.
———. "The Hidden Language." Translated by Annette Cowart and Reginald Gibbons. *Triquarterly*, no. 85, Fall 1992, pp. 317–35
———. "María Luisa Puga." Interview conducted by Gabriella de Beer. *Contemporary Mexican Women Writers: Five Voices*, by De Beer, U of Texas P, 1996, pp. 10–57.
———. *Las posibilidades del odio*. Siglo XXI, 1978.
Shirk, Henrietta Nickels. "Cancer Diaries: Writing as Fighting for Wellness." *Conference of College Teachers of English Studies*, vol. 64, Sept. 1999, pp. 30–39.
Snyder, Sharon L., et al. *Disability Studies: Enabling the Humanities*. Modern Language Association, 2002.
Szanto, George. "Civil Societies." *Brick*, vol. 54, Spring 1996, pp. 4–12.
Valdés, María Elena de. "Crítica feminista de la identidad en 'Inmóvil sol secreto.'" *Journal of Hispanic Research*, vol. 1, 1992, pp. 239–48.

Liliana Pedroza

Small Acts of Resistance: The New Woman Confronts Social Conventions in the Narratives of Silvia Molina

Quiero cambiar; ser otra: la que siempre quise y no pude. (I want to change; be another: the one I always wanted and could not be.)

—Silvia Molina, *Dicen que me case yo*

Silvia Molina, born in Mexico City in 1946, is a storyteller with a wide register whose work includes chronicles, essays, short stories, children's stories and novels, and fictionalized historical accounts. She studied anthropology, and later Hispanic language and literature, and has been a university professor in Mexico and in the United States. Her beginnings in literature are closely associated with the rise of women authors who started publishing in the late 1970s and early 1980s, such as María Luisa Puga, Ethel Krauze, Ángeles Mastretta, and Brianda Domecq, writers born in the 1940s and 1950s who confronted literature from new social circumstances.

For a course that includes works by Silvia Molina, I suggest assigning research for the first class session on the Mexican sociohistorical context and on women's social movements in Latin America in the twentieth century. Following this discussion, students can be directed, individually or in teams, to write a short report on the social evolution and judicial guarantees for women in various Latin American nations. Students can then discuss and compare the different countries, their social progress and the impact of those circumstances, to then center discussion on Mexico. This can be followed by readings of essays by Rosario Castellanos in *Sobre cultura femenina* (*On Feminine Culture*) and *Mujer que sabe latín . . .* (*Woman Who Knows Latin . . .*), or readings of her short stories in *Los convidados de agosto* (*The Guests of August*) and *Álbum de familia* (*Family Album*), as well as the readings suggested in this essay's appendix about the feminist movement, to help students understand the era preceding the arrival of new women writers.

The 1970s was a period when women were making demands for equality. Nearly two decades after women finally won the right to vote, in 1953, through an amendment to article 34 of the Mexican Constitution (making women over twenty-one citizens),[1] in 1971 article 4 of the General Population Law was amended to set forth the equality of spouses to decide on family planning issues. Thus in the 1970s groups such as Lucha Feminista (Feminist Fight), Grupo Autónomo de Mujeres Universitarias (Autonomous Group of University Women), and the group of feminist lesbians called Lesbos founded the Frente Nacional por la Liberación y los Derechos de la Mujer (National Front for the Liberation and Rights of Women) to pursue rights related to four fundamental issues: voluntary motherhood; the need for day-care centers; protection from discrimination under the Federal Labor Law for female workers such as household maids, seamstresses, and those working in small businesses; and sexual violence in all of its forms. In 1975 the United Nations proclaimed International Women's Day, which would advance all these demands.

Silvia Molina then was in her twenties and nearing publication of her first book. In the air were debates about the decriminalization of abortion, assertions of female sexuality and pleasure, and repudiations of the use of the female body as a sexual object. In this context, literature had an important role, not only in offering female characters as protagonists or eroticism employed as a rhetorical exercise, but also in presenting new discourse. Works by the women who started writing in the 1970s reflect new approaches stemming from that social moment.

Having first studied anthropology, and after her travels and work in such countries as France, Belgium, the United States, and England, Molina embarked on an evaluation of female roles in Mexican society. It is important to place her in this context because such a vital experience guides her female characters: they confront traditional roles, including the figures of the mother and the patriarch (father or husband), the lady of the house, and the nanny or maid, as well as other women from the same generation as Molina. These characters seek to taste the freedom glimpsed through feminist movements. Their small acts of resistance in domestic settings reveal the early literary exploration of this woman writer, who deliberately contextualizes her era and her nation's experiences.

University students in upper-level literature courses conducted in Spanish would find the following texts by Mexican women writers accessible: Domecq's *Bestiario doméstico* (1982; *Domestic Bestiary*), Puga's *Accidentes* (1981; *Accidents*), Krauze's *Intermedio para mujeres* (1982; *Intermission for Women*), María Teresa Priego's *Tiempos oscuros* (1988; *Dark Times*), Mastretta's *Mujeres de ojos grandes* (1990; *Big-Eyed Women*), and Marilú Pando's *La yegua de la noche* (1993; *The Mare of the Night*). I recommend splitting the class into groups and then having each group reading one of the works. During discussion in class, students will begin to see how these authors converged in describing women's roles from childhood to old age, including puberty to maturity, and concerns about birth and death, sexual awakening, marriage, and children. From here they can identify diverse narrative moods and styles used to approach these topics, including irony, nonchalance, humor, and feistiness.

Following these group readings of other writers, I suggest assigning all three of Molina's early short-story collections, *Lides de estaño* (1984; *Tin Disputes*), *Dicen que me case yo* (1989; *They Say I Should Get Married*), and *Un hombre cerca* (1992; *A Close Man*), which define her early trajectory, both for the manner in which she approaches concerns about life and in the treatment of her characters. In each book a specific stage of life is treated as a narrative axis. Reading these works chronologically will help students study the behavior of Molina's characters through their lives—infancy in the first book, youth in the second, and maturity in the third.

Childhood and Adolescence: Transitions

Lides de estaño is brief, almost an initiation for the writer on life topics: memories from childhood and adolescence, and first love. The painful chain of events in the stories helps the protagonist mature or face life in a different way. The loss of illusions, death, and deceit are heavy blows that force characters to transform themselves to tell their stories with nostalgia, astonishment, or disenchantment.

In some of the stories, Molina uses reminiscence to talk about childhood. In "Amira y los monstruos de San Cosme" ("Amira and the Monsters of San Cosme"; *Lides* 27–32) the narrator, from a temporary distance, tells a story about school. As an adult, the narrator reflects upon the relationships between adults and children, whether parents and children or teachers and pupils. She measures the distance between them and shows how the desires of each are mismatched. The world of adults is a territory that is conditioned by how one ought to appear in front of others, while the actions of children are ruled by their personal tastes and desires. Therefore adults and children speak different languages, and communication between them is impossible, since they have different means of surviving in their environment.

The protagonist of "Amira y los monstruos de San Cosme" is enrolled—"sin alternativa ni discusión" ("without choice or discussion"; 27)—in a Catholic, bourgeois school, outside her normal context: her father is of Arabic descent and does not care about religion, and her mother is a nonpracticing Catholic.[2] Inserted into this new environment as one would introduce an artifact into a museum, she has to develop resistance mechanisms to cope with her family's move from a middle-class to a higher-class neighborhood, her father's lack of time for his family because of new work responsibilities, and her mother who, in her unanticipated new social position, becomes frivolous and distant. Growing up will not be easy when the closest bonds this protagonist has are her familiar and clandestine relationships with the nine nannies she has per year, or when her parents have regular appointments with the principal to address her indiscipline. Her resistance is based on being no more than what her nature dictates, because at her early age she does not understand the contradiction between discourses at home and in school: "a mis rabiosos seis años gritaba por gritar; nunca medité el por qué de mi repugnancia al colegio" ("at the furious age of six I yelled just for the act of yelling; I never thought about why school disgusted me"; 29). Her resistance manifests through her imagination. To create a world different from the one in which she deals with adults is an imperative if she is to survive the oppression she is facing, because, again without asking her opinion, the protagonist's mother decides her daughter should take piano lessons.

The narrator describes her mother's will as something that cannot be questioned or compromised with. Her will is a decree that the protagonist must comply with. The girl, without any say about her preferences, attends piano lessons for eight months. The teacher, tough and indifferent toward her, becomes the target of her imagination. The piano teacher will become a monster, one she compares to the dinosaur skeleton in the Museum of Natural History at her school, haunting students and luring them with soft music to trap them. Violence, not only psychological but also physical—when the teacher slams her face onto the piano—does not inspire in her notions of an adult world of care and protection, thus her imagination invents a way to understand or escape the world she is facing. Many years later, the narrator discovers that her fable for her brief stay in Catholic school has been repeated and augmented as a legend through generations, a sign that relations between children and adults have not changed.

Adolescence will be another difficult stage of life, when the body and the scope of life are transformed with time. "Ya no te voy a leer" ("I Will Not Read You Anymore"; 17–19) provides an example of that transformation; it is a retrospective short story told by a female character about her passage into maturity, her first romantic encounters and sexual initiation. In a bourgeois context, two young people surrender to their sexuality (despite social norms that dictate that they may only meet in specific sites and with adult supervision). Longing for freedom, they manage to escape their watchers and, inspired by the Marquis de Sade's novel *Justine*, they replicate the novel's game of resistance to pleasure and perversion. The story is brief, and the events run fast. The protagonist is forced to grow up quickly because of her circumstances: the death of her mother, her father's second marriage, and her own rushed marriage. But throughout this process, the decisions about events related to her are made by other people. She believes she herself has decided things, when in reality she has only been driven by circumstances; the freedom she used to enjoy led to impediments in her life quest, since she stopped being the character defined by social norms, the chaste young woman virtuous for marriage. She then has to construct herself as another character, that of Justine, without it really being her. In this masquerade where everybody has a role, the protagonist discovers that detaching from family history—tradition and the hypocrisy behind tradition—also means breaking the chains.

The Social Role: No, I Don't Want a Husband

Marriage is a topic associated with preestablished social molds that Molina regularly criticizes. Her second collection, *Dicen que me case yo*, with a title extracted from a poem by the Portuguese writer Gil Vicente,[3] is a provocation of social norms. The collection is written with humor, irony, and even uneasiness from the point of view of the married woman, the divorced woman, and the mistress. The central characters tell the story of the eventualities of marriage and the roles they ought to take on in society.

Most of Molina's main characters come from middle- or upper-class society, the social medium that Molina criticizes for its rules to be followed toward the only possible aim: marriage. Thus the characters must attain certain levels in the sociocultural hierarchy and maintain the image of chastity—even if it has been lost. The rules are not so rigid for characters of the lower classes, such as in the story "Lucrecia," from *Lides de estaño*, which is about a nanny whose only dream is to flee with her boyfriend (51–56). Here fleeing (*fuga*) has equal status with marriage. The ambition is the same as that of the higher-class characters in the other stories, but the image that the nanny and her boyfriend project to their peers does not have the same relevance. For this reason the succession of events in the story is not considered a scandal by its characters, as it would be in higher spheres.

Dicen que me case yo is an act of resistance to social conventionalism. Although marriage is an unavoidable social event in the life of a Mexican woman and also perceived as conferring superiority over those who remain single, Molina creates subversion by presenting female characters who are detached from conventional social formulas. "Recomenzar" ("Recommence"; 79–92) is the narration of a personal search once social duties have been met. The protagonist, María López, earned her degree as an elementary school teacher, following a gender-specific role; she is married but because of cancer was not able to give birth. In her critical moment, she recognizes that she feels conflicted not because she cannot become a mother, but instead because she is not the woman she wanted to be: she did not get to study what she wanted to, and she married not because she wanted to, but because it was an opportunity, a chance she could not miss.

> Soy así—le aseguré—, porque así me impusieron. . . . Siempre pensando que la vida es ésta que llevo, que me enseñaron. Sin haber sospechado que había otras cosas, que yo pudiera cambiar. Quería tener un hijo porque así aprendí que tenía que ser, porque como todas mis amigas esperaba el día de comprar una cunita, de tejer chambras, de bordar baberos. (81)

> I'm this way—I assured him—, because it was imposed on me. . . . Always thinking that life is this way, the one I was taught. Without suspecting that there were other things that I could change. I wanted to have a child because I learned that is what I had to do, because like

> all my friends I was waiting for the day to buy a little cradle, to knit baby clothes, to embroider bibs.

In an act of solitude, because her discourse is misunderstood in her environment, María faces her disease and gazes on her aspirations from the outside, as in a reverie. This character has had to remain on the edge of life, so now she wants to change before the opportunity runs out. In confronting these ideas, she narrates her life from childhood and recognizes the emptiness of her parents' relationship, their emotional failures and demands for what they believed their existence should be. María wants to be different but still does not know who she is. That is what she wants to discover.

In "Por una voz" ("By a Voice"; 93–100), a single woman, who is a research assistant at the university and the story's narrator, must face the process of getting an abortion by herself. Accompanied only by a taxi driver, she confirms the news of her pregnancy to the clandestine clinic where she will get the abortion. Her status as a pregnant single woman forces her to hide the events from her family; she suffers from loneliness. The narrator wishes she could change her reality; the writer she meets at the hospital tells her it is possible. That wish is why she invents a new identity for the taxi driver. Unbeknownst to him, as he sings during the ride, the driver is her companion in this trance. Here she feels anchored to life and to the possibility of starting over.

Bonding and Subordination: That Fragile Balance

"Hospital," from the collection *Un hombre cerca*, reveals the transition from childhood to adulthood through a young protagonist who is forced to care for her sick father (55–63). The grudge they both hold is a silent battle, for neither one starts a dialogue. The protagonist, who narrates, faces the events in fear and rancor because of a lack of closeness with her father. She is afraid because she does not know how to take care of a stranger: "De niña quise a mi padre, pero no recordaba haber estado acunada en sus brazos ni, mucho menos, haberlo visto desnudo" ("As a child I loved my father, but I don't remember being cradled in his arms, much less seeing him naked"; 60). She feels rancor when she discovers her own reasons for her distance. As she meditates on the family past, she realizes that the father represents the symbolic castration of her mother, who was denied access to sexual, personal, and professional plenitude. Now that the mother is dead and the father is sick, the protagonist's sister, Luisa, replaces the mother figure and takes charge of the father, leaving the protagonist to reject her sister, for Luisa represents a repetition of the traditional, submissive female role.

Near the end, in a confrontation between father and daughter, the once strong and authoritative father figure is dismantled by sickness and old age. Ruined and helpless, he does not ask for help and has a bowel movement on the hospital bed. The protagonist is a spectator who watches in uneasiness the ironic weakness of the patriarch. There is something brewing inside her as she recognizes that seeing him in the nude is also an affront to him. The protagonist lets Luisa take charge of her soiled father and abandons the hospital, thereby breaking traditional bonds and killing her father symbolically, while also deciding to pursue her own path, one that will permit her to be the woman she has decided to be.

These short-story collections demonstrate the impact of the 1970s on Molina. If *Lides de estaño* comprises reflections on the transit from childhood to adolescence, *Dicen que me case yo* and *Un hombre cerca* are reflections on prescribed social roles for women. Although it comes through more clearly perhaps in *Un hombre cerca*, each collection has a discursive narrative, exposing ideas over the action of the characters. Thus the author explains, rather than shows, the emotions that lead the characters to act in one way or another. This method weakens the short story as a narrated series of actions, but the stories gain strength through discourse. Molina responds to her social environment and era through literature. This is her way of explaining—even to herself—her rebellion against established norms and her characters' search for new models for contemporary women. Her books are part of the mosaic of works by women writers born in the 1940s and 1950s, whose publications led to the so-called boom of literature by women in the 1970s and 1980s. They are the voice—deliberately or not—of a historical moment for women.

Notes

1. The amendment was enacted on 17 December 1953.

2. Translations in the essay are mine unless otherwise indicated.

3. Vicente was born in Portugal in 1465 and died in 1537. He wrote the poem, a Christmas carol, in Spanish; it starts as follows: "Dicen que me case yo: / no quiero marido, no" ("They say I got married: / I don't want a husband, no").

Appendix: Suggested Reading

ANFER. *Participación política de la mujer en México: Siglo XX*. ICAP, 1984.

Barrancos, Dora. *Mujeres en la sociedad argentina: Una historia de cinco siglos*. Editorial Sudamericana, 2007.

Bedregal, Ximena. "Reflexiones postelectorales: Posibilidades, desafío y límites del movimiento feminista." *Debate Feminista*, vol. 2, no. 4, Sept. 1991, pp. 259–65.

Bianchi, Susana. "Peronismo y Sufragio Femenino: La ley electoral de 1947." *Anuario IEHS*, vol. 1, 1986, pp. 255–96.

Bonifaz de Novelo, María Eugenia. *La mujer mexicana: Análisis histórico*. Talleres de Litoarte, 1978.

Eltit, Diamela. *Crónica del sufragio femenino en Chile*. Servicio Nacional de la Mujer, 1994.

Works Cited

Castellanos, Rosario. *Álbum de familia*. Editorial Joaquín Mortiz, 1971.

———. *Los convidados de agosto*. Ediciones Era, 1964.

———. *Mujer que sabe latín . . .* SEP/Diana, 1979.

———. *Sobre cultura femenina*. Ediciones de "América," Revista Antológica, 1950.

Domecq, Brianda. *Bestiario doméstico*. Fondo de Cultura Económica, 1986.

Krauze, Ethel. *Intermedio para mujeres*. Editorial Océano, 1982.

Mastretta, Ángeles. *Mujeres de ojos grandes*. Ediciones Cal y Arena, 1990.

Molina, Silvia. *Dicen que me case yo*. *Dicen que me case yo*, by Molina, Ediciones Cal y Arena, 1989, pp. 77–141.

———. *Un hombre cerca*. Ediciones Cal y Arena, 1992.

———. *Lides de estaño*. 1984. *Dicen que me case yo*, by Molina, Ediciones Cal y Arena, 1989, pp. 11–70.

Pando, Marilú. *La yegua de la noche*. Joaquín Mortiz, 1993.

Priego, María Teresa. *Tiempos oscuros*. Instituto de Cultura de Tabasco, 1998.

Puga, María Luisa. *Accidentes*. Martín Casillas Editores, 1981.

Nathanial Gardner

Symbols, Codes, and Points of Focus in Silvia Molina's "Mentira piadosa"

To literature students, the process of becoming a published author can be a mystery. While students can remove the blindfold by taking a creative writing course, it is relatively uncommon for literature students to learn about the creative process and how this process can influence the codes, symbols, and points of focus in a writer's work. My introduction to how writers become published authors came through Mexico, where literary genealogy is commonplace and where being the protégé of a member of the literary establishment often leads to professional opportunities. This genealogy is a key lesson for literature students. Indeed, it helps them comprehend one of the cornerstones of the creation of new writers in Latin America. With noteworthy exceptions such as the writer Margo Glantz, perhaps nowhere has this proved to be truer than in Mexico, where this tradition gained momentum in the second half of the twentieth century. José Luis Martínez and Christopher Domínguez Michael described the phenomenon in *La literatura mexicana del siglo XX* (*Twentieth-Century Mexican Literature*): "La generación de Emiliano Pérez Cruz accedió masivamente a los talleres literario, que pasaron de la élite estilística a la institucionalización multitudinaria" ("Emiliano Pérez Cruz's literary contemporaries [those born in the 1940s and 1950s] strongly participated in the literary workshops, which went from serving a stylistic literary elite to becoming institutions for the masses"; 256).[1] Such comments provide a crucial introduction to the topic, underlining the great importance of the literary workshop tradition.[2]

However, the impact of literary workshops is undertaught and under-researched, so it may require a bit more contextualizing by teachers, which can greatly help students understand the literary world and literary content. I demonstrate this point through a case study of the literary workshop run by one of Mexico's most prominent authors, Elena Poniatowska—which has shaped a generation of writers—and its likely influence on one such writer. First, we consider the workings and context of the literary workshop, followed by a close reading of works by one of Poniatowska's most successful students, Silvia Molina. Such a process can help students and others approach close reading and understand how this technique enables us to identify codes and symbols that are transmitted through literary genealogy. Hence, I will show how these reappearing foci and interests, or what Tom Gibbons calls "patterns of imagery," can be understood as one of the fruits of the literary workshop (84).

When I teach close reading, I divide the students into small discussion groups (three to four students per group) to encourage in-depth discussion of the points explored. Topics to be analysed in class as well as in discussion groups are presented through electronic presentation platforms (i.e., *Prezi*), which I have made available through the class *Blackboard* page to allow students to prepare for class. After introducing the context, I start the section of the class that analyses the symbols, codes, and themes by having students do a brainstorming activity in small discussion groups, which allows them to identify the findings of their own close readings, after which guided classroom discussion is used to probe deeper questions.

Giving a brief lecture on the history of literary workshops helps the students gain an understanding of the local context. For example, Elena Poniatowska has stated that her journey as a writer began with her newspaper articles for *El Excelsior* (Méndez-Faith 2). The principles of her own writing workshop, or *taller*, can be traced to the Centro Mexicano de Escritores (Mexican Writers' Center), an institution set up by Margaret Shedd in 1951 (initially with support from the Rockefeller Foundation) to provide Mexican students with literary influences from the United States. Soon the center had key figures from Mexican letters leading it: Alfonso Reyes, Julio Torri, Rosario Castellanos, Juan José Arreola, and

Juan Rulfo, among others (Cruz García). It was during Shedd's time as general director of the center that Poniatowska received direct tutelage from both Arreola and Rulfo. The center required students to meet weekly, and to read their work to each other and to their teachers to receive critiques. As is generally known, Juan José Arreola—a Mexican master of the short story—coached Poniatowska when she was writing her first creative work, *Lilus Kikus*, published in 1954 in his literary anthology *Los Presentes*.[3] Her other early writing coach, Juan Rulfo, is wellknown for creating characters of great literary depth. At this point I review with my students some of the key characters in his text *Pedro Páramo* (1955), which we previously studied, to underline the usefulness of a comparative framework.

A recognized and award-winning author herself by the late 1960s, Poniatowska was invited to become the writing coach for the literary workshop that now carries her name. Inaugurated on 12 July 1972, it was originally housed in El Instituto Kairos in central Mexico City and was later relocated to a private residence in San Angel, Mexico City (Ávila). The group met every Thursday from 10:30 a.m. to 2:30 p.m. and began with a discussion on a literary classic that the students were reading, after which students read their own work for critiques by Poniatowska and by classmates. Students were offered the opportunity to publish their best pieces in *La libreta universitaria* (*The University Notebook*), a local university press publication, as well as in *Palabraísmos* (*Words Derived from Words*), a literary magazine printed by a local, privately owned press.

Turning to Silvia Molina, one of the more successful students of Poniatowska (in terms of publications), we find that Poniatowska's literary influence becomes clear. For example, Molina has acknowledged during interviews that Poniatowska taught students to write about their own experiences and interests (Gardner 46–48), as well as to "escarbar en el ser humano" ("interrogate human experience"; 47); she cites a principal factor of Poniatowska's coaching: the guidance to create characters of depth who exhibit curiosity about the marginalized people of Mexico.

The wealth of studies that center Poniatowska's work on the subaltern make it clear that she is a writer who has shown a profound interest in marginalized communities. A short article posted on *Blackboard* can bring this point into focus for the students: Jean Franco and Ilan Stavans, as well as newly minted PhD students (Fuentes, *Espacio* and Introduction; Leah Cruess), all have relevant writings in this area. When discussing marginality with students it is useful to outline, or identify, specific ways that

Molina's characters are marginalized, which—depending on whether students are familiar with Poniatowska's works—can show both differences and influence.[4]

Although a number of scholarly texts explain in clear terms the basic tenets of close reading, and most agree that to read closely means to acquire a greater understanding of literature by approaching a work's codes, themes, symbols, and figures while also considering use of time, action, and vocabulary, I recommend assigning Gibbons's *Literature and Awareness: An Introduction to the Close Reading of Prose and Verse* because it is clearly written and facilitates student engagement. Frank Lentricchia and Andrew Dubois's *Close Reading: The Reader* has also brought positive results for the same reasons. Next, I have students read short interviews with Molina (revealing important points, such as her degree in anthropology), and I provide a list of questions to encourage close reading and prepare students for engagement through discussion. The close reading tools, plus classroom and discussion-group commentary, help students identify the nature of the lasting effects of a workshop experience. As an example, Molina's short story "Mentira piadosa" ("Reasonable Lie") offers students the opportunity to consider this influence and writing from their own experiences.

Upon launching a close reading of this story, I embark on the exercise to brainstorm ideas about codes, themes, symbols, and figures. Inevitably, the theme that most frequently rises to the surface is subalternity (often understood by students as resulting from power imbalances and abuse, causing loneliness, and so forth). By focusing on the two protagonists, Carmela and Eugenia, who meet at an elite school in the socially progressive La Condesa neighborhood in Mexico City, students discern that each is indicated as being located on the periphery of experiences. Carmela, the narrator (who is from a more stable socioeconomic background), enjoys the vantage point of studying the other: Eugenia, the new girl in her class. While Carmela suffers the stigma of being the youngest girl in their final year of *secundaria* ("high school") and of not yet having entered puberty, Eugenia suffers from the attention she draws for being well developed for her age. Also, Eugenia stands out as marginalized after her abrupt transfer from her old school to the new one (until Carmela befriends her). Closer reading, however, soon reveals forms of abuse that appear to play a stronger role in the marginalization of Eugenia. A prereading question regarding Eugenia's bruises can help students achieve a more nuanced understanding of such symbols. Initially, the text appears to link subalternity to physicality, but then symbols modify to a degree as the narrative develops. Underlining these discussion points in class helps students understand that the process of close reading requires attention to literary details.

Students benefit from discussing Tom Gibbons's "patterns of imagery" evident in the description of the adult Carmela (84). Considering the opening (and closing) line of the story makes evident Molina's studies in anthropology: "La observo detenidamente mientras habla. Pienso en lo que ha dicho y callo" ("I observe her closely while she talks. I think about what she said, and I say nothing"; 67). Molina does not disclose what Eugenia says or how Carmela responds, and this elliptical treatment of the scene suggests that Eugenia's story does not offer closure but rather raises more questions. Although the reader has not anticipated it, a case study has begun. As we continue reviewing the development of the story (and the lives of the protagonists beyond graduation from high school), I make it clear that the story explores the lives of two marginalized young women trying to function within the upper classes. We identify the symbols suggesting that Carmela overcomes her marginality (through her education, stable marriage, and government employment), while Eugenia appears to remain trapped in her marginalized status (unable to maintain stable relationships and disengaged from the workforce). In close reading, students point out symbolic differences revealed early on, for example, between the two girls' backpacks (since the school requires standard uniforms, no difference in attire is noticeable), Carmela has a leather backpack (71), and Eugenia only a canvas bag (68). As Carmela's thoughts are evaluated, the story shows that she is self-aware, not only of what drew her to Eugenia, but also in recognizing her privilege: she feels guilty for her advantages over Eugenia (71).

Notwithstanding Carmela's early understanding of her higher status relative to Eugenia, the latter is always able to maintain the upper hand because of her greater life experience. Also, Carmela is fascinated by Eugenia: "Viéndola, era inevitable pensar en un misterio" ("Seeing her, thoughts of mystery were unavoidable"; 68). Later on, the bruises (symbols) on Eugenia's body supply a new mystery that retains Carmela's budding anthropological interest until Carmela feels tricked by Eugenia into accompanying her to what she discovers is a clandestine abortion clinic. There Carmela is forced to recognize that the object she is fixated on can manipulate the anthropologist. The exploration of this point allows classroom discussion to identify subaltern agency as a narrative theme.

The adult Carmela still possesses anthropologist-like interests and continues in search of answers. Resentful that she was manipulated into accompanying Eugenia to the abortion clinic, she appears unsympathetic to her old classmate. This point could be used to explore how Carmela also marginalizes Eugenia. Likewise, students can identify that Carmela is developed with greater nuance. For example, her motivations are openly explained: "Decidí irme. Había esperado de esa reunión solo la verdad, porque estaba segura de que me había contado una estúpida mentira cuando sucedió aquello" ("I decided to leave. I had only been hoping for the truth in that meeting, because I was sure that she had told me a stupid lie when all of that happened"; 75). Eugenia, on the other hand, requires a more nuanced interpretation of codes and symbols. Questions to pose include the following: Who left the bruises on her leg? What is her relationship with her stepfather's friend? Why does she choose to confide in Carmela? Carmela's threat to leave the clinic appears to convince Eugenia to offer the reader the story Carmela wishes to hear.

Eugenia argues to her that they are not so different: "La condición era que llegara acompañada. Dije que eras mi hermana. Después de todo nos parecemos: una mentira piadosa" ("The condition was that I bring someone with me. I told them you were my sister. After all, we look like each other: a white lie"; 81). This phrase reminds Carmela that their relationship might not follow the paradigms she expected it to, and students can find points for discussion in Eugenia's comment. In class, they can discuss the implications of Eugenia's lie regarding the entire narrative: if Eugenia was capable of telling a white lie to others, then why should students accept her responses to Carmela as trustworthy? How might the lie affect how students interpret the signs and symbols within the narrative?

Just as a close reading has helped students consider Carmela's motives and Molina's anthropological training, it begins to elicit other questions that can help point to influences on Molina by a writing coach. Why did Eugenia need the abortion? The text suggests, without fully disclosing it, that the pregnancy may have resulted from her relationship with her stepfather's friend. Students can also discuss the notion of a lie that is *piadosa* ("pious") and the term's double meaning. While Eugenia lied to obtain the support she needed (by getting Carmela to accompany her to the abortion clinic), the story's explanation of the lie allows readers to have compassion for Eugenia by putting themselves in her shoes. This, of course, is one of the main thrusts of Poniatowska's writings: to understand the subaltern's experience.

As students consider the focus of "Mentira piadosa" on the subaltern, certain patterns of imagery come into view. The curious teenager becomes the anthropologist as the narrative develops. The character she observes, Eugenia, represents the periphery as a newcomer to her school, but also as a woman systematically cast aside, by her mother, her stepfather, her husband, her teachers, and so forth. Not just Carmela, but all the characters who come in contact with Eugenia marginalize her in one way or another. These patterns of imagery permit students to discuss the underlining of patterns of abuse suffered by women. When literature students reflect on the portrayal of emotions within this narrative, they ascertain that while both Carmela and Eugenia suffer from the effects of subalternity, Eugenia is subaltern to all.

While Carmela's envy, curiosity, betrayal, and unwillingness to forgive are plainly manifest within the text's vocabulary, the reader can only intuit Eugenia's emotions. Observing that she has lied and manipulated on various occasions, the reader only once sees her deeper thoughts placed on display. Upon her impromptu confession, her self-loathing becomes evident, which suggests that erasure of the subaltern would solve its problems: "La gente habla de felicidad, pero la verdadera felicidad es cuando ya no te importa si te mueres . . ." ("People talk about happiness, but true happiness is when you don't care if you die . . ."; Molina 81). Such strong self-critique mirrors the behavior of Poniatowska's protagonist Jesusa Palancares in the 1969 novel *Hasta no verte, Jesús mío* (*Until We Meet Again*) and Jesusa's thoughts on Mexican identity: "Si yo tuviera dinero y bienes sería mexicana, pero como soy peor que la basura, pues no soy nada" ("If I had money and material goods, I would be Mexican, but since I am lower than trash, I'm nothing"; 213). The fact that each writers' characters emphasize that point, along with a strong theme of marginality, suggests influences, and perhaps ideological links, between the writing coach and her student. Such conclusions can be gleaned by literature students through close readings and consideration of the dynamics of the literary workshop in the transmission of ideas across generations of writers.

Reading published work by a writing coach together with the published work of one of her students can enrich understanding of the influences facilitated by writing workshops and the themes identified through close readings. In the case of Poniatowska and Molina, the emphasis in the work of both writers is on marginality, writing from one's own experiences, and the treatment of the voices of the marginalized. "Mentira piadosa" offers an opportunity for students to examine the influence of Molina's writing coach and the importance of workshops in the development of literary work, and to learn a classic technique of literary study, close reading. Indeed, such an opportunity is essential for students to achieve greater understanding of Mexican literary history and the literary industry as a place where one learns the craft of being an author and as a livelihood. By making use of stories like this one, students begin to comprehend literature within its own context, adding to the richness and texture of our understanding of Latin American cultural processes.

Notes

1. Translations in this essay are mine unless otherwise indicated.

2. Research for this article has been supported by the research network Traducción, Ideología, Cultura, which is based at the Universidad de Salamanca.

3. The original form of *Lilus Kikus* was as a novella of twelve chapters. This work is at times confused with a later rerelease of the novella in an edition that also included several unrelated stories and that was titled *Los cuentos de Lilus Kikus*. Later, a translation of four of the stories and the novella was titled: Lilus Kikus *and Other Stories by Elena Poniatowska*.

4. Further discussion on subaltern studies and Latin America can be found in Rodríguez.

Works Cited

Ávila, Rodrigo. Interview. By Nathanial Gardner. July 2002.

Cruz García, Ricardo. "Fuentes y 'La Poni.'" *Cuadrivio Semanal*, 1 Mar. 2014.

Franco, Jean. *Plotting Women: Gender and Representation in Mexico*. Columbia UP, 1989.

Fuentes, Cristina. *Espacio y marginalidad en la narrativa mexicana del siglo XX*. 2014. U of California, Irvine, PhD dissertation.

———. Introduction. *Elenísima*, by Michael Schuessler, Diana, 2003, pp. 13–14.

Gardner, Nathanial. *Through Their Eyes: Marginality in the Works of Elena Poniatowska, Silvia Molina, and Rosa Nissán*. Peter Lang, 2007.

Gibbons, Tom. *Literature and Awareness: An Introduction to the Close Reading of Prose and Verse*. Edward Arnold, 1979.

Leah Cruess, Susan. *A Study of Elena Poniatowska's* Amanecer en el Zócalo*: The Contemporary Mexican* Crónica *in Translation*. Mar. 2014. U of Ottawa, PhD dissertation.

Lentricchia, Frank, and Andrew Dubois. *Close Reading: The Reader*. Duke UP, 2003.

Martínez, José Luis, and Christopher Domínguez Michael. *La literatura mexicana del siglo XX*. CNCA, 1995.

Méndez-Faith, Teresa. "Entrevista con Elena Poniatowska." *Inti: Revista de Literatura Hispánica*, vol. 1, no. 15, 1982, pp. 1–8, digitalcommons.providence.edu/inti/vol1/iss15/7/.
Molina, Silvia. "Mentira piadosa." *Un hombre cerca*, Cal y Arena, 1992, pp. 66–82.
Poniatowska, Elena. *Hasta no verte, Jesús mío.* Ediciones Era, 1969.
Rodríguez, Ileana, editor. *The Latin American Subaltern Studies Reader.* Duke UP, 2001.
Rulfo, Juan. *Pedro Páramo.* Cátedra, 1983.
Stavans, Ilan. *A Critic's Journey.* U of Michigan P, 2010.

Manuel F. Medina

Narrative Spaces, Gender, and Sephardic Identity in Rosa Nissán's *Novia que te vea*

This essay introduces a student-centered approach to teaching *Novia que te vea* (1992; *Like a Bride*) by the Sephardic Mexican writer Rosa Nissán. It advances the study of form and content in terms of teaching textual analysis, and relevant cultural issues, to undergraduates and graduate students. It shows how to help students identify narratological components (narrative voices and other elements that focalize a narrative) and how to embark on such topics as gender in Jewish society, tradition and renewal across generational bridges, and the crossing of Jewish and Mexican cultural borders within the context of Mexico City. It helps students grapple with the complexities of contemporary Mexico City society through both a Sephardic perspective and an understanding of the role of women in the late twentieth century.

Rosa Nissán received recognition as a Mexicana writer in 1992 when her first novel became an immediate best seller. Her second novel, *Hisho que te nazca* (1996; *Like a Mother*), continues the story where *Novia que te vea* leaves off.[1] What aided in propelling her instant success was the fact that the Costa Rican Jewish film director Guita Schyfter was looking for a screenplay about the experience of Jews, and that Elena Poniatowska (Nissán's writing workshop coach) suggested Nissán's work to her. Schyfter incorporated a parallel story with Nissán's novel *Novia que te vea*, creating a homonymous film; released in 1992, the film received a great reception at the Ariel Awards ceremony, earning sixteen nominations and winning five awards.

Nissán's third novel, *Los viajes de mi cuerpo* (*The Travels of My Body*), pinpoints a departure from her previous topics, relating the story of Lola Luna, a woman who sets out to discover life as a divorcée in Mexico City. Nissán has also authored a collection of short stories, *No solo para dormir es la noche* (1999; *The Night Is Not Only for Sleeping*), where she showcases her talents and craftsmanship as a fiction writer. Nissán more recently released *Trrri biutiful leidis* (*Three Beautiful Ladies*), a trilogy collecting the previously published travel chronicles *Las tierras prometidas: Crónica de un viaje a Israel* (*The Promised Lands: Chronicle of a Trip to Israel*) and *Horizontes sagrados: Diarios de viaje* (*Sacred Horizons: Travel Diaries*), the second of which centers on her travels to India; and a new chronicle that shares the trilogy's title, where she relates that she is content living by herself, now in her seventh decade.

Nissán's first novel appeared in Mexico at a time when a few other Jewish women authors had begun reflecting on issues of cultural identity, family practices, and memories in their own narratives. The success of the novel can be traced to an engaging style that helps deliver Nissán's accounts through the narrative voice of a girl who makes observations while growing up. The main character marries at age seventeen, by the end of the novel, but the book's most important quality is that it allows audiences to glimpse the world of Sephardic society and explore with the writer issues of gender and national identity. The novel helps readers lift the veil of mystery, identify stigmas assigned to Jewish populations, and understand the core values of a culture that is both Mexican and Jewish and that may seem foreign to some students.[2]

The female protagonist of *Novia que te vea*, named Eugenia (in Spanish) and Oshinica, the name she inherited from her Sephardic grandmother, relates the story (in a form somewhat like journal entries), beginning when she is eight years old with a description of her apartment and neighborhood, and then of the family's relocation to a neighborhood with other Sephardic families. Oshinica describes other children, the household maid, and her mother's friends—in spaces connected to home and school—as well as the Lagunilla market where her father and grandfather operate a men's clothing business, and finally, activities at the Jewish Community Center in Mexico City (Centro Deportivo Israel). She only ventures away from these spaces once when she attends a high school academy, where she begins to learn about careers and mingles with non-Jews, but she also knows she is destined to marry soon. Her point of rebellion is when she rejects her parent's prospect (who is invited to the home) and instead chooses her own husband, Lalo, who is also Jewish, and who promises he will allow her to study after marriage. As *Novia que te vea* ends, Oshinica narrates details of the wedding and plans for a honeymoon in Acapulco, the first trip she will take away from her family, now as a wife and woman. She has transitioned from childhood into adulthood.

Is It an Autobiographical Text?

Novia que te vea has elements that classify it as life writing or autobiographical fiction. There are several similarities between the main character, Oshinica, and Rosa Nissán. Born in Mexico City to immigrant parents, the author and character each grow up in families that follow Sephardic traditions. Students can be assigned some of the many interviews with Nissán to deduce this, and they may also observe the cultural practices and ideological positions regarding gender roles shared by the author and the protagonist.[3] Each of them lives life in the thin margin that separates their national and ethnic cultures. Similar topics appear in Nissán's travel chronicles, such as *Las tierras prometidas*, where the author speaks freely without using a fictional character as a filter.

What Are the Characteristics of the Narrative Voice?

The use of the narrative voice of a young girl who becomes a young woman stands as one of the novel's most memorable achievements. Never diverting from this pattern, the novel uses Oshinica's narration to center her life in Jewish space in contemporary Mexico City. Fictional accounts that use narrators who reflect on their childhoods often describe events using what the narratology expert Franz Karl Stanzel calls acting and contemplative beings (290). As the narrator recounts an event from childhood, the portrayal of the event comes to readers through the focalization of the child who experienced it. Such narrators usually make comments from an adult perspective that they have gained through chronological distance from the event. To better explain this concept in *Novia que te vea* I ask a student to read aloud a passage that illustrates this narrative technique. The text offers plenty of examples and opportunities to show the technique in action (such as the extract that follows).

Nissán's talent lies precisely in keeping the narrator within character, literally never letting Oshinica go off script to provide adult perspectives, comments, or reflections. Written as if it were a personal journal, *Novia que te vea* allows readers to move through the story at the same time as Oshinica lives it. And this technique allows access to the protagonist's views of the world as she experiences them and not later, when they may be embedded with a filter of nostalgia or when she has achieved some chronological distance. Darrell B. Lockhart proposes that Nissán uses a child narrator who, through her youthful perspective, can look for an identity of her own rather than accepting the one imposed on her by tradition (166–67). Oshinica voices personal feelings about the traditionally assigned duties for boys and girls as they move toward adulthood. Her words carry social commentary and criticism, especially when she explains her reasons for selecting models to imitate:

> Do I want to look like my mom, my grandmother or my aunt? No. I'd rather look like my grandfather, my dad, or even my brother. Those women are so boring, and they're dumb as well!! Well, I guess my mom isn't so dumb, but she's not all fun and games either. My grandmother can't even go to Sears by herself, and it's only two blocks away. But she goes secretly with Uba. Women are supposed to stay at home; it doesn't even occur to them to go rowing. . . . At least I don't get bored, because I get to go outside and always beat the guys at soccer or baseball. (Nissán, *Like a Bride* 20–21)

This passage can provide excellent discussion for students; they can then be asked—in small groups—to identify other such passages where Oshinica comments on her cultural traditions.

Such a narrative strategy of commenting on life and cultural practice appears throughout the novel, and at times it is used to address sensitive subjects. However, Oshinica also relinquishes her narrative voice so that others can elaborate on adult themes. Readers learn about the Jewish Diaspora from a book read by Trivia, a seventeen-year-old girl who attends youth meetings. And Oshinica introduces the topic of divisions, including different teachings, among diverse groups of Jews in Mexico by reading a letter received by her teacher in school, where an unidentified author from Israel declares: "Dear Friends: I have noticed in Jewish Mexico there are sharp differences among the three predominant groups. That is a real pity, although it seems natural for them to exist, because your parents grew up in different parts of the world, and upon arriving on the new continent, they wanted to continue their own way of living, eating, marrying, educating their children, and burying their dead" (85). Afterward Oshinica moves on to the next topic, her class on "boring" biology, letting readers draw their own conclusions about differences among the Jews living in Mexico, who are separated by place of origin. The protagonist remains on the outside of this complicated and serious "adult" matter (86).

Can This Novel Be Labeled Jewish Literature?

Students can be directed to the introduction to *The Location of Culture* (1–18), a short reading by theorist Homi K. Bhabha on third spaces, which helps them consider contexts for understanding cultural hybridity and strategies to translate social differences in order to define Jewish identity (10). Bhabha sustains that a bridging of borders occurs in in-between spaces rather than in completely defined and clearly marked areas (4). Beginning early in the novel, students can examine how Oshinica sits in the space that joins and at the same time separates her two religions and ethnicities—Jewish and Catholic, Jewish and Mexican: in the first chapter she performs a Hail Mary so that her parents will not transfer her out of the Catholic school, which is named after the Virgin of Guadalupe, a hybrid symbol of Mexican and Catholic identity. She shows reluctance to trade this school for a Jewish school, which would offer a less Mexican and surely non-Catholic experience. Thus readers learn early on of Oshinica's struggle to inhabit this in-between space.

This identity conflict also is demonstrated through the protagonist's two names, Eugenia and Oshinica. Later in the novel, when Oshinica relates her genealogy, readers see that her Mexican identity document lists her as Eugenia, which is the Spanish translation of her grandmother's name, Oshinica, whose heritage is a mixture of Turkish and French (Nissán, *Like a Bride* 48). Her family's use of the non-Spanish Oshinica causes personal conflict; she negotiates her identity according to corresponding spaces. As she grows up and moves into the Jewish neighborhood, she welcomes her otherness, introducing herself as Eugenia, adding that some people call her "Oshi." This triggers a conversation about her national origin. She assumes her Mexican nationality with pride but clarifies her parents' non-Mexican national status: "My parents aren't Mexican, but I am. I was born here" (111–12). Yael Halevi-Wise explains that Oshinica presents herself as a Mexican Jew with inherited allegiances and responsibilities to two cultures (271). Interestingly, during her brother Moshón's bar mitzvah, Oshinica's grandfather refers to her as "Eugenia" rather than using her Jewish name (Nissán, *Like a Bride* 90). This action might suggest a conscious effort by her grandfather to fit into his newly adopted land in a process of cultural assimilation rather than mere cultural adaptation. By calling her Eugenia, he embraces his granddaughter's Mexican national identity and places it ahead of her Jewish identity.

The title of the novel itself presents another culture, by using a saying from Ladino, the heritage language of Sephardic Jews, *Novia que te vea*, which means "May you soon be a bride" (whereas the title of Nissán's second novel is a saying in Ladino that means "May you soon have a son"). And in fact, the sprinkling of phrases and vocabulary in Ladino in the novel serves to delimit and emphasize the novel's spaces. Oshinica gets invited to a *posada*, a sort of pre-Christmas party celebrated in Mexico, and thus not part of Jewish culture. Her father reacts to Oshinica's request for permission to attend the party by speaking in Ladino to accentuate their otherness and remind Oshinica in their own language of her culture, her "other" identity (138). Halevi-Wise maintains that the use of the Ladino language of Oshinica's ancestors (which traveled with them from Spain in the late 1400s) represents an attempt to bridge two cultures, that of Oshinica's Sephardic heritage and that of her birth country, Mexico. The novel offers a space, if only textual, where both cultures can coexist (Halevi-Wise 274).

How Are Gender Roles Assigned?

This text is also ideal for examining gender role issues because it questions, revises, and subverts those roles. As Oshinica enters her teenage years, she becomes aware of how she fills the male gaze. She purposefully begins to dress to entice. Once students discuss the male gaze (through their own experience), they can be asked about her examination from the female gaze. Ultimately, she defies the cultural tradition of parents selecting a spouse for their child through a matchmaker, for she convinces them that she will accept a marriage proposal from Lalo. Also, she gets Lalo to promise to allow her to continue pursuing an education, and, importantly, not to ask for a dowry. She thus subverts tradition. These acts stand as a great accomplishment for a girl raised in Jewish tradition, and they charge the protagonist's statements with ideological implications.

Oshinica's father informs Oshinica that she will only leave the house once she gets married: "Women leave home with their husbands; you can go wherever you want with him" (Nissán, *Like a Bride* 77). At a family gathering, Oshinica observes how the domestic duties fall exclusively on the women, "All the women must get up to help, because the table belongs to the men" (91), and she notices that her brother, who is two years younger, is entitled to male privileges as of his bar mitzvah at age thirteen. She also ponders gender inequalities in temple functions, where once she is a teenager, she can no longer sit with her father on the main floor. She learns that women are not allowed to carry the sacred book because of their monthly menstruation, which makes them unclean, as her aunt states: "'we are impure, that's why. It's an honor that we don't have . . . , my little darling' she said hugging me. Isn't that strange? We are impure" (94).

Finally, critics have noted Nissán's dual role of contesting gender roles for both mainstream Mexican society and Sephardic culture. Elizabeth Coonrod Martínez observes that the novel makes visible the traditionally unseen Sephardic woman within the context of the migrant Jewish population in Mexico, because "Nissán both recuperates Jewish pilgrimage and formation as a Mexican immigrant population within that nation's history and restores the seemingly invisible Sephardic woman to her own community" (103). César Ferreira comments that, by using personal experience as a point of departure, the novel claims a space for women's voices within Mexican society (70). The novel represents a narrative of empowerment: a female narrator takes control of the storytelling process, her life, and her choices, within a joint context of cultural tradition and mainstream society. Students can be guided to identify these dual accomplishments through group work.

Novia que te vea is a novel that students find enjoyable, that likely only requires four class periods of discussion, and in which students can analyze narrative voice and other elements that focalize the story, which serve to question and subvert traditional values and gender roles. Through the voice and observations of a little girl who becomes a seventeen-year-old on the threshold of marriage, students can examine the novel's limitations and avenues for analysis, and discussions will open up topics of national identity, migration, religious and cultural practices, and women's roles. Oshinica must constantly negotiate cultural borders within all the spaces she inhabits and identify her own third space. Just as Lockhart suggests that Oshinica can choose her own identity (166–67), *Novia que te vea* moves the definition of *Mexican* to that of *Jewish*, that of *religious* to that of *secular*, and that of *male* to that of *female*. A Sephardic Jew can be culturally Jewish and Mexican and both follow and rebel from cultural and religious practice. But in this novel the stigma of Jewish people as others (even as "evil," as a child says to Oshinica in a public playground [41]) is removed. Through this novel, students learn to confound and see beyond stereotypes, and to assess cultural differences and gender role prohibitions.

Notes

1. In 2002 the two novels were published together in English translation as Like a Bride *and* Like a Mother; in the process of translating them, the archaic Ladino was lost, having been rendered simply in English along with the rest of the text.

2. The Sephardic Jews have an ancient history, having been ejected from Spain in 1492 because of the nationalization of Christianity. Many of them subsequently migrated to the Ottoman Empire (now Turkey and other nations), and in the early twentieth century extensive groups migrated to Latin America.

3. For interviews with Nissán, see Hind (133–42); Bermúdez Barrios (255–62).

Works Cited

Bermúdez Barrios, Nayibe. *Sujetos transnacionales: La negociación en cine y literatura*. Universidad Autónoma de Ciudad Juárez, 2009.

Bhabha, Homi K. *The Location of Culture*. Routledge, 1994.

Ferreira, César. "Una nueva versión de la infancia en México: *Novia que te vea* de Rosa Nissán." *Revista de Literatura Mexicana Contemporánea*, vol. 4, no. 9, Oct. 1998 / Jan. 1999, pp. 66–70.

Halevi-Wise, Yael. "Puente entre naciones: Idioma e identidad sefardi en *Novia que te vea* e *Hisho que te nazca* de Rosa Nissán." *Hispania*, vol. 81, no. 2, May 1998, pp. 269–77.

Hind, Emily. *Entrevistas con quince autoras mexicanas*. Iberoamericana / Vervuert, 2003.

Lockhart, Darrell B. "Growing Up Jewish in Mexico: Sabina Berman's *La bobe* and Rosa Nissán's *Novia que te vea*." *The Other Mirror: Women's Narrative in Mexico, 1980–1995*, edited by Kristine Ibsen, Greenwood, 1997, pp. 159–73.

Martínez, Elizabeth Coonrod. "Rosa Nissán: Cultural Memory and the Mexican Sephardic Woman." *Mosaic*, vol. 37, no. 1, Mar. 2004, pp. 101–18.

Nissán, Rosa. *Hisho que te nazca*. Plaza y Janés, 1996.

———. *Like a Bride*. Like a Bride *and* Like a Mother, translated by Dick Gerdes, U of New Mexico P, 2002, pp. 1–212.

———. Like a Bride *and* Like a Mother. Translated by Dick Gerdes, U of New Mexico P, 2002.

———. *Novia que te vea*. Planeta, 1992.

———. *Los viajes de mi cuerpo*. Planeta, 2003.

Stanzel, Franz Karl. *A Theory of Narrative*. Cambridge University Press, 1988.

Jessica Burke

The Reader and the Text in Carmen Boullosa's Fragmented Narratives

A prolific writer dedicated to her craft, Carmen Boullosa has written novels, theater, poetry, short stories, and essays, in addition to her work in television. Through a fragmented discourse that reflects her characters' fragmented notions of self, Boullosa creates parodic, self-reflective novels that center on a plot but also engage with their own creation as texts and with the practice of storytelling as an art. The personal histories that she creates in her novels dialogue with and question the official history that often has excluded or silenced certain groups. Boullosa gives these marginalized groups a voice and a space from which they can express themselves. The physical body and the body of the text are both works in progress, requiring the active participation of the reader in the construction of their meaning. Boullosa's narrators struggle to define themselves under the pressure of expectations put forth by both society and the genre of the novel itself.

I have found teaching Boullosa's narratives both challenging and rewarding. Undergraduate students accustomed to more traditional narrative techniques may initially struggle with a fragmented narrative that questions its own reliability. However, given the proper introduction to Boullosa's work, an upper-division class is able to appreciate the complex relation Boullosa constructs between characters' bodies, characters' sense of self, and the text that contains them.[1] A good place to start is with background on the fragmented novel in Mexican literature. Carol Clark D'Lugo's *The Fragmented Novel in Mexico: The Politics of Form* is a useful resource for establishing a literary history of the fragment as a metaphor for national identity. From a general discussion of fragmented narrative and its relation to Mexican history, we move to Boullosa's work in particular, where fragmentation allows for reconfiguration of physical and textual bodies, and of identity. Our class discussions consider how dismantling instituted notions of gender, identity, body, and narrative allows Boullosa to create a space for reinvention of the self, and of novelistic form. We talk about why it is important to dismantle such instituted notions: specifically, those related to gender identity and gender roles. I posit questions to the class about feminine archetypes in Mexican history, from La Malinche, to La Virgen de Guadalupe, to Sor Juana Inés de la Cruz. It is helpful, if time allows, to have students read critical material related to these figures and their impact on women's writing in Mexico.[2] These readings find a natural place in the course design when I am teaching a course on women's writing in Latin America, or in a course on Mexican literature, in which reading the predecessors of Boullosa allows us to consider her creative project within the larger context of Mexican narrative. I am careful to point out that Boullosa is uneasy with the categorization of writers based on their gender, and we talk about why that is. What are the expectations for literature written by women? Does gender impact how and what women write? Why does Boullosa resist being lumped together with other women writers of her generation? These are all helpful questions to stimulate class discussion on the relation between gender and writing, in preparation for our study of Boullosa's work.[3]

Boullosa's texts are not as widely read as those of her more mainstream contemporaries, perhaps because of their complexity and lack of narrative flow. Students may be familiar with the works of more widely recognized writers such as Isabel Allende or Laura Esquivel, and it is helpful to survey the class on the type of novels they are accustomed to reading. Critics situate Boullosa's writing within postmodern debates because of its self-reflective, fragmentary, and often parodic nature, so I spend time in class summarizing the trends of postmodern narrative and its problematic relation to history. In several of her narratives, Boullosa inserts herself into the text as a character. At times referring to herself as "Carmen" or "Boullosa," and at others as "la autora" ("the author"), she subjects herself to the questioning and even ridicule of her own characters and narrators.

Regardless of who is narrating, the narrators maintain an intimate connection with their perceived audience. The reader is always kept close, whether directly invoked in the text or not. At times it seems that Boullosa's narrators rely on the reader more than the reader can rely on the narrators, which creates an interesting dynamic in terms of reader response. Titling her work with such disclaimers as "Ingobernable" ("Ungovernable"), "Teatro herético" ("Heretical Theater"), or "Papeles irresponsables" ("Irresponsible Papers"), Boullosa's intent often seems to be to disconcert the reader and call into question the expectations one brings to a text. The reader is taken on an imaginative adventure with multiple side trips, and sometimes the narrative path falls back on itself. We cannot expect a linear progression of plot or a traditional and reliable narrator who will guide us to a "natural" conclusion of the story, but as readers we can expect to form an integral part of the meaning of the novel, since it is through the reader that the text gains meaning.

While the reader may be directly incorporated into Boullosa's texts, the metafictitious nature of the narrative will not allow us to stay there, caught up in the story. The self-aware text needs a reader in order to construct itself as a narrative, yet it demands a critical reader who will never forget the creative, inventive process at hand. Boullosa's engagement with her readers invites us to discuss as a class our response as readers to this imposed relationship. I ask my students about their reaction to Boullosa's narrators: Are they uncomfortable? intrigued? amused? confused? Sorting out their own reader responses allows for a discussion of the author's intent and the overall impact that narrative technique has on our processing of the story.

Boullosa's characters and narrators are subjects who have been marginalized by traditional literary and historical narrative; they are women, children, immigrants, natives, Romani, prostitutes, pirates, slaves, vampires, cannibals, and ghosts. Instead of providing types to be assimilated into a certain historical framework, Boullosa's protagonists break the mold with their complex and often hybrid natures. Their marginal position in society does not prohibit their right to a voice in Boullosa's texts but rather allows them to provide alternative testimonies to history. When discussing *historias* ("stories") versus history, I provide a theoretical framework by talking about Hayden White's reading of historical writing as narrative prose discourse and Michel de Certeau's concept of historical writing as dialogue with the ghosts of the past. Linda Hutcheon's definition of historiographic metafiction is particularly useful in contextualizing Boullosa's novels that take place (partially or entirely) during the colonial period. In *Son vacas, somos puercos* (1991; *They're Cows, We're Pigs*, 1997), *Duerme* (*Sleep*), and *Llanto: Novelas imposibles* (*Weeping: Impossible Novels*), we hear testimonies from marginalized characters whose stories are noticeably absent from historical narratives of the time. Each of these novels resuscitates historical figures only to problematize their existence and the possibility of finding historical truth. The shadowy marginal spaces from which Boullosa's narrators write grant them a certain narrative freedom. They are not responsible for telling the story of a nation; they are simply telling their own stories. These voices, however, are frequently broken ones, torn in their attempt to represent, and pulled in different directions by social and narrative pressures. The narrators struggle with their sense of autonomy and identity, and through them is revealed the author's struggle with the autonomy and identity of her text.

The plurality of narrators and perspectives in Boullosa's texts are a testimony to her resistance to adopting one version of any historical event or figure. For example, the obsession with creating a true history of Moctezuma stalls the many narratives that compose *Llanto*. Inspired to write about the famous Aztec emperor, the writers in the novel must abandon their attempts after realizing that creating a true history of Moctezuma is impossible. The voices in *Llanto* each offer a different version of the life and death of Moctezuma, all of which are truncated by the inability to continue. The resulting text—Boullosa's text—is the compilation of several "impossible" novels. Thus the only "possible" novel about Moctezuma is one that narrates the impossibility of accurately representing him. Boullosa resurrects Moctezuma as a character in the novel, but he dissolves into thin air at the end, unable to maintain a corporeal form in modern-day Mexico.

Faced with the impossibility of a cohesive true story, we are forced to treat all perspectives as equally valid, thus contesting the grand, totalizing historical narratives of the past. Such monolithic narratives that situate all events within their proper context do indeed presume that a certain sense should be made of the information at hand. It is this narrative aspect of history that concerns Boullosa, a concern shared by many of her contemporaries.

Contextualizing Boullosa's approach to narrative in this way permits a rich discussion of the relation between history and literature. When confronted with such a big subject, I like to start by breaking the class into small groups and having them discuss the topic and then prepare some summary comments to share with the class. A follow-up question for discussion could be, "What can fiction contribute to historical perspective that historical writing does not?" Both of these questions lay the groundwork for understanding the creative project of Boullosa in her novels set in a historical past, as these works are the result of careful readings of literary and historical texts. Her novels set in colonial times were inspired by sixteenth- and seventeenth-century accounts of the Spanish conquest and colonization of the Americas, and her first two novels, *Antes* (1989; *Before*, 2016) and *Mejor desaparece* (1987; *Just Disappear*, 2009), both set in childhood, were inspired by memories and journals that she kept as a child. Boullosa's consultations of these historical and personal documents revealed inconsistencies, contradictions, and gaps, all of which contributed to the fragmentary nature of her novels, which openly acknowledge their own inconsistencies, contradictions, and gaps. What we know as reality is mapped out through a process of recollection, interpretation, and postulation, a process limited by language and memory. In Boullosa's narratives, the gaps in memory and knowledge are either filled with imaginative invention or left glaringly open, revealing the absence of a monolithic truth (personal or historical) that would unite the various fragments of the text.

While Boullosa's work indubitably questions history as a narrative, it does not deny history as its own source and inspiration. Among Boullosa's novels inspired by historical figures, *De un salto descabalga la reina* (2000; *Cleopatra Dismounts*, 2002) is a rewriting of the character of the Egyptian queen Cleopatra. Diómedes—Cleopatra's scribe and the novel's narrator—insists that he "almost" captures Cleopatra's true testimony (109), but he is challenged by both external and internal obstacles. This text doesn't come close to being a historical novel in the traditional sense. Although it includes historical events and figures, it also includes Cleopatra's abduction by a mythical bull that carries her across the sea and deposits her on the shore of the land of the Amazon women. This highly eroticized, imaginative history of Cleopatra seeks not to paint a historical portrait of the woman, but rather to create a very human, intimate, creative, and sensual character who *could* have been Cleopatra and who is just as real as any other textual projection of the Egyptian queen. Narrated by the man who betrayed her, the novel lends voice to Cleopatra, but always through a filter. She dictates her testimony to her scribe, but he admits that he edits it as he sees fit, cutting out sentences that seem incoherent to him (31). He also confesses that the words that he attributes to Cleopatra are altered by the Roman authorities. Diómedes vows to try again to capture Cleopatra's true testimony but repeatedly fails: "Casi, casi, casi . . . Casi hablaba así, como aquí he anotado, casi fueron así sus palabras, o casi lo serían . . . si no fuera porque Cleopatra me dijo unas muy otras" ("Almost, almost, almost . . . She almost spoke this way, as I have noted here, her words were almost these, or almost would be these . . . if it wasn't for the fact that Cleopatra told me something different"; 109; my trans.). The scribe's struggle to capture the true essence of Cleopatra mirrors Boullosa's own literary project. While Boullosa does not pretend to represent the real Cleopatra, her text does engage with others who have made this attempt. By having her narrator openly acknowledge the influences that affect his narration, Boullosa reminds us that no writing takes place in a vacuum, and that all writers are influenced by social, political, historical, cultural, linguistic, and literary factors that shape how and what they write.

Boullosa's novels engage with writing as a profession, as a passion, as a struggle, and as a creative outlet. Torn between his desire to create the perfect novel and his laziness when it comes to actually writing it, Vértiz, the protagonist of *La novela perfecta* (2006; *The Perfect Novel*), seems to have found the perfect solution when his neighbor, Lederer, approaches him with a new invention that will allow the writer to imagine his novel and record it without the use of words, by means of a sensor placed under the writer's tongue. The images from the writer's imagination are projected into the space of the laboratory, where Vértiz's characters take on lifelike qualities that far surpass those of any written character. Despite this amazing new technology, which revolutionizes (and subverts) the writing process, Vértiz is distracted by tangential stories, his own lack of focus, and his jealous suspicion of Lederer's intentions, both with his novel and with his wife. The partial "novel" made possible by Lederer's invention lacks structure and discipline and eventually runs amok. A machine malfunction renders its characters discombobulated, fragmented, and creates a whirl of images and objects in the laboratory that ultimately kill the machine's creator, along with the possibility of creating a "perfect novel."

Written and set in Brooklyn, New York, *La novela perfecta* was inspired by Boullosa's reading of the work of Jorge Luis Borges and Adolfo Bioy Casares as a youngster. While her novel certainly echoes the style of fantastic literature, it also pokes fun at the writing profession and the literary marketplace. Driven by economic gain, the protagonist of *La novela perfecta* is initially delighted that he can create a novel without wrestling with language and the proper form. If Vértiz's perfect novel had ever been finished and reached a "reading" public, its readers would have experienced the novel exactly as its creator did. The reader would see, hear, and even smell the characters, leaving little room to imagine them as one does characters on the written page.

La novela perfecta opens the door for a class conversation on the nature of the novel. Can a novel still be a novel if it is imagined and not written? What is technology's role in the creative process? What is the future of the written book? Are we to deduce a moral to this story? Is Lederer's invention a modern-day Frankenstein's monster, created to remind us of the limits and dangers of science? One can see how Vértiz's virtual novel, on the brink of perfection, might be attractive to both writers and readers, but what is the price of abandoning written form? Lederer's marvelous invention is destined to fail, since it is unable to contain the images produced by the writer's unbridled imagination, revealing how easily the creative project can get out of hand if imagination is the only element in the "writing" process. Lacking structure and discipline, the potentially perfect novel spirals out of control, coming to a violent, chaotic, and abrupt end. As in *Llanto*, we are left with a novel that narrates the impossibility of producing the desired narrative.

Boullosa's narratives frequently have a sinister undercurrent that questions the humanity of the world we have created for ourselves. Her protagonists—marginalized by history and traditional narrative—find in her fiction a space in which to redefine their place in society. Fearing the other, they are simultaneously drawn to it, and they constantly seek an identity that is other—one that might represent them in all of their complexity. Torn between the past and the present, plagued by fears and doubt, they turn to the text as a place to leave testimony of their struggle, as a record of their experience. Boullosa's narrators cling to the narrative process and to the reader to escape dissolution. The text is their one hope for immortality.

The question of transition is central to the physical, metaphorical, and textual bodies of Boullosa's narratives. The transitional nature of those narratives can be appealing to university students, who are undergoing their own transitional experience. Boullosa's characters are morphing and growing. Their identities are works in progress, even as the novels conclude. Likewise, the text itself is a work in progress, requiring the active participation of the reader as interpreter, participant, and witness. In Boullosa's texts, the body becomes the site of a renegotiation of social identity. Bodies fade, disappear, dismember themselves, appear in partial form, and even cannibalize each other. The fragmentation of physical bodies within the larger, fragmented textual body of the novels is what allows Boullosa's characters and narrators to reconfigure themselves as they see fit. There is freedom in the fragmented narrative; the space between the fragments is a space for the possible, and sometimes for the impossible. Within a literary production that is as diverse as it is extensive, the intimate relation between body, identity, and the writing process is at the core of the creative (and destructive) narratives of Boullosa.

Notes

1. I teach Boullosa's narratives (in Spanish) in advanced undergraduate courses, in which students have had at least one prior course in literary study in Spanish. Most students at this level are Hispanic studies majors, native or heritage speakers of Spanish, or both.

2. Some short readings I've used in class include Roberto Goizueta's "Our Lady of Guadalupe," Sandra Messinger Cypess's "La Malinche as Palimpsest" in her book *La Malinche in Mexican Literature* (1–13), and Rosario Castellanos's essay "Otra vez Sor Juana" ("Again Sor Juana") in *Narrativa* (467–70).

3. Students might benefit from a brief lecture on how the field of gender studies has approached the topic of women's writing. The questions posed by scholars could be presented to the class for discussion, followed by a theoretical summary to fill in any gaps.

Works Cited

Boullosa, Carmen. *De un salto descabalga la reina*. Editorial Debate, 2002.

———. *Duerme*. Alfaguara, 1994.

———. *Llanto: Novelas imposibles*. Ediciones Era, 1992.

———. *La novela perfecta*. Alfaguara, 2006.

———. *Son vacas, somos puercos: Filibusteros del mar Caribe*. Ediciones Era, 1991.

Castellanos, Rosario. *Narrativa*, 1989. *Obras*, vol. 1, FCE, 1989–98. 2 vols.

Certeau, Michel de. *The Writing of History*. Translated by Tom Conley, Columbia UP, 1988.

Cypess, Sandra Messinger. *La Malinche in Mexican Literature: From History to Myth*. U of Texas P, 1991.

D'Lugo, Carol Clark. *The Fragmented Novel in Mexico: The Politics of Form*. U of Texas P, 1997.

Goizueta, Roberto. "Our Lady of Guadalupe: The Heart of Mexican Identity." *Religion and the Creation of Race and Ethnicity*, edited by Craig R. Prentiss, New York UP, 2003, pp. 140–51.

Hutcheon, Linda. *A Poetics of Postmodernism*. Routledge, 1988.

White, Hayden. *Metahistory: The Historical Imagination in Nineteenth-Century Europe*. Johns Hopkins UP, 1973.

Rabi'a Hakima

Navigating Unanswerable Questions in Carmen Boullosa's "So Disappear"

The Mexican author Carmen Boullosa's work is a valuable addition to a world literature curriculum that seeks to expand the traditional canon. Boullosa is author of an impressive body of work that includes eighteen novels, twelve collections of poetry, four plays, and two short-story collections. She has received numerous literary awards, and several of her works have English translations. To undergraduates, she may not have as much name recognition as other Latina authors, but the volume and complexity of her work warrants her inclusion in an undergraduate survey course.

Although Boullosa lives and teaches in New York, she was born in Mexico City in 1954 and remains loyal to her home language, choosing to write in Spanish, but good translations exist. When teaching Boullosa's story "So Disappear," I choose the translation by Heidi Neufeld Raine because I find it to be the closest representation of the poetics of the original. When teaching a work available in multiple translations, the instructor contends with two levels of removal from the original text. The first is caused by the subjectivity of the translator, who has made individual choices about how to recreate the original text in new language, and the second involves the instructor's subjective decisions about which text is most accurate or most accessible to students. I bring up these concerns with my students when we read works in translation, so that we can acknowledge the limitations of the translated text before we proceed with our investigation.

First published as part of her 1987 novel *Mejor desaparece* (*Just Disappear*, 2009) and later excerpted in translation in an anthology of short stories by Latin American women writers titled *Out of the Mirrored Garden*, the short account "So Disappear" presents a challenge for students who are accustomed to reading narratives that have clearly defined settings, characters, and situations. In "So Disappear," a first-person narrator who identifies herself as a "married woman" discusses her fraught relationship with entities that she calls "children." The narrator describes her present circumstances in a stream-of-conscious format: she repeats herself, at times contradicts herself, presents facts that may be metaphorical and metaphors that may be facts, and, at one point, even implores her audience to continue paying attention, as if aware that the structure of the narrative is distracting. The story's use of first person, a potentially unreliable narrator, and a nonlinear structure causes students some initial hesitancy about studying this text. Boullosa's poetic and painterly style defies interpretation for the novice reader.

My four-step process includes the use of dialogic teaching (a method that emphasizes student-centered, student-led discussion), and close reading to guide students to a deeper understanding of the text. This process begins with questions to which there are clear answers in the text, determining what we can know. The second step is to ease into the questions that are more difficult to answer. The third step is to have students seek answers to these questions through a process of close reading and group discussion. The final step, and perhaps the most important, is to help students understand why the text's unanswerable questions should be appreciated as part of the fabric of the story.

I have taught Boullosa's "So Disappear" in sophomore world literature survey courses at a four-year university in Alabama and in multicultural literature courses at a community college in northern Illinois. I enjoy teaching the work because its nonlinear narrative structure breaks up the monotony of canonical texts to which students have been previously exposed, inspiring students to read more. More than anything else, the value of this text in a literature course is the intellectual challenge it presents to students. The educational backgrounds and interests of the students in world literature survey courses at four-year institutions, and in multicultural literature courses at community colleges, make the teaching of Boullosa's short story especially appropriate.

My world literature students at the four-year university often have limited interest in the study of literature. These students take world literature as a required course, and some feel that the course is an imposition and not directly relevant to their chosen major or career path. For these reasons, they need to have their experience of literature expanded by a story that is nontraditional and surprising. Furthermore, students enrolled in world literature have taken first-year composition courses and have developed some of the reading and writing skills commensurate with sophomore-level English, which supports their ability to process Boullosa's text.

Community college students who take my multicultural literature course are not required to take first-year writing courses as a prerequisite for literature. This makes them less likely to have the skills necessary for the self-driven study of literature. These students may have difficulty reading deeply and may be less able to read critically and formulate responses to texts. The community college students choose from a range of courses to satisfy their humanities requirements and are not required to take literature specifically; thus, some have selected the course because they are already interested in the subject matter and want to study literature from diverse cultures. This initial interest serves as an advantage in their reception of Boullosa's text.

To open discussion of this text, I offer background information about the author: that she is a contemporary Mexican writer with an affinity for elements of narrative fantasy and feminist themes. I briefly discuss some of her other works. I also solicit from students their preliminary reactions to the text. Both world literature and multicultural literature students are quick to express their unease. Some students proclaim that "She's crazy!" making little distinction between the author of the text and its first-person female narrator. Acknowledging the students' opinions of the text is an important first step. I ask students if the impulse to label the narrator as insane is a function of the text, and whether its elements raise questions about the narrator's sanity or lead readers to question their own assumptions about the proper way to tell stories. These informal questions serve to separate author from narrator, prompting students to consider the details of the text as intentional choices by a thoughtful author. These questions also caution students to avoid rushing to the easy conclusion that the text represents insanity and that no real meaning is to be gleaned from it.

Students are thus primed to wonder why the text is constructed as it is and see this is as an answerable question, despite their continued uneasiness.

I then give students a set of prepared questions to guide their reading of this text, questions to alleviate some of their anxiety as they focus on what they can know for certain about the text. The opening question is "Where is this story set?" Others include: "How would you describe the location?" and "What evidence supports your answer?" In small groups, students discuss narrative details that they have noticed about the physical location of the narrator. Typically groups consist of two or three students. I circulate and check in with particular groups to make sure that all members remain actively involved in answering the questions. All students must be engaged in the excavation of the text, making meaning on their own. If they are reticent, I ask questions to build on the group's discussion. For example, as they list the details that describe the children, if one student is not volunteering information, I ask whether they agree or disagree with the last thing suggested. This requires that they take a position. Once they have done this, the door is open to invite them to provide more textual evidence by asking why they agree or disagree. The student must then either say more about a passage already discussed or choose an additional passage. This problem is rare, however, in small group discussions, because students are reassured by the fact that their task is simplified by its concentration on the knowable rather than the uncertain.

When we return to the large group for debriefing, students share their group responses about the setting, relating that the narrator is in a room in a house. The secondary questions are crucial to the process because they remind students to use textual evidence to anchor even their most obvious claims about the text. To support their descriptions of the story's setting, they will cite passages such as the first page, where the narrator states that she prefers to remain confined in her room. As they provide more details about the surroundings and more evidence, they may say that the room is small, because the narrator says, "I like to walk the room as if it were impossible to count the steps needed to cross it, as if the room were as wide as the earth and fit in the palm of my hand." The room has a terrace, they notice, because the narrator says, "I like to drink coffee alone, very slowly, lock myself in my room, look out at the terrace and see nothing on the horizon" (4). I do not find it necessary to note that the text does not exactly say that the room is small; it simply implies that the room is not vast. What matters is that students are examining the translated words, and reasoning out their possible meanings in their quest for practical information. At this point, someone invariably points out that the phrase "nothing on the horizon" might indicate that the narrator's house is not near others or, taken metaphorically, that the narrator anticipates a bleak future. In moments like this, the focus on answering the knowable questions with close attention to the text causes students to notice moments that offer easy entry into the more abstract elements.

My discussion guide prompts students to describe other things beyond the room. The narrator speaks of a restaurant in which her husband has lunch with his colleagues (5), and, frequently, of the children, who would "like to be far from here, running through fields, breathing pure air" (7). Students offer these details as evidence that the narrator's room and house are in a town or city rather than a rural area. For a different type of text, such questions would be useful perhaps only for a quiz to check if students had completed the reading. For "So Disappear," on the other hand, these questions require enough close examination of the text that answering involves an intellectual process, not just regurgitation of information.

One of the major questions that students have initially and throughout our discussion of this text is, "Are the children real?" At times passages suggest that the children are not real: "I've never seen them. Not once. I don't know what they look like but I know everything about them" (4). At other times, the narrator describes the children in enough detail to suggest that they are real: "I talked about their caked hair against their lowing, childish heads, about their filthy ears and their disgusting socks stuck to their feet like potato skins" (13). These often conflicting thoughts about the children focus student readers on the question of the children's existence and the narrator's sanity. Uncertainties like this one can be presented in the form of easily answerable questions. My discussion guide does not ask if the children are real. Instead, it requires that students focus on the certainties about the children. Two sets of questions help ease students into the uncertainty: "What details are added throughout the story to describe the children? (What do they look like? What do they sound like? When did they arrive? How do they spend their time? How do they feel about the narrator?)," and, "How does the narrator feel about the children? What specific details support your answer?" These questions require, again, that the students return to the text for evidence to support their responses.

On the second day of discussion of "So Disappear," we begin with student presentations. My literature students are required to present on various texts throughout the semester; each student must select a short passage of no more than a paragraph from the day's assigned reading, present the results of a close reading of that passage, and facilitate a discussion generated by the presentation. This presentation prompt encourages dissection of a passage that is in need of close scrutiny. The prompt tells students to look for places in the reading assignment that are particularly dense or confusing and crucial to our understanding of the larger text. Presenters first read their passages aloud, then explain what insight or information has been gained from close scrutiny of the passages. They present any additional information that the other students need to know to fully understand the passages, and they explain why the passages are important in the context of the larger text. Finally, presenting students solicit and respond to questions and comments.

The second period spent on this text helps students build on the confidence they gained from the first day's discussion. Having a student at the helm takes the focus off the instructor and centers student responses and thinking. I can sit and listen to the conversation and only interject to draw a quiet student into the conversation. The only danger in the presentations is that a student may choose a portion of the text that is not particularly in need of close examination. However, Boullosa's text presents so many challenging passages that this outcome is not likely. If the analysis of a passage is lacking, I can always locate key points that can be expanded upon through dialogic teaching, in response to which, as noted by Alina Reznitskaya, students often "present lengthy, elaborate explanations of their ways of thinking [and] consistently engage in *meta-level reflection*, seeking clarification, *connecting ideas* across contexts and participants, and reflecting on levels of understanding" (448). In my classes, student presentations lead to the entire class closely examining the passage, considering how their interpretations of the passage differ from the presenter's, asking why they have differences or similarities of opinion or observation, and making note of when those opinions seem to be based on the details in the passage and when they are not. Students also bring up additional passages and make connections between the passage that was the initial focus and other important parts of the text. This is very helpful to them.

To offer an example, one student presented on the following passage in which the narrator talks about her husband: "I seldom think of him. If I don't reserve much space for him when I remember the two of us in the past—that past that others call happy—I leave him even less in the tedious present where the two of us are enveloped. Now I speak of him only because I believe I have to, if I want to make a more or less acceptable portrait" (Boullosa 5). The student presenter read the passage aloud and discussed his findings. He essentially argued that the narrator, who identifies herself as a "married woman" (11), does not love her husband or her children and is selfish and bitter. While this presentation did not seem to be the result of close reading, it raised questions that led to a lively discussion of additional uncertainties in the text. The students began to challenge or agree with the presenter and offer evidence to support their claims about the narrator's relationship with her husband and the narrator's state of mind.

As we wrap up our second day of discussion on this text, I prompt students to consider the question "How do the uncertainties in the text contribute to the meaning of the text?" In asking them why the text is structured as it is, I direct attention back to the thematic questions. What do these discussions we have had about the children's existence and the narrator's feelings about her husband suggest about the expectations placed on married women? We can connect our earlier questioning of the narrator's sanity to the quoted monologue above in order to indicate that we have perhaps bought into or are aware of the expectations placed on women to marry, procreate, and devote themselves to their families. Ultimately, the children do not have to be definitively real or imaginary to expose the societal construct that is being challenged by the story. Students can discover that the perception of the narrator as insane comes out of society's very rigid expectations about how women are supposed to think and behave.

In "Should College English Be Close Reading?" Don Bialostosky points out that close reading has its limitations. He says rightly that the danger of the emphasis on close reading is "that our students come to college English convinced that they can't understand . . . literature, . . . because they have learned to distrust their initial uptake [in favor of a close] reading that will satisfy what they have learned is an institutional demand for deeper, hidden, symbolic meanings" (112). He suggests that too much focus on close reading could potentially have students fail to see the proverbial forest for the trees, that if they are too focused on isolating words and images in a text, they may overlook the context and a larger meaning. I have found, however, that in the teaching of Boullosa my focus on close reading poses no real danger of dismissing a more general reading in favor of minute details. Students will have difficulty solidifying their own initial reading of the text, so close reading is absolutely essential to their comprehension. Close reading also encourages students to take charge of the reading process, because they begin to understand that, for a text that initially looks impenetrable when viewed broadly, close reading can open a gateway to understanding.

Works Cited

Bialostosky, Don. "Should College English Be Close Reading?" *College English*, vol. 69, no. 2, 2006, pp. 111–16.

Boullosa, Carmen. "So Disappear." Translated by Heidi Neufeld Raine. *Out of the Mirrored Garden*, edited by Delia Poey, Anchor, 1995, pp. 4–17.

Reznitskaya, Alina. "Dialogic Teaching: Rethinking Language Use during Literature Discussions." *The Reading Teacher*, vol. 65, no. 7, 2012, pp. 446–56.

Part II

Chicana Writers and Their Precursors

Marcel Brousseau

Jovita González and "Her People's History": Teaching Borderlands Culture through Close Reading and Archival Practice

Given the deep involvement of the Texan writer Jovita González de Mireles in education, as a student, teacher, advocate, and author of textbooks, her work provides a crucial voice in a course on the diverse history of the borderlands. The critic Tey Diana Rebolledo calls her a "foremother" for Chicana writers, whose work in the early and middle twentieth century extends the historical scope of Mexicana and Chicana cultural production (27). Thus González's two early novels, *Caballero: A Historical Novel* and *Dew on the Thorn*, unpublished until after her death,[1] are important texts for classes on Mexicana, Tejana, Chicana, and Latinx narratives. Each novel is situated in south Texas, with themes focused on historical transitions of power.

Caballero, written with Margaret Eimer (as Eve Raleigh), depicts "South Texas Mexicano history" in the mid–nineteenth century through the ranch family of Don Santiago de Mendoza y Soria, immediately following the upheaval of the Mexican-American War (Garza-Falcón 112). In a novel evaluating "new ways and the old, the loss of land, and violent conflict between . . . the U.S. Army, the Texas Rangers, the *Americanos*, the border Mexican landowner families, the peon class, the clergy, and [the new, white] pioneers" (Garza-Falcón 116), important details include the functions of day-to-day life, food preparation, and celebrated traditions.

While *Caballero* takes a relatively coherent novelistic form, *Dew on the Thorn*, according to the introduction by José Limón, "may best be understood as a moderately unified set of literary, which is to say fictionalized, sketches fashioned into a short novel" (Limón, Introduction xv). González herself summarized the manuscript as "sketches . . . deal[ing] with a border family of Mexican ranchmen, descendants of a family that held a grant from the viceroy. Date 1906." She describes this turn-of-the-century historical setting as "when Americans from the middle west came in great numbers to develop what is now the Rio Grande Valley." *Dew on the Thorn* stitches together, in González's words, "much folklore," with political dialogues inspired by her ethnographic fieldwork and historical research (González, Correspondence; qtd. in Limón, Introduction xxv).[2]

The critical epilogue by María Cotera in *Caballero* provides historical and cultural context that positions the novel as a challenge to the Chicano literary canon, one that "gives voice to the Chicana speaking subject" (González and Raleigh 339). Limón's introduction to *Dew on the Thorn* likewise elucidates the material history of the manuscript and González's political importance as an author. Earlier, in *Dancing with the Devil*, he identifies González as an integral "precursor" in the project of writing about Mexican Americans (12), who found herself "entangled [among] sites of [dominant, white patriarchal] power represented by [her longtime mentor J. Frank] Dobie, her own race/class affiliations, and her larger community" (74–75).

The range of criticism of González's writing indicates that her work complicates or challenges established literary genealogies based on national literatures, Chicano Movement politics, or Chicana feminism. Leticia M. Garza-Falcón examines González's writing as representative of "the stories of a 'gente decente' [who] assert[ed] themselves against . . . Anglo American white supremacist views" (x). Louis Mendoza regards *Caballero* as a medium for "provid[ing] [literary] insight into a world of [female and underclass] experience that had not been represented in historical representations of the [middle to late nineteenth century]" (33). Cotera's *Native Speakers* articulates González's complex relationship with Dobie, while also comparing González to the African American folklorist Zora Neale Hurston and the Dakota ethnologist Ella Cara Deloria to establish knowledge about "the politics and poetics of women [of color] writing culture" (2). Nicole Guidotti-Hernández departs from previous critiques to argue that González's texts "enact their own form of epistemic and discursive violence through the stock caricatures, outright denials, racist portrayals, and erasures of African Americans and Texas Indians" while also reviving the voices of "the socially or physically dead [who] represent a forgotten and unresolved past" (135, 139). Donna M. Kabelen de Bichara examines González's writings as "contribut[ions] to the preservation of a distinct cultural heritage that involves the spheres of New Spain, Mexico, and the United States" (5). Priscilla Solis Ybarra rethinks González's work through an ecocritical lens, examining how her writing confronts "modernity's interference with the Mexican American relationship with the land" (85). Amanda J. Zink argues that González's writings critique "Texas Mexican domesticity [as a system of] patriarchal control" and explore how "Anglo domesticity . . . offer[ed] Tejanas an alternative gender role" (110).

González locates her maternal family in Texas dating back to the mid–eighteenth century, as "colonizers who had come with Escandón to El Nuevo Santander" (*Dew* ix).[3] She traces her father's family as a line of educators and artisans from Nuevo León, Mexico. At her birth, González's parents were living at Las Víboras ranch in Roma, Texas. Her parents eventually moved the family to San Antonio, where González graduated from high school. Obtaining a teaching position in Río Grande City, she saved her wages to pay for tuition at the University of Texas, where, in 1930, she earned a master's degree in history. From 1930 to 1932 González was president of the Texas Folklore Society. By the end of the 1930s, she had married the educator Edmundo E. Mireles and was living in Corpus Christi, employed as a teacher of Spanish and Texas history at W. B. Ray High School. Mrs. Mireles, as she was known, was "a tough and demanding teacher . . . with a good sense of humor" and was dedicated to teaching "South Texas Mexicano history." She continued to research "her people's history . . . , the true history of the land grants and how the land had been taken away from the Mexicanos" (Garza-Falcón 97–98). This research found its way into her novels, which as Limón asserts, she continued to work on in the years before her death in 1983 (Introduction xxiv).

Teaching Strategies for *Dew on the Thorn*

González's novels, particularly *Dew on the Thorn*, can be taught as "contrapuntal re-presentation[s]" of dominant history, suitable for undergraduate courses in literary, ethnic, or cultural studies (Cotera, "Refiguring" 87). González's writing provides an interdisciplinary object of study that elucidates the complicated past and present of Texas and the borderlands of Mexico and the United States (87–89). A contrapuntal reading practice allows students to explore the "intertwined and overlapping histories" of the borderlands, while also engaging issues of power, race, class, gender, and textual production (Said 18). My process guides students to do this visually and verbally, based on close readings.

Limón and Cotera suggest comparing *Dew on the Thorn* to Captain John Gregory Bourke's 1894 *Scribner's* essay "The American Congo" (Limón, *Dancing*; Cotera, "Refiguring").[4] A productive method for counterposing these depictions of the era and the region is to have students work in groups to storyboard the texts, an activity where students recast prose as a film. Each student team uses a three-by-three grid to extrapolate images for a film narrative. Students sketch and caption the images with contextual detail or direct quotations, and they must choose a genre for their film (e.g. action, romance, documentary). In my undergraduate comparative literature class,[5] students' storyboards articulated important distinctions between the dominant historical text (by Bourke) and González's text. One group likened Bourke to a guide in a nature documentary, framing images of flora and fauna lining the Rio Grande as Bourke's steamer traveled downriver. The viewer is interpellated as a consumer of scenery of, in Bourke's words, "prickly pears and other distinctive agriculture [including] mesquite, boars and roadrunners, tortoises, ponies, and Mexican laundresses working on the river bank." For this course, we initially read Mary Louise Pratt's "Introduction: Criticism in the Contact Zone" (*Imperial Eyes* 1–11) to help contextualize the "radically asymmetrical relations of power" in the borderlands of Mexico and the United States. In summarizing their storyboard, students criticized Bourke as what Pratt calls a "seeing-man," a "male subject . . . whose imperial eyes passively look out and possess" (7).

Another group developed a storyboard for a documentary based on chapter 1 of *Dew on the Thorn*, using the visual motif of the Rio Grande as a natural and political border around which conquests by Spain, Mexico, and the United States play out. A storyboard of chapter 2 rendered the drama of rancho life in action scenes, beginning with an aerial shot of the ranch, climaxing in flamboyant depictions of González's popular stories of the devil, and closing with music. By storyboarding González's and Bourke's texts, students ascertained how each writer uses rhetoric and manipulates genre conventions to construct knowledge. The activity concluded with students reflecting on the forms and conventions they used:

How did they choose their mode of drawing? How did they edit for content? What did they learn about the borderlands as a site of intertwined histories and asymmetrical relations of power?

Intertwined histories are apparent from *Dew on the Thorn*'s first chapter, in which the Olivares's family story is mapped onto historical south Texas. In another undergraduate class,[6] students expressed gratitude for Gonzalez's counterhegemonic origin story of Texas, highlighting Spanish and Mexican presence over Anglo power. However, applying close-reading techniques to chapter 1 also led to classroom discussion about a dialectic of civilization and barbarism in Gonzalez's description of an "Indian infested region" and a language of domination in the account of the Spanish "subdu[ing] the warlike Indian tribes" (3, 4).

After class discussion, students can be assigned a close-reading essay where, by reading short passages of text, they elucidate *Dew on the Thorn*'s range of voices and ideologies, as well as concepts of gender, material culture, folk culture, religion, and violence. Considering a dialogue about the impending collapse of the rancho culture between the protagonist Don Francisco and the local priest Padre José María, my student Lucibella Hernandez notes in her essay how "the repetition of the verb 'to see' four times within [half of page 176], as opposed to verbs such as 'thinking' or 'feeling,' further instills in the reader the unfortunate reality of Manifest Destiny." By focusing on González's use of verbs, Lucibella asserts a connection between characters who "see" the future and the reader, who sees the past through the act of reading. Such language, she argues, enables the reader to look for and to visualize social inequality as a visible phenomenon of the past, present, and future. By reading, one sees the "other side of Texas history" and witnesses the ongoing realities of "racial hierarchies" and of "indigenous people who are often glossed over."

In her essay, my student Daniela Rascón analyzes material culture as a metaphor for social relations. Closely reading the scene (midway through the novel) of the *posada* ceremony, she focuses on the "personification of the *piñata*," identifying tonal shifts in language that elicit empathy for the piñata, which "foolishly . . . swayed and bowed much to the delight of the children" (González, *Dew* 93). In Daniela's reading, this description, which "illustrates submissiveness, . . . is countered by . . . the piñata's 'executioner,' the decorated stick." The scene symbolizes a class system in which the piñata "represent[s] the peasant class and the work that they do for the aristocracy . . . while the stick represents the violence used to enforce the caste structure." Reflecting this metaphor back upon the novel's social milieu, she reaches a devastating conclusion: "By describing the peasants (*piñata*) as mindless, and the aristocracy [as "blindfolded children"], González leaves the reader with the idea that maybe this system of conquest is incvitablc bccause the parties involved might not be aware of their participation in it." In this elaborate analysis, Daniela locates what Guidotti-Hernández calls the "epistemic and discursive violence" embedded and "unresolved" in the folkloric motifs of González's text, and in the mores of the rituals they describe (135, 138).

Archival Research Projects

Both *Caballero* and *Dew on the Thorn* bear the marks of archival reproduction, which as noted by Suzanne Bost, "has particular significance for scholars in Latino/a literary studies" (625). The publication of González's work indicates the ways in which "Latino/a literary studies has been growing backward in time, to establish a lost or erased tradition, at the same time that it grows forward" (625–26). As mentioned above, the introductions framing both books contextualize their salvaging from González's papers and reveal the "mess" inherent in archival knowledge (618). In both works the editors make use of bracketed text and numbered notes to index "marked out" or "crossed out" passages and illegible typing by González and Eimer and by González, respectively.

As a result of Limón and Cotera's editorial accountability, *Caballero* and *Dew on the Thorn* are intricate texts that open a window into the González archives while also presenting readable surfaces. Students were intrigued by the authorial and editorial subjectivity on display in *Dew on the Thorn*. Writing for an online discussion board, Daniela wondered why González would cross out a passage in which a ranchero, Don Ramón, "talks about how times are changing as 'Americans are moving in,' and how the only *gringo* he likes is 'one under seven feet of dirt,'" but leave in "the [passage] that follows in which Don Ramón thinks the culprits could be within their own community." Martin Sanchez, Jr., responded by noting another omission, in which "González crosses . . . out [her description of the peon household] but chooses to leave the description of the [wealthy] Olivares household." Asking more media-specific questions, another student drew a connection between the symbolic content of *Dew on the Thorn* and the book's mediality by focusing on the narrative role of characters like Antonio Traga-Balas and the messages they carry, such as love notes. The student wondered how these characters alter the meaning of the messages they carry and then extended this inquiry to the material novel itself, asking what González's message might be for readers and how effectively Limón conveys it. These questions reveal that the visible ambiguity of Limón's editing allows students to analyze knowledge production as subjective and contingent upon social and material factors.[7] Whether questioning González's privileging of certain social dynamics or criticizing Limón's position as messenger, students absorbed themselves in *Dew on the Thorn*'s problematic of the archive.

When teaching at the University of Texas, Austin, I extended the class's engagement of archival work by asking students to undertake guided research in the Nettie Lee Benson Latin American Collection. For their final research essays, they were to locate objects that intrigued them and analyze these documents in terms of their materiality, content, and form. They needed to creatively translate a document they had analyzed to another genre, and reflect on their translation. In so doing, students mirrored the praxis of editors Limón and Cotera—by locating, appraising, and transforming historical materials. Asking students to respond to the archive, first, as it is visible in González's text, and second, by immersing themselves in special collections, helped them "embrace permeability, multiplicity, and uncertainty in [their] scholarship" and understand "making meaning [as] a radically inclusive and continually open process" (Bost 628).

"Desire for a subaltern literary precursor," as noted by Bost, inspired Limón and Cotera to reproduce González's writing for today's audiences. The traces of their editing are "rooted in the present and always subject to future transformation" (626). For undergraduate students, it can be a transformative experience to embark on careful close readings of these early novels, and to develop research skills based on working with images, critical and linguistic details, and attention to archives. One could imagine that as a lifelong educator, González would be gratified to know that her literary writings prove inclusive and flexible examples for a pedagogy that develops the ability of students to analyze power relations, race and gender, literary techniques, and archival practice while they also study "her people's history" (Garza-Falcón 98).

Notes

The author wishes to thank, first and foremost, his students at the University of California, Santa Barbara, and at the University of Texas, Austin. Their work with the writing of Jovita González, with archival materials, and with their own narratives was consistently inspiring and humbling. The author also wishes to thank the archivists at UT's Nettie Lee Benson Latin American Collection, particularly Margo Gutiérrez, Carla Alvarez, and A. J. Johnson, for making the archive a place of possibility for students. Finally, the author wishes to thank Katherine Kelp-Stebbins for her always brilliant pedagogical advice.

1. *Caballero: A Historical Novel* and *Dew on the Thorn* were published in 1996 and 1997, respectively, having been retrieved from the E. E. Mireles and Jovita González de Mireles Papers at Texas A&M University, Corpus Christi. *Dew on the Thorn* was published as part of Arte Público Press's Recovering the U.S. Hispanic Literary Heritage Project. In a 2012 article, the founder of Arte Público Press, Nicolás Kanellos, identified González as one of a number of historic Latinx writers whose work was nearly lost because of the "often purposeful erasure" of the "Hispanic heritage" of the United States (373).

2. As Limón also notes in his introduction to *Dew on the Thorn*, González changed the temporal setting of the novel from 1906 to 1904. Additional publications by González that are currently available include the collection *"The Woman Who Lost Her Soul" and Other Stories*, which brings together folkloric tales that González recorded during her anthropological career, and *Life Along the Border: A Landmark Tejana Thesis*, which reprints her 1929 master's thesis. I have used *"The Woman Who Lost Her Soul"* to exemplify the genre of folklore in an introductory class on Latinx literature at the University of Oregon.

3. Nuevo Santander was a Spanish province in New Spain, comprising what are now most of south Texas and parts of the Mexican state of Tamaulipas.

4. Bourke, a soldier and ethnographer, served as commander of Fort Ringgold in Rio Grande City from 1891 to 1893. His essay reflects "his two careers—war and anthropology" in its historical and ethnographic commentary; it also functions as a travel guide, encouraging economic development and tourism in south Texas (Limón, *Dancing* 29–31).

5. I taught this class at the University of California, Santa Barbara, in summer 2014.

6. This discussion took place in a class that I taught in fall 2015 and 2016 and that was cross-listed in the Departments of English and Mexican American and Latina/o Studies at the University of Texas, Austin.

7. These comments are taken from discussion boards for my classes at the University of Texas, Austin, fall 2015 and 2016.

Works Cited

Bost, Suzanne. "Messy Archives and Materials That Matter: Making Knowledge with the Gloria Evangelina Anzaldúa Papers." *PMLA*, vol. 130, no. 3, May 2015, pp. 615–30.

Bourke, John G. "The American Congo." *Scribner's Magazine*, vol. 15, no. 5, May 1894, pp. 590–610.

Cotera, María Eugenia. *Native Speakers: Ella Deloria, Zora Neale Hurston, Jovita González, and the Poetics of Culture*. U of Texas P, 2008.

———. "Refiguring 'the American Congo': Jovita González, John Gregory Bourke, and the Battle over Ethno-historical Representations of the Texas

Mexican Border." *Western American Literature*, vol. 35, no. 1, Spring 2000, pp. 75–94.

Garza-Falcón, Leticia M. *Gente Decente: A Borderlands Response to the Rhetoric of Dominance.* U of Texas P, 1998.

González, Jovita. Correspondence with Dr. John Joseph Gorrell. E. E. Mireles and Jovita González de Mireles Papers, Special Collections and Archives at the Mary and Jeff Bell Library, Texas A&M University, Corpus Christi.

———. *Dew on the Thorn.* Edited by José Limón, Arte Público Press, 1997.

———. *Life along the Border: A Landmark Tejana Thesis.* Edited by María Eugenia Cotera, Texas A&M UP, 2006.

———. *"The Woman Who Lost Her Soul" and Other Stories: Collected Tales and Short Stories.* Edited by Sergio Reyna, Arte Público Press, 2000.

González, Jovita, and Eve Raleigh. *Caballero: A Historical Novel.* Edited by José E. Limón and María Cotera, Texas A&M UP, 1996.

Guidotti-Hernández, Nicole M. *Unspeakable Violence: Remapping U.S. and Mexican National Imaginaries.* Duke UP, 2011.

Kabelen de Bichara, Donna M. *Telling Border Life Stories: Four Mexican American Women Writers.* Texas A&M UP, 2013.

Kanellos, Nicolás. "Recovering the U.S. Hispanic Literary Heritage." *PMLA*, vol. 127, no. 2, Mar. 2012, pp. 371–74.

Limón, José E. *Dancing with the Devil: Society and Cultural Poetics in Mexican-American South Texas.* U of Wisconsin P, 1994.

———. Introduction. *Dew on the Thorn*, by Jovita González, edited by Limón, Arte Público Press, 1997, pp. xv–xxvii.

Mendoza, Louis Gerard. *Historia: The Literary Making of Chicana and Chicano History.* Texas A&M UP, 2001.

Pratt, Mary Louise. *Imperial Eyes: Travel Writing and Transculturation.* Routledge, 1992.

Rebolledo, Tey Diana. *Women Singing in the Snow: A Cultural Analysis of Chicana Literature.* U of Arizona P, 1995.

Said, Edward W. *Culture and Imperialism.* Vintage Books, 1994.

Ybarra, Priscilla Solis. *Writing the Goodlife: Mexican American Literature and the Environment.* U of Arizona P, 2016.

Zink, Amanda J. *Fictions of Western American Domesticity: Indian, Mexican, and Anglo Women in Print Culture, 1850–1950.* U of New Mexico P, 2018.

Alberto Varon

Pre-Civil-Rights-Era Chicana Writing and the Impact of the Mexican Revolution: Josefina Niggli's *Step Down, Elder Brother*

In the 1930s and early 1940s, the Mexican American author Josefina Niggli (born in Monterrey, in northern Mexico, in 1910) wrote and produced several popular plays based in Mexican culture, including *The Cry of Dolores* (1936) and *Soldadera* (1938), during and right after participating in a highly touted MA program for playwrights at the University of North Carolina, Chapel Hill. In 1945, she published a novel in stories, *Mexican Village*, which was highly successful and led to a screenplay and a movie, *Sombrero*, starring Ricardo Montalbán. During the difficult war years she lived with her mother in San Antonio, Texas, where she wrote a second acclaimed novel, *Step Down, Elder Brother*, which was published two years after the first. Niggli's plays and first novel have been studied by contemporary scholars, but her work as a novelist is greatly undervalued and largely neglected, despite her pivotal position connecting pre– and post–civil rights moments. She could be dubbed an early Chicana writer, and one of few Mexicanas publishing novels (although composed in English) in the early to middle twentieth century. According to one study, Niggli "represented Mexicans both as citizens of America (in Texas and the Southwest) and as worthy neighbors to citizens of the United States" (Martínez, "[Re]Visioning" 106).

The significance of her second novel is that it is one of just a few novels by women set in the immediate post–Mexican Revolution period. It received high accolades in book reviews and other mentions when published in 1947, but it has been greatly overlooked in the decades since the Chicano Movement and has received sparse critical attention in the United States. Interestingly, the major Mexican novelist David Toscana prepared a translation to Spanish of the expansive novel, which was published in 2003 as *Apártate, hermano*, to acclaim as a northern Mexican text, and he expressed his delight for her understanding and capture of the immediate postrevolutionary period.[1] The novel explores the rapid economic growth and social change of that era, with an emphasis on cultural history. Equally impressive is its dramatization of the influences and competing national interests of the United States to the north and Mexico City to the south.

Step Down, Elder Brother depicts Monterrey, in northern Mexico, as a thriving industrial hub and follows the affluent de Anda family as they adapt to social changes brought by the revolution. The novel follows trips to a nearby village; to the city of Saltillo in the adjoining state, where it makes occasional references to Mexico City; to the industrial port of Veracruz; and across the border into the United States. Despite the novel's continental scope, at the time of publication in the United States, critical reception was limited to discussions of local color or regional fiction. Elizabeth Coonrod Martínez's critical biography in 2007 and the release of Niggli's collected works in 2008 have opened new opportunities to consider this important novel for courses on early-twentieth-century American literature and pre-civil-rights-movement Mexican American and Chicana experience, and new ways to link national literatures and to cross literary periodization.[2]

One of the great literary strengths of *Step Down, Elder Brother*, distinct from Niggli's work as a playwright, is how it intersects with a variety of different genres, styles, historical moments, and national literary traditions. My strategy in teaching the novel focuses on two approaches: formal and historical. Together, these approaches expand students' understanding of Chicana or Mexican American authorship as well as the historical contributions by Latinas more generally to cultural life in the United States. Focusing on these methods introduces students to some of the central and most important concepts in Chicana (and Latina) literary history: the cultural legacy of the Mexican Revolution in terms of mixed-race experience, Indigenous influence, contemporary philosophy, and issues of migration and immigration. Through its generic familiarity as a romance, the novel makes accessible some difficult ideas that emerge around these concepts and the novel's portrayal of class and gender. The Mexican Revolution allows for an important historical lesson, but one that sets the stage for a larger discussion of transnational movement between the United States and Mexico. The relations of the characters to the United States and to the Mexican capital take a back seat to their more regional affiliations, and the novel casts movement and migration as a bilateral issue, one not centered on national centers but on regional networks. Once students grapple with the revolution and its aftermath, especially its social and political impact, then they see the complexity of the Mexican Revolution as a regional or hemispheric phenomenon, affecting not just Mexico but the United States as well.

The novel begins with a relatively long, introspective account by a twenty-something young man living in 1940s Monterrey. Narrated by the de Anda family's eldest son, Domingo, the story delves into Indigenous culture, social class, and postrevolutionary politics, but also national challenges facing the developing nation. The plot reads like a telenovela or soap opera, and suggesting this perspective to students can elicit lively comments. But the telenovela as a category falls short of fully describing the complexity of this novel, its attachment to place and history, and the author's binational perspective. Niggli's novel challenges the ways in which the work of early-twentieth-century women writers were often confined within generic categories such as romance or local color, categories that belie a complex account of national and regional belonging.

In terms of romance, the narrative centers on the personal struggle of Domingo as he confronts social changes while working in his father's businesses, and on his obsession with a mysterious female, Márgara, whose father, Bárcenas, has a shady past connected to the revolution and is currently working as a photographer. Through the gradually unraveling mystery of Bárcenas's connections, the story delves into the broader social ramifications of the revolution. Monterrey serves as a microcosm of the new Mexican republic but also as a northern border city more directly under the influence of the United States.

Secondly, the novel blurs distinctions between race and class, criollo and Indigenous, allowing them to be mapped onto diverse national concerns at a moment when a new mestizo culture was being promoted. The novel invokes José Vasconcelos's vision of a cosmic (mixed) race,[3] which helps open discussions on Chicano culture and the development of borderlands identity. Students can examine the differences between Domingo and the character Mateo, Domingo's stymied ambitions to practice medicine, and the family chauffeur's interest in seeking employment in the family real estate office. Mateo will also embark on a relationship, seeking marriage, with Domingo's sister. Of all the characters, Mateo is the quickest to adopt the commercial mindset of the style of real estate speculation found in the United States, demonstrating entrepreneurial savvy. The characters' divergent approaches to the region's economic surge also highlight the larger social changes afoot in Mexico in the 1930s. The novel addresses land redistribution, the key facet of the new 1917 Constitution, which can prompt additional classroom discussion of twentieth-century history, the colonial legacy, and social class. While disrupting the elite class, land reform and accompanying social class reforms presented new opportunities for the postrevolutionary nation.

A readily accessible method of introducing the complicated legacy of the Mexican Revolution is through visual history. The text regularly refers to the Casasola collection of photographs (a photography studio founded by an expatriate Mexican consul worker, which provided photographs for early newspapers) on the 1910 Revolution.[4] Certain photographs recur as a strategic plot device, providing a visual reference to history. Students can research images from the revolution, bring examples to class for discussion, and be coached through ekphrasis, a visual-rhetorical exercise that empowers students to trust their critical reactions as they explore how visual iconography extends to broader histories and cultural circles. Images visually encode many of the ideals of the revolution and of Indigenous culture in Mexico, as well as other possibilities, and provide a basis for discussions extending to the recognizable iconography of Mexican and Chicano culture. This type of exercise can be enhanced with examples, perhaps from the murals of Diego Rivera and David Alfaro Siqueiros, or the iconic images of Pancho Villa, Emiliano Zapata, and the *soldadera* ("woman soldier"). Through a romance that exceeds its generic constraints, this novel demonstrates how categories of race and class intersect, tying in to discussions of how ideas and philosophies are nationally constructed with longstanding transnational connections.

Once students are familiar with Mexico's sociohistorical politics of the mid-century, conversations can move into how national literatures are artificially imposed on cultural movements. Students are frequently accustomed to conceiving of national cultures as inherently separate, and despite the prevalence of the term *globalization* in contemporary discourse, they still struggle to understand or imagine cultural movements across borders and through many cultural affiliations. This novel offers an opportunity for discussions on nationalism and transnational Chicana/o studies, helping provide students with a critical vocabulary.[5] As Yolanda Padilla points out about Niggli's *Mexican Village*, her work "brings to light the transnational networks at play in ostensibly nationalist practice [that] achieves an expansive view of the nation" (46).[6] Such short critical readings, including excerpts from Gloria Anzaldúa's *Borderlands / La frontera*, are helpful to students, as is assigning research for biographies on Niggli, which make these networks clear.[7] Niggli's own personal history intersects with the novel's account. Born in northern Mexico to European-heritage Americans, Niggli's personal biography complicates her position within Chicana literary history. Niggli was born and raised mostly in northern Mexico, where her father worked all of his adult life. Like other Mexicans, her childhood experience was marked by the early years of the revolution: she and her mother were intermittently sent to greater safety across the border, and, when she was a teenager, to San Antonio, where she completed a college degree at Incarnate Word College in 1931. She then pursued playwriting studies in North Carolina. After the mid-1950s she taught drama at Western Carolina University, where she completed a third novel on the Indigenous Virgin of Guadalupe.

Thus Niggli's own experience can be discussed in terms of how we associate Chicana writing with late-twentieth-century political identity and concepts of authenticity. To do so, it often helps to have students form small groups and identify what facets they consider to be the defining features of Chicana writing. Then, broadening to full class discussion, students can interrogate how the immigrant and binational status of Niggli may have affected her writing, and how her biography aligns with our expectations, especially in ways that trouble periodization of Chicana literature. Further discussion can lead to the exploration of topics such as geographies of place, cultural inheritance, and Chicana inclusion in the national literature of the United States.

Domingo's obsession for the mysterious, working-class woman Márgara leads Domingo to uncover secrets about the revolution even while there is an impending crisis in his own family, which leads to larger questions about his possible emigration to the United States. By staging this dilemma as a crisis of both personal and cultural significance, the novel leaves open several questions: As the eldest son, will Domingo lose his status in his family's legacy and inheritance? Will the former chauffer's marriage to his sister change the family dynamics and the chauffer's class status? Will his younger brother's baby by a household maid be born? In the end, he must choose between his love for Márgara and his attachment to home and family. Students are captivated by the dramatic crisis, which is performed at the border between Mexico and the United States, yet the scene lends itself to a discussion of both the costs of immigration and the symbolic effects of cultural border crossing. Finally, the novel places authority and leadership in his sister Sofia, the character who is most self-aware of how to navigate the social changes taking place, and who has accepted the changing racial identity and politics of the new society. This strong female character, in a novel that also speaks to a dissolution of authority by the "elder brother" of the novel's title, represents an interesting precursor to the female characters found in later-twentieth-century Chicana feminist writing.

Niggli's characters often represent diverse racial, ethnic, Indigenous, national, and regional backgrounds, speak to new understandings of mestizo identity, and employ Mexican cultural history—factors central to Chicana/o works.[8] Raymund Paredes describes Niggli as a "transitional" figure in Chicano literature who "simulat[ed] the flavor of Spanish through her English prose," and whose work marks the end of the romantic tendency in literature toward a more realist, protest-oriented literature, while still emphasizing the Mexican content and focus (90). Niggli's *Step Down, Elder Brother* draws in part on older literary forms, but also on new tendencies in giving the characters psychological complexity (comparable to that of characters in the early-twentieth-century novels of Edith Wharton), all in service to discussing the morals and obligations of individuals in class-stratified societies. As an allegory, the novel poses formal questions about how we read and interpret ethnic American literature; it asks us to consider the line between literature from a solely "American" perspective and that of Mexican or transnational literature. Class lectures can include discussions on diverse literary categories and styles, as this novel offers rich opportunities to expand discussions about the formal scope and range of Chicana literature.

Furthermore, instructors teaching classes in Latino, cultural, and transnational studies can encourage students to reframe national categories within a transnational frame by reading this novel. In considering the movement of people between the United States and Mexico, one way to understand transnational movement is by introducing and critiquing *México de afuera* ("Mexico from outside"), a concept used by critics to refer to expatriate Mexican ideological and cultural formations, often nostalgic, that are focused on a return to one's native land; these formations have been largely understood as a Mexican phenomenon that is foreign to cultural history in the United States and that is predominantly male oriented.[9] The concept of *México de afuera* encourages students to think about how ideas migrate across borders, how nations and cultures influence one another, and how Chicana writing dialogues with this central Chicano idea. The characters living in Monterrey are constantly negotiating the influence of their northern neighbor, the United States, even as they debate the state of the Mexican nation. Yet the novel, written in English and published in the United States immediately after World War II, has translated these Mexican national concerns into the context of the United States. Pointing this out to students opens discussion about the flow of peoples across national borders and reorients Mexican American literary history by placing the Mexican Revolution in a global history between the World Wars, where the revolution becomes indicative both of broader concerns inside and outside the nation and of the formative role they play within a national project in the United States.

The novel also offers instructors the opportunity to ask students to imagine the concerns of Mexicanas and Chicanas within national, transnational, and Mexican American literary history. This is especially useful when trying to affirm Chicana literary history as existing prior to the civil rights movement, and Chicana writers as long-standing participants in national life in the United States. For these reasons, Niggli's novel offers a powerful pedagogical tool that broadens beyond early Chicano nationalism and engages the Chicana presence in and contributions to literary and cultural history in the United States.

Notes

1. See Martínez, *Josefina* 283–90.

2. The novel was reissued in its entirety in Niggli, *"Mexican Village."* The lukewarm foreword by Ilan Stavans provides some useful biographical information but leaves it to the reader to attend to the complexity of Niggli's work (ix–xv).

3. *La raza cósmica* (*The Cosmic Race*), a philosophical treatise and ideology of a new race that combines all other races, was first published in 1925, when José Vasconcelos was Mexico's secretary of education. Vasconcelos unsuccessfully ran for president in 1929.

4. While part of a fictionalized narrative, the Casasola Photograph Collection (named after the photographer Alfonso Casasola) is real and is housed at the

University of Texas, El Paso, and in the Mexico City archives. Most of its contents are in accessible digital collections that allow for independent student research.

5. Gloria Anzaldúa's chapters "How to Tame a Wild Tongue" (75–86) and "Towards a New Consciousness" (99–113), from *Borderlands / La frontera*, are instructive, as is Rafael Pérez-Torres's work on *mestizaje* ("miscegenation"). These essays pair well with selections from the work of critics such as Benedict Anderson (9–36), Ernest Gellner (106–17), and Anthony Smith (66–71) and the philosopher Vasconcelos (7–40) to help students reflect on how nationalism creates cultural canons.

6. Orchard and Padilla provide a chronology of Niggli's life in the front matter of *The Plays of Josefina Niggli* and a short biography in their introduction (ix–xi, 3–33).

7. In addition to Martínez's critical biography and Stavans's foreword to Niggli's *"Mexican Village,"* students can consult online biographies of Niggli, such as Arrizón, "Niggli." They can also access a biography and conduct archival research through the Josefina Niggli Collection at Western Carolina University's Hunter Library: wcu.lyrasistechnology.org/repositories/2/resources/219.

8. Niggli's play *Soldadera* also beautifully captures the figure of the woman soldier, an important archetype for female participation in the social struggle of the Mexican Revolution and a symbolic representation for contemporary Chicana feminism.

9. For a discussion of *México de afuera*, see Bruce-Novoa; Kanellos.

Works Cited

Anderson, Benedict R. *Imagined Communities: Reflections on the Origin and Spread of Nationalism*. Revised ed., Verso, 2006.

Anzaldúa, Gloria. *Borderlands / La frontera: The New Mestiza*. Aunt Lute Books, 1999.

Arrizón, Alicia. "Niggli, Josefina Maria." *Handbook of Texas Online*, Texas State Historical Association, 1999–, tshaonline.org/handbook/online/articles/fnitt.

Bruce-Novoa, Juan. "La Prensa and the Chicano Community." *Americas Review*, vol. 17, nos. 3–4, 1989, pp. 150–56.

Gellner, Ernest. *Nations and Nationalism*. 1983. 2nd ed., Cornell UP, 2006.

Kanellos, Nicolás. *Hispanic Immigrant Literature: El Sueño del Retorno*. U of Texas P, 2011.

Martínez, Elizabeth Coonrod. *Josefina Niggli, Mexican American Writer: A Critical Biography*. U of New Mexico P, 2007.

———. "(Re)Visioning Mexican Intellectual and Peasant Life." *Experiments in Democracy: Interracial and Cross-Cultural Exchange in American Theatre, 1912–1945*, edited by Cheryl Black and Jonathan Shandell, Southern Illinois UP, 2016, pp. 105–25.

Niggli, Josefina. *Apártate, hermano*. Translated by David Toscana, Consejo para la Cultura / las Artes de Nuevo León, 2003.

———. *"Mexican Village" and Other Works.* Edited and with a foreword by Ilan Stavans, Northwestern UP, 2008.

Orchard, William, and Yolanda Padilla, editors. *The Plays of Josefina Niggli: Recovered Landmarks of Latino Literature.* U of Wisconsin P, 2007.

Padilla, Yolanda. "The Transnational National: Race, the Border, and the Immigrant Nationalism of Josefina Niggli's *Mexican Village.*" *CR: The New Centennial Review*, vol. 9, no. 2, 2009, pp. 45–72.

Paredes, Raymund. "Evolution of Chicano Literature." *MELUS*, vol. 5, no. 2, Summer 1978, pp. 71–110.

Pérez-Torres, Rafael. "Chicano Ethnicity, Cultural Hybridity, and the Mestizo Voice." *American Literature*, vol. 70, no. 1, Mar. 1998, pp. 153–76.

Smith, Anthony. *Nationalism: Theory, Ideology, History.* 2nd ed., Polity Press, 2010.

Vasconcelos, José. *The Cosmic Race: A Bilingual Edition.* Translated by Didier Tisdel Jaén, Johns Hopkins UP, 1997.

Shelley García

Crossing the (Genre) Border: Sandra Cisneros's Genre Innovation in *The House on Mango Street*

The 1984 publication of Sandra Cisneros's *The House on Mango Street*, and notably, its subsequent reissue through a commercial press a decade later, marks an important moment of mainstream awareness of Chicana literature (despite the fact Chicanas had already been publishing short stories and poems and had written novels that had received little outside attention). In the decades since, Cisneros's book (alternately called a novel or a collection of stories) has been assigned to classes from grade school through college, often as a way to illuminate the experiences of poor, working-class, urban Chicanos, from the perspective of a little girl.

This book relates the experience and observations of a young girl as she enters puberty and develops the ambition to become a writer, even while Cisneros subtly paints the sexist and racist antics of the girl's society. To fully appreciate Cisneros's work, however, readers need to acknowledge and study its groundbreaking form and poetic quality. *Mango Street* defies, even transcends, easy genre categorization.

In many ways, *Mango Street* reflects the advent of a more inclusive canon and the vital contribution women of color make to the literary landscape. And yet, the accounts in *Mango Street* are too often read as interesting cultural pieces, texts that simply document a girl's personal experience of nondominant cultures. An opening toward inclusion in the literary canon has been mistaken for the achievement of equitable treatment of literary works. While inclusivity is a necessary precondition, equitable treatment requires that readers analyze texts using similar methodologies. Not exploring the aesthetic and formal qualities of literatures by women and nonwhite authors communicates that those areas are somehow lacking. By categorizing Cisneros differently, readers imply that texts by female and nonwhite authors do not warrant, or cannot bear, deep aesthetic exploration.

To shift how readers engage these texts, we must focus on the formal aspects of these works. I advocate, specifically, for the lens of genre. To be clear, I do not advocate a return to New Criticism close reading, which ignores—or, worse, negates—the inextricable relation of texts to contexts. Instead, I advocate attentiveness to formal innovation and transgression to fully understand Cisneros's (and more broadly a Chicana) critique of dominant culture. This approach can be practiced in a graduate-level course or, with careful guidance, in a course for upper-level undergraduates.

Many instructors lack a significant education in genre as a field. We know and regularly engage with genres, but they operate primarily as natural categories. Unfortunately, this lack of training leaves us ill equipped to engage with texts that overtly innovate with or transgress genre boundaries. This essay offers two segments of metacritical analysis: first, a look into how *Mango Street* scholarship grapples with Cisneros's genre transgressiveness (or fails to), and second, a review of the body of work that reads *Mango Street* as fitting within a genre: that is, as a contemporary Chicana bildungsroman.

Much of the discussion about *Mango Street*, in classrooms or in published articles, engages details of the story line itself. Esperanza is incandescently charming, bold yet vulnerable, smart yet sullen. It is no wonder readers are captivated by such a narrator and her community. But discussions of characterization and theme, and of content broadly, miss Cisneros's formal innovations and her departure from tradition. A careful look at the scholarship reveals that the initial questions to be addressed when analyzing *Mango Street*—aside from scholarly arguments—are issues of identification and classification. The question "What is it?" is unavoidable. This question is sometimes directly engaged in the scholarship, sometimes only obliquely referenced. Nonetheless, the text requires that we, as readers and teachers, grapple with it. There is a lack of scholarly consensus regarding *Mango Street*'s genre. Further, the fact that *Mango Street* requires genre classification is itself a break with tradition. This book's indeterminacy and nonconformity with regard to genre sheds light on the entire genre system and its influence on our reading and interpretation. Cisneros's work reminds us how much we rely on genre classification to fill gaps, direct focus, and guide interpretations. By countering traditional form, Cisneros challenges genre's role in shaping our engagement with texts. She invites readers to consider how genre designations are decided and what implications they have for reading.

Though the book is composed of forty-four pieces that loosely follow the protagonist's experiences and that range in length from a few paragraphs to several pages, scholars like Yvonne Yarbro-Bejarano, Ellen McCracken, and Annie Eysturoy have decided *Mango Street* qualifies as a novel. More commonly, however, scholars avoid that designation, likely because the genre has specific criteria and a body of theory. Many scholars opt to use nongenre terms such as *story* to sidestep genre designation, or wider terms such as *text* or *narrative*. Whether referring to *Mango Street* as a text made up of a "collection of texts" (Gonzáles-Berry and Rebolledo 114) or a "work of fiction" (Yarbro-Bejarano 142), they avoid a genre designation with too rigid or too many (and ultimately conflicting) qualifications.

This same skirting of genre labels is visible when scholars highlight *Mango Street*'s poetic quality and emphasize Cisneros's literary identity as that of a poet first. Rather than confidently making a genre designation, they adapt the language of description: "poetic" (Yarbro-Bejarano 142; Klein 22; Quintana 66) or "lyrical" (Valdés 60) is used rather than "poem" or "poetry," which allows authors to describe the text's stylistic elements without committing to a definitive genre. Other scholars address the prose-poetry divide by claiming both for *Mango Street.* María Elena de Valdés describes Cisneros as a poet, the text as a novel, and the collection of forty-four pieces as "written in the manner of a young girl's memoir"—not in a daily journal, but rather in a "loose-knit series of lyrical reflections" (57). Valdés ultimately determines that each piece "can be seen as a self-contained prose poem," and, when reading them collectively, she finds "a subtle, yet powerful, narrative thread that unites the text" (58).

In keeping with Valdés's rejection of a binary choice, several scholars suggest that *Mango Street* is best understood as a genre hybrid or as some new, as yet unnamed, genre. Sonia Saldívar-Hull's analysis of Cisneros's work places *Mango Street* alongside Cherríe Moraga's *Loving in the*

War Years and Gloria Anzaldúa's *Borderlands / La frontera*. Saldívar-Hull labels all three as *mestizaje* texts, a "mixture of fiction and history" (85). McCracken's analysis of *Mango Street* identifies genre elements but also confirms the work's nonconformity. At points McCracken describes it as a "modified autobiographical novel, or Bildungsroman," but she ultimately prefers to categorize the text as "a hybrid genre midway between the novel and the short story" (64). In keeping with McCracken's description of *Mango Street* as belonging to a hybrid genre, Diana Klein offers perhaps the most beautiful genre description of Cisneros's text: "*The House on Mango Street* is the story of growing awareness which comes in fits and starts, a series of almost epiphanic narrations mirrored in a structure that is neither linear nor traditional, a hybrid of fictive and poetic form, more like an impressionistic painting where the subject isn't clear until the viewer moves back a bit and views the whole" (22).

Klein compares Cisneros's text to an impressionistic painting, and many other scholars have used similar art metaphors. Stella Bolaki, echoing Klein, characterizes the work as a collection of vignettes, which taken together create a tableau. Once it "hangs complete[,] we stand in front of a tapestry of static women confined in houses 'sitting their sadness on an elbow' . . . looking out the window all their lives" (109). Of the art metaphors used, the label "vignette" emerges as the descriptor of choice for the units that make up *Mango Street*. Erlinda Gonzáles-Berry and Tey Diana Rebolledo, María Herrera-Sobek, Julián Olivarez, Jacqueline Doyle, Reuben Sánchez, Alvina Quintana, Maria Karafilis, Kelly Wissman, Karen Martin, and Stella Bolaki all use "vignette" to describe the text's small components. Despite its common deployment in *Mango Street* scholarship, however, "vignette" is rarely defined. These art metaphors emphasize Cisneros's ability to craft images that are so powerful they capture life in ways only master painters rival; however, the reliance on art metaphors also highlights the insufficiency of genre terminology to describe *Mango Street*.

Alternative approaches to describing genre move away from literary designations of fiction, poetry, and prose and instead draw from other disciplines. Alvina Quintana describes Cisneros's work as an "ethnographic allegory of female experience" (61). Pedro Gutiérrez-Revuelta describes Cisneros's text as "las *historias* (historias del barrio)" ("the stories [neighborhood stories]"; 51; my trans.). Unfortunately, what Quintana and Gutiérrez-Revuelta gain in descriptive detail through their designations of ethnography and history, they lose in estimation of literary quality.

In some scholars' work, the process of determining a category figures less prominently. However, while such scholars never overtly ask what kind of work *Mango Street* is, the analysis itself sometimes makes clear how they respond to the question of the text's identity. Doyle, Wissman, and Laura Gutiérrez-Spencer in various ways read *Mango Street* as feminist revision. Doyle interprets Cisneros's work as a revision of the white feminist vision articulated in Virginia Woolf's essay "A Room of One's Own." Both Wissman and Gutiérrez-Spencer read Cisneros's text as critiquing and revising fairy tales. Still other scholars define the text by determining its audience—adults or children.

Scholars also consult commentary by Cisneros to identify *Mango Street*'s genre, including interviews, essays, and speeches about her life and writing, and especially her description of *Mango Street*'s origins at the famed Iowa Writer's Workshop. They pull from her own artful descriptors of her writing, noting in particular her inspiration and agenda to innovate literary forms. Such scholarship defers to Cisneros's explanation of intent in order to deal with Cisneros's generic innovation.

From the earliest responses to Cisneros's work to more recent commentaries, one thread of analysis remains consistent: reading *Mango Street* as a contemporary bildungsroman. Bildungsroman is the most popular genre designation for Cisneros's work, and the closest we come to scholarly consensus, and the bildungsroman analysis provides some of the text's most insightful readings as well as the most attentive observations regarding form. Nonetheless, even the most thorough bildungsroman genre analysis cannot capture the fullness of *Mango Street*'s genre innovations.

Early Cisneros scholarship tends to employ comparative readings of Cisneros's text and the work of another (usually male) Chicano author. By focusing on two texts, scholars establish a general perspective of Chicana/o youth experience and, to a lesser degree, point out the gendered differences in those maturation processes, all while working to establish the texts as part of the larger bildungsroman tradition. For instance, Gonzáles-Berry and Rebolledo compare *Mango Street* to Tomás Rivera's novel *Y no se lo tragó la tierra . . .* (*And the Earth Did Not Part . . .*), and Klein compares Cisneros's work to Rudolfo Anaya's *Bless Me, Ultima*. Klein, like Gonzáles-Berry and Rebolledo before her, brings attention to how each book differs from traditional bildungsromans written by white men and makes distinctions between Chicano and Chicana experiences, though primarily in terms of gender. All three scholars also discuss *Mango Street*'s innovative structure, but they have a complicated task: they argue for including the works they discuss in the genre of bildungsroman while simultaneously suggesting that these works are unique.

While the politics of these texts are progressive, perhaps even radical, the analytical approach is conservative. That conservatism is made clear by how scholars stress the commonalities in these works in order to admit them into the bildungsroman genre. The very process of genre classification (which employs comparison) privileges the more established member of any pair. Though seemingly neutral, the comparison in genre analysis is never between two equally weighted texts but between an established and a newer or less-established text. The problem is not with particular scholars or arguments. It is rooted in the power of the genre system, wherein even the most counterhegemonic perspectives are made to support the status quo. Ultimately, pressure to illustrate compatibility with traditional genres blunts a text's distinctiveness.

Following this early trend, scholars have moved in a different direction, acknowledging Cisneros's radical departure from the traditional bildungsroman. The recent trend in Cisneros scholarship has been to argue that *Mango Street* participates in the bildungsroman tradition while fundamentally remaking it. Leslie Gutiérrez-Jones argues that the bildungsroman is a white, patriarchal form that Cisneros strategically revises in order to write a story consistent with her politics and with Esperanza's development. Gutiérrez-Jones casts Cisneros's project as a battle against a white, patriarchal genre and literary legacy—akin to Esperanza's efforts to create a space for herself through her writing. Thus Cisneros carves out a literary home for herself and other Chicanas/os by "tactically appropriating" the bildungsroman (297).

Taking a similar approach a half-decade later, Karafilis reads Cisneros's text as "appropriating and modifying" bildungsroman (64). When Cisneros adopts and adjusts the traditional form to fit her needs, she not only speaks "to the options, futures, and responsibilities of [the] young narrator" but also comments "on dominant Euro-American society by revising or even rejecting some of its values and certain aspects of its literary traditions" (Karafilis 64). In other words, *Mango Street* gives voice to Chicana experience while also critiquing dominant culture.

Whereas early scholarship highlighted shared bildungsroman elements (seemingly to legitimize marginalized literatures by allowing them to gain membership in the long-standing genre), later scholars built on the previous work and went beyond it. Scholarship went from arguing that *Mango*

Street should be read as a bildungsroman to arguing that Cisneros strategically adapted the form. Despite this progress, the bildungsroman analysis still cannot fully articulate Cisneros's genre innovation. As mentioned previously, the early comparative approach is rooted in a conservative genre reading that encourages conformity and compliance. While the later scholarship moves beyond that pressure for sameness, correctly recognizing the challenges *Mango Street* poses to traditional bildungsroman analysis, it fails to go far enough. Cisneros is not simply remaking the bildungsroman; she is remaking the broader genre system.

Even scholars who recognize *Mango Street* as a radical departure from traditional form fail to address other aspects of genre. It could be argued that the consistent scholarly focus on the bildungsroman in *Mango Street* is because of the relatively straightforward method this genre designation provides for classifying an otherwise unclassifiable text. That it is possible to ignore the text's innovative formal aspects and focus solely on plot indicates that the genre is defined primarily by its content rather than, if at all, by its form. Questions of form (novel, composite novel, serial narrative, short-story cycle, vignettes) and style (poetic, prose, prosaic) may prove too complicated, thus scholars center discussion on Esperanza's development. While other elements of the text are more difficult to recognize and categorize, the coming-of-age idea is rather simple. A classification of bildungsroman thus encourages suspension of any further (or complete) genre categorization or discussions of innovation.

Early genre analysis of Cisneros's first book led readers to understand it as part of the bildungsroman tradition, whereas later analysis allowed readers to consider how *Mango Street* radically challenges and remakes that tradition. Each approach fails to recognize the larger challenge that *Mango Street* poses. Were Cisneros simply remaking the bildungsroman, then disrupting the inner form would be sufficient. The inner form (the coming-of-age plot) and the outer form (the work's forty-four segments, which are independent and yet cohere, and which, taken together, challenge genre categorization) are being renovated, so it is not enough to categorize Cisneros's text as an unconventional bildungsroman. Cisneros is not simply renovating a genre; she is transforming our understanding of genre. *Mango Street* exceeds the limits of the bildungsroman and spans multiple possible genres yet never fits one. Her book calls into question not just the bildungsroman genre but the very practice of genre classification.

It is important for the next generation of *Mango Street* scholars to engage even more deeply with questions of form and genre innovation. To that end, instructors should extend the discussion from sociocultural themes to matters of genre. The emergence of the work of Chicana writers in the 1980s reflects innovations not only of subject but also of form. Students should be invited to explore genre not as a neutral classificatory system but as a vital social system that transmits dominant ideology and that can be transgressed and even, in the case of *Mango Street*, transformed.

Works Cited

Bolaki, Stella. *Unsettling the Bildungsroman: Reading Contemporary Ethnic American Women's Fiction*. Brill / Rodopi, 2011.

Cisneros, Sandra. *The House on Mango Street*. Vintage Books, 1991.

Doyle, Jacqueline. "More Room of Her Own: Sandra Cisneros's *The House on Mango Street*." *MELUS*, vol. 19, no. 4, 1994. *JSTOR*, www.jstor.org/stable/468200.

Eysturoy, Annie O. *Daughters of Self-Creation: The Contemporary Chicana Novel*. U of New Mexico P, 1996.

Gonzáles-Berry, Erlinda, and Tey Diana Rebolledo. "Growing Up Chicano: Tomás Rivera and Sandra Cisneros." *Revista Chicano-Riqueña*, vol. 13, nos. 3–4, 1985, pp. 109–19.

Gutiérrez-Jones, Leslie. "Different Voices: The Re-*Bildung* of the Barrio in Sandra Cisneros's *The House on Mango Street*." *Anxious Power: Reading, Writing, and Ambivalence in Narrative by Women*, edited by Carol J. Singley and Susan Elizabeth Sweeney, State U of New York P, 1993, pp. 295–312.

Gutiérrez-Revuelta, Pedro. "Género e ideología en el libro de Sandra Cisneros: *The House on Mango Street*." *Critica: A Journal of Critical Essays*, vol. 1, no. 3, 1986, pp. 48–59.

Gutiérrez-Spencer, Laura. "Fairy Tales and Opera: The Fate of the Heroine in the Work of Sandra Cisneros." *Speaking the Other Self: American Women Writers*, edited by Jeanne Campbell Reesman, U of Georgia P, 1997, pp. 278–87.

Herrera-Sobek, María. "The Politics of Rape: Sexual Transgression in Chicana Fiction." *Americas Review*, vol. 15, nos. 3–4, 1987, pp. 171–88.

Karafilis, Maria. "Crossing the Borders of Genre: Revisions of the Bildungsroman in Sandra Cisneros's *The House on Mango Street* and Jamaica Kincaid's *Annie John*." *The Journal of the Midwest Modern Language Association*, vol. 31, no. 2, Winter 1998, pp. 63–78. *JSTOR*, www.jstor.org/stable/1315091.

Klein, Dianne. "Coming of Age in Novels by Rudolfo Anaya and Sandra Cisneros." *The English Journal*, vol. 81, no. 5, 1992, pp. 21–26.

Martin, Karen. "*The House* (of Memory) *on Mango Street:* Sandra Cisneros's Counter-poetics of Space." *South Atlantic Review*, vol. 73, no. 1, 2008, pp. 50–67. *JSTOR*, www.jstor.org/stable/27784760.

McCracken, Ellen. "Sandra Cisneros' *The House on Mango Street*: Community-Oriented Introspection and the Demystification of Patriarchal Violence." *Breaking Boundaries: Latina Writing and Critical Readings*, edited by Asunción Horno-Delgado et al., U of Massachusetts P, 1989, pp. 62–71.

Olivarez, Julián. "Sandra Cisneros' *The House on Mango Street*, and the Poetics of Space." *The Americas Review*, vol. 15, nos. 3–4, 1987, pp. 160–70.

Quintana, Alvina E. *Home Girls: Chicana Literary Voices*. Temple UP, 1996.

Saldívar-Hull, Sonia. *Feminism on the Border: Chicana Gender Politics and Literature*. U of California P, 2000.

Sánchez, Reuben. "Remembering Always to Come Back: The Child's Wished-for Escape and the Adult's Self-Empowered Return in Sandra Cisneros's *House on Mango Street*." *Children's Literature*, vol. 23, 1995, pp. 221–41. doi:10.1353/chl.0.0455.

Valdés, María Elena de. "In Search of Identity in Cisneros's *The House on Mango Street*." *Canadian Review of American Studies*, vol. 23, no. 1, 1992, pp. 55–72. *Project MUSE*, muse.jhu.edu/article/681089.

Wissman, Kelly. "'Writing Will Keep You Free': Allusions to and Recreations of the Fairy Tale Heroine in *The House on Mango Street*." *Children's Literature in Education*, vol. 38, 2007, pp. 17–34.

Yarbro-Bejarano, Yvonne. "Chicana Literature from a Chicana Feminist Perspective." *The Americas Review: A Review of Hispanic Literature and Art of the USA*, vol. 15, nos. 3–4, 1987, pp. 139–45.

Ashley Hope Pérez

Navigating Narrative Ambiguity in Ana Castillo's *The Mixquiahuala Letters*

Ana Castillo's experimental novel *The Mixquiahuala Letters* (1986) traces more than a decade in the friendship between the two main characters, Teresa—a Latina poet who composes the letters—and Alicia, a struggling artist, whose responses are not included. The slimness of the novel may suggest an easy read, but students are often challenged by the multiple sources of ambiguity in *The Mixquiahuala Letters*. Despite the intimacy of the letters, crucial aspects of the women's travels and travails are occluded, leaving readers to contend with uncertain motivations and gaps between events. Teresa's letters interweave reminiscences, third-person narratives, imagined scenes, and poetry, creating a variety of genres that sometimes belie the glaring absence of Alicia's responses. And, most significant of all, *The Mixquiahuala Letters* presents us with repeatedly diverging narrative paths that frustrate our desire for narrative closure.

Several Paths for Reading

An opening note to readers explains that the novel's forty numbered letters are arranged in "hopscotch" fashion under three different headings: "For the Conformist," "For the Cynic," and "For the Quixotic." Under each heading, letters (chapters) are arranged to indicate the order in which they should be read. This involves skipping over some letters, doubling back to others, and omitting some altogether. Most letters appear under all three headings—although sometimes in different positions—but a few are unique to each path. Despite the apparent modesty of these deviations, they generate different starting places, endpoints, and outcomes. For example, in one path Teresa ends up married with a son; in another, she has a son but no husband; in the third, she is childless and divorced.

The paths also generate different thematic emphases. Whereas the path labeled "For the Quixotic" stresses the power of female friendship to transcend crises, betrayals, and distance, the path "For the Cynic" offers a vision of female friendship as an inadequate stay against destructive heterosexual relationships and cultural and social pressures. The path "For the Conformist" makes especially prominent the possibility that the correspondence serves first and foremost as a tool for Teresa's self-definition, often at Alicia's expense.

It is notable that in spite of the ambiguity introduced by these competing visions of the novel's central relationship, critics have tended overwhelmingly to privilege aspects of the narrative that celebrate female friendship, liberated sexuality, resistance to sexist social expectations, and the evocation of a Chicana perspective. This is also the angle presented by the back cover copy of the 1992 paperback edition, published by Anchor Books, which highlights the "enduring friendship" between the women. These positive prospects appeal, to be sure, but *The Mixquiahuala Letters* offers much more—and asks more of us. The tensions between the paths unsettle any singular interpretation of the novel and the relationship it explores, demanding instead that readers pioneer a vision of Latina relationality robust enough to contend with all of the paths. In the next section, I describe the broad strokes of an approach that has allowed me to support undergraduates in navigating various forms of ambiguity in this complex narrative. I stress how our understanding of the narrative—and of the work of reading—changes when we hold the different paths in productive tension.

Strategies for Navigating the Paths with Students

I dedicate two weeks (two classes per week) to *The Mixquiahuala Letters* as part of a general education literature course for nonmajors, often teaching it near the end of a semester. Although my students generally express genuine interest in encountering perspectives different from their own, I have observed that they often have an unexamined expectation that fiction by nonwhite authors should be straightforward, so that they can access cultural information with as little struggle as possible. Because this expectation does not prime students to appreciate a book like *The Mixquiahuala Letters*, I take care to provide other frames for their encounter with the novel by emphasizing the significance of the novel's narrative experimentation and by foregrounding the value of grappling with narrative ambiguity. As we work with the novel, we explore what this ambiguity means for our understanding of culture, character, context, and our identities as readers.

I begin by asking students to consider how ambiguity is present to varying degrees in all narratives, from the other novels that we have read together, to the films and the daily stories that we share with others. Some ambiguity—like whether someone is motivated by jealousy or loyalty—may be resolved, as when a withheld piece of information is finally provided. Often, as we continue reading, ambiguity diminishes as textual evidence accumulates. In other cases, we may never be certain whether an event has taken place—or how we should interpret it. Ambiguity puts added stress on the reader's role in interpretation, revealing the story to be something that we can't simply consume, but that, in certain ways, we cowrite. Students often imagine that interpretation in these cases consists of deciding between possible outcomes, but instead I encourage them to focus on why an author wants to maintain the uncertainty in the first place. We start with the headings of the novel's three reading paths, which are identified in terms of who they are for: the conformist, the cynic, and the quixotic. These unflattering labels foreclose the prospect of our claiming a positive identity as readers so long as we limit ourselves to any single path; in this way, Castillo stresses the need for us to take a broader, more flexible view of the novel's characters and events.

I find it useful to have students complete a first reading that focuses on just one path, so I split the class up into groups that each focus on one of the three paths. (I generally assign the groups and the reading paths, although students with a strong preference can sign up for a specific path.) During the next two classes, students discuss observations and questions within their small groups. To avoid spoilers at this stage, our whole-group conversation focuses on broader questions related to the novel's experimental structure, such as the temporal ambiguities of the novel. We consider the dynamics between Alicia and Teresa in various letters, the nature of our access to Alicia's inner life, and the tensions between letter writing as a space of intimacy and as an opportunity for performance.

Once all students have read their assigned path from beginning to end, a simple exercise sharpens the differences between the narrative trajectories. In class, students complete the following sentence based on their reading path: "In the end, *The Mixquiahuala Letters* suggests that the friendship between Alicia and Teresa . . ." This prompt helps students make bold claims about the character and future of the friendship. I also ask students to assemble specific details and quotations to support their claims. These claims are shared with the whole class, and we get to see the dramatic differences in how readers of different paths responded to the prompt. For example, readers of the conformist's path often make claims focusing on how the friendship between Alicia and Teresa fails to free either from expectations of conformity and underscoring how their friendship reflects a search for the kind of love that neither can get from men. By contrast, readers of the quixotic's path typically emphasize the value of the women's friendship as the one constant in their lives, and readers of the cynic's path tend to see most clearly the dysfunctional dimensions of the relationship, including the mutual resentment that becomes evident in this arrangement of the letters.[1] The emergence of these broad patterns suggests real differences in what we experience as the story of the relationship, depending on which path we travel. In addition, there are often a few examples within each reading group that reflect a predominant theme of another path, suggesting that the reader was sensitive to qualities of the narrative that were made even more salient in another path.

This exercise sets the stage for students to finish the novel by reading the letters that do not appear on their path and by shadowing the other reading paths (tracing the sequence of letters as they would be read on that path to experience some sense of how the narrative unfolds when the letters are arranged differently). On our last day with the text, we finally have the common ground to discuss these patterns and the connections between the narrative and structural particulars of the novel and broader thematic and contextual considerations. Students discover that, in contrast to works that offer the more familiar satisfactions of coherence, *The Mixquiahuala Letters* requires a dramatic increase in their tolerance for ambiguity. Often, this means releasing the readier forms of reading pleasure—like the appealing notion of Teresa's letters as an attempt at "reaching out"—to engage with aspects of the novel that may bring discomfort or frustration. Although the challenges of Castillo's novel are significant, my students often describe it as the work that most changed their understanding of the possibilities of narrative representation.

Other Sources of Ambiguity

The multiple paths through the letters are the most dramatic source of ambiguity in *The Mixquiahuala Letters*, but other features also intensify this effect. It is useful to consider the range of genres embedded in the letters. Does Teresa have less of an obligation to be truthful, for example, in the poems that she pens? What about when she describes an episode as happening to "the two women" (Castillo 70)? What possibilities are opened—or closed—when she ends an account abruptly by reminding Alicia that she already knows what comes next (74)? In addition, the absence of dates on the letters means that we don't always know the temporal relation between the events and the writing of the letters.

Teresa's letters thematize fluidity and hybridity, particularly with regard to perceptions of the female body and sexual, ethnic, and cultural identity. This is especially evident in Teresa's portrayal of Alicia. Teresa clearly positions herself as a Chicana, but her letters leave open somewhat contradictory possibilities for reading Alicia's ethnicity. Teresa initially dismisses Alicia as "just another WASP" when they meet (50) but elsewhere includes Alicia in a strategic disavowal of whiteness: "couldn't they see by our color that we weren't gringas?" (69). Alicia's ambiguous ethnic identity is related to another matter: to whom does the narrative address itself? In Manuel Martín-Rodríguez's view, it matters that Alicia is "non-Chicana" because this enables Teresa (and Castillo) to reach out "cross-culturally to explain Chicana subjectivity and culture" (99). Of course, this assumes a non-Chicana reader, which seems in tension with Castillo's own declared intention to write for "another Chicana very similar to me" ("*MELUS* Interview" 140).

Although Alicia is the named addressee in a number of the letters, we can also imagine Teresa writing past her to a different, perhaps broader, audience. At one point, Teresa interrupts her message to Alicia with a comment that begins, "if anyone else happens to read this account . . ." (Castillo, *Mixquiahuala Letters* 95). My students have also raised the possibility that these are the sort of impassioned, anguished letters that stay in the desk drawer while more muted missives go in the mail. Or perhaps Alicia merely provides a pretext for writing to the world at large. Students begin to see the letters themselves as a fundamentally ambiguous performance: texts ostensibly directed at Alicia may also be a performance for another reader—or for Teresa herself—and may be delivered with a wink over Alicia's head.

We can see how ambiguity accumulates in and between different paths in the novel by tracking how Teresa strategically reconfigures expected values to elevate herself. As she tells it, Teresa gets more attention, as a *morena*, a woman with a darker complexion, than the fair-skinned Alicia; her voluptuousness trumps her friend's thin contours, and her Indian ancestry is valued over Alicia's uncertain heritage.[2] At times, this valorization of Chicana identity appears capacious enough to accommodate difference, as when Teresa addresses Alicia as "hermana" ("sister") and begins her letter with "i wish i could have convinced you how beautiful you are" before going on to catalog Alicia's assets, which she insists go well beyond any diplomatic reference to "inner beauty" (51). At other times, however, Teresa seems bent on the calculated deflation of Alicia's value: "you were . . . not especially pretty and bore no resemblance to the ideal of any man / you encountered anywhere" (50; spacing in original). This description of Alicia is echoed in milder terms elsewhere, but other textual elements—such as accounts of Alicia's easy connection with men—seem to belie Teresa's claims. In discussions of Alicia's appearance, as in all aspects of the narration, descriptions produced by Teresa must be situated in relation to her purpose and the needs she is fulfilling through her narration.

Of course, what we take to be Teresa's needs and purpose depends in large part on the path we take to a given scene—and where that path subsequently leads. We can see the impact of the arrangement of the paths' configurations by examining a letter that appears in all three. In one such letter, Teresa details a painful experience that happened to Alicia long before they met:

> You were seventeen and, at first, had wanted the child, romanticized motherhood, life with its father, struggling together, the way young people do. When Rodney stopped coming around, you were afraid to be exiled alone.
>
> A friend of a friend lent you her welfare card. The fee for a legal abortion was steep for a teenage girl. . . . At the clinic, you were alone, posing as a Puerto Rican woman who had already borne five children.
>
> The nurse looked up the records and shook her head disgusted by your supposed negligence. She drew up forms that were not presented to you until you were on the table, sedated, feet in stirrups and exposed to the world the way you had never been exposed before in your life.
>
> You were sterilized. (126)

Some critics take as a given the faithfulness of Teresa's rendition of Alicia's experiences and words here and elsewhere.[3] But strategic ventriloquism is an equally plausible explanation for how Alicia's "voice" emerges within Teresa's narration—or appropriation—of the event. This passage, like many others, reads differently depending in part on which of the paths we are traveling when we encounter it.

In the quixotic's path, this passage reminds us of the intimate secrets that bind the women to each other. Just a few letters prior to the sterilization narrative, Teresa has described her own, far more recent, abortion experience (114), and what follows in the final two letters of this path is an appeal for reconnection. By contrast, in the cynic's sequence, the sterilization narrative functions as yet another illustration of what Teresa sees as Alicia's brokenness, and it is followed by a letter that rails against Alicia for letting a man come between them (128–29). The next letter in the path abounds in negative evaluations of Alicia's physical appearance and personality (49–50), and the trajectory ends with a letter that accuses Alicia of traveling with one of Teresa's ex-lovers (131–32).

The resonances of the sterilization scene are even more troubling in the conformist's path, where it provides the cornerstone for Teresa's triumphant departure from the friendship in favor of the conventional roles of wife and mother. Just a few letters earlier in this path, Teresa writes to Alicia, "[Y]ou craved a family, to share life with a steady man, and children to sit around the table together" (112). By bringing up the sterilization experience at a time when Alicia longs for motherhood, Teresa rubs salt in the wound of her friend's unachievable desire. The pressure on this point continues in a letter unique to the conformist path. It includes a kind of gloating incredulity when Teresa realizes her friend has not revealed her inability to have children to her boyfriend: "[he] didn't know! . . . you were never going to have a baby. Never" (136). Teresa depicts Alicia's life in ruins but shows little patience for her struggle. Instead, she conflates her own happiness in the wake of heartbreak with the expectation that Alicia, too, ought to have moved on (129).

The final letter of the conformist's path effects a separation that is far crueler, albeit more subtle, than the breach effected by Alicia's supposed betrayal in the cynic's path. In it, Teresa recounts her visit to New York City to attend Alicia's first solo art show. She casually declares, "[T]oo bad we didn't get a chance to talk," underscoring her ability to do without Alicia in light of the husband and son around whom she has recentered her emotional life. Teresa has what Alicia cannot have (and what Teresa has portrayed her as desiring), yet she smugly wishes Alicia well in her search for "a place you'll want to go back to and call home too." These final lines of the narrative arc stress Alicia's lack in contrast to Teresa's fulfillment, allowing Teresa to simultaneously elevate her status and cut ties with Alicia. Teresa's imaginative extension into Alicia's experiences can index solidarity and intimacy, but it can also be read as a feat of ventriloquism that appropriates and manipulates the emotional content of Alicia's experience.

The diverging reading routes of *The Mixquiahuala Letters* demand that the reader navigate varied possibilities, some hopeful and others perverse. Castillo asks us to go beyond readings that would reduce the narrative to a single path, reckoning instead with unresolved contradictions and the many faces of Latina experience. Narrative ambiguity offers a stay against too-hasty satisfactions derived by flattening a text into a familiar form and provides an excellent learning and reflection experience for students. Especially when dealing with ethnic literatures, quests for coherence can come at the cost of attention to the text's particularity. Sometimes the more responsible reading entails keeping contradiction and ambiguity active, as *The Mixquiahuala Letters* asks that we do.

Notes

1. These insights are based on typical responses to the exercise by students in a number of class groups.

2. On this point, see Gonzáles-Berry 118.

3. For example, Manuel Martín-Rodríguez asserts that the embedded quotations attributed to Alicia allow us to "reconstruct much of what Alicia actually says" (97).

Works Cited

Castillo, Ana. "A *MELUS* Interview." By Elsa Saeta. *MELUS*, vol. 22, no. 3, 1997, pp. 133–49.

———. *The Mixquiahuala Letters*. 1986. Anchor Books, 1992.

Gonzáles-Berry, Erlinda. "*The* [Subversive] *Mixquiahuala Letters*: An Antidote for Self-Hate." *Chicana (W)Rites: On Word and Film*, edited by María Herrera-Sobek and Helena María Viramontes, Third Woman Press, 1995, pp. 115–24.

Martín-Rodríguez, Manuel M. *Life in Search of Readers: Reading (in) Chicano/a Literature*. U of New Mexico P, 2003.

Mary Jane Hurst

The Holy and the Ordinary: Lessons on Life, Love, and Language in Denise Chávez's *Face of an Angel*

Teaching Denise Chávez's *Face of an Angel* opens windows to literary and cultural issues within the American Southwest, but it also, more broadly, offers opportunities for exploring such topics as gender, language, American identities, and human nature itself. Winner of the American Book Award, the novel contains elements of bildungsroman, memoir, feminism, realism, Romanticism, and postmodernism, and it can be interpreted as an uninhibited representation of female sexuality and as an extended contemplation on spirituality, among other things. Richly developed and infused with joy, the work compares with novels by Leo Tolstoy and Charles Dickens but also shares truths with fiction by Alice Walker and Louise Erdrich (Hurst, "Transcendence" 29 and *American Voices* 2). A challenging yet versatile text, *Face of an Angel* works well in lower-level and upper-level undergraduate courses as well as in graduate courses in literature, American studies, cultural studies, and gender studies.

Face of an Angel is set firmly in southeastern New Mexico, not far from borders with Texas and Mexico, but place in the novel means more than literal geography. Chávez shares with many American writers that sense of home as a complex emotional and cultural site, a contested moral center. *The Great Gatsby*'s Nick Carraway describes his Midwest as both "the warm center of the world" and the "ragged edge of the universe" (Fitzgerald 3), and such an oxymoronic set of phrases could apply to Chávez's Southwest as well. Some students with Mexican American roots will be delighted to discover stories similar to their own, while others may be embarrassed by what may seem like revelations of family secrets, and still others may worry that classmates from other traditions and ethnicities will wrongly assume that they think or behave like the characters in the novel. People of any background may feel uncomfortable with the frank language or with certain characterizations, just as readers will likely encounter discomforting characters or situations in virtually every text on the syllabus. In academic environments rightly concerned about the hate and harm involved in stereotypes, it is worth taking time to differentiate an insider's portrayal of her own time, place, and culture from the assumptions and conclusions of an outsider. It will be helpful to acknowledge and sort through students' varying reactions and responses to the novel, perhaps through small group discussions or private journaling.

If a class situation lends itself to small group presentations, groups of students might be directed to discuss the presence of specific themes in this novel and to compare them with how they appear in other assigned readings. Certainly, sexual dynamics, gendered relationships, language use, religious or spiritual inquiry, and regional features would be among the list of themes appropriate for students to examine in *Face of an Angel*. Small group conversations often give students greater freedom to explore, discuss, and take risks. Working in small groups can also have a moderating effect on the expressions of students because they may listen and engage more intently when working together on an oral presentation, group paper, video, or other means of sharing ideas with the entire class. I have sometimes assigned different books to different groups within a class so that students are reading and comparing completely different texts (and not just different themes in the same set of texts), including books written by authors with obvious connections to each other (such as Chávez and Rudolfo Anaya or Sandra Cisneros) or by authors who would at first glance seem to have minimal common ground (such as Chávez and William Faulkner or Chang-rae Lee). This strategy maximizes students' in-depth exposure to literary riches. When small groups read different books but communicate regularly and interactively with the whole class, a dynamic and creative learning environment can flourish that facilitates more intense readings across a wide spectrum.

Another teaching strategy that I particularly like is to introduce a variety of critical theories (archetypal, reader response, psychoanalytic, deconstructionist, feminist, new historicist, etc.) and linguistic theories (including speech act and gender theories, among others) near the beginning of the semester, and then throughout the course to invite students to analyze or discuss particular texts from different theoretical perspectives. Depending on whether the students are first- or second-year students, upper-level majors, or graduate students, these assignments can be short and focused on one passage in one text, or they could be developed into semester-long papers or oral presentations using various media and multiple texts. *Face of an Angel* is an adaptive and richly rewarding novel, suitable and valuable for many types of students and many types of classes. This essay's appendix offers a highly selected list of resources that instructors and students, especially those who are new to *Face of an Angel*, may find helpful as they explore the cultural and theoretical contexts of the novel.

What Reed Way Dasenbrock said of Rudolfo Anaya and Leslie Marmon Silko holds true for Denise Chávez: all three are "in their very situations between two cultures, neither completely one nor the other. . . . These writers are where their formative cultures meet, and it is precisely for their representation of that meeting ground which can be a battle ground that these writers are Southwestern" (317). Of course, competing cultures and identities appear throughout American literature, as in canonical texts such as *The Scarlet Letter* or *Adventures of Huckleberry Finn*. In its language, *Face of an Angel* constructs these issues in contemporary settings. Though written in English, it conveys what Anaya has described in his own English-language fiction as "the rhythms of Spanish" (251), and Chávez further incorporates Spanish words and phrases in ways significant for gendered relationships and community affiliations. For instance, Manuel and Elena Dosamantes, ancestors of the main character, intentionally converse in Spanish to mark the special bond between them, but subsequent generations use Spanish less and less except when fighting or referring to something taboo. The main character, Soveida Dosamantes, charges that her brother, Hector, knows only enough Spanish to order drinks in Juárez. Soveida herself does not speak Spanish to any of her husbands or lovers; the one time it is spoken to her intimately is when Ivan once moans in the night, "'Te quiero, te quiero, te quiero.' I want you. I want you. I want you. In Spanish." With women, however, Soveida freely speaks Spanish or a Spanish-English mix. She claims that her favorite days are when she and her maid, Chata, clean the house together: "I love these Mondays with Chata. Talking in Spanish and laughing in no particular language" (Chávez, *Face* 215). Spanish fills a need for Soveida, connecting her in a deep way to her family and her culture.

Soveida's other outlet for Spanish can be found at her workplace, El Farol, a restaurant portrayed so realistically and amusingly that students who have worked in food service will instantly relate. The employees agree with the owner, who says with affection, "Hell, this cockroach-ridden, leaky-assed, chile-spattered, greasy-smelling pit of a restaurant is home" (461). The employees fight and argue with each other, share their joys and sorrows, and shut down the restaurant for funerals and weddings—including those of their regular customers—all while mixing their Spanish and English. Lavel, the African American cook whose substance abuse forms a running subplot, is described as "a vato loco ["a crazy dude"] . . . who loved to tell dirty jokes in Spanish" (301). The inability of Flavio, a new employee, to comply with Spanish instructions sends the head cook, Eloísa, into an indignant rage: "Shame on your mamá! What's happening to our kids? They don't speak Spanish no more!" until in her exasperation she recasts her Spanish instructions to Flavio—"Péguele a ese Tampico hasta que sangre chile"—into English, telling him to tenderize the steak Tampico and to add plenty of chile, or, as she translates herself, "Hit it until it bleeds chile" (294). Her outrage, of course, is not just about language loss but about the accompanying loss of family, community, and tradition. In an ironic twist, Mr. Tangee, a regular customer, chokes to death on this very steak while reading a book entitled *Deification of the Persona*, even as the Women Aglow, who happen to be in town for a convention, pray and sing around him.

Starting work at El Farol at age fifteen, Soveida is taken under the wing of Milia, who provides what Soveida's family cannot: calm, clear directions about life. Many of these lessons involve language, as does the first: "Now Soveida, I want you to listen. A person who listens is a good waitress, remember that. Do you hear a cough? It could mean someone is ready to order, or they need water. . . . Silence means the customer is either happy or mad. Things could go either way. Learn to know the difference" (106). Eventually, Soveida begins to write a book, which she calls "The Book of Service," recording the skills needed to work in a restaurant or to make one's way through the universe as an individual embracing one's identity, asserting one's human dignity, and connecting in meaningful ways to others. By writing their books, the author, Chávez, and her character, Soveida, claim power and authority over their language, over their lives as women, and over their relationships with others. In Chávez's earlier novel *The Last of the Menu Girls*, one of the characters asks, "What did it mean to be a woman? To be beautiful, complete? Was beauty a physical or a spiritual thing, was it strength of emotion, resolve, a willingness to love? What was it then, that made women lovely?" (53). Writing about this passage, María González has said that the "ability to write one's own story and her community's stories" is what makes women lovely (88). By this definition, Soveida grows in loveliness through her writing and through the intellectual and emotional processes that make her writing possible. The novel's emphasis on the empowering qualities of narrative can be inspirational to students.

Despite having a theological skepticism that dates to her childhood in parochial schools, Chávez told Elizabeth Brown-Guillory, "I grew up a Catholic, am still a Catholic, will always be a Catholic" (Chávez, "Denise Chávez: Chicana Woman Writer" 36). The mixing of gender identity, sexuality, spirituality, and religion is a prominent feature in Chávez's writing. The very title of this novel alludes to angels, with its nine sections labelled by the nine orders of heavenly beings who serve God—angels, archangels, principalities, powers, virtues, dominations, thrones, cherubim, and seraphim—even though the actions and language depicted in those sections might not be traditionally associated with Christian ideals. In fact, however, Soveida finds her deepest moments of grace and transcendence when physical and spiritual aspects of life are aligned, experienced together, and welcomed as integral parts of the human experience.

Subjected to sexual abuse, perhaps by her father but definitely by various young men and then by her very odd husbands, Soveida has complicated relationships with men. Her first husband is a sexually dysfunctional artist who likes to illustrate himself as a suffering Christ figure and who eventually commits suicide. Her second is a braggart who talks of his ambitions for greatness but spends his time cheating with other women and returning home late at night to force himself on Soveida. After divorcing him, she becomes involved with one of her professors, who considers himself far too important to be teaching in a community college. He too abuses Soveida, first intellectually with his scathing comments on her assignments, and then emotionally with his thoughtless sexual interactions. Humiliated, Soveida finds comfort with the professor's brother, a kind, mild-mannered, but married man. By the end of the novel, she is expecting the brother's baby and tells him, in a moment of grace and power, that she is pregnant with his child but expects nothing from him and will raise the child herself.

Hector, the brother of Soveida, is one of the more deplorable men in her life. He has inherited misogynistic patterns from their family and adds a readiness to deride women in public as well as in private, thereby "making the abjection of women the guarantor of his ethnic and masculine difference"—to borrow a phrase used by Marta Sánchez to describe the behavior of the protagonist in *Down These Mean Streets* (118). Hector describes his pregnant fiancée crudely: "She has the face of an angel and she likes to fuck" (Chávez, *Face* 375). Key to the novel's premise, the line provides the title *Face of an Angel*. As Chávez has explained in an interview, Soveida is shocked by Hector: "in a way she understands too well what he means, but in a way she cannot understand what he means. The fact is that if one enjoys any kind of sexuality, intimacy, for women it is immediately put into a certain category and we have this myth to deal with and these lies, really, these lies that we have lived with for so long" ("Denise Chávez: Interview" 168). Within the novel, men like Hector brutalize women to mask their insecurities and make up for the abuses to which they themselves have been subjected. Even more so, men like Hector abuse women because of a fundamental misunderstanding of human nature: they are unable to get beyond the binary thinking that classifies women into two categories, Guadalupe or La Malinche, virgin or whore. Complex and thoughtful consideration of such issues can be extremely relevant and meaningful to contemporary college students.

Throughout *Face of an Angel*, Chávez contrasts spiritual and physical dimensions of life as she juxtaposes religious concepts with sexual scenes. Chávez shows that women as well as men can be angelic or demonic, sexual or asexual, demonstrating a broad range of human behavior. As for Hector, his fiancée gratifies his animal nature, but he is so constrained by selfish desires that he cannot venture beyond stereotypes. He marries the fiancée but secretly takes on another lover who also becomes pregnant. Given the hurt that Dosamantes men have caused their wives and children, it is unsurprising that her mother and grandmother express no dismay at the end of the novel when Soveida announces she is about to become a single parent. Her grandmother declares, "It shouldn't frighten you. And in a way, you're lucky. . . . Your mother and I didn't do so good, maybe you can do better" (450).

One of the many pleasures of the novel is that it presents serious subjects respectfully but also includes comedic elements in its transcendent vision. Soveida's encounter with the Holy Tortilla, for example, underscores with ironic tones the mystery of human existence with its puzzling blend of animal and spiritual natures. When Soveida visits a shrine where someone claims to have seen the face of Christ on a tortilla, she is surprised by the humility and modesty of what she finds:

> You could see the black gas-burner grill marks on the Tortilla, which formed the image of a face, and it was definitely someone male. But it was hard to say whether the face was Christ's or any other man's with a full beard. Never mind, to the owners of the Holy Tortilla, the Tortilla was a sacred sign of God's appearance on this earth, the mark of God's grace.
>
> But to the side of the supposed Christ image were human bite marks. Someone hungry and in a hurry had obviously chomped down on the Tortilla before it was observed to be holy. (428–29)

The Holy Tortilla episode, filled simultaneously with funny, serious, reverent, and irreverent details, shows how holy moments can intrude unexpectedly into the lives of humans, who may be slow to recognize the presence of the sacred as they engage fully in the physical side of life "with the gusto of those human teeth marks attempting to grab hold of the divine" (429). The sacred and the profane, the holy and the ordinary, and the spiritual and the material mix freely, naturally, and sometimes surprisingly in this exceptional and delightful novel.

Note

With permission from Palgrave Macmillan, the present essay develops ideas from the following work in order to suggest new ways in which *Face of an Angel* might be taught and studied: Mary Jane Hurst; "Contours of the Future in Denise Chávez's *Face of an Angel* and Rudolfo Anaya's *Alburquerque*"; *Language, Gender, and Community in Late Twentieth-Century Fiction: American Voices and American Identities*, by Hurst, Palgrave Macmillan, 2011, pp. 139–70.

Appendix: Suggested Reading

Anaya, Rudolfo. *Bless Me, Ultima.* Quinto Sol Publications, 1972.

———. "'I'm the King': The Macho Image." *Muy Macho: Latino Men Confront Their Manhood*, edited by Ray González, Anchor Books, 1996, pp. 57–74.

Eysturoy, Annie O. *Daughters of Self-Creation: The Contemporary Chicana Novel.* U of New Mexico P, 1996.

Heredia, Juanita. *Transnational Latina Narratives in the Twenty-First Century: The Politics of Gender, Race, and Migrations.* Palgrave Macmillan, 2009.

Kessler, Elizabeth Ann Rodriguez. *Language, Nature, Gender, and Sexuality: Theoretical Approaches to Chicana and Chicano Literature.* 1998. U of Houston, PhD dissertation.

Madsen, Deborah L. *Understanding Contemporary Chicana Literature.* U of South Carolina P, 2000.
Naranjo-Huebl, Linda. "Faith, Hope and Service in Denise Chávez's *Face of an Angel.*" *Rocky Mountain Review*, vol. 61, no. 1, 2007, pp. 51–72.
Richter, Francine K. Ramsey. "Romantic Women and *La Lucha*: Denise Chávez's *Face of an Angel.*" *Great Plains Quarterly*, vol. 19, no. 4, 1999, pp. 277–89.
Saldívar-Hull, Sonia. *Feminism on the Border: Chicana Gender Politics and Literature.* U of California P, 2000.
Socolovsky, Maya. "Narrative and Traumatic Memory in Denise Chávez's *Face of an Angel.*" *MELUS*, vol. 28, no. 4, 2003, pp. 187–205.
———. *Troubling Nationhood in U.S. Latina Literature: Explorations of Place and Belonging.* Rutgers UP, 2013.
Yarbro-Bjarano, Yvonne. "Chicana Literature from a Chicana Feminist Perspective." *Feminisms*, edited by Robyn R. Warhol and Diane Price Herndl, Rutgers UP, 1991, pp. 732–37.

Works Cited

Anaya, Rudolfo. "Rudolfo Anaya." Interview conducted by Feroza Jussawalla. *Interviews with Writers of the Post-colonial World*, edited by Jussawalla and Reed Way Dasenbrock, UP of Mississippi, 1992, pp. 243–55.
Chávez, Denise. "Denise Chávez: Chicana Woman Writer Crossing Borders—an Interview." Conducted by Elizabeth Brown-Guillory. *South Central Review*, vol. 16, no. 1, 1999, pp. 30–43.
———. "Denise Chávez: Interview by Annie O. Eysturoy." *This Is about Vision: Interviews with Southwestern Writers*, edited by William Balassi et al., U of New Mexico P, 1990, pp. 157–72.
———. *Face of an Angel.* Warner Books, 1994.
———. *The Last of the Menu Girls.* Arte Publico Press, 1986.
Dasenbrock, Reed Way. "Forms of Biculturalism in Southwestern Literature: The Work of Rudolfo Anaya and Leslie Marmon Silko." *Southwestern Literature*, vol. 21, no. 3, 1988, pp. 307–19.
Fitzgerald, F. Scott. *The Great Gatsby.* Scribner's, 1925.
González, María C. *Contemporary Mexican-American Women Novelists: Toward a Feminist Identity.* Peter Lang, 1996.
Hurst, Mary Jane. "Transcendence and Mythic Vision in Leo Tolstoy's *Resurrection* and Denise Chávez's *Face of an Angel.*" *CCTE Studies*, vol. 77, 2012, pp. 29–37.
Sánchez, Marta E. "La Malinche at the Intersection: Race and Gender in *Down These Mean Streets.*" *PMLA*, vol. 113, no. 1, 1998, pp. 117–28.

Laura P. Alonso-Gallo

Deconstructing Mexican Masculinity in Denise Chávez's *Loving Pedro Infante*

A first reading of Denise Chávez's novel *Loving Pedro Infante* may lead readers to see it as a bildungsroman that takes the main character from an unhappy romantic relationship with a married man to a mature realization of her gender and ethnic identity. Alert readers, however, can discern a satire of the celebrated Mexican icon Pedro Infante and his melodramatic movies of the 1930s through the 1950s. Juanita Heredia argues that "the reception of Pedro Infante's films by spectators bridges generations and national spaces and leads to the formation of a transnational border feminism by the female protagonist" (40). The protagonist, Tere Avila, is a border-town girl who grows up obsessed with Infante's filmography. She conducts her life like that of the films' female characters and as a result, to find fulfillment, seeks a man who embodies Infante's ideal masculinity. The novel examines and then scorns Mexican paradigms of masculinity and femininity and the rigid Catholic moral and social codes evident in the films. To uncover such paradigms and codes, readers have to focus on the protagonist's desire to love and be loved, which is negotiated in both the social space of her hometown, Cabritoville, and the physical space of her body in its sexual and alimentary capacities.

The young, working-class Tere tells her first-person story in a free-spirited and fresh voice, revealing the deceitful mentality in which she—and other women before her—have been raised. Readers experience firsthand her passionate character and her plight in a world of forsaken and abused women, where society diminishes female worth and roles. Such is "the problem with most women," her friend Irma says regarding Catholic and patriarchal mores: "We're still playing out our parents' melodramas, our ancestors' locura ["madness"]. We're stuck either on the altar or in the gutter" (Chávez, *Loving* 230). A key issue in this novel is whether Catholic precepts have forged the *machista* ("male chauvinist") qualities of the Mexican character and shaped Mexican (and Chicano) cultural identity. The novel's melodramatic format provides a map to Chávez's parody of this cinematographic genre and finds its objective in questioning and exaggerating society's roles for women, based on the moral message of Infante's films. In an interview, Chávez spoke of her novel as an "obsessive love story . . . sad and crazy sometimes, like a telenovela" (Ikas 60). By narrating a love story from the framework of melodrama, a genre that evolved into the contemporary telenovela,[1] Chávez is able to challenge the genre's premise and replace its formulaic happy ending with an alternative, more realistic ending where the protagonist is not "saved" by the man through marriage.

This essay gives instructors a step-by-step guide to discussion of the novel's interwoven issues, from the Mexican masculine cultural model to the value of female identity in Mexican culture (and Mexican American or Chicano experience), and the influence of Catholicism on Mexican and Chicano gender relations and identity. I teach this novel to English majors in undergraduate courses in Latino/a literature that usually focus on national and cultural traditions. *Loving Pedro Infante* is an ideal text because it invites readers to explore Mexican historical, social, and cultural contexts and is an enjoyable read. But students require guidance from the instructor to fully understand its engagement of perceived Mexican and Chicano identity.

To begin, I have students write a synopsis of the novel, summarizing the story and highlighting crucial actions. Tere's story appears simple, embedded in a melodramatic plot: she is a young, divorced Chicana with no children, who falls in love with Lucio Valadez, a married man with a nine-year-old daughter. Their border community in New Mexico, Cabritoville, has a mixed population of Mexicans, Chicanos, and Anglo Americans. Tere is a teacher's aide at a local school and serves as secretary for the Pedro Infante Fan Club #256. All the members are women except for Ubaldo, a young, homosexual Chicano who shares a fervor for the Mexican actor with the sixteen women. Tere's expectations are grounded in melodrama: Tere seeks to be rescued by Pedro Infante, personified by Lucio. During the course of the romantic relationship, however, she gradually becomes disappointed in herself and with her community and breaks from the deceptive mentality. Given Chávez's use of parody to criticize life as a melodrama or telenovela, and the use of satire to condemn societal standards, it is important for students to discern the rhetorical value of Chávez's narrative and discursive strategies.

To help students identify the differences between parody and satire, I provide examples from classical literature: for example, Miguel de Cervantes's *Don Quixote*, a burlesque work where the hero is a tragic idealist. Just as students can understand how Don Quixote challenges the traditional worldview with an alternative vision, they can begin to detect how in Chávez's novel the image of Pedro Infante challenges the view that men are superior to women, that women should feel powerless and be reified as possessions, that romantic love is a conquering act, and that male supremacy comes through physical violence. Once students grasp the value of the parody, they are ready to enjoy the intellectual pleasure of reading the text. Just as Cervantes satirizes vices and societal customs through humor and is careful not to reveal hostility toward or disapproval of those behaviors, Chávez's novel parodies the iconic Infante figure in its discussion of women's identity.

Pedro Infante as a Model of Masculinity

Since the novel opens with Tere watching the classic film *La vida no vale nada* (*Life Is Worth Nothing*), I ask students to do research about the structure, elements, and dramatic value of this film for class discussion. They learn that the melodrama genre stresses the exaggeration of emotions, and sentiments associated with women's desires, that the target audience is female, that the moral message is that women should accept submission to men (as opposed to independence) and value virtue (as opposed to open sexuality), and finally, that men are the agents of power while women are victims and dependents.

When Tere is watching *La vida no vale nada* at El Colón Theater with her friends, she identifies the actor as a role model and object of desire:

"Pedro Infante could have been my father. . . . He is the man we want our men to be. And he's the man we imagine ourselves to be if we are men. The man we want our daughters to have loved" (Chávez, *Loving* 9). In that scene Tere introduces readers to a female audience that worships and is infatuated with Infante. The scene, which takes place two years after Infante's death, illustrates a cultural ideal of masculinity embodied by the actor-singer. If there is time, I screen the film in its entirety in class, as it lends well to discussion focused around the following questions: What is the central topic of the film? Is it romantic love? Is it romantic love between two people of antagonistic social classes? What is the purpose of humor in the film? How does the film's story line adapt the structure (setup, confrontation, and resolution) of melodramas and telenovelas? What is more dramatic, the facts or the feelings and emotions? Does the film have a happy or tragic ending? What message does the ending convey?

I have students do research online to find articles that describe Pedro Infante, and to draw a contrast between descriptions of his personality and his conduct in the film. During discussions we define the masculinity he evokes. For example, Tere pronounces him "Confident. Without fear. Puro chingón" (42),[2] which suggests his assertiveness, courage, and skill as an actor and as a musician. The articles students find often describe the actor as the prototypical Mexican macho: womanizer, romantic, seducer, good son and friend, party lover, and a man of many passions.[3] Much like Elvis Presley and Frank Sinatra, Infante played the same personality in all his films.[4]

Once we turn to *Loving Pedro Infante*, I ask students to look for references in the text that identify Infante as the ideal man. The character of Lucio is explanatory, for he personifies the actor not only in behavior and looks but also in his loose morals. Many other references are to be found in Tere's inner monologue and conversations with her friends, such as her weekly "Pedro-athons" with Irma (Chávez 115). During these film and collaborative cooking festivities, the two women highlight an ideal of masculinity and, by evoking their desire, attempt to liberate themselves from the parochial mentality of their community and the suffocating social space of Cabritoville, where racism and homophobia are rampant: "Black, gay, it's all the same thing [to them]. A sin against God, nature and Pedro Infante" (141).[5] Sharp readers will grasp the irony of these sacrilegious rituals: while the two friends declare themselves liberated from the social and moral dictates of their town, a place "twenty years behind the times" (26), governed by the youngsters' loose morals and the elderly's hypocrisy, they submit nonetheless to an archaic ideal of masculinity.

Femininity, Catholic Values, and Ethnic Purity

Tere's femininity is modeled after the behavior and desires of the Mexican divas in Infante's melodramas, at three levels: physical (pretty looks and sensuality), moral (discretion, submission, and maternal virtue), and ethnic or national (Mexican identity as pure, in contrast to Mexican American and Chicano identities). Thus Chávez satirizes the rigid moral codes that Infante's films present to Mexican (and Chicano) peoples. Readers understand through Tere's story that Catholic patriarchal ideology subjugates women and compromises their identity. This candid but sacrilegious statement by Tere corroborates the parody: "Pedro's right up there with Jesucristo and la Virgen de Guadalupe. Just thinking about both Pedro and Christ being carpenters makes me feel holy" (Chávez, *Loving* 121).

Chávez draws a subtle parallel between Tere and her namesake, Saint Teresa of Ávila, a prominent mystic writer of sixteenth-century Spain, who comes into play as another role model in the novel. Although seemingly anecdotal, such a connection actually carries significant weight in the story, and to appreciate it, instructors can provide students with background on traditional Mexican education. From colonial times to the mid–twentieth century, the study of the lives of the Catholic saints constituted a basis for moral education, especially for women.[6] Tere's inner discourse reveals that she aspires to be pure, strong, and a model of saintly behavior, just like Saint Teresa: "I'm always carrying on this dialogue inside my head. I talk to a Tere of Avila who isn't gastada, apagada y jodida ["worn out, turned off, and messed up"]" (11). Tere understands her Chicana identity and the sociocultural milieu of her environment to be key reasons for her misery: "What I haven't told you is *why* I hooked up with Lucio. I could give you the short answer, that I was jodida by birth, but that's too simple. The long answer has to do with who I am, and where I live" (46).

At this point, it helps to ask students to take on another research exercise, that of identifying the historical role of Saint Teresa of Ávila; by seeking information on her background, social experience, and personal religious goals, they learn the history of a nun who defied the patriarchy of the Catholic Church. Teresa Sánchez de Cepeda y Ahumada, later Saint Teresa, was a writer of prose and poetry, a reformer, and a mystic. Born well-to-do, she disapproved of class privileges among the religious orders, which appeared even among the Carmelites, an order of mendicant nuns. Aristocratic families, who had direct influence over the orders, were permissive about how seriously their daughters took the core commitments of poverty, obedience, and chastity when they joined the Carmelites. Students will find connections between Tere's modern-day, multiethnic Cabritoville and Saint Teresa's city, Ávila, under the rule of King Charles V, in an era when three main ethnic and religious groups of Spaniards lived together: the Old Christians, the descendants of Arabs, and Jews who remained in Spain as Marranos and conversos. Furthermore, Saint Teresa defied the church's masculine world by creating an original method of prayer for women to achieve spiritual perfection, something that had previously been exclusive to men.[7]

Once students have grasped Saint Teresa's personal and historical value, I ask them to make connections to the novel by analyzing Tere's personality, mentality, and behavior. Is there a parallel between Tere and the saint of Ávila? Do they live in similar social spaces? How is Cabritoville similar to Ávila? What are the gender politics in the two communities? How are the two women similar, what is their relationship to men, and in what ways do they conform to social and moral standards or rebel from them? The novel's use of symbolism in the names of people and places calls for interpretation, as do biblical references in Tere's inner discourse. *Cabrito*, for example, may refer to a libidinous goat or an immoral man; the name Lucio could suggest Lucifer; and the women loyal to Tere are Nívea Esther and Albinita, whose names connote purity and strength.[8] Students will recognize connections and contrasts between Tere and her namesake in the areas of fasting and eating; writing, praying, and talking; and spiritual union and sexuality.

Food and Sex

As discussed above, by commending the archaic ideal of masculinity depicted in Pedro Infante's films, Tere denies her value as a late-twentieth-century Chicana. At the same time, food becomes a sign of cultural and ethnic identity in the novel. By despising the allegedly contaminated and mixed food that is cooked and consumed at local restaurants, and by praising Mexican food as pure, she rejects a *mestizaje* ("cultural mixing"). Students can be asked to identify any symbolism in the nun's fasting and Tere's eating habits, and any connections between Saint Teresa's desire for perfection and Tere's desire for happiness. They can be guided to identify an apparent dichotomy between, on the one hand, the nun's fasting and Tere's eating disorder, and on the other, the text's explicit food images and sexual metaphors.[9] Tere eats passionately, an act that represents, on the one hand, an appetite for life, including the desire for romantic love, but also hunger for ethnic understanding. Since her love life remains unfulfilled, her hunger is never satiated. Even her eventual heartbreak is expressed in food terms: "The cabrón ["jerk"] *chewed up* my soul and *spat it out like a piñón shell* and left my *tamale husk* of a spirit there in the parking lot of Cabritoville Elementary" (Chávez, *Loving* 190; emphases added).

Tere is aware that she has committed the sin of adultery, but her desire for love was stronger than her will to live by a moral principle. She knows that Saint Teresa's discipline in fasting, writing, praying, and remaining celibate led to her spiritual communication with her beloved, God. But Tere's goal for love and her impure sexual activity, like impure food, do not lead to fulfillment. So instead of the happy ending of a melodrama, Chávez's protagonist comes to realize that the ideal image and virility of a Pedro Infante figure only perpetuates sexist cultural values of patriarchy that subjugate women. She scorns both her lover and Pedro Infante's prototypical masculinity: "He had diabetes. His hair was thin on top—don't tell me you didn't notice he wore a tupé" (317). At the end she understands herself as a woman and as a Chicana.

Notes

1. Following the melodrama genre, telenovelas seek to cultivate oversentimental reactions. See Altman; Battistuzzi.

2. *Chingón* is a colloquial term understood in English as "kicks ass" and "fucking great." So "puro chingón" would mean "a real fucking kickass," "supreme badass," or "just wonderful." The verb *chingar*, on the other hand, means literally "to fornicate," and when it refers to such an action commited forcefully by a man, it can have a positive connotation in terms of his virility and macho qualities, but it also has a negative connotation.

3. References to Pedro Infante are frequent in Mexico, both in popular culture and in the media. In 2017, the hundredth anniversary of the actor-singer's birth, special conferences and events were held throughout Mexico, celebrating how his image shaped a Mexican national identity (comparable to the national identity established by figures like Frank Sinatra, Humphrey Bogart, Gary Cooper, and Elvis Presley in the United States). Students can search the Internet for this information. In the appendix I have provided several articles in Spanish and English for instructors and students.

4. See González Marín; Alfaro Gómez; de la Mora; and Monsiváis. González Marín sees the body of Infante as an object of desire not only for women but also for "un público masculino que oscilaba entre la fantasía erótica y la admiración" ("a male audience that fluctuated between erotic fantasy and admiration"; 13; my trans.). Infante's womanizing, drinking, and partying were justified as passionate manifestations of his character. Alfaro Gómez examines various critical

works on masculinities and the sociocultural role of men like Pedro Infante in nineteenth-and twentieth-century Mexico. De la Mora argues that Infante contributed to building and disseminating the macho as a national model of manhood. Monsiváis analyzes Infante as a charismatic Mexican icon who promoted positive traits, such as optimism, familial and romantic love, camaraderie, sensitivity to social injustice, and graciousness.

5. The "Pedro-athons" can be interpreted as rituals that parody the Catholic Eucharist and confession. See Alonso-Gallo 103–04.

6. Raised by a Catholic mother, Chávez attended a Catholic school in Las Cruces, New Mexico (Ikas 59). Traditionally, Catholic primary education uses biographical stories of saints to provide role models for girls and to reinforce Christian values. See Socolovsky; McCracken for critical analyses of memory, religion, and sexuality in *Face of an Angel.*

7. It is ironic that Saint Teresa, a descendent of Jewish converts who surmounted the limitations placed on women, became an ambassador of Spanish Catholic spirituality (see Bilinkoff; Du Boulay; and Weber). Tere will end up recognizing the patriarchal expectations for women when she finally rejects Pedro Infante's iconic masculinity and assumes her own agency.

8. For a thorough interpretation of religious allusions and symbols in the novel, see Alonso-Gallo 104, 107, 109.

9. For a discussion of food and sexual metaphors in the protagonist's discourse, see Alonso-Gallo 108–09.

Appendix: Suggested Reading

"After 100 Years, Mexican Idol Pedro Infante Remembered for His Modesty." *Latin American Herald Tribune*, 17 Nov. 2017, www.laht.com/article.asp?ArticleId=2446395&CategoryId=13003.

Morales, Vanessa. "Pedro Infante: Así fue el accidente que impidió que triunfara el amor." *Univision*, 14 Apr. 2017, www.univision.com/entretenimiento/pedro-infante-asi-fue-el-accidente-que-impidio-que-triunfara-el-amor.

"Pedro Infante: Macho, seductor y mal educador." *WikiMéxico*, Conaculta, www.wikimexico.com/articulo/pedro-infante-macho-seductor-y-mal-educador.

Porter, Tom. "Who Is Pedro Infante? Here's What You Need to Know about the Mexican Screen Icon Celebrated in a New Google Doodle." *Newsweek*, 18 Nov. 2017, www.newsweek.com/who-pedro-infante-heres-what-you-need-know-about-mexican-screen-icon-being-715945.

Posada, Jorge. " El mito de Pedro Infante continúa inagotable: La leyenda cumple cien años." *El Nuevo Herald*, 18 Nov. 2017, www.elnuevoherald.com/opinion-es/trasfondo/article185283953.html.

Tello, Judith Amador. "Analizan estereotipos masculinos del cine mexicano." *Proceso*, 23 July 2015, www.proceso.com.mx/411415/analizan-la-masculinidad-de-el-cine-de-oro.

Vancini, Betzabé. "Adiós Pedro Infante: La nueva construcción de la masculinidad en el hogar." *Periodico Central*, 5 Apr. 2017, periodicocentral.mx/2017/

columnistas/tu-yo-y-el-ello/item/5141-adios-pedro-infante-la-nueva-construccion-de-la-masculinidad-en-el-hogar#ixzz51xlENIZS.

Works Cited

Alfaro Gómez, Cecilia. "De machos, héroes, afeminados y otros tantos mexicanos: Estudio historiográfico sobre las masculinidades en los siglos xix y xx." *Graffylia*, no. 10, 2009, pp. 133–44.

Alonso-Gallo, Laura P. "Food, Consciousness, and Feminism in Denise Chávez's *Loving Pedro Infante*." *Rethinking Chicano/a Literature through Food: Postnational Appetites*, edited by Nieves Pascual Soler and Meredith E. Abarca, Palgrave Macmillan, 2013, pp. 97–115.

Altman, Rick. *Film/Genre*. British Film Institute, 1999.

Battistuzzi, Mariano. "La matriz narrativa del melodrama mudo." *Creación y Producción en Diseño y Comunicación*, no. 56, 2013, pp. 57–61.

Bilinkoff, Jodi. *The Avila of Saint Teresa: Religious Reform in a Sixteenth-Century City*. Cornell UP, 1989.

Chávez, Denise. *Face of an Angel*. Farrar, Straus and Giroux, 1994.

———. *Loving Pedro Infante*. Farrar, Straus and Giroux, 2001.

De la Mora, Sergio. *Cinemachismo: Masculinities and Sexuality in Mexican Film*. U of Texas P, 2006, pp. 1–20.

Du Boulay, Shirley. *Teresa of Avila: An Extraordinary Life*. Blue Bridge, 2004.

González Marín, Daniel. "¿Es que no sabes que eres un hombre? Star system y masculinidades en cinco actores del cine mexicano." *Miradas al cine mexicano*, edited by Aurelio de los Reyes García Rojas, vol. 1, IMCINE, 2016, pp. 1–45.

Heredia, Juanita. "From Golden Age Mexican Cinema to Transnational Border Feminism: The Community of Spectators in *Loving Pedro Infante*." *Aztlán: A Journal of Chicano Studies*, vol. 33, no. 2, 2008, pp. 37–59.

Ikas, Karin Rosa. "Chávez, Denise: Novelist, Playwright, and Actress." *Chicana Ways: Conversations with Ten Chicana Writers*, U of Nevada P, 2002, pp. 46–65.

McCracken, Ellen. "Voice and Vision in Chicana Religious Practice: The Literary Re-elaborations of Mary Helen Ponce, Denise Chávez and Sandra Cisneros." *Mexican American Religions: Spirituality, Activism, and Culture*, edited by Gastón Espinosa and Mario T. García, Duke UP, 2008, pp. 242–60.

Monsiváis, Carlos. *Pedro Infante: Las leyes del querer*. Santillana Ediciones Generales / Ediciones Raya en el Agua, 2008.

Socolovsky, Maya. "Narrative and Traumatic Memory in Denise Chávez's *Face of an Angel*." *MELUS*, vol. 28, no. 4, 2003, pp. 187–205.

La vida no vale nada. 1955. Directed by Rogelio A. González, performances by Pedro Infante and Rosario Granados, Cozumel, 2003. DVD.

Weber, Alison. *Teresa of Avila and the Rhetoric of Femininity*. Princeton UP, 1990.

Margaret Cantú-Sánchez

Norma Elia Cantú's *Canícula* and Gloria Anzaldúa's *Borderlands / La frontera* in a Multiethnic Literature Classroom

Norma Elia Cantú's *Canícula: Snapshots of a Girlhood en la Frontera* is an innovative text that rejects the traditional formatting and modes of literary novels by intermixing pictures and short vignettes. At times the stories seem to describe the images being conveyed, while at other points readers must call upon their imagination, active reading skills, and experience to fill in the gaps of imagery. Cantú herself points out the discrepancy between the images and the text, calling her work "fictional autoethnobiography," a blend of fiction, autobiography, and ethnography with a heavy emphasis on the themes of memory, border crossing, and identity politics (Cantú xi).

Similarly, Gloria Anzaldúa's landmark critical and creative text *Borderlands / La frontera* explores what it means to exist in the Rio Grande Valley region in southeast Texas near the Mexican border. Like Cantú, Anzaldúa resists traditional literary structure in favor of blending history, fiction, autobiography, creative writing, and philosophy to examine Mexican American identity. The use of *Canícula* in conjunction with *Borderlands* in an undergraduate class with a multiethnic group of students allows for a thorough exploration of identity using a pedagogy that I refer to as a *mestizaje* of epistemologies—a blending of cultural and formal, institutional education ideologies.

My pedagogical orientation emerges from my understanding of both Laura Rendón's sentipensante (or "sensing-thinking") pedagogy and Anzaldúa and Cherríe Moraga's foundational theory in the flesh: "[a] theory in the flesh means one where the physical realities of our lives—our skin color, the land or concrete where we grew up on, our sexual longings—all fuse to create a politic born out of necessity" (Anzaldúa, "Entering" 23). While these texts and this approach are often used in graduate-level courses, I find that they are adaptable to a multiethnic literature class for lower-level undergraduate students (or students in a community college). Use of a pedagogy based on a theory in the flesh helps students contemplate the impact of writings by Chicanas, which can lead to an evaluation of their own identities that entails calling upon their lived experiences and prior knowledge. In a similar fashion, Rendón's sentipensante pedagogy merges both sensing and thinking, asking "instructors to work with individuals as whole human beings—intellectual, social, emotional, and spiritual" (135). This pedagogical strategy encourages students to write and relay their own stories or engage in activities that ask them to think critically about their own identity politics.

From a theory in the flesh and sentipensante pedagogy emerges a *mestizaje* of epistemologies, where I, as the instructor, ask students to critically examine how identity comes about through the exploration of the institutional knowledge found in schools in the United States and the cultural knowledge found in students' homes and communities. This pedagogy emerges especially through students' exposure to texts like *Canícula* and *Borderlands*, where they encounter protagonists who experience a conflict of identity directly related to their residing in the Texas-Mexico borderlands. In addition to reading these texts, students are directly asked to contemplate this idea of identity conflict by engaging in critical freewriting about examples in their own lives and in society, history, and mainstream media. Students then share their examples with one another during a pair-share activity. Students also begin to make these connections through online journaling on *Blackboard*, where they are asked to respond to the readings by sharing their own personal experiences, anecdotes, and cultural knowledge. Some give examples from their lives of having to adapt to the English language at school while retaining their native Spanish in the home environment because that is the only language their parents know.

Before discussing *Canícula* and *Borderlands*, I give a brief introduction to Mexican American history and literary studies. To help students understand this notion of Mexican American history and identity, I go back to the inception of such concepts beginning with the Mexican-American War and the Treaty of Guadalupe Hidalgo that emerged from it. The ending of that war is especially significant because of the compromise made regarding the ownership of some of the southwestern states, including Texas. The annexation of Texas by the United States signaled a great shift in culture and identity for Mexicans already residing there; suddenly they became Americans, in name if nothing else. Thus, the emergence of Mexican American identity starts. The treaty attempted to assure that Mexican residents would retain their lands and language and be treated equally with Anglo Americans, but history reveals that this is not what happened. Students are shown a map of Texas, with a focus on Laredo and Nuevo Laredo, which reveals the proximity of the two cities and demonstrates how the border that resulted from the Treaty of Guadalupe Hidalgo ultimately separated families like Cantu's and others who were already residing in those areas, and therefore why this idea of being Mexican never went away.

To further aid in the examination of *Canícula* and *Borderlands*, students are briefed regarding some of the overriding themes in these texts, which include the blurring of borders and nonlinear structures, the sharing of family and cultural history, and the blurring of Mexican and American identities. Students are instructed to look out for these themes while contemplating the importance of the lack of simple genre identification, keeping in mind how these themes add to our understanding of Mexican American identity. Students are also asked to keep notes while reading, on points of the story that resonate, confuse, or connect to any historical context, personal stories, or current events. In addition, as students continue to read, they are asked to reflect in an online journal upon certain themes, concepts, stories, or confusing points, which allows for further discussion to occur between them.

Having read the first few vignettes of Cantú's text, students engage in a freewrite about their initial reactions to the text. Discussions of these freewrites take place in pairs and then with the larger class. Most students initially find the structure of the book confusing since the opening photographs often do not correspond with the text, and the vignettes often switch between past and present. These discrepancies in structure allow for critical awareness of traditional versus nontraditional linear formats.

Upon further exploration of Cantú's text, students at times respond to its blurring of fact and fiction by explaining that they are not sure what to trust. Despite these initial reactions to *Canícula*, students begin to inquire critically, using such labels as autobiography and fictional autobiography to discuss the blurring of boundaries, borders, and identities that occur in the real world. Working through points gleaned from the critical article by Timothy Dow Adams on this text, students begin to understand that all writing is "to a degree autobiographical *and* fictional" (57). We explore these ideas with exercises about the act of remembering. Students are asked to reflect upon the process of recalling certain momentous events from their lives. Examination of the process of remembering often reveals diluted, blurred, and even exaggerated impressions that can be interpreted as fictionalized. Memory is based on fact, but the act of remembering forces our minds to fictionalize some elements of our memories. But does this mean that our memories are not valid?

Discussion can then turn to the photographs that open each vignette. While photographs can appear to offer factual representations of reality, students begin to see that Cantu's use of these images in conjunction with vignettes offers an alternative understanding of fact versus fiction. At times the images being described do not match the details in the story. For example, in "Bueli" the narrator mentions four people even though only three are pictured: "In the photo, Bueli sits in her high-back rocking chair, her sillón where she'd rocked all of us to sleep, surrounded by Tino, Dahlia, Esperanza, and me . . ." (24). Some students remark that these details may be an attempt to confuse the reader, while others note that sometimes our memories do not coincide with the images or stories we tell. To emphasize this point, I ask students to look for an image on their phone. Using that image, they must write down the story behind it. After taking time to write, students work in pairs to examine this idea of remembering versus the images presented on their phones. Many soon note that the details in their stories do not match up with the images depicted, revealing the complexity of remembering, storytelling, and pictures. Adams points out that the use of images in an autobiography implies accuracy of fact, when really images blur the boundaries between nonfiction and fiction. More importantly, *Canícula* "also asks its readers to continue to consider those categories," which are reflective of the "complexities and ambiguities of life on the border" (70).

Cantú demonstrates how, like the blurring of fact and fiction that occurs with the use of images and words, blurring also occurs when it comes to identities on the borderlands. This is especially exemplified in the vignette "Mexican Citizen," whose accompanying images are identification cards for immigrants to the United States, from the narrator's childhood and adolescence. The tape over the signature and the description of the narrator's skin tone as "blanco" ("white") on one document and "moreno" ("brown") on the other reflects the narrator's ability to transition smoothly to the various countries associated with each color: "In short, she's considered white for purposes of entering the United States but brown for entering Mexico" (Adams 62). What we see then is the idea of identity as fluid, the blurring of which makes it possible for immigrants to live in two worlds. The evidence of this blurring allows students to further contemplate their own identities and how they may or may not be subject to similar influences depending on where they live, who they interact with, how they have been educated, what memories they have, and so on.

Students, regardless of gender, respond well to Cantú's reflections on what it means to be a Mexican American woman. Although part of a younger generation, they indicate relating to the feelings expressed by Cantú regarding the awkwardness that adolescence brings, as well as the disconnect between Anglo and Mexicana approaches to beauty and hygiene. In "Body Hair," Cantú explains that she was made fun of because "we [Chicanas] don't yet shave, much less pluck our eyebrows, or wear makeup—our parents forbid it" (61). Students discuss how customs in different cultures or households can at times cause feelings of rejection or shame, affecting one's sense of identity.

After reading Cantú's book, we begin Anzaldúa's *Borderlands* and continue exploring notions of fluid identity. Here our class discussion commences with background information on the author and my presentation on some of the book's major themes. We consider Anzaldúa's working-class background; her positionality as a woman in a predominantly male-oriented culture, both in the United States and in Mexico; and her experience in the borderlands of the Rio Grande Valley in Texas. Once again, students encounter a work that consists of a nontraditional blurring of genres, in this case fiction, poetry, memoir, history, and literary and cultural criticism. Anzaldúa also uses many languages in the book, including English, Spanish, Spanglish, and Nahuatl.

Students provide their first impressions of the text by journaling on *Blackboard* and by completing an in-class freewrite. Reactions have ranged from slight confusion to shock, disbelief, and anger. Interestingly, most students' reactions are not so much to how the content is presented; rather, they are surprised to learn about certain historical events described by Anzaldúa in her narrative, stating that such information has been left out of their classes on history in the United States. For example, Anzaldúa refers to the harsh impact of the Treaty of Guadalupe Hidalgo, which left "Mexican citizens on this side, annexed by conquest along with the land. The land established by the treaty as belonging to Mexicans was soon swindled away from its owners. The treaty was never honored and restitution to this day, has never been made" (29). Students directly respond to such information through journaling, freewrites, class discussions, and the sharing of similar family stories of land being stolen, accounts of personal discrimination and prejudice in school, and an awareness of belonging and not belonging to the United States.

Female students, especially those who claim Mexican American backgrounds, may relate to the description by Anzaldúa of how women are silenced or kept from opportunities in her cultural community. Explaining that for her there were not many choices when it came to choosing her future, Anzaldúa says, "[T]here used to be only three directions she could turn: to the Church as a nun, to the streets as a prostitute, or to the home as a mother" (39). Female students often find themselves sharing similar stories of being scolded by their fathers, grandfathers, and other relatives for making plans for their future.

Since I teach at St. Mary's University in San Antonio, a Hispanic-serving institution in which more than fifty percent of the students identify as Hispanic—and most of those are from Anzaldúa's borderlands, the Rio Grande Valley—this text often hits home both geographically and culturally. The course, however, is a core curriculum literature requirement on multiethnic literature, which all students must take, no matter their major. In our discussions, anger ensues because students feel that parts of their cultural history have been purposefully omitted from their schooling. In contrast to students who identify culturally with Anzaldúa, those of non-Latino/a background are often in agreement and accepting of their peers' observations, though some admit to being unable to relate to or fully understand the anger and discrimination Anzaldúa speaks of.

Another element that garners attention from students is the code-switching that Anzaldúa periodically uses. About half the class responds favorably to the use of Spanish and English because they are bilingual, but the others express the frustration of not knowing Spanish. And yet all respond well to the section "How to Tame a Wild Tongue" after I ask students to consider whether they have encountered moments in their lives when they have been silenced by others. Many students identify with being silenced because of racism, sexism, and internalized racism. Specifically, students are asked to pair up to answer the questions of who has been silenced and who does the silencing throughout history and in the present day, while also coming up with solutions to combat such acts of silencing. Students indicate that various minority groups like Native Americans, immigrants, and women have been and continue to be silenced. Solutions they pose include educating others about various cultures, groups, and communities through literature and history.

The "linguistic terrorism" discussed by Anzaldúa is another topic that opens discussion among Chicano students whose speech traverses borders (38). Criticism of both Mexican and American culture allows for further discussion of identity especially regarding language: "if you want to really hurt me, talk badly about my language. Ethnic identity is twin skin to linguistic identity—I am my language. Until I can take pride in my language, I cannot take pride in myself" (81). Students are asked to respond to this quote, arguing whether they agree with the idea that language is identity and vice versa. Often, they notice this blurring of boundaries, this border crossing as it pertains to language and identity. Many take note that writing and language allow them the ability to communicate, express themselves, and share experiences with each other.

The emphasis on this shifting between borders is further asserted in Anzaldúa's chapter "The Path of the Red and Black Ink," which focuses on writing as a means to reach what she deems mestiza consciousness or a specific awareness of identity. The focus on awareness as it pertains to identity and writing calls to mind Anzaldúa and Moraga's theory in the flesh and more specifically my use of a *mestizaje* of epistemologies, because through writing—specifically writing that addresses the question "What is my culture?"—students contemplate awareness of their identity politics and question how that politics has been formed or is being formed by society. Students respond to questions of what their cultural identities are, how they are constructed, and by whom before we begin the course material and again at the end of the course, after we have gone through the various readings, which directly address such questions of identity.

Anzaldúa further points out that "writing produces anxiety. Looking inside myself and my experience, looking at my conflicts, engenders anxiety in me" (94), and this is true for students as well, since they find it difficult to acknowledge or place themselves within their writing, to admit that what they know is valid and important, especially in an English course.

In this same section on writing, Anzaldúa emphasizes the importance of art as another method to process awareness; she explains: "my people, the Indians, did not split the artistic from the functional, the sacred from the secular, art from everyday life" (88). With this in mind, students are asked to contemplate their notion of identity by doing a creative identity presentation in which they discuss who they are through a creative medium such as painting, sculpture, dance, or writing.

The culmination of this course, with a focus on multiethnic literature and a particular emphasis on identity, really comes together through the creative identity presentation. Students are asked to reflect upon the texts we have read thus far, while contemplating the various themes that have arisen in *Canícula* and *Borderlands*, and to question, deconstruct, and reconstruct their own identity. The result is often a myriad of unique presentations ranging from interpretive film representations of identity questioning, to collages of family photographs, interviews with family members, and even historical explorations of cultural backgrounds.

A course in multiethnic literature is a strategic space in which to bring these two books—and writing by contemporary Chicanas—into focus. The innovative structure and creative autobiographical nature of *Canícula* and the critical and creative nature of *Borderlands* provide excellent terrain for a basic discussion of literary form connected to Latina identity in an undergraduate course. While young adult students can examine the nature of critical discussion by Chicana writers from the borderlands in order to then explore their own identity and that of their family members and community, the writing exercises help them recognize their own balance of sources of knowledge.

Works Cited

Adams, Timothy Dow. "'Heightened by Life' vs. 'Paralyzed by Fact': Photography and Autobiography in Norma Cantú's *Canícula*." *Biography*, vol. 24, no. 1, Winter 2001, pp. 57–71.

Anzaldúa, Gloria. *Borderlands / La frontera: The New Mestiza*. Spinsters / Aunt Lute, 1987.

———. "Entering the Lives of Others: Theory in the Flesh." *This Bridge Called My Back: Writings by Radical Women of Color*, edited by Cherríe Moraga and Anzaldúa, 2nd ed., Kitchen Table Press, 1983, pp. 21–22.

Cantú, Norma E. *Canícula: Snapshots from a Girlhood en la Frontera*. U of New Mexico P, 1995.

Rendón, Laura. *Sentipensante (Sensing/Thinking) Pedagogy: Educating for Wholeness, Social Justice, and Liberation*. Stylus Publishing, 2008.

Carol E. Pearson

The Personal and the Historical in Lucha Corpi's Detective Novels

The literary works by Mexicana and Chicana authors that emerged in the 1980s and 1990s, which reveal those authors claiming public voices and agency, have many layers and intersections that can inspire a variety of paths and techniques for teaching them. As Susan Baker Sotelo affirms, "Chicano detective fiction is a particularly suitable subject matter for the secondary and undergraduate student of literature and cultural diversity" (1–2). Lucha Corpi is an excellent example for her detective fiction and for her participation in the Chicano Movement in the late 1960s in the California Bay Area and on the campus of the University of California, Berkeley (Brinson Curiel).

Born in Veracruz, Mexico, in 1945, Corpi arrived in California at age nineteen during an era of international student movements. The series of detective novels she would later publish (*Eulogy for a Brown Angel*, *Cactus Blood*, *Black Widow's Wardrobe*, and *Crimson Moon*) includes previously unrecounted threads of Chicano and Mexican experiences through the point of view of detective-protagonists Gloria Damasco and Dora Saldaña. Published in the 1990s, these novels illustrate a key discourse of the Chicano Movement and signature aspects of Mexican and Mexican American history. This essay illustrates a multicultural approach to teaching these works in an upper-division undergraduate topics class in Chicano literature. Multicultural pedagogy instills a process of dialogue in cultural analysis, in which students have more responsibility for their own learning and for recognizing, as Laurie Grobman states, "that knowledge is socially constructed. Decentered methodology compels us to be creative in finding ways for students to obtain knowledge of cultural and literary traditions without simply lecturing at them, perhaps through individual or collaborative student class presentations, a wide range of secondary readings, or guest speakers" (227). As Grobman affirms, when we "bring students into the debates of multiculturalism," we are able to "teach them that multiple perspectives exist and [that such perspectives can] aid in broadening their visions" (237).

Since students in topics courses often have diverse levels of ability in Spanish, the class could be taught in both Spanish and English. The choice of language, whether by the writers themselves or by the professor and the students, constitutes a topic of discussion in itself (Rebolledo 171; Anzaldúa 75–86). Depending on its demographics, such a class might have differing mixes of second language learners and heritage language learners. Thus, the dynamics of language use as introduced and profiled by Chicana authors become an important theme in such a classroom.

A central question for instructors can be, What themes are important for students to examine in a class of this type, especially before they study Lucha Corpi's work? At the beginning students can be assigned selections from *The House on Mango Street*, by Sandra Cisneros, including particularly the sections "Hairs" (7), "My Name" (11), and "A House of My Own" (132), which address issues of identity and agency. After reading, students can form small groups and work to brainstorm and extract possible themes and questions. Keeping notes from this group work, they can report to the class in a larger discussion that facilitates greater understanding. Readings from Chicana cultural criticism can then be assigned and, again, discussed in small groups, followed by full class discussion. I like to assign the preface (ix–xi), introduction (1–9), and first chapter (11–28) from Tey Diana Rebolledo's *Women Singing in the Snow*, an engaging and insightful overview of Chicana authors and themes. Rebolledo describes the many struggles evidenced in Chicana work, including those in support of the Chicano Movement, where Chicanas were relegated to the sidelines and struggled to find voice and agency outside the enclosed sphere of the home. Their act of writing becomes a form of resistance that includes cultural experience, community, and self-agency (all identifiable in

Cisneros's and Corpi's novels). Moreover, a strong oral tradition exists in Chicano culture that constructs and preserves communal history, and in which women have been active participants (Rebolledo 6, 7, 117–30). By seizing and subverting language, Corpi's works profile many of these traits and construct varied possibilities for Chicana subjects and portrayals through the following themes: resistance through the construction of a Chicana private-eye figure; the importance of dreams, visions, and memory; the importance of solidarity with the movement and partnerships with men; tensions between the need for solidarity with the movement and the right of individuals to participate; and the inscription of Chicano history.

Other assigned readings can include women's voices, such as that of Apolinaria Lorenzana, discussed in the accounts of the journal *Crítica* (Lorenzana), women characters in Rolando Hinojosa's novel *El condado de Belken: Klail City* (*Belken County: Klail City*) and Tomás Rivera's novel . . . *Y no se lo tragó la tierra / And the Earth Did Not Part*, and themes in the poetry in Margarita Cota-Cárdenas's *Marchitas de Mayo*, each providing contrast and comparisons for the themes in Corpi's novels. After earlier readings, students are ready to embark on independent analysis; each student will choose a theme to explore in the process of reading *Crimson Moon*. After a first reading the novel is discussed in class, then a second reading can be pursued, with guidance, to find examples of selected themes.

The unit on Lucha Corpi and her novel *Crimson Moon* is a three-week sequence for my class (with reading done outside of class). Reading comprehension quizzes are posted on *Blackboard*, one for every five chapters, and they are due the day before class discussion. During weeks 1 and 2, students work in small groups (grouped by choice of theme), report on discussions to the class, and seek examples to illustrate (or counter and question) their themes found in *Crimson Moon*. The instructor rotates through the small groups to guide the discussions and answer questions.

During the second week, students work individually to write a five-page paper analyzing *Crimson Moon* through their chosen theme and citing other readings from the course. Rather than being based on research outside of course readings, this paper is based on discussions and analysis conducted throughout the course. The rough draft of the paper is due at the end of the second week of the unit. Week 3 begins an academic-style miniconference, in which students present five- to ten-minute versions of their papers in panels grouped by theme and answer questions at the end of the panel's presentations. This allows students to present a polished version of their thoughts. Since the sources are the course materials, the presentations serve as both a review and a reflection on the issues raised by *Crimson Moon*. Using Rebolledo's critical assessment as a framework, students can embark on critical analysis by seeking connections to other novels and poetry from the class, to the readings about Chicano culture, and to their own experiences. The following discussion provides some examples of themes, sociohistorical context, testimony, struggles for survival, and instances of agency and subjectivity in the novel *Crimson Moon*.

A Subversive Protagonist

Students can begin by identifying the characteristics of the protagonist in *Crimson Moon*. To provide context, instructors can note that a Chicana private eye is a subversive figure (Rebolledo 5, 95–103, 116). Gloria Damasco, the protagonist of Corpi's first three detective novels, is bright, observant, logical, and incisive. She opposes anything "that might put into question a woman's intellectual ability" (*Eulogy* 48). Corpi's detective novels make allusions to the long tradition of detective literature and to the famous examples of Holmes and Watson, Poirot, and Marlowe. Traditional themes of murder, family intrigue, and danger are all present here, as in canonical detective novels (Pearson 42). Students, with guidance, can seek the ways in which Corpi's novels depart from the patterns of classic, male-authored detective stories and instead reproduce many of the characteristics of Chicana writing profiled in Rebolledo's critical analysis, including the presence of dreams, visions, and memories (4–9, 117–30).

Dreams, Visions, and Memories

Each novel in this series contains an important dream or vision. The instructor can help students identify the vision or memory that drives the plot of *Crimson Moon*: the rape of the writer and activist Ramona M. Serna by a notorious FBI agent and infiltrator, with the collusion of a second infiltrator, on the occasion of a Third World Liberation Front protest at Berkeley on 19 February 1969. This memory is part of Ramona's testimony, around which the plot turns. Elizabeth, Ramona's friend, has her own dark memories of that day (12–13). Elizabeth's account resonates with that of Ramona as told to another writer, Vincent. Students may point to Vincent's manuscript as a separate focal point of the novel; Vincent's sister Beatrice, who is the neighbor of Dora Saldaña (a private eye and associate of Gloria's), hires Dora to find her brother. Vincent's manuscript documents many of Ramona's memories—written in the first person—including the abuse by the FBI agent and infiltrator (67–68).

Students might point out that the rape of Ramona had lifelong consequences—and not just for Ramona. For one, she becomes pregnant; her baby is adopted by Elizabeth and becomes her eldest daughter, Irene. In addition, the FBI agent, Pretty Boy Patterson, raped at least three other Latina women, which had consequences on their lives, some of which are played out in the unraveling of the plot. One of those women, Felicia, is involved in the Crusade for Justice movement in Denver in the days of Corky Gonzales's leadership. Felicia's son (as a result of the rape) returns to Denver years later and becomes involved with Vincent and the subject of an investigation by Dora. Thus, memories and dreams are key elements in Corpi's writing;[1] through these personal memories, Corpi's characters bear witness to the events that have shaped and informed Chicano history.

Solidarity with Community, Partnership with Men

Students might choose to examine other key elements in Corpi's work: the sense of solidarity with the Chicano community and the vision of partnership with men in the Chicano Movement (Rebolledo 5, 71–72). Gloria and Dora become collaborators and business partners in their private detective company. Gloria also works with her lover and eventual business partner and husband, Justin Escobar, providing an example of respectful work with male characters. In *Crimson Moon*, the two principal protagonists are Dora and Justin (Gloria is absent from most of the book, as she is with her mother on a trip to Lake Tahoe). Dora and Justin each work on separate cases that in the end coalesce.

Students following this theme can be guided to see that many of the cases taken on by Gloria, Dora, and Justin reflect a sense of solidarity with their people. This attitude stands in contrast with that of traditional male detective characters, who tend to be cynical. Gloria reveals her emotions and reactions to the reader and is compelled by personal empathy for the victims to take cases. Dora practices self-examination: of the two women, she is perhaps closer to the traditional figure of a private eye: "No doubt about it, she was a loner. Maybe that was partly the reason she had chosen to become a private investigator" (*Crimson Moon* 5). And yet, she follows Gloria's pattern in taking a case because of her empathy for an acquaintance.

When Gloria asks why she took on Beatrice's case, Dora explains, "Beatrice reminds me so much of my mother" (10).

Individual versus Communal

Rebolledo describes the conflict felt by many Chicanas between their right to participate publicly in the movement and their profound identification with, and obligation to, their families and the private sphere (100; Pearson 44). Students tracing this theme can point out that in *Crimson Moon*, Ramona is affected by her mother's (and by extension society's) censure. Ramona knew her mother's disapproval was poisonous and battled against it all her life: from her friend Elizabeth's point of view, "Angelina 'Lena' Serna was a moral tyrant who saw her daughter's past and present life as nothing less than evil. . . . Ramona swore she did not care what her mother thought of her; as long as she had her writing, she could live with her mother's disapproval. But Lena's lack of love and support had always been at the center of Ramona's low self-esteem" (15).

Students might discover another interesting example of the struggle between the individual and the collective in a description of inner conflicts caused by the movement during the Third World Liberation Front student strike. Two fictional long-time activists and members of the arts community in Oakland, Art Bello and Myra Miranda, describe that struggle: "We spent so much time questioning each other's loyalty and ethnic credentials that we couldn't see the real enemy right under our noses" (20).

Inserting Cultural and Historical Context

Students interested in historical context can find examples in Corpi's work, since Corpi often inscribes elements of Chicano history by including many events that have been nearly forgotten. For example, *Eulogy* is set in 1970 on the day of the National Chicano Moratorium Committee march to Laguna Park in Los Angeles. *Cactus Blood* deals with a confrontation between United Farm Workers activists and local farmers in the late 1960s in California's San Joaquín Valley. *Black Widow's Wardrobe* highlights the Mexican archetypal figure of La Malinche (Pearson 44–45). And in *Crimson Moon*, students will be able to identify Corpi's inclusion of such events in Chicano history as Chicano student activism in Berkeley and Oakland, the Crusade for Justice protests in Denver, the current-day contexts of Chicano artists and writers, the Zapatista movement, and the plight of Latin

American immigrants (whether documented or not) in the United States. Rebolledo emphasizes the importance of "being a witness to the historical, social and cultural processes" that form the writer and notes that "[b]ecause the history of the Chicana experience in the United States defines our particular *mestizaje* of feminism, our theory cannot be a replicate of white feminism nor can it be only an academic abstraction. The Chicana feminist looks to her history . . . to learn how to transform the present" (x, 6). As an author, Corpi practices this belief in the importance of archiving history within her stories. As an example, students might point to statements about the Third World Liberation Front strike in Berkeley in 1969, in which Bello and Miranda ironically describe the value and the pain of memory:

> "You know, bro', we should really try to write about our experiences at Berkeley back then, before senility sets in." [. . .]
>
> "You do it. [. . .]" Art said, half in jest. "I don't think I can revisit Berkeley in the sixties yet. In the wake of the English Only and anti-Bilingual Ed initiatives and the end of affirmative action by the U. C. Regents, I'd be afraid to confirm how . . ."
>
> "How much of our bloody souls we left there and for what?" Myra said, completing Art's statement.
>
> "Damn right! We seem to have gained so little for the next generation of Chicanos. [. . .] Too painful to go into that inferno even for a poet." (44)

Much of the plot in *Crimson Moon* hinges on the presence of FBI infiltrators in both the resistance movement in Berkeley and Oakland and in Denver in the 1960s and 1970s. Elizabeth attests to this when she tells Justin:

> I know Ramona was raped . . . by . . . Pretty Boy. Patterson and [Willie] Oz were undercover feds who infiltrated the Third World Liberation Front at Cal, the Black Panther Party and the Crusade for Justice in Denver, among other militant groups. They had carte blanche when it came to their covert activities. . . . Patterson believed in nothing but himself. He felt certain he could get away with anything, including rape. And he did. (97)

Other elements of Chicano history that students might find intriguing and poignant include the novel's inscription of some of the history of the Mexican Americans in Denver in the 1960s by the infiltrator Willie Oz, who describes the Crusade for Justice and Corky Gonzales in an empathetic yet cynical manner (110). As Sotelo states, Corpi "incorporates Chicano history and elements of the classical whodunit. [She] explores the activism of the 1960s and 1970s, the role of Chicanas as leaders, poets, laborers, and the double marginalization of women of color in the United States by racism and patriarchal privilege. . . . One transformation . . . is the use of the mystery novel to communicate an alternative ideology" (78).

The inscription of Chicano history is one of the most powerful themes in Corpi's work: whether in her revision of Ramona's story, her inclusion of specific aspects of the Chicano Movement, or her subversion of the traditional private-eye figure, Corpi tells the story of her people. She also often refuses to offer a tidy explanation: at the end of *Crimson Moon*, actions by Irene's sister cause the death of Ramona, Irene's birth mother. "The transition from the personal to the historical complicates the personal," and the reader finds "no easy answers, but rather is left to ponder complexities" (Pearson 49).

The growth of Corpi's characters is never separated from the experience of the collective. Their "anger and anguish come from seeing the pain of their people, from witnessing the deaths [and violations] of individual brothers and sisters and the collectively experienced hardships and struggles, while many of their best efforts go unrecognized and unrewarded" (Pearson 50). The novels by Corpi gather up her people and give them a history. She and her protagonists Gloria and Dora make contributions as women and yet "maintain a connection to, and the support of, their people and the movement" (Pearson 50).

Note

1. Dreams are crucial in many of Corpi's works—in *Delia's Song* and *Black Widow's Wardrobe* in particular.

Works Cited

Anzaldúa, Gloria. *Borderlands / La frontera: The New Mestiza*. Aunt Lute Books, 2012.

Baker Sotelo, Susan. *Chicano Detective Fiction: A Critical Study of Five Novelists*. McFarland, 2005.

Brinson Curiel, Barbara. "Lucha Corpi." *Chicano Writers, First Series*, edited by Francisco A. Lomeli, 1989, pp. 91–97. *Dictionary of Literary Biography*, vol. 82, Gale, 1978–. 385 vols.

Cisneros, Sandra. *The House on Mango Street*. Alfred A. Knopf, 1994.

Corpi, Lucha. *Black Widow's Wardrobe*. Arte Público, 1999.

———. *Cactus Blood*. Arte Público, 1995.

———. *Crimson Moon*. Arte Público, 2004.

———. *Delia's Song*. Arte Público, 1989.

———. *Eulogy for a Brown Angel*. Arte Público, 1992.

Cota-Cárdenas, Margarita. *Marchitas de mayo (sones pa'l pueblo)*. Relámpago, 1989.

Grobman, Laurie. "Toward a Multicultural Pedagogy: Literary and Nonliterary Traditions." *MELUS*, vol. 26, no. 1, Spring 2001, pp. 221–40.

Hinojosa, Rolando. *El condado de Belken: Klail City*. Bilingual Review Press, 1994.

Lorenzana, Apolinaria. "Memorias." *Nineteenth Century Californio Testimonials*, special issue of *Crítica*, edited by Rosaura Sánchez et al., U of California, 1990, pp. 1–14.

Pearson, Carol. "Writing from the Outside In: Constructs of Memory and Chicanas as Private Eyes in Three Detective Novels by Lucha Corpi." *Interdisciplinary Literary Studies*, vol. 4, no. 1, Fall 2002, pp. 38–51.

Rebolledo, Tey Diana. *Women Singing in the Snow: A Cultural Analysis of Chicana Literature*. U of Arizona P, 1995.

Rivera, Tomás. . . . *Y no se lo tragó la tierra / And the Earth Did Not Part*. Justa Publications, 1977.

Leigh C. Johnson

Feminist Consciousness and Community Activism in Novels by Ana Castillo and Demetria Martínez

Creating an upper-level general education literature class, often comprising students from diverse backgrounds, involves thinking strategically about how students will encounter social and political issues in the texts they are assigned. This essay presents guided discussion of such issues by engaging thought on hemispheric interconnectedness and social activism through two important texts by Chicanas: Ana Castillo's *So Far from God* and Demetria Martínez's *Mother Tongue*. Here students encounter characters who face domestic violence, anti-LGBTQ violence, war, political violence, and poverty. Searching for larger societal solutions to the problems presented by the texts can often cause students to feel discouraged or frustrated by their perceived impotence in the face of systemic racism, violence, and sexism.

For these foundational texts in Chicana literature, discussion strategies are necessary to help undergraduates not majoring in English analyze them and think critically about oppression, racism, and sexism. The following strategies do not imply that the two texts must be taught in the same class to have an impact; they can be considered individually. It is worthwhile, however, to think about what kind of class can best integrate these texts. These full-length novels work well in upper-level classes on contemporary literature or on topics in American literature or Chicana and Latina literature, and in an introduction to gender studies. As a literature professor, my goal is for students to recognize in literature a transnational, hemispheric feminist movement and possibilities for agency, thus I use writing and literary theory as tools, which I explain below.

To help students in upper-level classes better understand the foundations of Chicana and other feminist theories, and the transformative power of these texts, I also assign chapters 2, 5, and 7 from Gloria Anzaldúa's *Borderlands / La frontera* (37–45, 75–86, and 99–120) and the following essays: Norma Alarcón's "Chicana Feminism: In the Tracks of 'the' Native Woman," Cherríe Moraga's "A Long Line of Vendidas" (*Loving* 90–145), and Patricia Hill Collins's "Shifting the Center: Race, Class, and Feminist Theorizing about Motherhood." Through these accessible readings students begin to ground the fiction in theory, with guidance from me. For instance, Collins argues that women whose communities expect them to educate, care for, nurture, and discipline children in the face of colonial oppression and racism perform radical motherwork that "challenges social constructions of work and family as separate spheres, of male and female gender roles as similarly dichotomized, and of the search for autonomy as the guiding human quest" (47).

This idea of motherhood as feminist activism is easily applied to both novels and can be discussed by students. I regularly teach feminist theories in general education and liberal arts core classes to nonmajors who then participate successfully in discussions. The student body at my university is diverse in terms of race, ethnic background, level of preparation, religion, and socioeconomic status, and given those differences, students find questions, and some answers, in these theoretical approaches. One could supplement some of these primary texts with quotes or summaries from the work of other theorists, such as Amy Kaminsky's discussion of indigenous feminisms: "With exposure to different forms of feminism, indigenous feminism recognizes itself as such and develops itself from within, borrowing from whatever is useful in foreign feminism" (22). With these tools, students can interrogate the ways in which characters in the two novels act with agency despite the odds against them in a country in which they wield little political and economic power.

Castillo's novel is somewhat complex, but when students approach it thinking about questions of social justice and feminist action, it becomes clearer and more manageable. Each of the five main characters, Sofi and her four daughters, Esperanza, Fe, Caridad, and La Loca, has a specific approach to feminist agency. Through each character's confrontation with the globalized patriarchal network of violent oppression, a possibility for action is explored and rejected or affirmed. For instance, Esperanza studies Chicano politics at the university, becomes involved in the American Indian Movement and its traditions, and chooses journalism as a way of engaging in feminist action. But she encounters gender problems within the Chicano Movement, and disillusionment when her boyfriend, Rubén, leaves her for a white woman. As a journalist, she is sent to Saudi Arabia, where she is killed by a bomb. Her voice is then co-opted as a tool for media complicity in a transnational project of oil exploitation, thus revealing how her nation (the United States) promotes discrimination and violence. It would seem that she has failed to act on the agency she might have had as an educated Chicana.

The other characters fare little better. Fe, in pursuit of the American dream—a house, kids, and social mobility—takes a job at a weapons factory where the exposure to dangerous chemicals renders her sterile and leads to cancer. Caridad, after a horrific experience of sexual violence in which her "nipples were bitten off" and she was "stabbed in the throat," retreats to the mountains as a hermit, becomes a healer, and develops a love interest in Esmeralda, a woman from Acoma pueblo (Castillo, *So Far* 33). After Esmeralda is raped, she and Caridad choose death. Sofi's youngest, later called La Loca, dies at age three, comes back to life at her funeral, and flies to the top of the church. She spends the rest of her life tending to her sisters before their deaths, talks to animals, and spends time with La Llorona, a ghost from Mexican legend, at the river. Surprisingly, at the end of the novel, La Loca has contracted HIV and cannot be cured, despite the efforts of *curanderas* (women healers) and her doctor; she appears to have become a vessel for the ills of the nation. For Sofi, the tragedy of losing her daughters leads her to establish a community of mothers who can support one another: Mothers of Martyrs and Saints.

When systems of institutionalized racism and sexism continue to affect women of color in the United States, motherwork becomes necessary to ensure the dignity and survival of women. Motherwork, then, does not have to be performed only by mothers, but by women who are committed to what Castillo calls "an incorporation of mothering qualities into our value system [that] would radically change our world" (*Massacre* 186). Mothers of Martyrs and Saints is a powerful tool for Sofi and other mothers to reclaim some power over the loss of their children; in some ways it allows them to mother an entire community in lieu of their families, which are no more. Returning to the essay by Collins, students can discuss how the resolution of the novel reflects the "loss of individual autonomy" and "submersion of individual growth for the benefit of the group" (50). These additional burdens placed on women contrast with the view that motherwork is simply a celebration and valuation of women's traditional roles. Instead, motherwork is both an effort to confront violence within the family to ensure the survival of children and an impetus to confront violent racism from government, business, and religious institutions, and to advance the concerns of women, children, and men.

Because there are five main characters in Castillo's novel, it is helpful to sort out the ways in which each character functions symbolically within the narrative. Using a mapping device or some other visual organizer in class helps students to identify what kind of violence each woman has endured and the activist approach she selects to resist violence, and to consider what larger networks of oppression exist to stymie her efforts. To help identify how each character engages with a community, students create charts to describe the characters' activities and pursuits of social justice. They take turns volunteering ideas for the chart and begin to see what kinds of activism are effective. Most crucially, they identify what does not work: how environmentalist and neoliberal approaches and approaches that include only the perspectives of white people do not take into account the social, cultural, environmental, spiritual, and economic mores of marginalized communities; more effective approaches are those that sprout organically from community needs. If the class is large, groups of four students could discuss an assigned character (and possibly secondary characters, such as Esmeralda, Doña Felicia, or others) before the full class discusses these issues and fills in the chart.

Martínez's novel *Mother Tongue* highlights two central characters, María, the young Chicana protagonist who house-sits and contemplates her future, and José Luis, a Salvadoran refugee sheltered by the homeowner, with whom María falls in love. Emotionally adrift since her mother's recent death, the nineteen-year-old María seeks to develop a political consciousness of women's roles. Early on she recognizes that "[t]o love a man more than one's self was a socially acceptable way for a woman to be insane" (27), but in the ensuing plot she appears to have forgotten this idea. Left to care for José Luis by her godmother (the homeowner), she develops an attraction for him and fantasizes that they will get married to solve his visa problem. Imagining that lovemaking can "take the war out of him for a few hours," María realizes later that "the war left his body by way of [hers]" (103). Their intimacy culminates in mutually shocking realizations, each of which can be difficult for students to grapple with, but students may be able to relate to María's age and innocence.

The sanctuary movement in the United States in the 1980s should be explained, especially with regard to how it sought to provide shelter for Salvadorans fleeing a brutal war. I often assign Martínez's poem "Nativity for Two Salvadoran Women," and her essay "A Moment in History" (*Confessions* 109–12), to introduce the movement and establish Martínez's authority on the topic: Martínez was a journalist who interviewed and accompanied sanctuary volunteers who helped move refugees across the border, and as a result she was taken to court by the federal government.

This novel inspires students to make strong connections between texts when it follows the other literary and theoretical readings, as there are correlations between the themes in this novel and in the other works, such as domestic violence, the globalized nature and impact of war, and child sexual abuse in a patriarchal system. The short account furthermore pursues a hemispheric course, moving from El Salvador through Mexico to Albuquerque, to Canada, and back to El Salvador, and through the characters' identities and experiences as global citizens. A final image of María's son, also named José Luis, committing to learning Spanish and working with environmental contamination issues in China shows this novel, like Castillo's, bringing its Chicanx characters to full participation in global, human concerns.

Narrative structure is crucial to the understanding of this novel. For a class activity, I ask students to start with the setting, to visually map it, working in small groups, then to take their maps to the whiteboard. From there, they can expand them to include relationships between characters and networks for social justice and activism, which radiate from a local center vertically and horizontally out to the larger world.

After students have read and mapped the text, I ask them for examples of narrative genres that appear in *Mother Tongue*: recipes, horoscopes, urgent action bulletins, letters, newspaper articles, *testimonios* ("testimonials"), journal entries, poems, and María's actual prose. I ask them to discuss what purpose each genre serves and whose voice it privileges. This activity primes students for the greater discussion on activism and transnationalism: How does María imagine her activism? Who is she saving? How does that change over the course of the novel? In what ways does the younger José Luis use transnational or global networks to enact change? These plot-based questions lead to a crucial question for literary studies in general: how might the humanities work with other disciplines to bring awareness to social justice issues?

Opening up this discussion of Western feminists' good intentions is important for students' understanding of global feminism and responsibility toward others. To some extent these narratives rely on feminist mestiza subjects within the United States as voices of reason or rescue, even though they provide support for other women's actions. In *So Far from God*, Esperanza hopes to advance herself and her community through her work covering American involvement in the war in Iraq, but her investment in neoliberal war games causes her untimely death. In *Mother Tongue*, María, consumed with her efforts to please her godmother by rescuing (rather than just caring for) a refugee in her godmother's absence, thinks she can take the war out of him (because of her youthful infatuation) and present him to the white, liberal sanctuary movement. Meanwhile, she suffers in silence her own experience of childhood sexual abuse.

To help students identify the ways that relationships create powerful avenues for care and activism, I have them do a class activity that uses four categories of relationships to determine where deep commitments develop and are sustained in the two novels. In four different groups, students think about how the texts present one of the following types of relationships: between men and women, men and men, women and women, and parents and children. Students create a diagram showing how the characters' experiences connect, then they think about the strength of those bonds as a form of liberation. They should draw these on the board and identify the major strength and major weakness of each relationship. Each group should also respond to the question of which way the balance is tilted. In both texts presented here, the parent-child relationship sparks activism and social change. Sofi, despite challenges and dysfunction, wants to protect and support her children; the loss of her daughters leads to her widespread social engagement. After doing this activity, students realize that the strength of the bond between parent and child reflects Collins's contention that motherwork "challenges social constructions of work and family as separate spheres, of male and female gender roles as similarly dichotomized, and of the search for autonomy as the guiding human quest" (47). The radical potential for activism and change is realized through an ethics of care for family that then extends globally.

Students can consider whether the pressure of motherhood is more intense for Chicanas and discuss how the cultural expectations around motherhood can be limiting or empowering—and sometimes both simultaneously. As Anzaldúa declares in *Borderlands / La frontera*: "Educated or not, the onus is still on a woman to be a wife/mother—only the nun can escape motherhood" (39). In delineating these expectations for women, Anzaldúa might appear to say that motherhood is a negative cultural expectation; however, feminist reformulations of how mothering can effect significant change in a community are worth examining as complementary to radical feminist activism. Because a traditional role for Chicanas in the family has been to pass cultural values along to children, women who refuse to replicate the subjugation of women within their mothering are performing feminist motherwork. Sofi as mother, and the others through their writing and activism, embrace the "fourth choice" Anzaldúa also posits, which is "entering the world by way of education and career and becoming self-autonomous persons" (39). Such discussions can be helpful to students in engaging ideas about their own families and lives, especially for those who are mothers or first-generation college students and children of single parents. The conversation around these texts validates the seeming contradictions within these roles and empowers students.

Through these two novels, students begin to grapple with issues that continue to shape their lives as they interact with a world in which the American dream beckons but remains elusive. As noted by Amy Kaminsky, "When a text brings together the emotional charge that reading usually displaces onto fiction with reporting of real-world events, readers are confronted with a disquieting need to act on the facts on the basis of their emotional response to them" (53). This way of reading and experiencing texts is a gift to students as they comprehend that, as subjects in the United States (with intersectional identities and privilege), they can evaluate complicity in reproducing narratives of the American dream, imperial forms of feminism, or false progressiveness. As students grasp how they are always already marked by their positions, they can begin to critically analyze their own production of values. In classrooms, the opportunity to challenge unseen privilege complements the creation of a space where students can access options for transforming that privilege, and for finding healing through narratives.

Works Cited

Alarcón, Norma. "Chicana Feminism: In the Tracks of 'the' Native Woman." *Cultural Studies*, vol. 4, no. 3, 1990, pp. 248–56.

Anzaldúa, Gloria. *Borderlands / La frontera*. 4th edition, Aunt Lute Books, 2012.

Castillo, Ana. *Massacre of the Dreamers: Essays on Xicanisma*. Plume, 1994.
———. *So Far from God*. W. W. Norton, 1993.
Collins, Patricia Hill. "Shifting the Center: Race, Class, and Feminist Theorizing about Motherhood." *Mothering: Ideology, Experience, and Agency*, edited by Evelyn Nakano Glenn et al., Routledge, 1994, pp. 45–66.
Kaminsky, Amy K. *Reading the Body Politic: Feminist Criticism and Latin American Women Writers*. U of Minnesota P, 1993.
Martínez, Demetria. *Confessions of a Berlitz-Tape Chicana*. U of Oklahoma P, 2005.
———. *Mother Tongue*. One World Books, 1994.
———. "Nativity for Two Salvadoran Women." *Three Times a Woman: Chicana Poetry*, by Alicia Gaspar de Alba et al., Bilingual Press, 1989, pp. 132–33.
Moraga, Cherríe. *Loving in the War Years*. South End Press, 1985.

Sheila Marie Contreras

Domestication and Resistance in the Short Fiction of Alma Luz Villanueva and Helena María Viramontes

Chicana art, history, literature, and science have always been necessary to the undergraduate curriculum, because of their contributions and their significance to the historical record of the United States. Long before the current period of demographic growth, Mexican Americans and other Latinx people were present in American artistic, cultural, and political life.[1] Consider the role of Spain in the early colonization of the continent: the first European settlement in what is now the United States was St. Augustine, Florida, established in 1565, and the first European language spoken in the Americas was Spanish. The military conquest of new lands for the Spanish crown rooted Spanish speakers in the southwestern United States as early as the late seventeenth century, and it is in these early mestiza/o communities that we can locate the origins of the Chicana presence in the United States, rather than in immigration patterns of the twentieth and twenty-first centuries. Based on contemporary statistics, researchers predict that by 2065 Latinx people as a group will compose twenty-four percent of the population in the United States (Cohn), yet Chicanas remain starkly underrepresented in school materials and course content.

When particular communities are virtually absent from the curriculum, as is the case with Chicanx people, the absence suggests a lack of accomplishment in those communities, which then governs how individuals, including people of color, perceive and assess themselves and others. Inarguably, students of color are positively influenced through exposure to curricular material that acknowledges their existence. Undergraduate students learn which groups of people are important—the producers of high art, hard science, and trustworthy leadership—from the materials they encounter in school. Chicana literature, in particular, has a minimal presence in American literature surveys, which belies its rich history. The short stories I discuss here, therefore, will bring new content choices to teachers of American literature, Chicanx and other Latinx literature in the United States, women's literature, and young adult literature, strengthening the body of texts available to teachers and suggesting new interpretative strategies. Although male characters are few in these short stories, the girls and women in them still suffer under male power and privilege. These literary texts enable instructors to introduce students to Chicana feminist content, an opportunity that must be carefully managed to avoid reinforcing stereotypes associating Chicanos with predatory masculinity, Chicanas with subservient femininity, and both with poverty.

In order to enhance student and instructor critical vocabularies, the following feminist interpretations of two short stories utilize specific terms and concepts, such as gender, patriarchy, heteropatriarchy, enforced heterosexuality, gender nonconformity, domestication, and intersectionality. Gender refers to the imagined construction of male and female identities and is not necessarily consistent with sex, the biological and physiological traits that enable human reproduction. Gender remains one of the principal organizing tools of society, and gender hierarchies produce relations of power that privilege men. Patriarchy, the male domination of social, economic, political, and religious institutions, is linked to enforced heterosexuality, which refers to political, legislative, and social practices and beliefs that privilege heterosexuality and criminalize homosexuality, and to gender conformity, which refers to behavior that aligns with dominant beliefs about how women and men should act, dress, and speak. The link between patriarchy and homophobia is represented in the critical term *heteropatriarchy*. I define domestication as practices that socialize girls and women to accept and find their value in an identification with social divisions of labor that classify housekeeping and caretaking as women's work. Girl and women characters throughout Chicana and other women's literature rebel against patriarchal authority by refusing to accept the limits enforced by family and society. Literary analysis is enriched when readers understand that these characters have other identities that also shape their experience and view of the world. One can be a woman, Mexican, lesbian, and working class all at once. Interpretative approaches that consider multiple identities and experiences simultaneously are referred to as intersectional analyses.

Chicana literature is best analyzed from a perspective that acknowledges the racialized, gendered, classed, and sexualized aspects of character that inform narrative meaning. Two collections of short stories by Chicana writers provide rich and nuanced explorations of female experiences from the perspectives of young girl and adult women characters. Alma Luz Villanueva's *Weeping Woman: "La Llorona" and Other Stories* and Helena María Viramontes's *"The Moths" and Other Stories* are complex, poetic texts that chronicle the emergence of young girls into adult worlds of responsibility and sexuality. In the title stories of their collections, Villanueva and Viramontes each create narratives of girls coming of age and entering phases of life in which they are increasingly sexualized and forced to adapt to their changing bodies and the changing attitudes toward them, even as they resist these imposed restrictions and unwelcome transformations. The two stories focus on relationships between and among women and girls, a theme notable for its privileging of their experience in the absence of, although not without the influence of, men.

The adolescents and early teen characters struggle with familial and social expectations that contrast with their understandings of themselves. As the girls come to consciousness about their shifting roles, readers encounter complex critiques of patriarchy and religion. Reflecting on and navigating the challenges of their circumstances, characters reveal to us the devastating effects of horizontal policing among women, and the degree to which the reproduction of the patriarchal family relies upon the authority of girls and women who are both constrained and enabled by the gendered norms of behavior enforced in family and public cultures. Close attention shows how women and girl characters police or monitor behavior to promote compliance with codes of conduct that work against their own interests as a group and, often, as individuals. But horizontal policing serves to elevate some women by creating negative examples against which these so-called upstanding women can be positively judged as they attempt to secure favorable standing within a social structure that systematically disempowers them.

Villanueva's "La Llorona / Weeping Woman" is a story about mothers and daughters, and about the close relationship between a seven-year-old girl, Luna, and her maternal grandmother, Isidra (*Weeping Woman* 1–7). It is also the story of the conflicted relationship between Carmen, Luna's mother, and Isidra, who lives with her daughter and granddaughter. While Isidra represents warmth and security in her caretaking of Luna and her transmission of traditional Mexican cultural values, Carmen represents the harsh realities of assimilation and patriarchy in her treatment of her mother and her daughter. The central symbol of the story is La Llorona, the weeping mother of Mexican folklore who appears near water seeking the lost children that she is said to have murdered. A Mexican oral tradition, the account of La Llorona is a cautionary tale meant to keep children away from bodies of water and safe from drowning. It creates a fear among children that the grieving mother might take them if they wander too close to water.

Male characters are barely present in Villanueva's story, which nevertheless illuminates the dangerous situations into which girls are born and that women face daily in patriarchal society, specifically, objectification and sexual violence. The action occurs primarily in domestic spaces, underlining the significance of the family, most importantly, girls and women, in reproducing patriarchal social structures and practices that exclude and harm women. The story opens in the kitchen, as Isidra's cooking envelops Luna in familiarity, comfort, and safety. Here, Isidra educates Luna about Sonoran culture and folktales by telling her the story of La Llorona.[2] The grandmother's version paints a picture of a loving mother who drowns her children to protect them from the brutality of the Spanish colonizers, a departure from the less sympathetic and more widely circulated version of the folktale, in which she kills her children to secure the affections of a distracted lover.

A subsequent scene disrupts the calm as Luna awakens to the sound of Carmen and Isidra arguing about the presence of a man that Carmen has invited to the home. The child hears a cry of pain or fear from her grandmother, and rushes to her assistance: "she ran into the dimly lit front room where her mother stood over her cowering grandmother, her fist raised again." "It's a sin, making me make the bed for you and that man," Isidra charges, finally telling Carmen, "You aren't a daughter of mine! My children are dead!" The scene culminates with Luna's intervention to protect her grandmother from Carmen's physical threat: "Don't touch her or I'll kill you. I'll kill you if you touch her again!" (4). As Luna steps in, she aligns herself with her grandmother against Carmen, disciplining and policing the mother who has been symbolically killed by both her mother and her daughter. While Carmen is the character with more power, the situation nevertheless is an example of horizontal policing. Isidra's claim that Carmen's behavior is sinful invokes the authority of church patriarchy in the condemnation of her daughter.

When Luna is sexually assaulted in a park, the narrative provides the only example of Carmen's caretaking: "By the time Luna got home, Carmen had called the police." After the physician confirms the assault Luna experienced, Carmen advises her daughter on the bus ride home: "Keep this to yourself. Nothing happened to you anyway, cry, baby" (6). Here, Carmen rejects the responsibilities of maternal nurturing, leaving readers to wonder what violence has been normalized in Carmen's own life that she would so diminish the severity of Luna's experience. Her lack of sympathy contrasts with Isidra's gentle treatment of the child, inviting harsh judgment of Carmen's gender nonconformity. Both adult women are versions of La Llorona, and whereas Carmen figures as the murderous mother of patriarchal folkloric convention, Isidra figures as the loving mother of the tale's feminist reinvention.

The story ends at the beach, where Isidra has taken Luna, presumably to seek La Llorona's healing and protection. The final scene depicts a confluence of Isidra and La Llorona as both step forward to comfort the child. The different responses to the assault—Carmen takes Luna to the doctor while Isidra takes the child to the ocean—may prompt readers to reconsider judgment of Carmen as irresponsible and neglectful. Similarly, readers might look with new insight at Isidra's choices, even as Isidra sees La Llorona for the first time since leaving Mexico many years before, as revealed in the last line of the story: "She looked tall and strong as she came towards them, weeping and singing" (7). The La Llorona folktale easily elicits discussion in class; below are suggested questions.

Find out if students are familiar with the La Llorona folktale. Ask them to share their own versions, and then ask the class how Isidra's story differs. Do students like La Llorona? Do any of the characters resemble La Llorona?

Why does Carmen downplay the violence of the rape? What kind of violence does Carmen accept in her own life? Why does she insist to Luna that "it's nothing"?

What is Isidra doing in the final scene? Does it seem a viable way to address Luna's situation?

How do we expect mothers to act? Who is the "better" mother in the story and why?

These fractured bonds between women are also evident in Viramontes's short story "The Moths," where alliances similarly skip a generation without finding a hold in the mother-daughter relationship (*"Moths"* 21–28). The story shares the perspective of a fourteen-year-old unnamed narrator who is caring for her dying grandmother. Alienation is a strong theme, since the narrator and main character is an outcast in her own family. She does not fulfill expectations of femininity or delicacy and does not take to learning the assigned skills of her gender, like sewing and crocheting: "I wasn't even pretty or nice like my older sisters and I just couldn't do the girl things they could do" (23). The narrator is courageous and daring, defying traditional gender expectations. We learn early on that she has experienced physical violence in her own family, which she then uses to protect and assert herself: "I began keeping a piece of jagged brick in my sock to bash my sisters or anyone else who called me bull hands . . ." (23). Her sisters band against her, excluding and blaming the narrator for their father's anger toward their mother, who is held accountable for the daughter's failure to conform: "Then he strategically directed his anger at Amá for her lousy ways of bringing up daughters . . ." (25). A meditation on and chronicle of a girl's relationship to her grandmother, "The Moths" is also about the deep absence of exile: "In the early afternoon, Amá would push her hair back, hand me my sweater and shoes, and tell me to go to Mama Luna's. This was to avoid another fight and another whipping, I knew" (24). The quotation suggests a daily occurrence in which the narrator is blamed for any fighting and receives the whipping. Her mother sends her away to protect them both.

Perhaps the strongest testament to the main character's intellectual independence and critical insight is her response to organized religion. At one point, she seeks solace in a church, only to find it empty of comfort: "I was alone. I knew why I had never returned" (25). Only at Abuelita's house does she feel that her "bull hands" are transformed into competent, gentle, life-giving tools as she helps with the gardening and, eventually, nurses her grandmother. When she senses Abuelita's "gray eye upon me," she is able to feel "safe and guarded . . . like God was supposed to make you feel" (24). Compelled by a strong sense of justice and reciprocity, the narrator insists on caring for Abuelita: "Really, I told Amá, it was only fair" (23). She rejects patriarchal and religious authority but never questions her responsibility to her grandmother. As she spends hours holding Abuelita's hand and tending to her last needs, the narrator connects with her own purpose and strength, as well as with her sorrow and pain. Alone with

Abuelita at the hour of her death, she invents her own ritual preparation of the dead: "With the sacredness of a priest preparing his vestments, I unfolded the towels one by one on my shoulders . . ." (27). Her ritual creates a sacred space not provided by the religion that she has rejected and that her father demands she accept.

"The Moths" is a story about cycles of abuse: the scars on Abuelita's back, the broken relationship between Abuelita and the narrator's mother, the mother's subservience to a husband who beats her daughter. The physical abuse exists alongside the absence of physical affection and the dismantling of alliances between women. But in her resistance, the narrator forges a new path marked by strength, integrity, and intelligence in the midst of rejection by family and community. Her final acts of physical connection with a woman who had never kissed her or shown her much physical affection, but who had made her feel safe and loved, bring the narrator to an awareness of her deep longing for her own mother. The final moment of the story is painful to those drawn into sympathy with this girl, who faces a devastating transition in life, as well as a moment of maturation. As the narrator realizes her own feelings of abandonment, she also comprehends her mother's victimization and powerlessness.

There are cultural references—mostly in relation to Abuelita—that will resonate with readers who share a Mexican or other Latinx cultural background. There are a few Spanish words and phrases in the family dialogues, but little else to mark the family as Mexican. Some readers might associate the father's authoritarian behavior with Latino masculinity, a stereotype that instructors might dispel by creating awareness of the presence of patriarchy across cultures. Students may relate to the profound responsibilities placed upon the narrator, her lack of support, and the limiting expectations that society has for women. Conversation in class can also address the horizontal policing and conflict between women family members that enable continued patriarchal rule in the household. Below are some prompts for class discussion:

Discuss the relationship between the narrator and her grandmother. How and why does the grandmother care for her? Does the narrator seem to appreciate that care?

Describe the narrator's relationship with other family members.

Why is the narrator uncomfortable in church? What are her thoughts on religion?

Discuss the narrator's mother and her relationship with her husband and mother.

What do you think happens next? Write the scene after the ending of the story, and discuss.

Diversification of course content is central to increasing academic success for Chicanx students and to transforming social relations of power. Inarguably, students benefit from curricular material that acknowledges their existence and that comes from their communities. The addition of Chicana literature, history, art, and science to the undergraduate curriculum will bring awareness of the diversity and complexity of Chicanx lives to all students.

Notes

1. *Latinx* and *Chicanx* are relatively new gender-neutral terms formulated to include nonbinary people and those who identify as women or men. These terms are replacing *Latina/o* and *Chicana/o*, which were developed earlier to rectify gender conventions in both Spanish and English that exclude women.

2. Sonora is a state in Mexico that borders Arizona.

Works Cited

Cohn, D'Vera. "Future Immigration Will Change the Face of America by 2065." *Pew Research Center*, 5 Oct. 2015, www.pewresearch.org/fact-tank/2015/10/05/future-immigration-will-change-the-face-of-america-by-2065/.

Villanueva, Alma Luz. *Weeping Woman: "La Llorona" and Other Stories.* Bilingual Review Press, 1994.

Viramontes, Helena María. *"The Moths" and Other Stories.* Arté Público Press, 1985.

Peter Schmidt

Lesson Plans for Four Stories in Sandra Cisneros's *"Woman Hollering Creek" and Other Stories*

The stories in Sandra Cisneros's *"Woman Hollering Creek" and Other Stories* (1991) are assigned frequently in high school and college courses in English, both for cultural reasons and for their representation of young girls and women who are making their way in the world. The following teaching strategies for Cisneros's short fiction focus on two stories that explore childhood—"Eleven" (*"Woman"* 6–9) and "Barbie-Q" (14–16)—and two that treat difficult passages into adulthood, "Woman Hollering Creek" (43–56) and "Little Miracles, Kept Promises" (116–29).

These lesson plans provide teachers with resources to help high school and college or university students of all ethnicities appreciate these stories' richness and wisdom regarding coming-of-age experiences and the bicultural history of the United States and Mexico. Students will be taught to appreciate and evaluate the stories as literature by attending to Cisneros's varied vocabulary, powerful sentences, daring metaphors, allusions, and story structure. All four stories also have rich and ambiguous endings that inspire students to debate how best to interpret them. These are stories without simplistic or feel-good resolutions.

Students are guided to identify and research key references such as La Llorona, La Malinche, and La Virgen de Guadalupe, or Tonantzín, and to present their findings to the class. They will better understand the experience of life in these stories as bicultural, comprising both Mexican-indigenous heritage and religious-cultural influences and the influence of popular culture in the United States on girls' and womens' identities (such as through Barbie dolls). Students will reflect on how popular commercial and religious cultures enforce negative stereotypes (especially regarding race, class, and Mexicana and Chicana identities), yet these stories also teach students to question and undo those cultural scripts.

Cisneros's tales highlight the experience of trauma and then narrate how such pain may be at least partially healed within communities. Discussing these stories with guidance from the lesson plans should help students not only appreciate Cisneros's storytelling prowess but also reflect on their own paths and influences.

To begin, have students discuss the following comment by Cisneros about an admired Catalán writer, Marcè Rodoreda: "It is this precision at naming the unnameable that attracts me to Rodoreda, this woman, this writer, hardly little, adept at listening to those who do not speak, who are filled with great emotions, albeit mute to name them" (*House* 123). Consider also sharing the point made by the poet and critic Harryette Mullen that *"Woman Hollering Creek"* contains "stories of a variety of women trying various means of escape, through resistance to traditional female socialization, through sexual and economic independence, self-fashioning, and feminist activism, as well as through fantasy, prayer, magic, and art." Each lesson plan suggests opening discussion in a different way.

"Eleven"

The story "Eleven" uses a dramatic tone, so have two to three students read portions of the story aloud for effect. Then proceed with class discussion using the following guidance:

The eleven-year-old girl is never named, although some of her classmates are. Ask for possible reasons why an author would not name her main character. Also, notice that the girl speaks her thoughts to "you"—directly addressing the reader. How does this observation contribute to an interpretation of the story?

Why is the girl so upset about a sweater? How does Cisneros use the present tense and vivid imagery to place the reader in the girl's imagination? For example, have students examine the paragraph in the middle of page 8, from the sentence that begins "But when the sick feeling goes away and I open my eyes . . ." to the phrase "Not mine, not mine, not mine."

What occurs in the classroom—between the teacher and the girl, and between the girl and her classmates—that upsets the girl? What does Mrs. Price say to the girl, and why does the girl behave as she does? (Is the teacher certain that the red sweater is the girl's?) Ask students how they feel about how the teacher treats the girl.

How old is the girl? Call attention to the opening statement she makes about the paradox of age (6–7), as well as to the title. At age eleven, most girls are entering adolescence: how is that important for the story?

While the teacher's humiliation of the girl is unforgettable, this story is arguably not just about victimization. Ask if students agree or disagree, and ask them to point to evidence in the story to support their interpretations.

The last two pages of the story contain two references to the family's upcoming birthday celebrations for the girl, particularly the cake her mother will bake. Ask why, in the final sentence, the girl imagines the events of her day as a tiny "runaway balloon" floating away from her?

Nearly the entire story is composed of words that the girl says not to the teacher or her classmates but only to herself. Help students discover this fact, and discuss its importance. Ask them to consider the possible relevance of Cisneros's comment about the influence of Rodoreda, and to discuss any remaining unanswered questions about "Eleven."

Teachers may use some of the above topics to focus discussion, and have students write reflection papers on others.

"Barbie-Q"

The story opens with the narrator addressing a friend and listing what's "yours" versus what's "mine."

Is this story really just about individualism and ownership? And is the friend the reader? After discussion of the previous story, possible responses can include an acknowledgment that the readers are present too as part of the girls' circle of friends.

Ask students to point out a few examples of the girls' comments and discuss their impact. For instance: "Only Ken's invisible, right?" (14); "see there?" (15); and the "so what" and "who's to know" questions in the story's last paragraph (16). How do these examples help enter into the larger questions the story pursues regarding how consumers create imaginary worlds using popular cultural commodities?

Ask when quotation marks are used by the narrator. Students will say that they only appear around the names of Barbie doll costume sets, which have been copyrighted by Barbie's corporate owner and creator, Mattel. Ask if the narrator's voice changes at those junctures (often sounding as if the language of Mattel advertising has become part of the narrator's inner voice), as in this example: "the 'Career Gal' ensemble, snappy black-and-white business suit, three-quarter-length sleeve jacket with kick-pleat skirt, red sleeveless shell, gloves, pumps, and matching hat included" (15). Have students debate interpretations of this example. Is it an instance of what the cultural critic Theodor Adorno would call "pseudo-individuality" (Adorno and Horkheimer 120–67)—of how our individualism has been completely defined by commodities, the things we possess?[1] Or do students disagree with that negative interpretation?

Encourage students to examine the girl characters' descriptions of interactions between the various Barbies. Ask them to consider this key quotation: "Every time the same story. Your Barbie is roommates with my Barbie, and my Barbie's boyfriend comes over and your Barbie steals him, okay? Kiss kiss kiss. Then the two Barbies fight. You dumbbell! He's mine. Oh no he's not, you stinky!" (14). What is that "same story"? Are the girls learning through their Barbie dolls to see themselves as sex objects for an absent male gaze? Or are they play-creating a female-centered rivalry, friendship experience, and sense of community, a "we"?

In the final paragraph, what is being asserted in the "so what?" and "who's to know" questions (16)? Does the girls' play reinforce the idea that women's worth is defined by who gets the man, who receives his gaze, so that the man's power is present even when he is absent? Ask whether the girls are mock fighting each other for the "boyfriend" in order to *imitate* that behavior, or whether the rivalry is genuinely felt.

Race and class intersect with gender in this story. Except for the Barbie dolls' burnt feet, which the girls joke about, thus giving the story its title, the dolls represent an ideal of white female beauty and the means needed to purchase them, since the dolls the girls play with are used. By playing with these dolls, are the girls learning to devalue their identity as working-class Chicanas? Or does the community that the girls create by playing together and saying "so what?" supersede a desire to be like the Barbies?

One possible summary of the story suggests that it is about the successful brainwashing of the girls as consumers, and that their enthusiasm for the dolls covers up their shame (Rivera 43).[2] A different argument could be that the girls' enthusiasm and their concluding questions reflect their pride and assert their feelings of community, a "we" that they themselves have made. Is the question "who's to know?" a boast rather than an admission of shame? Which of these two readings do students find more persuasive, and why?

Cisneros's story arguably doesn't offer a definitive conclusion about whether the girls' behavior is good or bad; it just presents it in their voices. Is the story's lack of engagement in judging the girls' interactions with a product of the Mattel Corporation a strength or a weakness?

Students should be given room to debate the above considerations, especially about how to summarize the story, which will generate good discussion and focused reflection papers.

"Little Miracles, Kept Promises"

This story includes several short notes that accompany the small charms left at a shrine, in the manner of ex-votos, to honor the Virgin Mary (or other saints) for miracles that involved healing. These *milagrito* ("miracle") notes often have the form of the organ or body part that has been healed: "miniature charms depicting parts of the body such as the heart, hands, and legs. Placed at a shrine that is considered to have miraculous power, they are attached to the clothing of the saint's statue responsible for the miracle" (Pineda 368). At times they are also a prayer for help. Collectively, these *ofrendas* ("offerings") and their notes tell the story of a community.

Ask students to consider how the story begins. Is it a portrait of a community or a collection of individual problems? What do the *milagrito* notes reveal about their authors? See, for example, the notes by Adelfia (Cisneros, *"Woman"* 117), Barbara (117–18), Arnulfo (120), and Teresa (121–22).

What is the implication of the story's double title, "Little Miracles, Kept Promises"?

In acknowledging Mary, are the characters placing agency and power outside themselves and solely in her? Or do you think her succor also ignites a kind of power in the characters? Encourage students—in small groups or in reflection papers—to indicate passages that support their arguments, and to discuss the power and mystery of religious and cultural beliefs in contemporary society.

Some of the *milagrito* notes reveal happy resolutions, while in others the reader doesn't know if the prayer was answered. Why do you think Cisneros included such a mix?

What general themes emerge about the challenges for the community identified in this story and about how they are met?

Near the conclusion to "Little Miracles," the story's format changes. Instead of just a brief note, we get an extended transcription of the thoughts and experiences of a particular person, Rosario "Chayo" De Leon, of Austin, Texas. This concluding sequence (124–29) acts as a portrait of the artist as a young woman experiencing a transformation in how she thinks about herself and her destiny: Chayo bears some resemblance to both Cisneros and the painter Frida Kahlo.

This final section is presented as an extensive note or prayer to La Virgen de Guadalupe that gives thanks for the strength Chayo received to begin a new life as an artist; the note is accompanied by a long braid of Chayo's hair, which has been cut off and pinned to the saint's statue. Carmen Rivera interprets the gift of a braid as signifying "rebirth" (48), stressing this quotation from Chayo: "my head as light as if I'd raised it from water" (Cisneros, *"Woman"* 125).

Key to Chayo's emergence as an artist is her discovery of a connection between La Virgen de Guadalupe, Mexico's patron saint, and the Aztec or Nahua earth goddess, Tonantzín, whom Chayo comes to realize is Guadalupe's antecedent.[3] Chayo considers these three sacred women—the Virgin Mary, La Virgen de Guadalupe, and Tonantzín—as a trinity of women who give her confidence to be an independent artist.

At first Chayo associates La Virgen de Guadalupe with subservience and suffering and refuses to allow images of her: "For a long time I wouldn't let you in my house" (127). Have students discuss whether this declaration represents an act of rebellion, and further, how Chayo is affected by the constant comments she hears from family and friends urging her to abandon her dreams of being a painter and instead be a more conventional, less "selfish" woman. Note that Chayo hears these voices criticizing her even when she's alone. Finally, what qualities does Chayo admire in Tonantzín? How does discovering a possible link between Tonantzín and La Virgen de Guadalupe change the meaning of this saint for Chayo? If necessary, have students do research online to learn more about Tonantzín and La Virgen de Guadalupe, then have them share and discuss their findings.

The main goal of this lesson on "Little Miracles" should be for students to discover why Tonantzín, La Virgen de Guadalupe, and other sacred deities inspire Chayo to have confidence in herself as a woman artist. Chayo's long *milagrito* note ends the story by giving thanks to these sacred figures (129). These deities also provide support—"kept promises"—for all the other characters.

"Woman Hollering Creek"

This is a story in which social and geographic spaces are marked by thresholds or border crossings where the expectations of characters are dashed. Yet out of those same spaces may emerge new possibilities. This story explores both outcomes.

Have students seek references in the story to thresholds, borders, arroyos, and even edges. Who are the dominant figures at these boundaries and in these spaces, and how does the character Cleófilas relate to them? Have students work in groups to make lists of references and discuss them. Are the rulers of these spaces or borders all male?

Ask students if great expectations become dashed. Have them find examples. What are the potential causes for the changes that Cleófilas experiences? Help students discover that these are repeated entrapments, not just changes. Have the class read the following passage closely, even aloud; it describes when Cleófilas is first beaten by Juan Pedro:

> Instead, when it happened the first time, when they were barely man and wife, she had been so stunned, it left her speechless, motionless, numb. She had done nothing but reach up to the heat on her mouth and stare at the blood on her hand as if even then she didn't understand.
>
> She could think of nothing to say, said nothing. Just stroked the dark curls of the man who wept and would weep like a child, his tears of repentance and shame, this time and each. (Cisneros, *"Woman"* 48)

Why does this passage use "it" in the first sentence, where the pronoun's referent is so unclear? Although the passage opens with the phrase "the first time," it ends with the phrase "this time and each": What does this shift suggest? Although the quotation stresses that Cleófilas is "speechless, motionless, numb," does it also suggest that she has a voice and agency, even at this low point in her life?

Cleófilas describes how she had been waiting for "passion" in her life, which she learns about from the telenovelas (44). Have students read carefully the narrator's description of what Cleófilas calls the most popular telenovela, *Tú o Nadie* (*You or No One*; 44–45). Who is the speaker and who is being addressed? What is the effect when the story directly addresses its readers? Have students note the powerful authority that the narrator claims when describing what *real* passion is: "Somehow one ought to live one's life like that, don't you think?" (45). Ask how a woman *should* live her life.

Advanced students can do brief research on the storytelling concept of free indirect narration and explain what free indirect speech is and why they think Cisneros employs this narrative technique for the telenovela passage. Does the author endorse this view of the world, of what women should feel and believe? Are there other moments in "Woman Hollering Creek" when the free indirect narration technique is used?

Have students identify what the story suggests about how men understand themselves (in the workplace, bars, etc.), and especially what the "ice house" section suggests. What is "the truth" that the men in the story want to tell each other (48)? How does this section function within the story as a whole? Help students recognize how Cisneros's story deftly uses dramatic irony to critique how telenovelas teach their viewers to internalize the perspective that love equals suffering and that women have to accept and endure this, even when they are beaten: "the pain all sweet somehow. In the end" (45).

Does this story suggest that men and women internalize scripts about gender roles from popular culture, and that Cleófilas is doomed to do this forever? Or is there any hope for her to cross the threshold to a new way? What are the parallels and differences between the commercial or popular cultural influences in this story and in "Barbie-Q"?

Have students discuss the portraits of Graciela and Felice in "Woman Hollering Creek." What roles does Cleófilas give these two women, and how does she describe them? How do these women challenge definitions of womanhood? Do they appear to be influenced by stereotypes in popular culture, such as those drawn from telenovelas? Ask students to notice how Cisneros relates this information, using primarily dialogue.

Finally, what meanings are derived from "crying" or "hollering" over the course of the story? Have students consider examples such as this one: "No one could tell if the woman had hollered from anger or pain" (46). Ask students how they understand Felice's scream at the end of the story and Cleófilas's response, described as "gurgling out of her own [Cleófilas's] throat, a long ribbon of laughter, like water" (56).

What role do other sounds play in the story? Many are not just referred to but enacted. A stimulating final exercise for students can be to identify such sounds as the melancholy sound of the pecan tree leaves (44), the "*rrrr*" of sewing machines, and the narrator's exclamation, "*¡zas!*" (45). Can students see any connection between these sounds and the story's final sentence, and if so, what impact it has for the ending of the tale?

Suggestions for further research projects on all four of these stories by Cisneros are available online (Schmidt).

Notes

1. For brief summaries of Adorno, see Ross; Parker.

2. For Rivera's main discussion of *"Woman Hollering Creek,"* see pages 42–51.

3. Tonantzín's temple was built on Tepeyac hill on the outskirts of Tenochtitlán, which is now Mexico City. A Catholic church was first built on that site in the early colonial era; now the site features the modern basilica honoring La Virgen de Guadalupe, the indigenous, brown-skinned Mexican religious figure of cultural importance in Mexico, throughout Latin America, and for Chicanos in the United States. See Gonzáles-Berry.

Works Cited

Adorno, Theodor W., and Max Horkheimer. "The Culture Industry: Enlightenment as Mass Deception." *Dialectic of Enlightenment*, by Adorno and

Horkheimer, translated by John Cumming, Herder and Herder Press, 1972, pp. 120–67.

Cisneros, Sandra. *A House of My Own: Stories from My Life*. Knopf, 2015.

———. "*Woman Hollering Creek" and Other Stories*. Random House, 1991.

Gonzáles-Berry, Erlinda. "Review of *Woman Hollering Creek and Other Stories*, by Sandra Cisneros." *The Americas Review*, vol. 20, no. 1, Spring 1991, pp. 84–85.

Mullen, Harryette. "A Silence between Us like a Language: The Untranslatability of Experience in *Woman Hollering Creek*." *MELUS*, vol. 21, no. 2, Summer 1996, p. 8.

Parker, Holt M. "Toward a Definition of Popular Culture." *History and Theory*, vol. 50, May 2011, pp. 147–70.

Pineda, Ana María. "Imagenes de dios en el camino: Retablos, Ex-votos, Milagritos, and Murals." *Theological Studies*, vol. 65, no. 2, 2004, pp. 364–79.

Rivera, Carmen Haydée. *Border Crossings and Beyond: The Life and Works of Sandra Cisneros*. Greenwood Publishing Group / ABC-CLIO, 2009.

Ross, Alex. "The Naysayers: Walter Benjamin, Theodor Adorno, and the Critique of Pop Culture." *The New Yorker*. 8 Sept. 2014, www.newyorker.com/magazine/2014/09/15/naysayers.

Schmidt, Peter J. "Sandra Cisneros 2: Optional Online Research Projects for Students, on Four Stories in Sandra Cisneros' *Woman Hollering Creek and Other Stories*: 'Eleven,' 'Barbie-Q,' 'Little Miracles, Kept Promises,' and 'Woman Hollering Creek.'" *Academia*, swarthmore.academia.edu/PeterSchmidt/Teaching-Documents-(Lesson-Plans-and-Syllabi-etc).

Part III

Comparative Notions

Anne M. McGee

Bridging the Border: Guiding a Comparative Study of Nellie Campobello's *Cartucho* and Sandra Cisneros's *The House on Mango Street*

Mexicana and Chicana literatures are often treated as distinct, unrelated literary traditions within academia, and they are frequently taught in different languages by faculty in separate departments. As a result, the complex connections that exist between these literatures, and hence between Mexicana and Chicana experiences, are often discounted by literary scholars and ignored in the university classroom.[1] In my classes in Spanish, I bridge this disciplinary gap through a close reading and comparative analysis of Nellie Campobello's *Cartucho: Relatos de la lucha en el norte de México* (*Cartucho: Tales of the Struggle in Northern Mexico*)—which is one of the few works of the Mexican Revolution written by a woman—and Sandra Cisneros's *The House on Mango Street* in Spanish translation (*La casa en Mango Street*). While superficially it may appear that these texts, which were written in different languages and historical contexts, have little in common, students are quick to discover the various thematic and structural components that they share.

Each text is composed of a series of vignettes, which are narrated primarily from the perspective of a young female narrator who tries to make sense of the violence that pervades her particular community. The use of vignettes works to present both individual and collective narratives, as each narrator gives voice to the stories of others who are otherwise voiceless. In *Cartucho*, the narrator, Nellie, relates her perspective on death and violence during the Mexican Revolution in northern Mexico at an intimate, domestic level.[2] The young Chicana narrator in *The House on Mango Street*, Esperanza, reveals the difficulties and violence of growing up in the urban barrios of Chicago in the 1960s and 1970s. Childhood trauma thus marks the life of each narrator, as each remembers the past through the writing process in the present. Because of these similarities, the texts lend themselves well to comparative readings in the undergraduate classroom, while providing students with opportunities to examine the various connections between Mexicana and Chicana literatures.

As *Cartucho* and *The House on Mango Street* are available in both English and Spanish, they can be utilized in a variety of courses.[3] Moreover, each text is written in a direct, matter-of-fact style, which makes it accessible to undergraduate readers who are taking a college-level literature class for the first time. For my class Introduction to Hispanic Literature, I have successfully integrated selections from *Cartucho* and *The House on Mango Street*. This class is taught in Spanish and is a prerequisite to all upper-level literature courses in Spanish at my institution. Most language departments offer this type of introductory literature course in one form or another. In my class, students develop the analytical skills necessary for more advanced study of Hispanic literatures through the reading and analysis of selected literary texts from both Spain and the Americas. I organize the class into three units, which focus on narrative fiction, poetry, and drama respectively. Each unit begins by introducing students to the genre to be studied, and to basic terminology related to the study of that genre, before moving on to selected readings.

In this introductory course, I use the textbook anthology *Aproximaciones al estudio de la literatura hispánica* (*Approaches to the Study of Hispanic Literature*), as it includes detailed introductions to each genre represented and to each author and the context of his or her work, as well as vocabulary notes and detailed questions for discussion (Virgillo). Unfortunately, anthologies such as this one seldom include many women or Latinx writers. To address this deficiency, I close the narrative fiction unit by having students comparatively read selections from *Cartucho* and the Spanish translation of *The House on Mango Street*. Having previously followed the textbook more strictly when teaching this unit, I find students to be more receptive to these alternative readings. This is especially true for heritage learners, who often closely identify with the characters in each work.

Reading the two texts comparatively not only introduces the class to Mexicana and Chicana voices but also serves as a valuable exercise for students after they have read the more canonical selections from the textbook. The new readings complement the earlier ones in a number of ways. The unique use of vignettes in *Cartucho* and *The House on Mango Street* offers an alternative to the traditional short stories included in *Aproximaciones*. This allows students to debate issues related to genre both in class and in short writing assignments, as they attempt to define and place the vignettes in relation to more familiar forms of narrative: that is, the short story and the novel. *Cartucho* is composed of fifty-six individually titled vignettes arranged into three sections—"Hombres del norte" ("Men of the North"), "Fusilados" ("The Executed"), and "En el fuego" ("Under Fire")—which together present a fragmented and chaotic view of the bloodiest years of the Mexican Revolution, during which men come through the young narrator's town of Parral, Chihuahua. Similarly, *The House on Mango Street* is made up of forty-four vignettes in which Esperanza describes episodes from her life and the lives of other women and children in her barrio. In each text the vignettes can be read individually or as parts of a larger composition.

In many ways this use of vignettes evades classification, and the structure of each text has been the subject of scholarly debate. Christina Dubb argues that the use of vignettes instead of linear narrative in *The House on Mango Street* "highlights the idea of living in the borderlands because she [Esperanza] is placed in an in-between space even in form" (223). According to Anna Marie Sandoval, this type of experimentation with genre, especially the use of short stories and fragmented forms, is typical in "the border zones of Mexicana and Chicana literatures," just as breaking with traditional genres "is often another strategy of resistance" (16). Although in an introductory class students do not read either collection in its entirety, they are able to consider a number of vignettes from each work and discuss the possible literary functions of this structure. In more advanced classes, I also have students read interviews in which the authors discuss their work, and this use of form, in more detail.[4]

In addition to the use of vignettes, the marginal position of the narrative voice in each text and the themes discussed also complement earlier readings. When students begin reading either text, they are quick to assume that the childlike voice with which both Nellie and Esperanza retell events from their childhood is genuine and unfiltered. The nearly complete lack of adult reflections in each text, coupled with the matter-of-fact way Nellie repeatedly recalls violent scenes of death and the unaffected manner in which Esperanza describes incidents of abuse and prejudice, leads the reader to believe that both narrators are children incapable of fully understanding the events that they witness and retell. Yet upon closer reading students discover how each text uses silences strategically, and that the adult voice of each narrator does rise to the surface from time to time, revealing that the appropriation of a childlike voice also serves a literary purpose.

I ask students to consider how their reactions to the vignettes, and to the violence in them, is influenced by their perception of each narrative voice, and we discuss how this would be different if either narrator revealed her adult voice early on. Scholars and readers alike often confuse the narrative voice in each text with the voice of the author, particularly in the case of *Cartucho*. We explore how each narrator serves as a compiler who chronicles, and thus edits, stories from her particular community. Discussions of the use of narrative voice lead students to discover the various themes that the two texts have in common. Students begin to assess both individual and collective responses to violence, trauma, and their impact on childhood. While these themes are explored in earlier readings in the textbook, I find that students more readily identify with the voices in *Cartucho* and *The House on Mango Street*.

I dedicate two weeks (two classes per week) to selections from these texts, and we generally consider eight to ten vignettes from each. In more advanced classes, I require students to read each work in its entirety. In the first week we spend one class session on each work, and in the second week we discuss them comparatively. As students are often unfamiliar with the historical context in which each work takes place, I give brief *PowerPoint* presentations on both the Mexican Revolution and the Chicano Movement of the 1960s before I assign the readings. I specifically cover the years of the Mexican Revolution in which *Cartucho* takes place, roughly 1916–20, and I include images from my own travels to Parral, Chihuahua.

In my introductory presentation on Cisneros's work, I play music from the time period, including the 1967 hit "Apples, Peaches, and Pumpkin Pie," by the multiracial pop group Jay and the Techniques, which Esperanza's neighbor Marin sings over and over while standing in her doorway in the vignette "Louie, His Cousin, and His Other Cousin" (Cisneros, *House* 23–24). Additionally, I post links to online biographies of each author on the course's *Blackboard* site, as required reading, and provide notes on unfamiliar vocabulary. I create a document in *Google Docs* that serves as a glossary where students can post words in Spanish that they had to look up or do not understand. Each new section of the course can edit and add to this glossary. I also post content-based questions for each assigned vignette on *Blackboard*, which students must answer before class. At the beginning of each session, students go over their responses in small groups. This is a useful exercise as it allows students to check their comprehension. More advanced students also benefit, as they explain their answers to classmates who may have more difficulty with the material. While initially it requires additional time on the part of the instructor, providing students with materials that support their comprehension, such as reading questions and a glossary, allows the instructor to dedicate more class time to literary analysis and discussion.

For the first week, I assign eight vignettes from *Cartucho* for the first session, and eight from *The House on Mango Street* for the second.[5] Although we may not discuss every vignette during the first week, they are all eventually covered. In these two initial classes we discuss the works separately, but I use the same basic structure for each session. While students discuss the content-based reading questions in small groups, I circulate and resolve any issues that may arise. Then each group receives a handout that outlines the three main points, with guiding questions, that they need to discuss. First, students examine the basic structure of the text, the vignette, with the following prompt:[6]

> The *Oxford English Dictionary* defines a vignette as "an ornamental or decorative design on a blank space in a book or among printed matter" or "any embellishment, illustration, or picture unenclosed in a border, or having the edges shading off into the surrounding paper." Do today's readings correspond to this definition, and if so, how? How does the vignette compare to other narrative forms we have studied thus far? What possible literary functions does it serve? Please discuss examples from the text that support your points. Be prepared to share your conclusions with the rest of the class.

The handout also provides two additional prompts that ask students to examine the use of narrative voices in each text and then to develop a list of the themes that recur throughout the vignettes. As they generate their lists, I encourage students to find examples of how each theme is treated, and to mark important passages that support their interpretations. I dedicate a large portion of the class, usually around thirty minutes, to such guided small-group discussions. Then each group reports back to the entire class on their particular findings, and I record the results on a white board while moderating the discussion whenever necessary. I try to avoid lecturing as much as possible. In most cases this activity is very effective in encouraging participation, since providing students with questions to guide their discussions gives them a framework on which to build their own interpretations and analysis. Utilizing the same handout to discuss each work also prepares students to examine the works comparatively.

The second week of class is dedicated to comparative analysis. In preparation, I ask students to reread the assigned vignettes, noting any relevant similarities or differences. At the beginning of the third class, I ask students to pull out their worksheets from the previous week and to compare and contrast each text's structure, use of narrative voices, and common themes. Students quickly discover that despite the differences in the texts, there are significant similarities that warrant additional analysis. Next I divide the class into three groups and assign each group two to three vignettes to examine in more detail. For example, the first group is assigned "Agustín García" and "Desde una ventana" ("From a Window") from *Cartucho* and "My Name" from *The House on Mango Street.* In "My Name" Esperanza describes how she was named after her great-grandmother, who refused to marry and was kidnapped by Esperanza's great-grandfather during the Mexican Revolution when he "threw a sack over her head and carried her off . . . as if she were a fancy chandelier" (Cisneros, *House* 11). Likewise in "Agustín García" Nellie's fourteen-year-old cousin, Irene, climbs up a chimney to avoid a similar fate. Esperanza further states that her great-grandmother spent the rest of her life watching the world from her window, a legacy she hopes to avoid: "I have inherited her name, but I don't want to inherit her place by the window" (Cisneros, *House* 11). This is the same space that the narrator Nellie inhabits in "Desde una ventana," in which she describes scenes of death that she observes from her window. By discussing these three vignettes, students make direct connections between the lives and historical contexts of the characters and note that Esperanza's great-grandmother and Nellie are from the same generation, as both are female survivors of the revolution.

The second group is assigned "Él" ("He") and "José Beltrán" from *Cartucho* and "Geraldo No Last Name" from *The House on Mango Street.* These vignettes relate the death of a member of the narrator's community. Students note how the victims in each account—two young revolutionaries in *Cartucho* and an undocumented restaurant worker in *The House on Mango Street*—are figures ignored by official history and only recognized through the memories of a child narrator. The third group discusses "El general Rueda" ("General Rueda"), in which Nellie witnesses the rape of her mother, and "Red Clowns," in which Esperanza struggles to recall her own sexual assault at a carnival. Students discuss how the characters are traumatized by rape, even into adulthood. They also note the strategic use of silences in each vignette and how understanding them requires active reading, for neither narrator discusses the precise details of her trauma. Many students do not realize the sexual nature of the attacks in a first reading of these vignettes, so here they have to be guided more closely. Students spend the majority of the session on this comparative activity, and during the final class each group presents its findings and leads a discussion with the whole class on its assigned readings.

Then, as we conclude the narrative unit, I distribute a list of topics for the final take-home essay, with two options on *Cartucho* and *The House on Mango Street*:

> Debate: *Cartucho* and *The House on Mango Street*: a valid comparison? Now that you have engaged in a comparative reading of both works, discuss whether a valid comparison can be made between these two texts from different literary traditions and written in different languages. Does reading the works comparatively help us to better understand them? If so, then how? Write a comparative analysis using two to four vignettes from the texts. Make sure to consider the use of narrative voices (and their literary function), the structure, and the themes in each work. In a brief essay argue whether a comparative reading of the two texts is valid. Use examples from the texts to support your ideas.
>
> Open topic: *Cartucho* and *The House on Mango Street*. As discussed in class, these two works treat many of the same themes (violence, sexual assault, death, roles for women, etc.). In a short essay, comparatively analyze how these works treat a particular theme using two to four vignettes. How is the theme treated in each work? What do the different instances have in common? How are they different? What does this reveal about the theme? Explore how each text approaches and treats the same theme and discuss how a comparative reading helps us to better understand each text.

I encourage students to incorporate additional vignettes if they wish, and explain that they cannot write about the same grouping of vignettes discussed in their small groups. Overall, I find that students are eager to work on new vignettes, and find that many make comparisons that I myself had never considered.

Reading *Cartucho* and *The House on Mango Street* together gives students an introduction to comparative literature and allows them to explore the multiple ways in which Mexicana and Chicana literatures are interconnected. Furthermore, it opens students' eyes to matters in Mexican and American histories and experiences. While I have outlined how to incorporate these texts into an introductory literature course, they could easily be used in advanced literature and culture courses as well. Analyzing these texts comparatively helps bridge the borders between Mexicana and Chicana cultural production.

Notes

1. While there are few comparative studies of Mexicana and Chicana literatures, a work that makes an important step in this direction is Sandoval, *Toward a Latina Feminism*. For comparative readings that focus specifically on *Cartucho* and *The House on Mango Street*, see Gano; McGee.

2. I refer to the principal narrative voice of *Cartucho* as Nellie, and the book's author as Campobello. The degree to which *Cartucho* is autobiographical is a matter of much debate.

3. Although I outline in this essay how I incorporate comparative readings of the texts into an introductory literature course, I have used the same techniques in more advanced literature courses as well as in courses on Latin American civilization and culture. For an English translation of *Cartucho*, see Campobello, Cartucho *and* My Mother's Hands (1–90).

4. For interviews with Sandra Cisneros in print, see "Returning" and "Do You." For an interview with Nellie Campobello, see "Nellie Campobello."

5. I assign two or three vignettes from each of *Cartucho*'s three sections, including "Él" ("He"; Campobello, *Cartucho: Relatos* 47–48), "Agustín García" (54–55), "Zafiro y Zequiel" ("Zafiro and Zequiel"; 64), "José Antonio tenía trece años" ("José Antonio Was Thirteen"; 65), "Nacha Ceniceros" (66–67), "El general Rueda" ("General Rueda"; 83–84), "Las tripas del general Sobarzo" ("General Sobarzo's Guts"; 85), and "Desde una ventana" ("From a Window"; 88). From *The House on Mango Street* I assign the following vignettes: "My Name" (Cisneros, *House* 10–11), "Louie, His Cousin, and His Other Cousin" (23–25), "Marin" (26–27), "Those Who Don't" (28), "There Was an Old Woman She Had So Many Children She Didn't Know What to Do" (29–30), "Geraldo No Last Name" (65–66), "No Speak English" (76–78), and "Red Clowns" (99–100).

6. All course materials and readings are in Spanish whenever possible, but I have included only English translations of course materials.

Works Cited

Campobello, Nellie. Cartucho *and* My Mother's Hands. Translated by Doris Meyer and Irene Matthews, U of Texas P, 1988.

———. *Cartucho: Relatos de la lucha en el norte de México.* 1940. 2nd ed., Era, 2000.

———. "Nellie Campobello." Conducted by Emmanuel Carballo. *Diecinueve protagonistas de la literatura mexicana del siglo XX*, by Carballo, Empresas, 1965, pp. 325–38.

Cisneros, Sandra. *La casa en Mango Street.* Translated by Elena Poniatowska, Vintage Español, 1994.

———. "Do You Know Me? I Wrote *The House on Mango Street.*" Interview. *Revista Chicano-Riqueña*, vol. 15, no. 1, 1987, pp. 77–79.

———. *The House on Mango Street.* Revised ed., Vintage Books, 1991.

———. "Returning to One's House: An Interview with Sandra Cisneros." Conducted by Martha Satz. *Southwest Review*, vol 82, no. 2, 1997, pp. 166–85.

Dubb, Christina Rose. "Adolescent Journeys: Finding Female Authority in *The Rain Catchers* and *The House on Mango Street.*" *Children's Literature in Education*, vol. 38, no. 3, 2007, pp. 219–32. *Infona*, doi:10.1007/s10583-006-9032-2.

Gano, Geneva M. "Campobello's *Cartuchos* and Cisneros's Molotovs: Transborder Revolutionary Feminist Narratives." *The Journal of Transnational American Studies*, vol. 6, no. 1, 2015, pp. 1–28. *eScholarship*, eScholarship.org/uc/item/8dm6d1fz.

McGee, Anne M. "Two *Niñas Traumatizadas*: Points of Contact between Nellie Campobello's *Cartucho* and Sandra Cisneros's *The House on Mango Street.*" *Journal of Ethnic American Literature*, no. 8, 2018, pp. 80–108.

Sandoval, Anna Marie. *Toward a Latina Feminism of the Americas: Repression and Resistance in Chicana and Mexicana Literature.* U of Texas P, 2008.

Virgillo, Carmelo, et al. *Aproximaciones al estudio de la literatura hispánica.* 7th ed., McGraw-Hill, 2012.

David S. Dalton

Borderlands, Race, and Gender in Novels by Helena María Viramontes and Rosario Castellanos

When designing courses on border studies, teachers may find it tempting to confine class discussions to the Mexican border with the United States. Teachers often focus only on Mexico's northern border because, in addition to separating the two nation-states, this marker separates the Global North from the Global South. But we do students a disservice when we emphasize only the one border because this approach limits the scope of potential analyses. If we extend classroom understanding to also include the Mexico-Guatemala border, students can gain a deeper understanding of how border discourses contribute to constructs of race, gender, and ethnicity across space and even over time (Villalobos 4–10). As such, I propose examining Helena María Viramontes's *Under the Feet of Jesus* (1995) and Rosario Castellanos's *Balún Canán* (1957; *The Nine Guardians*, 1992) together in a class. Each considers a Mexican border: in Viramontes's novel the border with the United States directly affects the experience of the protagonist, Estrella, and her migrant family in California, while Castellanos's novel highlights racial and gender hierarchies in Chiapas, a state that borders Guatemala and that is culturally closer to its neighbor than to Mexico City. *Under the Feet of Jesus* focuses primarily on interpersonal relationships between migrant workers, and only peripherally on societal racism. Each novel calls attention to how borders shape and influence societal discourses on race and gender.

Both authors focalize their novels through prepubescent or early adolescent girls. The novels are especially accessible for college classrooms because their plots revolve around different forms of initiation, which students may have experienced—or be experiencing—in their own lives. The female narrators live in a world where privileged people enjoy claims to citizenship that marginalize certain races: people of Mexican descent in *Under the Feet of Jesus* and Amerindians in *Balún Canán*. The texts differentiate legal citizenship—a bureaucratic status achieved through birth or naturalization—from cultural citizenship, which "locates the substantial meaning of citizenship in the everyday practices of sharing space . . . and exchanging ideas" (Lim 221; see also Reyes-Benítez 252–55). I find it useful to discuss how a character's group identity becomes a form of cultural citizenship in the novels. Such approaches allow students to recognize how notions of citizenship and legality play out along real-life borders. In *Under the Feet of Jesus*, Estrella faces marginalization because of her age, gender, and ethnicity. The unnamed narrator of *Balún Canán* belongs to the dominant Ladino (mixed-race) class, but she lacks full cultural citizenship because of her age and gender. The peripheral status of the characters allows them to document cases of oppression without being seen or interrupted.

I teach *Under the Feet of Jesus* first because it is more readily accessible in terms of topic and setting to most students in the United States. To flesh out the novel's racial critique, I ask students to read the introduction to *Racial Formation in the United States: From the 1960s to the 1990s*, by Michael Omi and Howard Winant. These scholars argue that race, far from self-evident, is a social formation that nation-states produce to govern their economies of production and other social goods (4). When viewed from this vantage point, the daily struggles of Estrella and her family become clear manifestations of a society whose economy depends on Mexican and Chicano subservience. When the family arrives at their "new" bungalow at the beginning of the novel, the narrator emphasizes the home's age and disrepair. Viramontes does not explicitly discuss race beyond noting that the family moved because Estrella got into a fight with her friend, another migrant in the next bungalow who is an Anglo American girl. Nevertheless, the family's poverty is intimately linked to ethnicity; their living conditions evoke those of other migrant workers during the 1970s and later.

Under the Feet of Jesus suggests that public schools in the United States play a key role in inculcating racialized modes of production in young migrant children, an act that ensures that the system will continue indefinitely. The family's mobile lifestyle forces Estrella to bounce from school to school. Rather than find inspiring mentors, she runs into teachers like Mrs. Horn, a woman who never compliments her intricately braided hair but always tells her she is dirty (25). Estrella's experience in public schools leads her to view education with skepticism not because she is unintelligent—she reads better than the girl whom she fought does—but because her teachers affirm that her Mexican identity makes her inferior. In a graduate course, my students and I discussed this scene alongside a reading of Louis Althusser's "Ideology and Ideological State Apparatuses." As students read this theoretical work, it became clear that, for the migrant children of the novel, schools become a key site for "reproduc[ing] the means of production" because they proactively direct Mexican children to the fields. Undergraduate students may not have read any work by Althusser, but instructors can still help them see how Estrella will encounter greater obstacles in her education than will people in more privileged circumstances.

For this reason, I invite students of all levels to compare Estrella's education to their own to discuss how public schools in the United States currently challenge or reproduce racialized structures of power. Students map Estrella's journey from the classroom to the workplace through small-group discussions and short writing assignments. Estrella starts working when she is young to help her family; she follows the migrant trail with them and labors full-time in the fields. By early adolescence, she begins to recognize injustice there as well. For example, when two harvesters faint from working in the scorching heat (*Under the Feet* 83), the employers do nothing to improve worker safety. Instead, the migrants have to help those among them who may have heat exhaustion (83–84). As instructors, we should help students understand that most migrant workers' employment depends on contractors and a complex matrix of power in which a combination of race, ethnicity, and legal status makes Mexican and Chicano workers cheaper to employ than their white American counterparts. While this structure of power allows migrant workers to find work, it also marginalizes them and gives them few legal resources for confronting abusive employers.

The human toll of the poor working conditions and low pay becomes especially clear in the novel when the teenage migrant worker Alejo and his cousin steal peaches from orchards and later sell them at a discount on the black market. When they sneak in and pick peaches during nonworking hours, a crop duster suddenly comes through to spray the trees and douses Alejo with a dangerous amount of pesticide. He cannot go to the doctor because he lacks money and because he took ill while breaking the rules. Alejo's actions, which some students may classify as petty crime, can lead to interesting class discussion: Why is he stealing? Is he having trouble subsisting? What would happen if he were caught? The lens of racial formation provides students with useful perspectives: Alejo steals peaches because of his great need, which inadvertently puts him underneath the crop duster's sweep through the orchard, and he cannot visit a clinic because he has neither the right racial background nor the right socioeconomic status.

Beyond showing how systemic racism forces Mexicans and Chicanos to take greater risks than their white migrant counterparts, the novel also emphasizes how access to medicine and proper health care is racialized. Alejo's emergency also coincides with an initiatory experience in the life of Estrella. As her mother tries to care for the boy (who has no family nearby), Estrella develops romantic feelings for him. It is fruitful for students to discuss how a racialized economy of production has brought these two characters together. Given the opportunity—through writing assignments, presentations, or exams—students can flesh out their understanding of the overriding racial and economic paradigms that directly affect Alejo.

Instructors need to be careful when explaining the racialized nature of Alejo's inability to receive health care, particularly when working with students who are not familiar with (or remain skeptical of) critical race theory. Some students may point out that very few doctors would refuse to provide care just because of the patient's race or ethnicity, while students who have undocumented family members will understand the fear of this outcome and its likelihood. Alejo's predicament, and whether he survives, is left unanswered by the novel. In her desperation, Estrella takes Alejo to a mobile clinic, where the nurse requests $15.00 but settles for $9.07 when Estrella proves that she has no more money. The nurse believes that she has done Estrella a favor, but Estrella feels robbed after the nurse refers Alejo to a nearby hospital, where she will once again be charged. In an important moment in Estrella's development, she enters the clinic with a crowbar and violently demands a refund. She justifies her actions by saying, "You talk and talk and talk and talk to them and they ignore you. But you pick up a crowbar and break the pictures of their children and all of a sudden they listen real fast" (151). As students grapple with the two different ways in which the nurse and Estrella interpret the $9.07 consulting fee, they can gain new insights into how poverty and racism operate in the borderlands and in the larger society in the United States.

After discussing *Under the Feet*, students are ready to tackle *Balún Canán*, a novel that uses a seven-year-old female narrator to navigate the complex systems of oppression in Mexico's southernmost state, Chiapas. Because *Balún Canán* has been translated as *The Nine Guardians*, instructors can teach both of these novels in an English-language class. This juxtaposition of texts will enrich students' understanding of such different border regions. The child narrator in *Balún Canán* helps readers understand how societal oppression and attitudes are handed down from generation to generation. At one point, she reasons, "El español es privilegio nuestro. Y lo usamos hablando de usted a los superiores; de tú a los iguales; de vos a los indios" ("Spanish is our privilege. And we use it with a 'your honor' to superiors, with a 'thou' to our equals, and with a 'ye' to the Indians"; Castellanos, *Balún Canán* 38; Castellanos, *Nine Guardians* 40). Whether instructors teach this novel in English or in Spanish, it is important for them to explain that there are three ways to say "you" in Chiapanecan Spanish: *usted*, *tú*, and *vos*. The use of these words has evolved in a unique way within the Chiapanecan context to reflect the rigid hierarchies of power. Indeed, the fact that such a young girl would recognize her society's rigid views on race and language emphasizes the extent to which her parents and local leaders have used the language to inculcate institutionalized racial hierarchies.

In teaching *Balún Canán*, instructors should explain colonially imposed racial hierarchies in Mexico and in Guatemala, a country where no revolution has challenged the colonial racial order; such hierarchies continued into the mid–twentieth century.[1] Students can quickly understand that regional opposition to federal mandates in Mexico might be likely, and that given its borderlands status, Chiapas would share more commonalities with Guatemala than with central Mexico. Castellanos's novel points out that most workers in Chiapas speak only Mayan languages like Tzeltal, and the majority have not had access to school instruction. Thus, they are unaware both of the postrevolutionary Constitution of 1917—which guarantees equal rights and access to education—and of the newer policies of President Lázaro Cárdenas (*Balún Canán* 100 and *Nine Guardians* 99–100). The landed class in Chiapas is opposed to these changes and impositions by federal officials in Mexico City, and the novel clearly demonstrates the landed class's refusal to accept rights for the Amerindian people. The fact that the novel is set in the early twentieth century needs to be stressed, as students will likely be aware of present-day practices and of the reality that indigenous people are still disrespected in the state.

Federal representatives close down unsatisfactory schools to undermine the authority of local, longstanding elites (including the narrator's parents). In one particularly memorable moment, a federal inspector exerts his privilege to shame a rural teacher and shut down an underperforming girls' school (Castellanos, *Balún Canán* 48–52 and *Nine Guardians* 49–52). Since the inspector never authorizes a new school, the narrator is forced to remain home—thus eliciting her female disadvantage—while her brother continues to attend classes at his boys' school. Thus the novel documents a diversity of schools: one for Ladino boys, one for Ladina girls, and a separate one for indigenous children of both genders to be instituted (as a result of the victorious revolution). Class discussions can help students understand that the societally defined roles for people of specific races and genders result in distinct educational experiences.

Chiapas's ties to Guatemala become even clearer when the Ladina smuggler-vendor Doña Pastora arrives at the family home to sell contraband. Seated with the narrator's mother, Zoraida, she refuses to transact business until Zoraida tells her indigenous servants to leave the room. The young narrator witnesses the ensuing conversation in silence. The young girl's continued presence may symbolize her racial and familial privilege, but it also shows how her age and gender make her invisible to those around her.[2] Zoraida tells Doña Pastora that she cannot purchase anything because she lacks the money (Castellanos, *Balún Canán* 47 and *Nine Guardians* 48). Even though the novel is focalized through the eyes of the young narrator, it makes clear that the family's recent financial hardships come from government initiatives to "liberate" (read: assimilate) the local Mayan indigenous farmhands by giving them the "privilege" of attending school during work hours and by partitioning some of the land of wealthy families to create cooperative communities for the indigenous people who have always worked that land. Zoraida claims ignorance of the political situation and states that she only knows what her husband, César, tells her about the family's finances. When Doña Pastora realizes that Zoraida truly cannot buy anything, she offers to sell a secret: a safe crossing point into Guatemala. Zoraida misunderstands the offer, thinking that the woman is offering her husband a career in contraband.

This short segment—consisting of just over two pages—is key to understanding the central role of the border in constructing notions of race and gender in Castellanos's depiction of the community in Comitán. Indeed, Doña Pastora tells Zoraida that if things continue as they are, then she and her family will need to relocate to Guatemala, where, unlike in postrevolutionary Mexico, their privileged position in the racial hierarchy will be preserved. In asserting that Guatemala is a better place for Zoraida and her family to live, Doña Pastora confirms that Ladino Chiapanecans have more in common with their peers in Guatemala than with people in Mexico City. While these differences did not cause major problems for the local elite prior to the 1910 Revolution, the new government endangers the social status of Ladinos. Those who relocate south—where they may acquire new landholdings because of their Ladino status—will be able to maintain their way of life by exploiting indigenous farmworkers. César does not do this, however; instead, he loses his ranch after an indigenous revolt. When discussing this novel, I ask students to think of as many social hierarchies as they can (e.g., race, gender, age, marital status, and legitimacy at birth), and then to tie these hierarchies to Chiapas's border status. They soon see that Chiapas remains a liminal space geographically as the novel ends, and most of the locals maintain their racist views. The balance of power, however, has shifted ever so slightly, since indigenous voices now register in political conversations.

This essay has suggested an approach for teaching Viramontes's *Under the Feet of Jesus* alongside Castellanos's *Balún Canán*. Both novels are set near borders—Chiapas is just north of Guatemala, and California lies to the north of Mexico. The presence of a major border in each work offers great opportunities to discuss continuing constructs of race with students: in *Under the Feet of Jesus* Mexican and Chicano migrant workers are coded as foreign, socially borderline figures precisely because they (or their ancestors) come from Mexico. As such, they are denied the privileges that citizens of the United States have. In *Balún Canán* the proximity of the border to Guatemala leads the Chiapanecan elite to think that they can circumvent new federal rules and cling to colonial racial and cultural paradigms. The stories are narrated by young female protagonists whose relative marginalization allows them to perceive acts of discrimination without drawing attention to themselves. Using these two novels and supplementary texts, instructors can design a course for undergraduate sophomores or juniors in which students examine how the protagonists' age, gender, and race interface in the context of a border-minded society.

Through readings and class interaction, students can engage their peers' observations, discuss societal boundaries and assumptions in relation to a physical border, and engage discourses on race and gender.

Notes

1. Smith; Lund can help students understand constructs of race in Guatemala and Mexico, respectively. They also identify key differences between the two countries.

2. I like to assign Cypess because it is approachable for students of all levels and because it provides an excellent explanation of the young narrator's social position.

Works Cited

Althusser, Louis. "Ideology and Ideological State Apparatuses." 1970. *Marxists Internet Archive*, www.marxists.org/reference/archive/althusser/1970/ideology.htm.

Castellanos, Rosario. *Balún Canán*. 1957. FCE, 2007.

———. *The Nine Guardians*. Translated by Irene Nicholson, Readers International, 1992.

Cypess, Sandra Messinger. "The Narrator as Niña in *Balún Canán* by Rosario Castellanos." *El niño en las literaturas hispánicas*, edited by J. Cruz Mendizabal, Indiana U of Pennsylvania P, 1978, pp. 71–78.

Lim, Jeehyum. "Reimagining Citizenship through Bilingualism: The Migrant Bilingual Child in Helena María Viramontes' *Under the Feet of Jesus*." *Women's Studies Quarterly*, vol. 38, nos. 1–2, Spring-Summer 2010, pp. 221–42.

Lund, Joshua. *The Mestizo State*. U of Minnesota P, 2012.

Omi, Michael, and Howard Winant. Introduction. *Racial Formation in the United States: From the 1960s to the 1990s*, 2nd ed., Routledge, 1994, pp. 1–13.

Reyes-Benítez, Iris Yolanda. "La estructura lingüística en *Balún-Canán*: El lenguaje como instrumento de dominio." *Revista de Estudios Hispánicos*, vol. 21, 1994, pp. 251–67.

Smith, Carol A. "Race-Class-Gender Ideology in Guatemala: Modern and Anti-Modern Forms." *Comparative Studies in Society and History*, vol. 37, no. 4, 1995, pp. 723–49.

Villalobos, Elizabeth. *Asesinos fronterizos: Performance de transgresión de los derechos humanos en el imaginario social del norte y sur de México*. 2014. U of Kansas, PhD dissertation.

Viramontes, Helena María. *Under the Feet of Jesus*. Dutton, 1995.

Elena Díaz Björkquist

Brianda Domecq's Novel *La Santa de Cabora* and a Southwest Chautauqua about the *Curandera* Teresa Urrea: A Personal Narrative

She scooped me up and didn't let me go. Her story gripped my imagination. A poor, illegitimate girl goes from rags to riches and becomes a spiritual healer to thousands of people, especially those working under harsh conditions in late-nineteenth-century Mexico. The Mayo and Yaqui Indians revered her as a saint, but the Mexican dictator Porfirio Díaz called her "a dangerous girl" for instigating rebellion among the "Indios" and exiled her, putting her on a train to the United States, where she healed people from one end of the country to another.

The incredible story of Teresa Urrea, La Santa de Cabora—or Teresita—reads like a movie script. Researching her life led me in directions I never thought possible. I first learned about Teresita in a Chicano studies class at Sonoma State University in the early 1970s. Her story intrigued me, but I never had time to pursue further research. When I moved to Arizona in 1999, I unpacked books and papers and found a yellowed photocopy of an article by Richard Rodríguez and Gloria Rodríguez, published in the early Chicano journal *El Grito*, that I'd read years earlier and saved with the idea that someday I would learn more about Teresita. I reread it and found her life as fascinating as I had before.

Coincidentally, and without knowing of my interest, my cousin Carlos gave me a copy of a novel published in 1990 by the Mexicana writer Brianda Domecq, *La insólita historia de la Santa de Cabora*. As I devoured it, friends told me about a request for proposals by the Arizona Humanities Council for scholars to perform in Chautauqua, a living history program, about a person important in Arizona history. The performances in 2000 were all to take place in Arizona State Parks. I knew this was my opportunity to research and, as an added bonus, portray Teresita. In writing the proposal, I gave a brief summary of her life and her significance to Arizona history. William Holden, in his book *Teresita*, describes her as living in the Arizona towns of Nogales, Solomonville, and Clifton, as do other historians. I found Gillian Newell's thesis, *Teresa Urrea: Early Chicana? The Politics of Representation, Identity, and Memory*, which postulates that Teresita was one of the first Chicanas because she spoke Spanish and had Mexican customs when she arrived in the United States as a young woman. Her exile forced her to learn English and adjust to the customs of her new country. She also exemplified an early-twentieth-century working single woman who supported herself and others.

The Arizona Humanities Council requested that I include in my proposal my photograph, so I had one taken at an old-time photography studio. I wore a makeshift nineteenth-century costume. I submitted the proposal and had a feeling that I would be selected. During the 1960s Chicano Movement, professors taught the story of Teresita, but now she was mostly forgotten. It was time for her to be known again. Many scholars applied (with diverse projects), but only two other scholars and I had our proposals selected. Thus began my journey of presenting Teresa Urrea throughout Arizona, and I never dreamed that the presentations would also take me to California, New Mexico, and Texas and would eventually earn me the prestigious Arizona Public Humanities Scholar Award from the Arizona Humanities Council.

I had only three months to prepare for the first presentation, in front of the Arizona Humanities Council staff and representatives from the Arizona State Parks system, who also funded my proposal, and for the second, which I would perform for the public in the historic Pinal County Courthouse in Florence, Arizona. During the preparation period, I researched Teresita's life, found a costume, and wrote a monologue to memorize.

As I delved into all the material that I could find about Teresita, I kept returning to Domecq's book. I learned that the Bilingual Press at Arizona

State University had published an English translation of the book in 1998, *The Astonishing Story of the Saint of Cabora.* I ordered the book because my presentation had to be in English, and having it would save me the time needed to translate the Spanish into English.

In my research I found various versions of her life story, explanations for what happened to her, and conclusions drawn from possible misinformation. I surmised that not much was really known about her in the historical record.[1] Alex Nava, in his article "Teresa Urrea: Mexican Mystic, Healer, and Apocalyptic Revolutionary," notes that Teresita describes her own life in interviews given to newspaper reporters. I decided to include in my presentation quotes from these interviews that matched what I had gleaned from several historians.

Historians all agree that Teresita was born on 15 October 1873 in Rancho de Santana, Ocoroni, in Sinaloa, Mexico. With what I gleaned from my sources, I wrote and memorized this opening to my monologue:[2] "My mother was a poor Yaqui Indian, her name was Cayetana Chávez. My father, Tomás Urrea, was a wealthy hacendado. I am not a legitimate child." Abandoned by her mother, she grew up in a hovel, was mistreated by her aunt, and was bullied by her Yaqui peers for looking different (since she had green eyes, reddish-brown hair), and they teased her that she was the bastard daughter of the hacendado, don Tomás Urrea. After describing her early years, historians differ on what happened next. Some opine that she confronted her father and demanded to be accepted as his daughter. Others claim that because he had only sons and no daughters, he decided to accept her. In an interview, Teresita stated that her father sent for her when she was sixteen years old to live at Rancho Cabora (Vanderwood). I chose to use her explanation in my portrayal.

Most historians agree that at Cabora Teresita met Huila, the household cook and a *curandera*, or healer, who taught her the use of herbs and massage for healing purposes. However, historians and other writers do not give Huila much of a role, almost as if they don't find her to be important enough in Teresita's life. Domecq, Holden, and the Chicano novelist Luis Alberto Urrea (*Hummingbird's Daughter*) are the exception. They not only include Huila in their accounts but paint a picture of the *curandera* as a teacher critical to Teresita's early training and as someone Teresita would later emulate when she became a healer. Since Huila became Teresita's teacher, she represents Teresita's future path. From Huila, Teresita learned Yaqui Indigenous remedies, which kept her in touch with her roots and led to her own healing practices.

In 1889, Teresita went into a trance, which Holden and Luis Alberto Urrea explain was a reaction to being accosted by a ranch hand and perhaps raped. Holden's account came from José C. Valadez in *La Opinión*.[3] Other accounts, like Frank Bishop Putnam's article on her life, suggest that Teresita fell into a cataleptic state. Still other writers thought the trance was due to a concoction that Huila prepared for her (to overcome fright). Domecq wrote that falling off a horse caused Teresita to go into the trance. This version of the event parallels what happens to the nameless researcher in Domecq's novel, who falls as she climbs down from the hill where Teresita dug up the red soil that she used in her cures. In preparing my portrayal of Teresita, I chose the explanation in which the trance was a reaction to the tea that Huila prepared for her.

When Teresita recovered, she exhibited healing powers that attracted large numbers of people to Cabora to receive her cures, which involved touch, massage, or herbal concoctions. A newspaper reporter wrote that about ten thousand people camped at the rancho, over several weeks, as she ministered to them. Because of the miraculous nature of her healings, Indigenous peoples in northwest Mexico began to call her La Santa de Cabora. Lauro Aguirre, a spiritist and activist from Guaymas who opposed the Díaz regime and who attested to having known Teresita, described Teresita's view that "Prayers should be offered with profound feeling, should be soul-stirring and heartfelt. She objected to the prayers of priests—empty, external, impersonal, without feeling; simply memorized passages" (qtd. in Nava 503). The Catholic clergy in the region denounced Teresita, and word of her reached Díaz, who was watching for insurrections in the late 1880s. The army was dispatched to the region to stop the Yaqui and Mayo Indigenous people from protesting the takeover of the last of their lands by large ranch holders. Teresa encouraged the Indians to pray directly to God. Rodríguez and Rodríguez write that she supported the Indians in defending their lands. At one point Mayo Indians attacked the city of Navojoa, yelling "Viva La Santa de Cabora" as they looted the town and killed its defenders in reaction to injustices committed against them by the Díaz regime. This event focused attention on Teresita; the Mexican government accused her of instigating rebellion. Not much later, in 1892, President Díaz exiled her and her father from Mexico.

In another portion of the monologue that I created using my research, I spoke as Teresita, saying: "I have seen the many wrongs, before my eyes children not yet three years old have been lynched, hung from trees, babies torn from mother's arms, their brains smashed on the ground. And this not in war but by order of the military commander of the Sonora district to keep the Yaqui down."[4]

Historians differ about when Teresita became politicized. Some think she was political from the time she began giving sermons that the Indians should get their land back. However, I agree with Domecq that Teresita at first believed in social justice and gradually became more political as she observed how the Indians were treated. She spoke out against the atrocities committed against them by the Mexican government. She continued to speak out even after she was exiled. A pharmaceutical company in Los Angeles hired her and had her travel throughout the United States to represent its products, but she also healed those who presented themselves to her with various illnesses.

In Domecq's novel, Teresita's friend and assistant Mariana Avendaño is depicted as unmarried. Other sources, such as Holden, picture her as brought to Teresita by her husband, Fortunato, to be cured of paralysis. In all of these accounts, Teresita cured her, and Mariana and her husband remained by Teresita's side. Mariana accompanied Teresita until her death and afterward took Teresita's two daughters to Mexico. In all accounts except Domecq's, Mariana is not fully fleshed out. Like she does with Huila, Domecq does more to portray Mariana as Teresita's helper and friend. However, Domecq does not leave the impression that Mariana, in addition to Teresita's father and Huila, played one of the most important roles in Teresita's life.

Domecq paints a multifaceted picture of Teresita as a young woman in search of herself, who had little knowledge at first, but who came into her power as she grew older. Her strength and perseverance, however, were evident from the start. She wanted to be recognized by her father, Tomás Urrea, and prepared herself to rise from poverty. Later, she defied her father when she chose to continue her healing practices at Cabora. In Nogales, she chose without her father's permission to have her photograph taken in a manner that portrayed her as a saint. After moving to Clifton, Arizona, she defied her father again by marrying a man he disapproved of, a Mexican miner named Guadalupe Rodríguez, who immediately tried to take her back to Mexico and was arrested and imprisoned in the United States.[5]

Domecq depicts Teresita's entrance into the United States as going unnoticed by the residents of Nogales. Teresita and her father moved into a dilapidated house in Nogales that brought her back to her humble beginnings. Neighbors snubbed her and complained about the Indians who came to her house, according to Domecq. In newspaper interviews Teresita states that when she alighted from the train, she was greeted by hundreds of admirers. She also claimed that merchants in Nogales gave her a house. I think the truth was probably somewhere between the two descriptions of her entrance into the United States. For my presentation, I chose to use the version that I gleaned from newspaper articles, because it presented a happier picture of her life after her arrest in Mexico (for several newspaper reports, see Irwin 234–36).

In December 1891, before Teresa and her father were removed by Díaz's troops in May, a rebellion by the men of Tomóchic, Sonora, in defense of their invaded territory brought the full force of the Mexican army, which killed all the men, then soldiers set fire to the church where the women and children were sheltered, leaving them to burn alive. General José María Rangel ordered his soldiers to set fire to the whole town. Díaz blamed Teresita because Tomochitecos yelled, "Viva La Santa de Cabora."[6] Some historians wrote that this event occurred while Teresita and her father were still in Mexico, but others, as well as Domecq in her novel, wrote that it occurred after they moved to Nogales. This latter account made more sense to me, and I chose to present the timing of the rebellion that way. Domecq goes a step further, stating that the rebellion was what radicalized Teresita.

Researching Teresita's life was easier than putting together a costume. As I studied the material I had accumulated, I searched for a costume that recreated what Teresita wore in the early 1900s. A seamstress sewed a white gown similar to what women in the 1900s would have worn. I selected jewelry, and I found props to enhance my portrayal. I chose props that would be easy to transport and that showcased the simplicity of Teresita as a *curandera*, as she might have appeared in her last public interview. I gleaned most of my information about her from historians and from interviews that she willingly gave, so I thought it appropriate to incorporate the interview format into my presentation. I also thought the presentation would involve the audience, who would be asked to pretend that they were reporters.

Domecq begins her novel with an unnamed researcher. At first I didn't find this character to be necessary to Teresita's story because the story stood on its own. However, in my third reading of Domecq's novel, I identified with the researcher-protagonist, who traveled to northern Mexico to learn more about the figure of Teresita. Like her I pored over the information accumulated, searching for a Teresita that felt right to me. It wasn't until I let go of my research, stopped thinking like a historian, and began to think like a storyteller that I realized the significance of the researcher. In a sense I was like Domecq's protagonist, who loses her briefcase containing her research and, in the novel's epilogue, assumes Teresita's identity. I became Teresita in my portrayal in the Chautauqua living history program. Domecq's researcher doesn't have a similar outlet, so she winds up in a mental institution (in the late twentieth century), where she claims to be Teresita.

Domecq is the only woman who has written a historical novel about Teresita. Her own experience as a woman seems to have helped her portray Teresita in a realistic and sympathetic manner. From Domecq's writing, I felt as if I knew Teresita. The male authors gave accounts of her story but didn't make me feel who Teresita was or how she thought. Domecq put me in Teresita's thoughts. Her poetic language captured the events in Teresita's life so that I felt I experienced them myself.

When I portrayed Teresita, I felt her presence. A photograph taken of me at a performance in a black box theater confirmed that she was present. When laid out chronologically, photographs from before and after the performance showed me in a white costume against the black background. Sandwiched between them was a photograph in which ectoplasm arched from one of my outstretched hands to the other. When I met with my cousin Cachuri, a *curandero*, who didn't know that I was portraying a *curandera*, he told me that he felt the presence of a spirit within me. He said that if I didn't take precautions, the spirit could take over my life. From then on, only when I performed as Teresita did I give her spirit free reign. When Luis Alberto Urrea researched Teresita for his novel *The Hummingbird's Daughter*, he experienced several mysterious events that he attributed to her.[7]

The night before my first performance as Teresita for the grant I received from the Arizona Historical Parks and the Arizona Humanities Council, I was unable to reduce the presentation to the requested half hour. I'd gathered so much information in my research, it was difficult to narrow it down. In a Chautauqua, presenters are advised to portray only one incident in the character's life, following a short introduction of who they were. The presentations should be an hour total. I had half an hour to present Teresita, fifteen minutes to answer questions as her, and fifteen minutes to answer questions as myself, the scholar who researched her life. But since the audiences I presented to would probably not know who Teresita was, I decided to relate her entire life.

Over the course of seventeen years, I portrayed Teresita more than two hundred times in various venues, ranging from intimate rooms in libraries that held less than fifteen people, to large theaters with three hundred people in attendance. I wore out my original costume and replaced it with another. "Being" Teresita brought me unusual experiences. Once a man in the audience believed I was really her, overlooking the part of my presentation when the host introduced me as myself, the scholar. He came up to me afterward wanting me to heal him. I had other similar experiences. After a presentation, two Native Americans poured five gold coins into my cupped hands. They said I knew what the coins were for and asked me to bless them. By this time I had adjusted to being Teresita and felt okay to give a blessing.

Friends who saw my presentation told me that they didn't recognize me when I was being Teresita. When I portrayed her, she indeed scooped me up. Her message of peace and love resonated not only with me but also with my audiences.

Learning about Teresita would benefit students in either English or Spanish classes. It would allow them to delve into the life of a spiritual healer and the topic of *curanderismo*, folk and Indigenous medicine. Here I've discussed Teresita's life from her early years in Cabora to her arrival in the United States, but Domecq's novel traces her early life to her death. Students could immerse themselves in Teresita's life by reading Domecq's novel and by studying other aspects of Teresita's life such as what she did after leaving Nogales. To bring Teresita to life as I have, students could be asked to research various parts of her life and present a living history presentation for their class. This would not have to involve costumes but could involve dialogues between students portraying Teresita and the various individuals important in her life: for instance, an argument between Teresita and her father concerning what to do about the multitude of people gathered at Cabora for her healings and the impact of their presence on his ranch.

Researching Teresita's life has been an enriching experience for me. I started with Domecq's novel and wound up learning as much as I could about Teresita from other sources. I'm sure student researchers would find the exploration as rewarding as I did.

Notes

1. Editor's note: Elena Díaz Björkquist researched her performance piece before further work was published on Teresa, significantly, Irwin (a chapter of which cites newspaper articles about Teresa, both in Mexico and the United States; 195–261); and Urrea, *Hummingbird's Daughter* and *Queen*. Díaz Björkquist's

performance over seventeen years surely stimulated new interest in research on Teresa.

2. Sources include Aguirre.

3. A historian and militant revolutionary, Valadez published his serialized accounts, under the title "La Santa de Cabora y la insurrección de Tomóchic de 1892" ("The Saint of Cabora and the Tomóchic Insurrection of 1892"), in *La Opinión*, a Spanish-language newspaper in Los Angeles, over twelve successive weeks, between 28 February and 16 May 1937. The accounts only came out in book form posthumously in 1985, in a volume titled *Porfirio Díaz contra el gran poder de Dios: Las rebeliones de Tomóchic y Temosachic* (*Porfirio Díaz against the Great Power of God: The Rebellions of Tomóchic and Temosachic*). See Irwin 250.

4. Teresita learned of some of these acts of violence through her visions; see Holden; Putnam; and Irwin.

5. Clifton and Morenci were boomtowns in the late nineteenth century that were populated mostly by miners and that had a Wild West sense of law; see Gordon.

6. The Tomóchic rebellion, the subsequent siege of the town by the army, and the massacre of the entire community were related in twenty-eight articles published in a Mexico City newspaper, *El Demócrata*, between 14 March and 14 April 1893. The war correspondent who prepared them, Heriberto Frías, traveled with the army; later he published these accounts as a novel titled *Tomóchic*. As noted by Irwin, Teresita is a minor figure in Frías's account, although her image looms large in the background (221).

7. Luis Alberto Urrea, a self-described distant cousin of Teresa, created two novels on her life, in English, one of which, *The Hummingbird's Daughter*, ends with her crossing into the United States, and the other of which, *Queen of America*, relates the rest of her years, when she lived in the United States.

Works Cited

Aguirre, Lauro. *¡Tomóchic!¡Redención! Revoluciones recientes y futuras de México.* Imprenta de *El Progresista*, 1901.

Domecq, Brianda. *The Astonishing Story of the Saint of Cabora*. Translated by Kay S. García, Bilingual Press, 1998.

———. *La insólita historia de la Santa de Cabora*. Grupo Editorial Planeta, 1990.

Frías, Heriberto. *Tomochic: Episodios de la campaña de Chihuahua: 1892: Relación escrita por un testigo presencial.* 1893. Océano, 2002.

Gordon, Linda. *The Great Arizona Orphan Abduction*. Harvard UP, 1999.

Holden, William. *Teresita*. Stemmer House Publishers, 1978.

Irwin, Robert McKee. *Bandits, Captives, Heroines, and Saints: Cultural Icons of Mexico's Northwest Borderlands.* U of Minnesota P, 2007.

Nava, Alex. "Teresa Urrea: Mexican Mystic, Healer, and Apocalyptic Revolutionary." *Journal of the American Academy of Religion*, vol. 73, no. 2, June 2005, pp. 497–519.

Newell, Gillian. *Teresa Urrea: Early Chicana? The Politics of Representation, Identity, and Memory.* 1999. University of Arizona, thesis.

Putnam, Frank Bishop. "Teresa Urrea, the Saint of Cabora." *Southern California Quarterly*, vol. 45, no. 3, 1963, pp. 245–64.
Rodríguez, Richard, and Gloria Rodríguez. "Teresa Urrea: Her Life as It Affected the Mexican-U.S. Frontier." *Readings from El Grito, 1967–71*, edited by Octavio Romano, Quinto Sol, 1971, pp. 179–99.
Urrea, Luis Alberto. *The Hummingbird's Daughter*. Back Bay Books / Little, Brown, 2005.
———. *Queen of America*. Back Bay Books / Little, Brown, 2011.
Vanderwood, Paul J. "Santa Teresa: Mexico's Joan of Arc." *The Human Tradition in Latin America: The Nineteenth Century*, edited by Judith Ewell and William H. Beezley, Scholarly Resources, 1989, pp. 215–32.

Emily Hind

Weight, Writing, and Privilege: Carmen Boullosa, Elena Poniatowska, and Rosario Castellanos

If location is the key to a good real estate deal, then likewise, context makes all the difference in a literature class. Placing authors' historical times into the larger framework of Mexican history and history in the United States gives learners a way to absorb literary pieces as logical if perhaps curious reactions to events, and not just as assigned readings that students may or may not identify with using contemporary standards. The following teaching plan aims to harness students' preexisting notions about migration, weight, and age, while exploring short texts by the Mexican-born authors Carmen Boullosa, Elena Poniatowska, and Rosario Castellanos. Each of the topics applies to all the writers, although for reasons of space I explore only one theme per writer. In honor of meeting students where they are, I usually begin a course with at least one contemporary text and then work backward chronologically. Thus, the outline below starts with a text by Boullosa and ends with a text by Castellanos.

Early in the semester I like to play a chronology game that involves dividing the class into two teams and asking a rotating member from each team to stand at the board and, choosing from a list that I have placed on the board, write down what the team believes is the year in which an event I describe aloud took place; I reinforce the knowledge of chronology introduced by the game by giving a written quiz at the end of class and allowing students to work collaboratively on it in groups of their choosing. For other quizzes that range beyond the list of years, I supply the last two digits of a year and ask the students only to fill in the century. These activities prove surprisingly challenging for many of them because they aren't accustomed to thinking about such broad historical context.

In an activity I pair with the chronology game, I write spontaneously on the classroom board a simple time line that I develop from right to left. Starting on the far right for a class on Mexican literature, I set up the following dates: 2010, the year of the Mexican bicentennial, which took place during President Felipe Calderón's bloody retaliations against narcotraffickers; 1910, the start of the Mexican Revolution; 1810, the beginning of the independence movement; 1767, when the king of Spain ordered all Jesuits to leave New Spain; 1691, when the nun Sor Juana Inés de la Cruz wrote her autobiographical feminist epistle *Respuesta a Sor Filotea de la Cruz*; 1521, when Hernán Cortés achieved the downfall of Tenochtitlán, which would become Mexico City; and 1492, when Christopher Columbus arrived wide-eyed in the Caribbean. After this basic setup, the instructor can then play the activity forward, adding additional dates of interest in chronological order.

Beginning with the topic of migration, which informs the class's analysis of Boullosa's work, the following dates of interest prepare students to compare Mexican history and the history of the United States. On the same time line, I can add the inauguration of Mexico City's first university in 1553. It took another eighty-three years for the northern colonies to open their first university, Harvard, in 1636, and thus no English-language equivalent to Sor Juana, a genius academic, exists in the history of the United States. The Declaration of Independence appeared in 1776, nearly a decade after the Spanish king expelled the Jesuits from the New World. This quick trip forward in time corrects the erroneous idea that Mexico is somehow less sophisticated than the United States by reason of a permanent lag in development. To the contrary, at the end of the eighteenth century much of the United States *was* Mexico, as illustrated by the map in Carlos Loprete's civilization and culture textbook (72). After students contemplate that map, the instructor may point out that the year 1848 marks the loss of a great deal of Mexico's land, thanks to an invasion by the United States and the Treaty of Guadalupe Hidalgo, which ended the Mexican-American War, called the US Intervention in Mexican history textbooks.

The United States also played a role in both the 1910 Revolution in Mexico and in the cartel violence of the twenty-first century: rebels, and later, cartel members, retreated strategically to Texas, which at both times was more stable than northern Mexico. In 1915 Mariano Azuela published the novel *Los de abajo* (*The Underdogs*) in serial form in a newspaper in El Paso, Texas; and during President Calderón's *sexenio* ("term of office"; 2006–12) the government's campaign of armed retaliation against cartels drew support from the United States. Within this larger context, students can consider the productive periods of three Mexican writers, and their short texts suggested here.

Boullosa's essay "El sueño mexicano" ("The Mexican Dream") remembers that in the 1830s and 1840s many African American slaves—thousands, according to Boullosa—fled the United States and what was then the Republic of Texas to Mexico, which refused to return the escaped people. Mexico had outlawed slavery and found itself in conflict with both the United States and Texas. As Boullosa points out, in 1850 the "Sueño Mexicano"—a capitalized phrase in the last paragraph of the essay—came to include not only black slaves but also hundreds of Seminoles who left a Texan reservation. Class discussion can compare the dynamics of the "Sueño Mexicano" for escaped slaves and for Seminoles and the American dream for later migrants to the United States.

Boullosa's essay "Más acá de la nación" ("Beyond the Nation") complicates the matter of race in Mexico by examining an image commonly found on an official Mexican textbook of the 1960s, which depicts a darker-skinned woman clothed in a Greek toga who allegorically represents Mexico.[1] Boullosa engages this image in her critique of the superficiality of this official celebration, evinced by the paucity of information available about the model for the image. Oral accounts name the model as Victoria Dornelas and indicate that she may have died of the effects of alcoholism, possibly after having lived in Paris. Supposedly, the painter Jorge González Camarena fell madly in love with Dornelas but never left his wife, "a not-at-all-Indian Frenchwoman" (Boullosa, "Más acá de la nación" 63). Boullosa adds that the painter and his wife are *güeros*, which in Mexican Spanish means people who are light-skinned or moneyed. The dual definition of *güero* recognizes the imbricated nature of racism and classism in Mexico.[2]

Boullosa's "Más acá de la nación" also reviews a variety of culturally specific terms for housekeepers, who occupy an overlooked and often denigrated sector of Mexican society. The wave of internal migration in Mexico during the second part of the twentieth century that brought women from the countryside to the national capital did not encourage employers to respect their cheap and easily replaced labor, and this practice continues. Students can examine how the speaker, Boullosa, stands at the crossroads of racial and class privilege. On the one hand, she is relatively light-skinned and, by her own admission, employs household help in Mexico City. On the other hand, in New York City, where she has a second home, she is seen as "Mexican" and "of color" (70). For class discussion, instructors can encourage students to imagine themselves in a social environment in which they are subjected to other people's positive and negative prejudices; students can contemplate themselves as actors in a complex network of license and bias, in other words. Are they near the top of the hierarchy in one social system and the bottom of another? What point is Boullosa making about migrant housekeepers' and her own Mexicanness?

Now in her eighth decade, Poniatowska is often lauded as Mexico's grand dame of letters, and her standing can be discussed along with her stories featuring household servants. Students can analyze a video of the ceremony in which Poniatowska was awarded Spain's eminent Miguel de Cervantes Prize in 2013. The video uses a soft focus that obscures the writer's facial wrinkles and age spots and in the process pixilates her gray and white hair to the point of blurriness, giving the impression of a halo (Poniatowska, *Elena*). Does this media process play in her favor? Poniatowska commented to me in an interview in July 2018 that she cannot find the time to color her hair: "Sí, yo nunca me pintaría. Me da una flojera infinita porque sabes que si te pintas tienes que ir cada mes o cada veinte días. Es horrible. Es espantoso" ("Yes, I would never dye my hair. The idea bores me to death because you know that if you dye it you have to go every month or every twenty days. It's horrible. It's terrifying"; Interview).[3] Poniatowska added that she cannot set aside time for cosmetic services with a dermatologist either. Thus hiding her age is not important to this prolific writer. Students can discuss how age is treated under the prejudices of contemporary youth culture, and how age might constrain students' perceptions of Poniatowska.

In a move to represent indigenous Mexican culture, during the ceremony for the Cervantes Prize, Poniatowska chose to wear an elaborate red and yellow huipil. Students can analyze their reactions to this attire and how Poniatowska represented Mexico. They can then read news reports on the event. One journalist praises Poniatowska, claiming that she has not changed since her cub reporter years: "A sus 82 años Elena Poniatowska sigue siendo la misma joven autora que entrevistaba celebridades, la misma mujer madura que enfrentó la historia inmediata de su pueblo a través de sus crónicas y reportajes, la misma mujer entregada a la pasión por vivir que es escribir" ("With her eighty-two years Elena Poniatowska continues to be the same young author who interviewed celebrities, the same mature woman who confronted the immediate history of her people through chronicles and reporting, and the same woman dedicated to the passion for life that is writing"; Valdés Medellín 81). What do students think about the idea of remaining "the same" through the decades?

"Las lavanderas" ("The Washerwomen") and "Esperanza número equivocado" ("Esperanza Wrong Number") provide topics for further discussion on age and ageism.[4] In "Las lavanderas," the narrative voice—ageless and disembodied—inserts itself explicitly only once, at the end of the fourth sentence, with the comment "siento como un gran ruido de manantial" ("I hear loud noise like running spring water"; Poniatowska 486). This first-person reference to the sound of distant traffic connects the narrator to the modern urban environment, leaving the washerwomen just outside it as they scrub clothes in the river and without the aid of a washing machine. The narrator's ability to make contact with modernity reappears at the conclusion of the tale, which features a canny and ironic comparison. A recently returned washerwoman, Lupe, blames her absence on her father's death, which was caused by a church bell that knocked him from the bell tower. In revenge, the community members put the bell in a jail. The other women characters accept this logic, and therefore, in terms of intellectual sophistication, it seems that the oldest, Doña Otila, does not differ much from the youngest, Conchita. The characters appear doomed to remain excluded from a modern society that would never bother to imprison an inanimate object for murder.

In "Esperanza número equivocado," the protagonist feels bitterly excluded from the narrative of marriage. Esperanza, the ironically named older, pessimistic, and unmarried household employee (whose name means "hope"), has a fortune-telling habit at the beginning of the story: she checks the wedding announcements in the newspaper and predicts the brides' futures, with outcomes slanted toward the "obsessive and malignant" (Poniatowska 488). In her youth, she enjoyed using the landline telephone to make social connections beyond the house. She kept mistaken callers on the phone—hence the story title—and sometimes dialed numbers randomly, hoping to strike up conversation with a stranger. Now that she is older, she both insists that no other household employee answer the phone and rejects surprise connections; for the concluding plot twist, she swears at an accidental caller: "y por favor, se me va a ir usted mucho a la chingada" ("and you'll do me the favor of going straight to fucking hell"; 488). Esperanza never married and appears sidelined by her age and circumstance; like the washerwomen, she is unable to see her predicament as clearly as the narrative voice appears to view it.

The best academic article I have found on the subject of household help has to do with the sustained yet always unequal relationship between Rosario Castellanos and her mother's former cook and nurse, María Escandón (Steele). A more recent biographical article, by Erin Gallo, mentions Cynthia Steele's piece and expands on it by tracing efforts by Castellanos to recast herself as an independent woman during gigs as a visiting professor at various universities in the United States during the 1960s. Gallo also mentions Castellanos's taste for valium (303–04). I recommend Castellanos's poem "Válium 10" for classroom use, even in a course that focuses on novels and short stories. Here and in other pieces, Castellanos circles the issue of food and the implied theme of body weight.[5] While instructors will want to distinguish Castellanos's literary voices from her own voice, the subject of fat appears in both her creative work and her personal letters.

Self-critical missives from Castellanos to her friend and eventual spouse Ricardo Guerra years before their marriage address the topic of weight. In a letter from Madrid dated 1951, Castellanos tells Guerra that she is "disparejamente gorda" ("unevenly fat"; *Cartas* 121). Another letter, written in Wisconsin in September 1966, hints at her thinness as a triumph; she informs Guerra: "Estoy bajando un poco de peso, lo que era necesario porque entre chicharrón y chicharrón, y botanita y botanita (ay), ya no era posible" ("I'm losing a little bit of weight, which was necessary because from chip to chip and snack to snack (ay), it wasn't possible anymore"; 184). In another letter to him, from October, she reports, "Ya puedo usar mucha ropa que en México no me venía. Si sigo así voy a llegar muy esbelta" ("Now I can wear a lot of the clothes that didn't fit me in Mexico. If I keep up like this, I'll arrive quite slender"; 202). By November, she declares that she has kicked her Mexican junk food habit: "Pero fíjate que a mí el antojito ya no se me antoja. Prefiero la esbeltez" ("But now guess what, junk food doesn't appeal to me anymore"; 228). In "Válium 10," weight figures in terms of the duties of meal planning, which are accomplished in concert with a private cook. The poem winks at high art in its use of Latin in the description of meal planning as an "ars magna combinatoria" ("art of great combinations") and manages irony, captured in the adjective "quotidian" in the line "el menú posible y cotidiano" ("the possible and quotidian menu"). That is, while the Latin phrasing aims for high culture, the notion of daily habits winkingly takes the tone down a notch.

The poem's struggle with grinding domestic routine prepares students to read the short story "Lección de cocina" ("Cooking Lesson"). This story adopts the point of view of a female narrator who has watched the housekeeper prepare food and who now, as a newlywed, must attempt the task herself. The meat that she takes from the package, described as frozen and then as bloody, serves as a metaphor for her young marriage, and as the protagonist gradually burns the steak meant for two, she sees that it is inedible. Students may judge the marital ideas as reflecting outdated patriarchy, but the sustained frustration with food might be recognizable to them. Castellanos broaches the contradictions of a capitalist society anxious for indulgence and discipline. The contradictory goals of cookbooks can vary from offering visual appeal to providing budget, quick-prep, or more complex recipes. The possibility of enjoyment fades, however, as the narrator turns from fretting that the steak may be too large for one meal to thinking that the shrinking and eventually overcooked serving best suits the garbage.

On the surface, the protagonist of "Lección de cocina" maintains an ambivalent attitude toward the need to nurture her own goals and the need to perform the role of a self-denying housewife. Students can discuss the endless pressures of economical cooking and cleaning, and pressures related to more indulgent self-care. The battle between economy and indulgence may explain why consumer societies promote restricted diets. In his amusingly titled *Eat Fat*, Richard Klein summarizes the diet historian Hillel Schwartz's answer to this contradiction: capitalism approves of diets because at first people spend more as a result of the special needs of a given diet, and later on, during the postdiet phase, they continue spending because of their altered and even increased appetites, which cause most dieters to regain lost weight and then some (Klein 144; Schwartz 246–47). In the 1980s, Schwartz incorrectly predicted that fat would become beautiful again, an aesthetic view that Klein, a decade later, also would like to see return (Klein 210–11). But in the 1960s Castellanos, despite her extensive work that has feminist leanings, was never able to accept her body.[6]

In conclusion, I offer a fourth topic that connects age, fat, and migration: the cool. Peter Stearns's excellent history of cool in the United States views this emotionally subdued mode of being as a consumption-friendly style: the cool are more passionate about objects than about people. It is surely no coincidence that after *American Cool*, Stearns wrote a history of fat. Of course, students know cool when they see it, without Stearns's help. The concept of cool—*padre* or *chido* in late-twentieth- and early-twenty-first-century Mexican slang—can be suggested to students in terms of the other topics. Instructors can ask: Is fat cool? Is older age cool? Is migrant status cool? Do the lines of cool cut across these categories, so that perhaps a fat young man could be cool, but not a slender elderly woman? As these topics complicate one another and place analysis in context, students who previously did not think of the instructor as cool may well reconsider.

Notes

1. Those textbooks belong to a series of *libros de texto gratuitos* ("free textbooks"), first published in 1960, that continues today. See "Comisión" for images of the textbooks: the cover in question appears twice in the "Catálogo histórico" ("Historical Catalog"), once with the caption "Generación 1962" ("Generation 1962") and once with "Generación 2014."

2. If Dornelas managed to paint her own canvases, that effort is now forgotten. Boullosa does provide a list of successful Mexican women artists and women artists residing in Mexico whom students can research, including Frida Kahlo, María Izquierdo, Nahui Olin, and Tina Modotti.

3. Translations in this essay are mine.

4. These two stories, which appear in Chang-Rodríguez and Filer's *Voces de Hispanoamérica* ("Voices of Latin America"), are actually older than the textbook acknowledges. Although they were reprinted in Poniatowska's early short story collection *De noche vienes* (*You Come at Night*), from 1979, Jörgensen notes that they first appeared under the section title "Herbolario" ("Herbalist") in *Los cuentos de Lilus Kikus* (*The Tales of Lilus Kikus*), from 1967.

5. Instructors can note that valium was first approved for use in 1960 and frequently prescribed to women by medical doctors for what was referred to in the mid–twentieth century as "women's problems." It would be helpful for students to read a short biography essay about Castellanos (e.g., Ahern, "Rosario" [*Latin American Writers*] or "Rosario" [*Spanish American Women Writers*]). Before her son's birth in 1961, she suffered from depression after several miscarriages. Her husband was regularly unfaithful during their thirteen-year marriage, and she divorced him in 1971.

6. For additional details on the attitudes of Castellanos's female characters toward fat, see Hind.

Works Cited

Ahern, Maureen. "Rosario Castellanos." *Latin American Writers*, edited by Carlos A. Solé and Maria Isabel Abreu, vol. 3, Scribner's, 1989, pp. 1295–302. 3 vols.

———. "Rosario Castellanos." *Spanish American Women Writers: A Bio-Bibliographical Source Book*, edited by Diane E. Marting, Greenwood Press, 1990, pp. 140–55.

Boullosa, Carmen. "Más acá de la nación." *Revista de Estudios Hispánicos*, vol. 46, no. 1, 2012, pp. 55–72.

———. "El sueño mexicano." Chang-Rodríguez and Filer, pp. 596–97.

Castellanos, Rosario. *Cartas a Ricardo.* Prologue by Elena Poniatowska, Conaculta, 1994.

———. "Lección de cocina." *Material de lectura*, selected and introduced by Nahum Megged, UNAM, 2008, www.materialdelectura.unam.mx/images/stories/pdf3/rosario-castellanos.pdf.

———. "Válium 10." Chang-Rodríguez and Filer, p. 460.

Chang-Rodríguez, Raquel, and Malva E. Filer. *Voces de Hispanoamérica: Antología literaria.* 4th ed., Thomson and Heinle, 2013.

"Comisión Nacional de Libros de Texto Gratuitos." *Gobierno de México*, 19 Feb. 2020, www.gob.mx/conaliteg.

Gallo, Erin. "The Political Becomes the Personal: Rosario Castellanos and the US Women's Liberation Movement." *Hispanic Review*, vol. 85, no. 3, 2017, pp. 295–313.

Hind, Emily. *"Femmenism" and the Mexican Woman Intellectual from Sor Juana to Poniatowska: Boob Lit.* Palgrave Macmillan, 2010.

Jörgensen, Beth. "Question about Poniatowska's 'Las lavanderas.'" E-mail message to Emily Hind. 15 Nov. 2017.

Klein, Richard. *Eat Fat.* Pantheon Books, 1996.

Loprete, Carlos A. *Iberoamérica: Historia de su civilización y cultura.* 4th ed., Prentice Hall, 2001.

Poniatowska, Elena. *Elena Poniatowska: Discurso completo, en su Premio Cervantes 2014. YouTube*, uploaded by Lared21TV, 23 Apr. 2014, www.youtube.com/watch?v=D3UwbRH-H7k.

———. "Esperanza número equivocado." Chang-Rodríguez and Filer, pp. 487–89.

———. Interview. By Emily Hind. 9 July 2018.

———. "Las lavanderas." Chang-Rodríguez and Filer, pp. 486–87.

Schwartz, Hillel. *Never Satisfied: A Cultural History of Diets, Fantasies and Fat.* Free Press / Collier Macmillan, 1986.

Stearns, Peter N. *American Cool: Constructing a Twentieth-Century Emotional Style.* New York UP, 1994.

Steele, Cynthia. "Power, Gender, and Canon Formation in Mexico." *Studies in Twentieth and Twenty-First Century Literature*, vol. 20, no. 1, 1996, pp. 65–100.

Valdés Medellín, Gonzalo. "Elena Poniatowska: Mexicana universal: Premio Cervantes 2013." *Siempre!*, 4 May 2014, pp. 80–81.

Part IV

Visual and Digital Strategies

Magdalena Maíz-Peña and Luis H. Peña

Life Writing, Biopics, Gender, and Media: Elena Poniatowska's *Tinísima* and *Leonora*

We have designed an upper-level undergraduate research seminar conducted in Spanish and titled Life Writing, Gender, and Representation: Bodies, Identities and Narratives, which engages undergraduate students in learning about Latin American and Latino life writing and contemporary visual and written discourses. We have found that undergraduate students can begin to grasp complex political, gender, and social issues, articulating innovative analytical models of life writing, with a focus on biofictions, as they examine Elena Poniatowska's two novels that are based on the lives of female artists, *Tinísima* (1992) and *Leonora* (2011), as part of a conceptual thematic unit. Taught in the Hispanic Studies Department at Davidson College, the semester-long course provides a theoretical framework that motivates juniors and seniors to examine subjectivities, sexualities, gender, and performativity, unsettling fictional and nonfictional discourses. Our primary sources include biographical and autobiographical narratives, urban chronicles, documentary photography, indigenous testimonials, an Afro-Brazilian journal, poetic self-portraits, writing about borders, visual narratives, performative discourses, biographical fiction, documentaries, graphic biopics, prison narratives, newsreels, animation, art installations, earth sculptures, Chilean tapestries, and material culture more broadly, among other possibilities.

Life writing is defined as a historical-cultural practice in diverse media, which materializes the subject in a hybrid genre and documents a condensed version of the subject's life as a visual, written, graphic, or cinematic narrative. Life-writing discourses encompass a diversity of enunciations, positionalities, intersectionalities, media, locations, spatial and temporal geographies, and contexts in relation to the biographical or autobiographical subject; the texture of that person's life; corporeal discourses; literary, cultural, or digital forms; and readers or spectators (Arfuch, *Vida*; Maiz-Peña and Peña; Smith and Watson, *Reading Autobiography*). Undergraduate students delve into epistemological questions on biographical markers, imaginative and referential frames, the instability of modalities of representation, and distinctive audiences, focusing on the analysis of visual, written, graphic, audible, performative, and material cultural artifacts and of cinematic lives, for which Poniatowska's novels are well suited.[1]

We begin the seminar by deliberating on the remarkable essay by Sidonie Smith, "Identity's Body," then, as we read each novel by Poniatowska, we ask students to map new *conocimientos y saberes* ("formal and informal knowledge") so that they problematize boundaries, surfaces, corporeal enactment, language, gender, and sexualities while arguing about subjectivity, the cultural body, location, temporalities, representational practices, and regulatory body politics. Bearing in mind Smith's incisive life-writing question "Whose history of the body is written?" (271–72), participants discuss such issues in *Tinísima* and *Leonora* while also deliberating about pertinent life-writing concepts such as narrative postures, embodiment, experiential histories, zones of transcoding, misrepresentation, erasures, gaps, and whitening.

Three life-writing conceptual units explore theoretical frameworks throughout the semester. In the first unit, Geographies and Forbidden Gazes, we discuss select excerpts from newspaper articles about Delmira Agustini (by Eleonora Croquer Pedrón), cultural journalism by Alfonsina Storni, a favela journal by Carolina Maria de Jesús, testimonial excerpts by Rigoberta Menchú, and essays by Gloria Anzaldúa. In the second unit, Dislocating Biographical Frames, Performative Narratives and Postfeminist Biopics, we concentrate on close readings that are attentive to gender and sexualities and on approaches to discussing Poniatowska's biofictional tactics in *Tinísima* and *Leonora*.[2] In the third unit, Graphic Narratives, Corporeal Memories and Global Legacies, which occurs in the final weeks of the seminar, we consider visual, written, cinematic, and material narratives by or about Frida Kahlo, Eva Perón, Ana Mendieta, the movement Madres de la Plaza de Mayo, the Chilean arpilleristas, and Doris Salcedo.

Scripting Performative Narratives and Biopics

The Italian American activist and modernist photographer Tina Modotti (1896–1942) and the English-born artist and writer Leonora Carrington (1917–2011)—each of whom lived many years of their lives in Mexico—left a legacy of innovative artistic explorations, distinctive visions, and political engagement. For the second conceptual unit, which is newly designed and focuses on performative narratives and biopics, students engage in a process of close reading of two biographical novels by Elena Poniatowska. We ask students to create an original manifesto on biographical fictional discourses, and then to write a daring script for a short documentary on Modotti or Carrington. Afterward they collaborate in pairs to create a postmodern biopic on one of these figures using the intuitive program *iMovie*. Preparation for this final cinematic project requires considerable discussion of Poniatowska's novels and the assigned theoretical life-writing readings. Discussing seminal concepts on biopic theory that are alluded to in cultural and visual studies by Carlos Monsiváis, Beth Jörgensen, and Andrea Noble makes students aware of the importance of frameworks, framing, interdisciplinarity, and postmodern narration. Students debate both works in depth before presenting their analysis and conclusions to the seminar participants. For the discussions on the life-writing works, we assign selected essays from Smith and Julia Watson's *Women, Autobiography, and Theory: A Reader* and *Reading Autobiography*, which students read alongside Poniatowska's novels.[3] Students' media projects must be limited to the theory of life writing, postmodern biopics, gender and sexualities studies theory, and issues related to Modotti or Carrington that concern the articulation of life writing, visual representations, and audiences.

The seminar calls for small group debates centered on the construction of selected cultural subjects by women writers. In their presentations, students must illustrate narrative strategies found in *Tinísima* or *Leonora*, which can include the biographical subject, meaning and textures of multilayered narratives, feminist techniques for framing a life, experimental documentation, the negotiation of conflicting themes, contemporary subjectivities, nonhegemonic or marginal history, and cultural memory. We encourage students working in small groups to formulate daring theoretical questions such as, What tactics does Poniatowska implement to reframe the lives of her subjects? What discursive strategies does she use to create multilayered textures situated in specific historical-cultural contexts? What innovative journalistic devices does she inscribe on her novels to generate postmodern ruptures? How does this Mexican author articulate epistemological discontinuities? Groups are prompted to theorize on the configuration of alternative life-writing templates: here they can identify the value of micronarratives, reflect on the implications of condensation, displacements, and the symbolization of "biographemes," which are relevant traces of an individual's life that textualize the subject (Arfuch, *Vida* 41). They also identify elements crucial to understanding the text such as the imaginative treatment of facts, embedded narratives, the function of intermediality, visual effects, the production of intimacy, and the fleshing out of female agency.

An additional supplementary reading that students might find constructive is the essay by Nora Erro Peralta, "Re(Creando) vidas, ¿biografía o ficción?" ("Re(Creating) Lives, Biography or Fiction?"). This provocative essay guides students to consider mapping life-writing strategies, journalistic tactics, transcultural lines of inquiry, and intermedial segments. Students are encouraged to consult the critical essay by Zaida Capote Cruz that deals with the challenges of composing a fictional narrative on Modotti's life (314) and the innovative project by María Claudia André on digital postmodern life-writing narratives (57). Another life-writing discourse that provides an alternative framework for approaching a biographical model is the graphic narrative *Tina Modotti: Una mujer del siglo XX* (2007; *Tina Modotti: A Woman of the Twentieth Century*, 2014), by the Spanish artist Angel de la Calle, which considers Modotti's complex life as a militant-artist. Finally, the documentaries *Leonora Carrington, imaginación a golpe fino* (*Leonora Carrington, Imagination with an Elusive Blow*), by Fernando Navarro Becker, and *The Flowering of the Crone: Leonora Carrington, Another Reality*, by Ally Acker, bestow innovative biopic discourses. Students could also choose to read Carrington's autobiographical, literary, and cultural pieces in *Memorias de abajo* (*Memories Below*).

Creating a Manifesto, a Script, and a Biopic

Reading the introduction to *Teaching Life Writing Texts* motivates students to think about their manifestos, and it preludes discussions about their scripts for a postmodern biopic on Modotti or Carrington (Fuchs and Howes 1–19). The introduction exposes them "to significant critical and theoretical work on gender, race, sexual orientation, class, disability, the status of indigenous peoples, and postcolonial politics and aesthetics" and foregrounds "issues of identity, subjectivity, memory, agency, history, and representation" (1). The reading provides key terms that students are required to annotate in their manifestos and that they will expand on in their *iMovie* projects.[4] This approach guides students to interpret and apply theoretical readings, and to engage in the critical selection of digital resources to produce their biopic. Such resources can include videos, recordings, photographs, paintings, lithographs, cultural documentaries, and performances that break generic boundaries.

Working in pairs, students first submit their life-writing manifestos to be evaluated then produce a collaborative script for a ten-minute biopic, which we review in order to provide suggestions for further research. Thus students must learn to work with a partner to outline a hypothesis, formulate arguments, discuss cinematic techniques, converse about audiences, and elaborate a concise visual storyboard. Their scripts should be based on the key concepts of biofictions laid out in their manifestos. The scripts should account for the instability of the genre; the implementation of special effects; the uncovering of hidden or erased aspects of the subject's life; and the historical context of other layerings, the importance of which has been noted by Gabriele Helms (100). Students present their scripts to the class and get feedback from other seminar participants. This experience of peer review incites them to establish a schedule to produce the short film, become familiar with *iMovie*, curate digital materials, and define archival procedures. They also follow specific guidelines and deadlines, so that they can exhibit their ten-minute collaborative digital project at the end of the semester.

The postmodern biopics of female subjects are then edited by students, who must integrate conceptual frameworks from the readings, discussions, and independent research. We ask students to call attention to the following life-writing elements when they are editing their biopics: identities, subjectivities, intersectionalities, life-lines (strands of the subject's life), agency, public memory, the fluidity of representation, power, framing, location of the subject, cultural politics, and audiences consuming a dissident life-writing model.

Creating the Frameworks of Postmodern Biopics and Media

Students learn so much more from their final projects in this seminar than they would in a less interactive and collaborative seminar (though this media project could be incorporated into a seminar conducted in English). They also learn in-depth, persuasive strategies to deconstruct the life of a female subject for a postmodern biopic—in the process of examining and interrogating George F. Custen's definition of a biopic as a cinematic composition of a life, a segment of a life, and the interpretation of the life of a real person whose real name is used (10). Students can broaden their understanding of biopics by consulting the recent seminal study by Bronwyn Polaschek, who defines the postfeminist biopic as a cinematic narrative "that depicts the life of a person from history" and that aims to expose the "real subject" behind the historical public persona (46). They can also consult scholarship by Dennis Bingham, interrogating, contesting and adding innovative elements as they reflect on the biopic as a cinematic discourse that "narrates, exhibits, and celebrates the life of a subject in order to demonstrate, investigate, or question his or her importance in the world; to illuminate the fine points of a personality; and for both artist and spectator to discover what it would be like to be this [actual] person . . . transformed into a character" (10).

The production of a postmodern biopic based on *Tinísima* or *Leonora* will integrate creative and critical skills, theoretical knowledge, research and writing abilities, cinematic experience, and digital literacy. Editing the biopic demands independent research and original conceptual frameworks related to the treatment of the subject's life, biographical markers, sexuality and gender biographemes, representation, cultural memory, private and public construction, and cinematic consumption. Students can be evaluated on their informed decision-making related to framing, cinematic intuition, and interpretation. The creation of a volatile, erratic, and fluid biographical profile will demonstrate their critical skills and the concrete articulation of a postmodern visual discourse. While they do not need extensive knowledge of staging scenes, interfacing media, or recording, editing, remixing, cutting, and fragmenting film (and some students will arrive with those skills), they might love to define critical narration and representational strategies. One invaluable learning outcome will be a greater awareness of local and global cultural contexts and audiences. A critical essay on teaching *Leonora* in an undergraduate seminar, by Aurora Camacho de Schmidt, also offers ideas to help guide students on a transcultural approach to Poniatowska's biographical writing, inciting them to construct oppositional reading frames to approach the female subject (9).

To fulfill one of the learning outcomes of the seminar, students are asked to deconstruct a single narrative by considering "the imposed fiction of a story, the creative use of fact, the translation necessary to make a life comprehensible and interesting" for contemporary audiences (Polaschek 46). A postmodern biopic is a contemporary cultural text that is inclusive of different viewpoints, and digital production inspires the creators of such a film to superimpose, rewrite, alter, intermix, and situate in the film "the complexities of the historical context of the setting of the film, and also of the actual context in which [it is] produced" (Polaschek 3).

The writing of an original script, development of a visual storyboard, and production of a postmodern biopic using *iMovie* motivates students in pairs to negotiate, make decisions, and materialize their own vision of an alternative script about a female biographical subject. Composing the biopic helps undergraduate students develop a unique critical position. They must rethink theories, conceptualize strategies for life writing and marking gender, integrate interdisciplinary knowledge, interface transcultural frames, refine critical skills, negotiate research topics, construct a hypothesis, select biographemes, write a short script, create a digital archive, and finally produce, edit, and add credits to the film while envisioning a target audience.

Poniatowska's creative writing about Modotti and Carrington embodies strategies to inscribe female bodies as texts and to theorize the interpretation of fictional biopics, challenging undergraduate students to embrace transcultural interpretations as they conceptualize and unfold life-writing narratives about female subjects in their postmodern biopics. Reading these texts mobilizes interdisciplinary thinking and, through pedagogical approaches, fosters the examination of the ethics and aesthetics of life writing, intimacy, and the bodily signatures of nomadic female subjects.

Notes

1. Both biofictional texts by Poniatowska have received important awards: Mexico's Premio Mazatlán de Literatura for *Tinísima*, and the prestigious Premio

Biblioteca Breve for *Leonora*. Our seminar has been taught twice and has included discussion of the production of postmodern biopics. The new unit, described in this essay, that focuses on Poniatowska's biographical fictions will challenge seminar participants to interrogate biography, biographical fictions, and biopics by fleshing out critical frameworks and theories of life writing in unexpected ways.

2. For the readings in unit 1, see Croquer Pedrón, *Escrito* 84–97, 113–20, and 98–105; Storni, *Nosotras* 25–27, 28–31, 49–51, and 129–32; de Jesús 1–47; Menchú 7–41, 80–104, and 148–75; and Anzaldúa 23–45, 47–73. For a critical understanding of Elena Poniatowska's works, consult Erro Peralta and Maiz-Peña, and for interdisciplinary pedagogical frameworks, see *Diálogo*, vol. 17, no.1, Spring 2014.

3. Other texts that can be consulted are Polaschek; Arfuch, *Memoria* and *Vida*.

4. These manifestos are a theoretical, conceptual, and cultural mapping of the postmodern biopic of a female subject as an alternative life-writing proposition that dismantles the hegemonic narrative in specific historical-cultural contexts. Consulting Polaschek will provide students with a solid analysis of this type of biopic so that they can apply postmodern biographical theories to their *iMovie* biopics.

Works Cited

Acker, Ally, director. *The Flowering of the Crone: Leonora Carrington, Another Reality*. Reel Women Media, 2017.

André, María Claudia. "Las crónicas femeninas de Elena Poniatowska en la construcción de un archivo digital." *Diálogo*, vol. 17, no. 1, Spring 2014, pp. 57–64.

Anzaldúa, Gloria. *Borderlands / La frontera: The New Mestiza*. 4th ed., Aunt Lute Books, 2012.

Arfuch, Leonor. *Memoria y autobiografía: Exploraciones en los límites*. Fondo de Cultura Económica, 2013.

———. *La vida narrada: Memoria, subjetividad y política*. Eduvim, 2018.

Bingham, Dennis. *Whose Lives Are They Anyway: The Biopic as Contemporary Film Genre*. Rutgers UP, 2010.

Camacho de Schmidt, Aurora. "Reading Elena Poniatowska's *Leonora* in an Undergraduate Seminar." *Diálogo*, vol. 17, no. 1, Spring 2014, pp. 9–21.

Capote Cruz, Zaida. "Biografía y ficción: El desafío de *Tinísima* de Elena Poniatowska." Erro Peralta and Maiz-Peña, pp. 314–20.

Carrington, Leonora. *Memorias de abajo*. Translated by Francisco Torres Oliver, Alpha Decay, 2017.

Croquer Pedrón, Eleonora. *Escrito con rouge: Delmira Agustini (1886–1914), Artefacto cultural*. Beatriz Viterbo, 2009.

Custen, George F. *Bio/Pics: How Hollywood Constructed Public History*. Rutgers UP, 2010.

De Jesús, Carolina María. *La favela*. Casa de las Américas, 1965.

De la Calle, Angel. *Tina Modotti: Una mujer del siglo XX*. 3rd ed., Ediciones Sins Entido, 2011.
Erro Peralta, Nora. "Re(Creando) vidas, ¿biografía o ficción? *Las siete cabritas* de Elena Poniatowska." Erro Peralta and Maiz-Peña, pp. 329–43.
Erro Peralta, Nora, and Magdalena Maiz-Peña, editors. *La palabra contra el silencio: Elena Poniatowska ante la crítica*. Ediciones Era / UNAM, 2013.
Fuchs, Miriam, and Craig Howes, editors. *Teaching Life Writing Texts*. Modern Language Association of America, 2008.
Helms, Gabriele. "The Generic Instability of Contemporary Life Writing in Canada." Fuchs and Howes, pp. 99–106.
Jörgensen, Beth E. "Fotoescritura: Biografía y fotografía en *Tinísima*." Erro Peralta and Maiz-Peña, pp. 267–86.
Maiz-Peña, Magdalena, and Luis Peña, editors. *Modalidades de representación del sujeto auto/biográfico femenino*. Universidad Autónoma de Nuevo León, 1997.
Menchú, Rigoberta. *Me llamo Rigoberta Menchú y así me nació la conciencia*. Edited by Elisabeth Burgos-Debray, Siglo XXI, 1992.
Monsiváis, Carlos. "Un cuarto de siglo." Erro Peralta and Maiz-Peña, pp. 321–28.
Navarro Becker, Fernando, director. *Leonora Carrington, imaginación a galope fino*. *YouTube*, uploaded by Canal 22, 12 June 2015, www.youtube.com/watch?v=e9iQx8m1JAc.
Noble, Andrea. *Tina Modotti: Image, Texture, Photography*. U of New Mexico P, 2000.
Polaschek, Bronwyn. *The Postfeminist Biopic: Narrating the Lives of Plath, Kahlo, Woolf and Austen*. Palgrave Macmillan, 2013.
Poniatowska, Elena. *Leonora*. Seix Barral, 2011.
———. *Tinísima*. Ediciones Era, 1992.
Smith, Sidonie. "Identity's Body." *Autobiography and Postmodernism*, edited by Kathleen Ashler et al., U of Massachusetts P, 1994, pp. 266–92.
Smith, Sidonie, and Julia Watson. *Reading Autobiography: A Guide for Interpreting Life-Narratives*. 2nd ed., U of Minnesota P, 2010.
———. *Women, Autobiography and Theory: A Reader*. U of Wisconsin P, 1998.
Storni, Alfonsina. *Nosotras . . . y la piel: Selección de ensayos de Alfonsina Storni*. Alfaguara, 1998.

Betsy A. Sandlin

Visual Teaching Strategies and La Malinche as a Cultural Icon

Powerful female figures—fictional, mythical, and historical—play an important role in the work of Chicana and Mexicana visual artists and authors, yet none has been imbued with as much symbolic meaning, at times highly contested, as the Mexican iconic figure La Malinche. Interpreter, slave, concubine, lover, traitor, victim, advisor, and mother: all of these identities and still others coexist in different versions of her story. Her original name was thought to be Malinalli, and in formal designation, Malintzín (later pronounced "Malinche"). The Spanish baptized her as Doña Marina. There is minor mention of her in the colonial record as the indigenous woman who was Hernán Cortés's interpreter and companion during the Spanish conquest of the Aztec empire. Cortés only mentions her a few times in his letters to Emperor Carlos V, referring to her as *la lengua* ("the tongue"). The chronicler Bernal Díaz del Castillo writes of her noble upbringing and her desertion by her mother, who sold her into slavery to protect the inheritance of a son.

La Malinche's story has changed over time. During the early colonial era she held a position of honor and was an important symbol for those seeking independence from Spain in the eighteenth century. Later, however, she was vilified by the Mexican revolutionaries. The word *malinchista* still carries the connotation of "traitor" and one who prefers foreign things. Octavio Paz, in his seminal book of 1950, *El laberinto de la soledad* (*The Labyrinth of Solitude*), identifies La Malinche as the symbolic mother of all Mexicans, for supposedly giving birth to the first child of mixed Spanish-Indian heritage. He infamously suggests that Mexicans are marked by being *hijos de la chingada*, or "children of violation," because of what he interprets as La Malinche's passive acceptance of her fate (88–113). Representations of La Malinche as Cortés's lover emphasize the danger of female sexuality, and Norma Alarcón describes the persistence of this image during the Chicano Movement in the United States, when La Malinche was viewed as an "evil goddess and creator of a new race . . . mother-whore, bearer of illegitimate children, responsible for the foreign Spanish invasion" (182).

By the 1970s and into the 1980s and 1990s, Mexicana and Chicana writers such as Rosario Castellanos, Gloria Anzaldúa, Cherríe Moraga, Carmen Tafolla, Lucha Corpi, Alicia Gaspar de Alba, and many others claimed and revised the image of La Malinche, bringing attention to her intelligence, resilience, and farsightedness. Their work often rewrites her story in the first person, giving her a voice of her own. As Luis Leal suggests, the feminist revision of La Malinche includes several strategies: characterizing Moctezuma as a tyrant, thereby reconfiguring La Malinche as a heroine who helped rescue her people from his iron-fisted rule; emphasizing her linguistic talent and superior intelligence; representing her as a peacemaker or bridge between worlds; revering her as a positive mother figure; supplying her with a more complete and complex history, especially by imagining her life before the conquest; and transforming her from passive victim into active participant in the conquest, in her relationship with Cortés, in the expression of her sexuality, and in the design of her destiny (277–80).

Approached as a cultural icon, La Malinche can be incorporated into a variety of college literature and culture courses. I have included her in Introduction to Latinx Literature, a course on Latin American culture before independence, advanced courses on Latin American women writers, and a course called Cultural Icons in Latin American and Latinx Literature. Studying La Malinche as a cultural icon through visual art and literature is an engaging way for students to grapple with several important issues: the biases of the historical record, the subjectivity of representation, and the role of cultural icons and the arts in exploring complex questions of identity.

Because visual representations easily draw students into a topic, class activities can evolve from simple descriptions to more complex analysis, interpretation, and finally, application of concepts. In the course Cultural Icons in Latin American and Latinx Literature, students begin by reflecting individually on the images shown to them, then they engage in small group discussions about the images, whole-class discussion of an assigned literary text, and finally, assigned individual creative projects. Each step in the process will be discussed in detail. Through this sequence, students are able to understand predominant versions of La Malinche's life story, gain insight into the social function of cultural icons, practice visual and literary analysis, identify strategies authors use to resignify La Malinche as a feminist icon, and apply their knowledge of cultural icons by creating original works.

First, students need to understand what cultural icons are. I assign the introductions to Robert McKee Irwin's *Bandits, Captives, Heroines, and Saints: Cultural Icons of Mexico's Northwest Borderlands* (xi–xxvi) and to David Scott and Kenyan G. Tomaselli's *Cultural Icons* (7–24). While neither work presents a comprehensive discussion of cultural icons as social phenomena, they do present jargon-free overviews that provide undergraduates with a common framework. Irwin, for instance, distinguishes between cultural icons and myths or legends, a subtle but interesting distinction for students to consider: "An icon . . . is not limited to a single story or cultural meaning. An icon more likely attains its status as such for its elasticity, its attractiveness to multiple peoples, and its ability to signify differently in multiple contexts" (xix). According to Irwin, an icon's meanings over time can vary "significantly according to the context in which the tellings of [its] stories have been produced and the ideological goals and prejudices of those who have produced those retellings" (xx). Likewise, Brenda R. Silver argues that cultural icons inspire "custody battles over who gets to define [their] meaning—over whose representation counts as 'truth'" (4). Cultural icons, then, are figures that have become a set of conflicting images, representations, and symbolic meanings. They are fictionalized versions of the people they were and may function as mirrors for society.

One advantage of approaching La Malinche as a cultural icon is that it allows instructors to incorporate into their classes a wide variety of visual images that are available online. Using visuals, including works of art, in the classroom is a way to generate student interest and increase motivation, reduce anxiety, and improve transcultural competence, particularly in the foreign language classroom (see Sederberg; Bush; Díaz; Barnes-Karol and Broner). By comparing and contrasting visual representations of La Malinche and practicing basic visual description, students are gently introduced to the complex idea that representation is subjective and the truth of an icon's story is in the hands of the artist and the eyes of the viewer or reader. Among many images of La Malinche that are easily located online are those from the *Florentine Codex*, where she has a central role (de Sahagún); the "Cortés and Malinche" murals by José Clemente Orozco, which portray the pair as Adam and Eve figures; the frightening painting *La Malinche: La lengua*, by the Cuban artist Rafael Zarza; the enigmatic and somber sculpture *Malinche*, by the Native American artist Jimmie Durham; and *La Malinche*, a small painting created by the Chicana artist Santa Barraza in 1996, which is fashioned in the style of a religious ex-voto and offers a positive, serene representation of Malinalli as a young woman (see Hughes and Reed for an image of the painting). La conquista, by the Mexican visual artist Alejandro Arango, is an interesting series of paintings, several of which refer to but also critique the Mexican muralist tradition and complicate the role of La Malinche in the conquest (see Eckmann for examples).

In advanced classes, I have contrasted portrayals of La Malinche with visual representations of another Mexicana icon, La Virgen de Guadalupe. The Chicana feminists Anzaldúa and Moraga have argued that Chicana women resist the limited binary represented by La Virgen / La Malinche (virgin/whore, good/evil, saint/sinner). Whatever visuals instructors choose, they should serve as a springboard for the idea that cultural icons have multiple, often conflicting representations.

Before I show visual images of La Malinche in class, I provide a brief overview of what we think we know about her life, as I do in the introduction to this essay. The work of Sandra Messenger Cypess and of Camilla Townsend is especially useful for this purpose. Afterward, I give students sticky notes, so that they can write down words that come to mind, one word per sticky note, as I click through some *PowerPoint* slides that show images of La Malinche. I never share these images with them before class, because I want to solicit their immediate reactions. I pause for fifteen seconds per slide to let them write on their notes. After all the images have been viewed, I put students in groups to share and discuss the words they wrote. I tell them to organize the words into a cognitive map or list, with categories such as "positive," "negative," and "neutral." I also ask them to identify the words that are most repeated. They can arrange their notes on the classroom walls if desired. This engaging activity paves the way for deeper discussion and analysis, guided by the following questions: How are the images of La Malinche similar? How do they differ? What social messages are being conveyed in the images? Are there any patterns in the words you wrote down? What might those patterns suggest? What does it mean that there are so many conflicting representations of the same woman?

After our initial discussion, depending upon time constraints, I choose one or more images for the class to revisit together. We discuss the chosen images in detail using a modified version of the learning method promoted by the organization Visual Thinking Strategies, which poses three questions to be addressed in order: What's going on in this image? What do you see that makes you say that? What more can we find? This method, codeveloped by Philip Yenawine, encourages close observation and critical thinking, since students must move beyond a superficial impression of an image in order to make deeper observations and to find evidence for their ideas and interpretations. Therefore, the Visual Thinking Strategies method results in more detailed observations than the initial sticky note warm-up activity described above. Finally, our work with visual representations in class prepares students to read literary texts that portray La Malinche. I ask students to think about the following guiding questions as they read: How can creative writing challenge predominant versions of cultural icons? How is La Malinche portrayed in the assigned literary texts?

There are many literary works to choose from for assigned readings, including the poem "Malinche," by the Mexicana author Castellanos; the play *The Eternal Feminine*, also by Castellanos; and poems by Chicana authors including Tafolla's "La Malinche," Corpi's "Marina," Angela de Hoyos's "La Malinche a Cortez y Vice Versa / La Malinche to Cortez and Vice Versa," Gaspar de Alba's "Malinchista: A Myth Revised," and others. The figure of La Malinche is also portrayed in novels and short stories, including Sandra Cisneros's collection *"Woman Hollering Creek" and Other Stories* and Laura Esquivel's *Malinche: A Novel.* Esquivel's novel is always a favorite with students—either in the original Spanish (*Malinche: Novela*) for advanced language learners or in English translation. It is a fictionalized account mainly from the perspective of La Malinche (called Malinalli in the novel) that imagines her life and relationships before, during, and after the Spanish conquest. The novel creates a fictional codex; this pictorial element can be used to transition from or link to the discussion of visual images of La Malinche in class. Themes explored in the novel include motherhood, dreams and visions, the power of language, and the role of religion and spirituality. Ultimately, Esquivel's novel is a sympathetic and empowering portrayal of La Malinche as a bridge between worlds. While reading the novel, we discuss ways in which its ideas are similar to or different from the visual images studied previously. We also consider Leal's list of feminist revision strategies to see which, if any, apply to Esquivel's version of La Malinche. Finally, I invite students to add additional revision strategies to Leal's list that they perceive in Esquivel's novel.

Following our discussion of the visual images and literary texts, I assign a creative project to assess whether students understand the concept of cultural icons and can apply their understanding to their new knowledge about La Malinche. For instance, I have asked students to dramatize parts of the novel on video or in front of the class. If writing is a main goal of the class, students can be asked to create a blog, present *Twitter* feeds, write original poems, or compose and perform original songs written in what they interpret to be La Malinche's voice. For an alternative activity that can be personalized to their interests, I have asked students to choose another cultural icon and write their own creative account or make a visual artwork to represent that person. Examples of icons students have chosen in the past include the singer Selena, the intellectual nun Sor Juana Inés de la Cruz, and the soccer star Diego Maradona, among others.

As observed by Townsend, who has closely studied Nahuatl and colonial documents from the era in which La Malinche lived, "The girl who had no choice in the matter but did as she was told would certainly never have guessed . . . that she herself would come to signify so many different things to so many different people that the truth about her could no longer be determined" (2). La Malinche is a fascinating figure for academics and students alike, precisely because her truth remains unknown, as she was unable to record her own account. The topic of cultural icons is an effective way to draw students into discussions quickly and to help them gain critical thinking skills and confidence as they move from initial observations and descriptions to more complex analysis of visual and literary texts. Like her ambiguous story, La Malinche as a cultural icon is flexible and can add cultural interest to a wide variety of courses at different levels. Students often become so interested in her that they leave class wanting to know more; perhaps that is the true power of La Malinche.

Works Cited

Alarcón, Norma. "Chicana's Feminist Literature: A Re-vision Through Malintzín /or Malintzín: Putting the Flesh Back on the Object." *This Bridge Called My Back: Writings by Radical Women of Color*, edited by Gloria Anzaldúa and Cherríe Moraga, Kitchen Table / Women of Color Press, 1983, pp. 182–90.

Barnes-Karol, Gwendolyn, and Maggie A. Broner. "Using Images as Springboards to Teach Cultural Perspectives in Light of the Ideals of the MLA Report." *Foreign Language Annals*, vol. 43, no. 3, 2010, pp. 422–45.

Bush, Michael D. "Facilitating the Integration of Culture and Vocabulary Learning: The Categorization and Use of Pictures in the Classroom." *Foreign Language Annals*, vol. 40, no. 4, 2007, pp. 727–45.

Castellanos, Rosario. *The Eternal Feminine*. Castellanos, *Rosario*, pp. 273–362.

———. "Malinche." Castellanos, *Rosario*, pp. 96–97.

———. *A Rosario Castellanos Reader*. Edited by Maureen Ahern, U of Texas P, 1988.

Cisneros, Sandra. *"Woman Hollering Creek" and Other Stories*, Vintage Books, 1992.

Corpi, Lucha. "Marina." Rebolledo and Rivero, pp. 196–97.

Cypess, Sandra Messenger. *La Malinche in Mexican Literature: From History to Myth*. U of Texas P, 1991.

De Hoyos, Angela. "La Malinche a Cortez y Vice Versa / La Malinche to Cortez and Vice Versa." Rebolledo and Rivero, pp. 200–01.

De Sahagún, Bernardo. *Historia general de las cosas de nueva España*. 1529. www.wdl.org/en/item/10096/#collection=florentine-codex.

Díaz, Erin M. "Expanding the Spanish Classroom: The 'Art' in Liberal Arts." *Hispania*, vol. 99, no. 3, 2016, pp. 436–48.

Díaz del Castillo, Bernal. *La historia verdadera de la conquista de la Nueva España*. 1576. Cambridge UP, 2010.

Durham, Jimmie. *Malinche*. 1988–92. *Artsy*, www.artsy.net/artwork/jimmie-durham-malinche.

Eckmann, Teresa. "Javier de la Garza and Alejandro Arango: Reevaluating Signs of Identity." *Anales del Instituto de Investigaciones Estéticas*, vol. 27, no. 86, 2005, pp. 55–93, www.redalyc.org/pdf/369/36908603.pdf.

Esquivel, Laura. *Malinche: A Novel*. Translated by Ernesto Mestre Reed, Atria Books, 2007.

———. *Malinche: Novela*. Atria Books, 2006.

Gaspar de Alba, Alicia. "Malinchista: A Myth Revised." Rebolledo and Rivero, p. 212.

Hughes, Bethany, and Lauren Reed. "Story Time: La Malinche." *Her Odyssey*, 15 June 2016, her-odyssey.org/2016/06/15/story-time-la-malinche/.

Irwin, Robert McKee. *Bandits, Captives, Heroines, and Saints: Cultural Icons of Mexico's Northwest Borderlands*. U of Minnesota P, 2007.

Leal, Luis. "La Malinche." *A Luis Leal Reader*, edited by Ilan Stavans, Northwestern UP, 2007, pp. 271–85.

Orozco, José Clemente. *Cortes y La Malinche.* 1923–26. Antiguo Colegio de San Ildefonso, Mexico City, oac.cdlib.org/ark:/13030/hb0m3nb2w4/?layout=metadata&brand=oac4.

Paz, Octavio. *El laberinto de la soledad.* Cuadernos Americanos, 1950.

Rebolledo, Tey Diana, and Eliana S. Rivero, editors. *Infinite Divisions: An Anthology of Chicana Literature.* U of Arizona P, 1993.

Scott, David, and Kenyan G. Tomaselli, editors. *Cultural Icons.* Left Coast Press, 2009.

Sederberg, Kathryn. "Bringing the Museum into the Classroom, and the Class into the Museum: An Approach for Content-Based Instruction." *Die Unterrichtspraxis / Teaching German*, vol. 46, no. 2, 2013, pp. 251–62.

Silver, Brenda R. *Virginia Woolf Icon.* U of Chicago P, 1999.

Tafolla, Carmen. "La Malinche." Rebolledo and Rivero, pp. 198–99.

Townsend, Camilla. *Malintzin's Choices: An Indian Woman in the Conquest of Mexico.* U of New Mexico P, 2006.

Yenawine, Philip. *Visual Thinking Strategies: Using Art to Deepen Learning across School Disciplines.* Harvard Education Press, 2013.

Zarza, Rafael. *La Malinche: La lengua.* 1975. *Cubarte Gallery*, www.galeriacubarte.cult.cu/g_obraexpo.php?item=254&tema=13&tipo=&page=6&lang=eng.

Carolina E. Alonso

Teaching Queer Chicana Writers through Historical Research, Blogs, and Podcasts

This essay discusses an upper-level undergraduate course in women and gender studies that is sometimes taught as a special topics or senior seminar and that is titled Chicana Lesbians: Their Contribution to Chicana/o Literature and Culture. The course provides students with critical and literary tools to identify and analyze the contributions of Chicana lesbians to Chicano literature, history, and culture. The pedagogical and technological strategies discussed here involve assigning narratives by María Amparo Ruiz de Burton, Gloria Anzaldúa, Cherríe Moraga, Carla Trujillo, Emma Pérez, and Alicia Gaspar de Alba.

These are writers who challenge three predominant forms reflected in early Chicana/o literature: coming-of-age novels, the (de)construction of traditional families, and the (re)construction of a historical discourse. While the course examines and problematizes these structures, it also empowers critical conversations on gender, sexuality, and ethnicity, conversations that continue to be necessary in the twenty-first century.

The design of this course helps students develop critical tools for reading and understanding literature, and multimedia competence for building their own discourse. For a semester of fourteen weeks, the course is divided into four sections: women writers' contributions before the Chicano Movement, the construction of the queer individual during and after the movement, lesbians and the Chicana/o family, and the (re)construction of a historical discourse. Narratives by the abovementioned authors and additional critical theory readings are assigned for each section. While students are doing the assigned readings, the instructor posts a weekly reading reflection on the class blog to facilitate in-class discussions and other assignments. The midterm exam helps students demonstrate critical and analytical skills, and better prepare for their final research paper.

The course follows a student-centered approach, in which the instructor serves as a facilitator who encourages active learning from the students. It also promotes a cooperative learning environment that emphasizes group work and builds a sense of community. Specific class activities include investigating online archives, reflection writing done in blogs, recording and uploading podcasts, and editing or creating new *Wikipedia* entries.

Women Writers before the Chicano Movement

The course is centered on the premise that in order to understand Chicana literature, as well as the history and experience of Chicanas/os and specifically of Chicana lesbians, the instructor must provide an overview of the trajectory of this literature beyond the last five decades. A process of historical revision and discussion should occur in the first weeks of the course. Such a survey should also include perspective on earlier women writers, from different social classes, who destabilized and contested a masculine and subsequently heteronormative hegemony, and should explain whether those writers wrote in English or Spanish. The rhetoric of resistance employed by women writers in the nineteenth and early twentieth centuries would later be palpable in the counterdiscourses of contemporary Chicana lesbian narratives.

As a research fellow for the Recovering the U.S. Hispanic Literary Heritage Project at the University of Houston, I worked with recovered material that gave me perspective not only on the historical resistance and literary contributions of Mexican Americans but also on the active role of women.[1] Thus I have found it crucial to introduce a genealogy of authors such as Ruiz de Burton, who published two novels in the 1880s (*Squatter* and *Who*). Her legacy is paramount for understanding the general discontent regarding the United States' denial of the rights of Mexican Americans, in violation of the terms of the Treaty of Guadalupe Hidalgo of 1848.

Her texts exhibit a sense of fierce resistance and complaints that will later be reflected in Chicana lesbian literature. Her novels, and the letters she wrote to Mariano Guadalupe Vallejo—an intermediary to the new system and an important figure for the original Californio population[2]—illustrate a woman who, although married to an Anglo man and coming from a privileged class, expressed the experience of displacement and injustice suffered by her people. Ruiz de Burton confirms the existence of early historical female contributions to Mexican American literature and culture.

By examining online archives, students begin to study the creation of discourse and to understand the rescue of the historical and literary legacy of Chicanas/os; I guide this examination by providing them access to the archives of the Arte Público Hispanic Historical Collection and of the Chicana por Mi Raza Digital Memory Collective.[3] Students enjoy the process of searching, reading, interacting with, highlighting, and printing materials from an online archive.

I ask students to use these online archives to find newspaper articles, biographies, essays, and editorials written by Mexican American women before 1970. Afterward, each student prepares a reflection paper that explains when and where one of these texts was published, and to analyze its content through critical theories discussed in class. Students then work in groups to create a time line with their articles' dates of publication. Afterward we design a virtual map, using *Carto*, to indicate the locations where the texts were published.[4] Such an activity visually reinforces the fact that Chicana women were active participants in the history of the United States, and that their participation has gone unrecognized in different parts of the country. Archival research also facilitates a class discussion about the homophobic discourse employed by some Mexican intellectuals exiled in the United States during the early twentieth century, and about how this discourse could have influenced Mexican and Mexican American sentiment toward homosexuality.[5]

The Construction of a Queer Individual

In the late 1960s and early 1970s the Chicano Movement sought its identity in Chicana/o literature in the United States, especially in coming-of-age novels, which had a fundamental role in promoting a Chicano consciousness and identity. Two novels that received the Quinto Sol awards, by Tomás Rivera and by Rudolfo Anaya, are recognized as pioneers in fulfilling this role. Later, Sandra Cisneros's *The House on Mango Street* became a standard for coming-of-age novels written by women.[6] Instructors can describe these examples to set up class discussion on how Chicana/o authors develop meaning through the subjectivity of their protagonists, inviting a critical and sagacious examination of society through the experience of the characters.

Another novel I've selected for this course is Trujillo's *What Night Brings*, a queer coming-of-age novel that students can analyze for how it rethinks Chicana stories. This novel narrates the story of Marci and her family, who live in California during the 1970s. Set in the decade of the Chicano Movement, Trujillo's novel presents main characters who depart from gender binaries and stereotypes, and the female protagonist (as well as other important characters) has a queer identity. *What Night Brings* thus destabilizes the traditional heterosexual coming-of-age story in Chicana/o literature.

After analyzing this novel, the class reflects on how Anzaldúa's and Moraga's groundbreaking critical texts validate experiences within the Chicana/o community that diverge from a heteronormative perspective. I assign two chapters of Anzaldúa's *Borderlands / La frontera: The New Mestiza*, "The Homeland, Aztlán" (23–36) and "How to Tame a Wild Tongue" (75–86), and two chapters from Moraga's *Loving in the War Years: Lo Que Nunca Pasó por Sus Labios* (*What Never Passed through Her Lips*): "La güera" ("The White Woman"; 50–59) and "A Long Line of Vendidas" (90–144). The students discuss how these authors challenge gender and sexual binaries, as well as considering the importance of intersectionalities in these autobiographical texts. Both writers use *testimonios* ("testimonies") to empower Chicana queer identities, paving the way for creative authors such as Trujillo, who on the acknowledgments page of her novel recognizes "Cherríe Moraga, Gloria Anzaldúa . . . who told me my stories mattered."

As we discuss these critical texts in class, students do reflective writing in blogs as homework assignments. The online platforms of most universities have a blog function; however, students seem to perform better with external blog platforms, such as *WordPress*, *Blogger*, and *Tumblr*. In *Using Blogs to Enhance Literacy: The Next Powerful Step in Twenty-First-Century Learning*, Diane Penrod establishes that students are in fact "blogging in record numbers" (18). According to her, this tendency will continue in the years to come. Penrod also highlights the benefits of blogging, which encourages fluency in writing, cooperative learning, and critical thinking (22). In addition, in this class the blog entries create a dialogue between students, who are encouraged to comment on their classmates' posts.[7]

Lesbians and the Chicana/o Family

The concept of the family is an important element of Chicana/o literature and was also emphasized during the movement. Most canonical Chicana/o literature highlights family representations in order to maintain and encourage the ideals of the movement. Moraga argues that individuals who did not accept or protect their roles, both sexual and gender-related, were excluded from the imagined Chicano family ("Queer Aztlán" 232–33). After two classes of critical discussion on the family and on Moraga's theories, students are ready to read the next two Chicana lesbian novels, *Faultline*, by Sheila Ortiz Taylor, and *Desert Blood*, by Gaspar de Alba. The main characters in these narratives live under family pressure that prevents them from developing or validating their queer identities. Students begin to identify this kind of family life as a metaphor for a panopticon (see Foucault); that is, these families impose a surveillance that makes the protagonists police themselves when acting outside the norm. The characters have to embark on self-exile, moving away from their families, their home environments, and, in the case of Gaspar de Alba's protagonist, from the community. Class discussions often move to how, while in this self-imposed exile, the protagonists reimagine and reconstruct their concept of family and family ties.

Like blogs, podcasts are another useful technological tool in this class. Podcasts are digital recordings uploaded to the Internet that can be downloaded to a computer or mobile device. Once a podcast has been downloaded to a device, it can be played even when the device isn't connected to the Internet. For the podcast assignment, students are placed in groups and given a discussion topic relating to the class themes or to a particular text. Each student prepares discussion points individually, and then the groups meet outside of class to discuss and record their conversations. The students then share their podcasts with the other groups. Students can upload their recordings to Web sites such as *PodBean*, which is free and user-friendly. After all of the podcasts have been listened to, the class has a general discussion.

Ultimately, this activity reinforces team-based learning, a technique of the student-centered teaching approach. In general, students who engage in group activities demonstrate better academic performance (Bradford et al. 35). Furthermore, the podcast assignment can improve students' oral proficiency and communication skills, and students enjoy listening to their peers' discussions on their cell phones or in their cars.

Reconstruction of a Historical Discourse

The final section of this course reviews how Chicana lesbians have used literature to rewrite the historical role of women in Mexican and Chicana/o discourse. A process of reimagining historical figures in Mexican culture was of interest to Chicana feminists in the 1970s, who often did so through art. Chicana artists such as Yolanda López challenged the traditional interpretation of the Virgen de Guadalupe, transforming its passive and submissive role to one of agency, as seen in López's "Portrait of the Artist as the Virgin of Guadalupe." Chicana lesbian writers also embark on this exercise of decolonizing historical icons and discourses that have silenced queer women. I use two historical novels, *Sor Juana's Second Dream*, by Gaspar de Alba, and *Forgetting the Alamo; or, Blood Memory*, by Pérez.

We also consider an essay by Pérez, "Queering the Borderlands: The Challenges of Excavating the Invisible and Unheard," where she describes historical voices that have been disregarded or overlooked, and whose accounts thus need to be reconstructed, as she does in *Forgetting the Alamo*. The protagonist is a cowgirl with homoerotic desires who is trying to survive the hostile environment of mid-nineteenth-century Texas. To help stay alive, she cross-dresses, and in her journeys she witnesses the injustices and atrocities of the era.

While Pérez inserts a queer woman in the history of Texas, Gaspar de Alba retells the story of one of Mexico's most important intellectual figures, Sor Juana Inés de la Cruz. This colonial figure is considered a protofeminist, but the Mexican cultural imaginary does not address her possibly queer identity. Gaspar de Alba's Sor Juana recognizes her own homoerotic desires, and she is constructed as the historical referent for Chicana lesbian writers. In the novel's postscript, Gaspar de Alba describes her as the "great-great-great, hundredfold-great-grandmother of my Mexican heritage" (459). With this declaration, and in the novel more broadly, Gaspar de Alba challenges the patriarchal and heteronormative interpretations of Sor Juana, known as the *décima musa* ("tenth muse").

These practices of decolonizing history and literature lead the class to a conversation on the visibility and representation of queer women of color in the twenty-first century. We then reflect on how exclusionary the Internet continues to be for certain groups. One of the final projects in the class is for the students, working in groups, to search for a *Wikipedia* entry about a Chicana lesbian author or her texts. If the entry already exists, they can edit it, adding information they have researched, or correct existing errors in the entry. They may also translate it into Spanish. Generally, students must also write a new *Wikipedia* entry that corrects the lack of visibility of Chicana writers.[8] This activity allows them to contextualize what they have learned, to continue practicing their research skills by documenting the sources they use to write their entries, and most important, to make Chicana authors and their work more visible. *Wikipedia* offers a training video and an entry on how to add a user account to the site. But before students post anything, the professor has to revise and approve the entries.

The activities listed above are examples of how modern technology can be used as a learning tool in the study of literature. The strategies and assignments used in this course facilitate its main objective, which is to assert the role of Chicana lesbian literature in the corpus of Chicana/o literature and in American literature more broadly.

Notes

1. Visit the Recovering the U.S. Hispanic Literary Heritage Project Web site to read about their mission and history: artepublicopress.com/recovery-program/.

2. A Californio is a descendant of Spanish colonists or is a native of California ("Californio").

3. María Cotera and Linda García Merchant created the Chicana por Mi Raza Digital Memory Collective, whose work can be freely accessed online: chicana pormiraza.org/.

4. *Carto* is an online mapping platform.

5. In his newspaper *Regeneración*, Ricardo Flores Magón consistently employed a homophobic discourse toward the Mexican politician and soldier Antonio I. Villarreal. See Flores Magón, "Patadas," "Coronel," and "¡Qué farsa!"

6. Rivera's . . . *Y no se lo tragó la tierra / And the Earth Did Not Devour Him* and Anaya's *Bless Me, Ultima* were the first two novels to receive the Quinto Sol publication award, in 1971 and 1972 respectively. (Estela Portillo Trambley won the award in 1975.) For information on the role of this award in building a canon for Chicana/o literature, see Dennis López. Cisneros's novel was published by Arte Público Press in 1984 and reissued in 1991 by Vintage Books.

7. All of the class entries are private and can only be seen and commented on by the students and the professor. Furthermore, it is important that the professor give precise instructions on word count, dates of submission, and other rules for the blog posts (such as the use of professional vocabulary and the need for students to be respectful when responding to classmates).

8. This assignment is based on the work of the Crunk Feminist Collective and other feminist groups, which for some years now have engaged in edit sessions where they have added or edited articles on *Wikipedia*. The collective adds entries about women and people of color that are written from a feminist perspective. Read the Crunk Feminist Collective's mission statement at www.crunkfeminist collective.com/.

Works Cited

Anaya, Rudolfo. *Bless Me, Ultima*. Quinto Sol Publications, 1972.

Anzaldúa, Gloria. *Borderlands / La frontera: The New Mestiza*. Spinsters / Aunt Lute, 1987.

Bradford, Jennifer, et al. "You Can Lead Students to Water, but You Can't Make Them Think: An Assessment of Student Engagement and Learning through Student-Centered Teaching." *Journal of the Scholarship of Teaching and Learning*, vol. 16, no. 4, 2016, pp. 33–43.

"Californio." *Collegiate Dictionary*. *Merriam-Webster*, 2020, www.merriam-webster.com/dictionary/Californio.

Cisneros, Sandra. *The House on Mango Street*. Arte Público Press, 1984.

Flores Magón, Ricardo. "El Coronel de los 41." *Regeneración*, vol. 4, no. 55, 16 Sept. 1911, p. 2. *EBSCOHost*, fortlewis.idm.oclc.org/login?url=http://search.ebscohost.com/login.aspx?direct=true&db=h6b&AN=70902720&site=ehost-live&scope=site.

———. "Patadas de ahogado del pederasta y asesino Antonio I. Villarreal." *Regeneración*, vol. 4, no. 53, 2 Sept. 1911, p. 2. *EBSCOHost*, fortlewis.idm.oclc.org/login?url=http://search.ebscohost.com/login.aspx?direct=true&db=h6b&AN=70852314&site=ehost-live&scope=site.

———. "¡Qué farsa!" *Regeneración*, vol. 4, no. 198, 8 Aug. 1914, p. 3. *EBSCOHost*, fortlewis.idm.oclc.org/login?url=http://search.ebscohost.com/login.aspx?direct=true&db=h6b&AN=70899694&site=ehost-live&scope=site.

Foucault, Michel. *Discipline and Punish: The Birth of the Prison*. Translated by Alan Sheridan, 2nd ed., Vintage Books, 1995.

Gaspar de Alba, Alicia. *Desert Blood: The Juárez Murders*. Arte Público Press, 2005.

———. *Sor Juana's Second Dream*. U of New Mexico P, 1999.

López, Dennis. "Good-Bye Revolution—Hello Cultural Mystique: Quinto Sol Publications and Chicano Literary Nationalism." *MELUS*, vol. 35, no. 3, 2010, pp. 183–210.

López, Yolanda. "Portrait of the Artist as the Virgin of Guadalupe." 1978. *Chicanas/Latinas in the U.S.*, almalopez.com/projects/ChicanasLatinas/lopezyolanda3.html.

Moraga, Cherríe. *Loving in the War Years: Lo Que Nunca Pasó por Sus Labios*. South End Press, 1983.

———. "Queer Aztlán: The Re-formation of Chicano Tribe." *Queer Cultures*, edited by Deborah Carlin and Jennifer DiGrazia, Pearson / Prentice Hall, 2004, pp. 224–38.

Ortiz Taylor, Sheila. *Faultline: A Novel*. Naiad Press, 1982.

Penrod, Diane. *Using Blogs to Enhance Literacy: The Next Powerful Step in Twenty-First-Century Learning*. Rowman and Littlefield Education, 2007.
Pérez, Emma. *Forgetting the Alamo; or, Blood Memory*. U of Texas P, 2009.
———. "Queering the Borderlands: The Challenges of Excavating the Invisible and Unheard." *Frontiers: A Journal of Women Studies*, vol. 24, nos. 2–3, 2003, pp. 122–31.
Rivera, Tomás. . . . *Y no se lo tragó la tierra / And the Earth Did Not Part*. Quinto Sol Publications, 1971.
Ruiz de Burton, María Amparo. *The Squatter and the Don*. Arte Público Press, 1992.
———. *Who Would Have Thought It?* Arte Público Press, 1995.
Trujillo, Carla. *What Night Brings*. Curbstone Press, 2003.

Ron Thomas

Developing Cross-Cultural Awareness and Digital Literacy through an Active Learning Project

This essay models a pedagogical exercise that could apply to many areas of literature in the United States, but that here I apply to novels by Chicana authors. I have been perfecting this classroom activity over several years in sophomore, upper-level, and graduate classes in American literature, having found that students enjoy it. The idea draws on the traditional assignment in which students create an annotated bibliography, but in this case using an electronic format. Each student must create a twenty-minute *PowerPoint* presentation on one of the authors on the course syllabus, using ten slides that annotate textual allusions to the wider world with the aid of images (in the form of JPEG, audio, or video files) and that include brief information about each image provided.

This active learning exercise teaches autonomy, research skills, and cross-cultural awareness. It offers an introduction to digital humanities and a path to research and discovery in areas of literature. Students are well-positioned to take advantage of this exercise in literacy beyond the alphabetic text, employing the new, empowering bibliographic paradigm of digitization. In pursuing this pedagogical exercise students can be inspired to bring voice and presence to the voiceless, impress their peers, and learn basic research and presentation skills.

What follows is a brief explanation of the exercise. Students taking my class can choose to present on Sandra Cisneros's *The House on Mango Street*, Margarita Cota-Cárdenas's *Puppet*, Estela Portillo-Trambley's *Trini*, Ana Castillo's *The Mixquiahuala Letters*, or Helena María Viramontes's *Under the Feet of Jesus*, among others. This exercise would not be possible without access to a smart classroom, which is now available to instructors at many universities.

On the first day of class, upon reading aloud key points from the syllabus, instructors should explain the exercise. "Everyone must make a twenty-minute *PowerPoint* presentation to the group on an author or text of your choosing from the reading list, which you will e-mail to me." Then open the class site on *Blackboard* or another platform (I use *Canvas*), where you will already have posted the instructions for this assignment, a model presentation, and three or four anonymous student presentations from previous classes. On the second day of class, remind students to consult these instructions and examples, stating that during the third class period you will ask them to sign up for an author, using a sign-up sheet that you have posted to the class site. In a hypothetical fifteen-week class that meets on Mondays, Wednesdays, and Fridays, has twenty-four students, and has a reading list of works by eight authors for students to choose from, three students would present on each author, making their presentations on any day their author is discussed except the first day of that discussion. There should be no more than two presentations per day.

When students in my class have chosen a work for this project, I ask them to look for allusions in the text to the broader cultural, historical, or natural world, then to surf the Web for images and information that clarify or contextualize the allusions. Next students create *PowerPoint* slides about the information, one slide per allusion. In each slide the image should appear on the right, and text should be added on the left: first, relevant facts about the image, then the quotation of the allusion from the text and a parenthetical citation. If needed, students might add a sentence or two explaining the significance of the slide. Figures 1–3 show sample slides that discuss allusions in Cisneros's *The House on Mango Street.*[1] The allusions are to Venus as the morning star, to Lewis Carroll's "The Walrus and the Carpenter," and to Giacomo Puccini's *Madama Butterfly*.

Presentations should include about ten slides on the chosen text, and about fourteen slides altogether. The first slide should serve as a title page and list the author and title of the chosen work, the presentation topic, the student's name, the class, and the date; the second slide should have a picture of the author and a brief bio; and the third slide should have a table of contents. Next come the ten slides about the chosen author's work, which may be titled individually. There is no need to include a works-cited list in the slides, but students should adhere to academic standards in using parenthetical citations, and the content they present should follow classroom decorum. Students should add a slide that provides some kind of conclusion, such as a question or comment or, if they know how to embed one, an audio or video file (e.g., of a poetry reading, a song, or a clip from an interview, concert, play, or movie), but the excerpt should be brief.

Students can be creative in how they prepare the slides about their chosen text. Some of the slides may just show images from the text (such as objects, characters, and settings), most should show quoted allusions from the text and images from the Web, and some may show images that gloss not the text but people, places, or events from the author's life. Even if the slides seem to students like a collection of random materials, students should try to organize their presentations around a topic, which should be specified on the first slide. Presentations should be at most twenty minutes long, including questions from the group. I ask students to e-mail me a copy of their presentations once they have prepared them, so that I can review them promptly and respond by e-mail with a critique that includes a score. Students post their finalized presentations to *Canvas* as models for others to consult going forward.

Presentations should occur at the beginning of class. In the hypothetical class described above, one or two presentations per class period would take up about fifteen percent of class time. Most important, the presentations draw other students into discussion of the text for that day. Students stay on task more effectively when they are given little reminders the week before they are to present; instructors could do this by reviewing the online sign-up list each day of class.

During each presentation, I try not to interrupt. At its close, I lead the class in polite applause then ask for questions or comments. The presenting student can address any errors made during the presentation by verbally restating those elements afterward. Other work that is not completed in class because of time taken up with presentations can always be summarized at the end of class or at the beginning of the next class.

In the last week or so of class, after all students have made their presentations, I administer a brief, anonymous survey regarding the *PowerPoint* exercise. I explain that the class's comments will help me fine-tune the exercise for next semester, and I provide twenty minutes at the end of class for students to complete the survey. On the survey sheet I list several prompts asking about such things as students' initial responses to the project, the helpfulness of the instruction sheet and the sample slides, my e-mailed comments about students' work, the time spent on the project, its weight in relation to the overall grade, especially memorable presentations or slides (and any weak or repetitive ones), and whether audio and video clips should be allowed. The survey also asks students what the exercise has taught them about technology, research, and presentations; close analysis of the text or appreciation of the writer's allusiveness; cross-cultural awareness of the text and of students' peers; self-empowerment or taking ownership of one's point of view; and definitions of literacy, ideology, race, gender, and class, among other things.

My hope is that this pedagogical exercise will provide new ideas for instructors about how to design interactive projects and help students develop critical thinking skills.

Note

1. In the model presentation that I share with students, three slides are dedicated to each of the works on my syllabus mentioned earlier. The model presentation has fifteen slides in total, including the three illustrated in this essay. The slides about *Puppet* discuss La Malinche, who is depicted as a character in the novella, alongside an image from the *Codex Azcatitlan*; allusions in the novella to the Franciscan missionary Bernardino de Sahagún alongside his portrait; and allusions to César Chávez, Dolores Huerta, and the United Farm Workers union alongside images of both people and the union logo. The slides about *Trini* discuss the novel's allusions to Mexican Christmas traditions alongside cartoon images of a nativity scene and a *posada* procession; a character's work sorting copper at a refinery in Smeltertown in El Paso, Texas, alongside an image of a historical marker commemorating Smeltertown; and the protagonist's migration journey alongside a screenshot of the route on *Google Maps*. The slides about *The Mixquiahuala Letters* discuss the experiences of the two main characters in the town Mixquiahuala de Juarez and their observations of Aztec religious relics alongside photographs of the town and some relics and an illustration of an Aztec god mentioned in the text; the two characters' adventures in a haunted house alongside images of personal items that are significant to this episode; and a character's mixed-media artwork, which is compared to the work of Frida Kahlo, alongside a photograph of Kahlo. The slides about *Under the Feet of Jesus* discuss the protagonist's work harvesting and drying grapes alongside an image of the Sun-Maid girl, the illustration for a brand of raisins; the novel's description of posters of Our Lady of Guadalupe, Elvis Presley, and Marilyn Monroe alongside the images themselves; and the description of a character making tortillas alongside an image of a *comal*, a griddle used to cook tortillas. The appendix includes titles on bibliography, Chicana feminist theory, and classroom pedagogy that helped guide me as I prepared these slides.

Appendix: Suggested Reading

Anzaldúa, Gloria. *Borderlands / La frontera: The New Mestiza*. Spinsters / Aunt Lute, 1987.
Arredondo, Gabriela F., et al., editors. *Chicana Feminisms*. Duke UP, 2003.
Bauer, Matthias, and Angelika Zirker. "Whipping Boys Explained: Literary Annotation and Digital Humanities." *Literary Studies in the Digital Age*, 2016, dlsanthology.mla.hcommons.org/whipping-boys-explained-literary-annotation-and-digital-humanities/.
Castillo, Ana. *Massacre of the Dreamers*. Plume, 1994.
Castillo, Debra A. *Talking Back: Toward a Latin American Feminist Literary Criticism*. Cornell UP, 1992.
Cazden, Courtney, et al. "A Pedagogy of Multiliteracies: Designing Social Futures." *Harvard Educational Review*, vol. 66, no. 1, Spring 1996, pp. 60–92.
Corpi, Lucha, editor. *Máscaras*. Third Woman Press, 1997.
De Leon, Jennifer, editor. *Wise Latinas: Writers on Higher Education*. U of Nebraska P, 2014.
Eliot, Simon, and Jonathan Rose, editors. *A Companion to the History of the Book*. Wiley-Blackwell, 2009.
Freire, Paulo. *Pedagogy of the Oppressed*. Revised ed., Penguin Books, 1993.
García, Alma M., editor. *Chicana Feminist Thought: The Basic Historical Writings*. Routledge, 1997.
Graff, Harvey J. *The Legacies of Literacy: Continuities and Contradictions in Western Culture and Society*. Indiana UP, 1987.
Herrera-Sobek, Maria. *Chicano Folklore: A Handbook*. Greenwood, 2006.
Martínez, Elizabeth Coonrod, and Gabriela Baeza Ventura. "A History of Latino-Focused Journals and Collaborative Research." *Diálogo*, vol. 20, no. 2, Fall 2017, pp. 1–6.
Moraga, Cherríe, and Gloria Anzaldúa, editors. *This Bridge Called My Back: Writings by Radical Women of Color*. 2nd ed., Kitchen Table, 1983.
Oropeza, Lorena, and Dionne Espinoza, editors. *Enriqueta Vasquez and the Chicano Movement: Writings from El Grito del Norte*. Arte Público, 2006.
Price, Kenneth M., and Ray Siemens. Introduction. *Literary Studies in the Digital Age*, 2016, dlsanthology.mla.hcommons.org/introduction/.
Rebolledo, Tey Diana, and Eliana Rivero, editors. *Infinite Divisions: An Anthology of Chicana Literature*. U of Arizona P, 1993.
Svinicki, Marilla, and Wilbert J. McKeachie, editors. *McKeachie's Teaching Tips, Strategies, Research, and Theory for College and University Teachers*. 13th ed., Wadsworth / Cengage Learning, 2011.

Works Cited

Castillo, Ana. *The Mixquiahuala Letters*. Bilingual Press, 1986.
Cisneros, Sandra. *The House on Mango Street*. Arte Público Press, 1984.
Cota-Cárdenas, Margarita. *Puppet*. U of New Mexico P, 2000.
Portillo Trambley, Estela. *Trini*. Feminist Press, 1986.
Viramontes, Helena María. *Under the Feet of Jesus*. Dutton, 1995.

Rising with the Tortilla Star

Venus often appears in the dawn sky as the morning star. In this vignette about Alicia, the planet gets renamed to fit her personal circumstance.

Alicia's father tells her that if she were asleep, the mice wouldn't bother her. She could then rise early with the "tortilla star" to make his "lunchbox tortillas" (31).

Alicia, whose mother has died, has inherited her "mama's rolling pin and sleepiness" but is "young and smart and studies for the first time at the university" (31). She takes "two trains and a bus, because she doesn't want to spend her whole life in a factory or behind a rolling pin" (31–32).

A good girl, and Esperanza's friend, Alicia "studies all night and sees the mice, the ones her father says do not exist." She's "afraid of nothing except four-legged fur. And fathers" (32).

Figure 1. *PowerPoint* slide about a scene in Cisneros, *The House on Mango Street*, in which making tortillas is discussed.

Edna's Ruthie

In "The Walrus and the Carpenter," a 108-line English ballad in chapter 4 of Lewis Carroll's *Through the Looking-Glass* (1871), the walrus and the carpenter entice the oysters out of their seabed onto the shore and proceed to eat them all.

Edna's grown daughter Ruthie wears mismatched socks, likes to play with children, laughs by herself, whistles "like the Emperor's nightingale," and "sees lovely things everywhere" (Cisneros 68), as if escaping from the moment. Having declined job offers when young, Ruthie "got married instead and moved away to a pretty house outside the city" (69). Esperanza doesn't understand why Ruthie is living on Mango Street if she doesn't have to, if her husband's going to come fetch her, yet he never does. Ruthie enjoys Esperanza's library books, but when Esperanza recites Carroll's poem, Ruthie tears up. After the last lines ("But answer came there none—and this was scarcely odd, because they'd eaten every one . . ."), she looks long at Esperanza, compliments her "most beautiful teeth" (69), and goes inside.

Figure 2. *PowerPoint* slide about a scene in Cisneros, *The House on Mango Street*, that features a ballad by Lewis Carroll.

A Smart Cookie

In his opera *Madama Butterfly*, Giacomo Puccini tells the story of a young Japanese girl in Nagasaki, Ciocio-san ("Butterfly"). Three years after her lover, an American naval officer, left her, he returns with his American wife to claim his love child by Ciocio-san, who consents to give up the child but commits suicide with a Hara-kiri knife.

Esperanza's mother speaks two languages, can sing opera, can fix a television, but is afraid to leave the house. Someday she would like to go to the ballet or see a play. She borrows opera records from the public library and sings along. "Today while cooking oatmeal she is Madame Butterfly, until she sighs. . . . I could have been somebody, you know?" She tells Esperanza to "go to school. Study hard. That Madame Butterfly was a fool. . . . Look at my *comadres* ["close friends"]." Izaura's husband left, and Yolanda's died. Then, suddenly, Esperanza's mother admits to having quit school because, though smart, she had no clothes and was ashamed. Disgusted, stirring the oatmeal again: "I was a smart cookie then" (Cisneros 91).

Figure 3. *PowerPoint* slide about a scene in Cisneros, *The House on Mango Street*, in which *Madama Butterfly* is mentioned.

Part V

Drama and Performance

Adrianna M. Santos

Reading, Witnessing, and Staging Virginia Grise and Irma Mayorga's *The Panza Monologues*

Works of Chicana drama stand out as transformative creations that have the potential to awaken students to social justice issues through the power of performance, and to expand students' ideas about whose narratives should be valued and whose stories told, to whom and in what spaces.[1] A Chicana feminist response to Eve Ensler's *The Vagina Monologues*, the performance piece *The Panza Monologues*, by Virginia Grise and Irma Mayorga, is an homage to Tejana Chicanas of south Texas and a celebration of the poetics of women's lives told through multiple voices, as well as a serious critical indictment of the social conditions of Mexican Americans in the United States. The play's collection of fourteen distinct monologues, which revolves around the *panza* ("belly"), reveals the daily lived experiences of Tejanas in San Antonio, Texas, the largest city in the United States with a Mexican American majority population. According to the Census Bureau, sixty-one percent of San Antonio residents identify as Hispanic. What's more, San Antonio, the seventh largest metropolitan area in the nation, is also one of the most segregated cities in the United States, marked by extreme income inequality that separates the privileged from those in poverty. The city has a long history of political engagement and creative activity by Mexican American women, but that history is often obscured by the dominant narrative of San Antonio. *The Panza Monologues* offers a glimpse into the everyday lives of Mexican American women in "San Anto," whose contributions have helped to shape the character of the city.

As Grise and Mayorga declare: "Now someone's *panza* story is a sacred story, and to share it with someone else is to tell them about the condition of your life" (41). The play engages compelling themes including public health, domestic violence, sexuality, reproductive justice, political protest, poverty, food insecurity, identity, and more. The material is particularly relevant to nontraditional, first generation, working-class, Mexican American, female, and queer students, but on a deeper level it examines universal human rights through a Chicana feminist lens. Study of this play is appropriate for both upper-division undergraduate courses in the arts and humanities (such as literature, women's and gender studies, ethnic studies, queer studies, or drama studies) and graduate courses. Articles on women's health and exposure to poverty and violence can effectively complement a reading of the play. Students can begin with Patricia Herrera's outstanding performance review in *Chicana/Latina Studies*, "Power to the Panza! Feminist Body Politics in *The Panza Monologues*," the title of which is taken from the play's final lines.

Teaching *The Panza Monologues* can be a cathartic experience for both teacher and students because of both the content and the critical interventions it encourages. In addition to reading the full transcript of the play, students could read portions of the additional material in the second edition of the play, which includes a history of San Antonio and a description of how the authors came to write the play while working together at Esperanza Peace and Justice Center. The second edition is a greatly expanded text that provides suggestions for performance and pedagogical interventions and makes a solid contribution to Chicana feminist theory and praxis by exploring innovative ways to reach the community outside traditional models. An impressive literary achievement in itself, it includes all of the tools necessary to investigate the play's production history and to contextualize the play. There is a complete guide to producing the play that the authors call a "DIY Production Manual," and a road map for encouraging further creative works to come out of "Panza Parties," in which groups come together to watch and discuss the performance DVD. Other effective classroom techniques include reader response strategies; suggestions for staging monologues with music, props, and costumes; and suggestions for creating original monologues inspired by the material.

The Panza Monologues questions gender and sexuality within the context of racial and economic injustice. Since 2003, the play has been performed by the solo artist and coauthor Grise in dozens of cities around the country, to critical acclaim. Theater groups have produced table readings of the material, and educators around the country have engaged students in classroom discussion of the play. Productions of the play have mostly occurred through women of color initiatives, or for people of color and queer cultural spaces, and have occurred in cities from Los Angeles to New York. The script was originally published by Evelyn Street Press in partnership with the Austin Latina/Latino Lesbian and Gay Organization. These ties to LGBTQIA communities are important for instructors to point out when framing for students the larger issues of gender and sexuality that are raised in the work. The performance DVD can be ordered through university libraries, and students can provide their own backdrop for their readings from the play, creating *PowerPoint* images of Chicanx cultural forms, playlists to enhance the mood, costumes that reflect their characters, props that aid in the staging, and PR materials for their shows, such as tickets and programs that include original artwork.

The material is best approached through the perspective of Chicana feminisms and Anzaldúan theory, Latinx theater and performance studies, and literary criticism by women of color. Importantly, many Chicana feminists and cultural critics argue for discovering unique theoretical concepts that diverge from European and American literary theory, such as those that can be derived from the embodied experience, which includes knowledge of (and immersion in) Chicana experiences. Centering the female body as a site of power and knowledge, Grise and Mayorga write:

> *Las diosas dijeron*:
> "Let there be *panza*!'
> And so it was.
> *La panza—esta parte tan importante de nuestro cuerpo.*
> *Allí va todo—*
> *los ovarios,*
> *la matriz,*
> *el vientre.*
> *Las diosas*
> prayed,
> lit *velas*,
> asked the moon.
>
> "Watch over our creation. You, who controls the waves, will control woman—her bloods, *cada factor, cada molinito de su cuerpo.*" (44–45)

It was within the context of the late-twentieth-century boom of Chicana creative activity that Grise and Mayorga developed this work, which focuses on Mexican American women in Texas. The surge of dramatic creativity in the 1980s and 1990s was made possible by the earlier work of women who resisted exclusion and stereotypical representations in Chicano Teatro. For a class focused on theater, the book *Luis Valdez—Early Works: Actos,* Bernabé *and "Pensamiento Serpentino,"* by Valdez, and *Teatro Chicana: A Collective Memoir and Selected Plays*, by Laura E. García and colleagues, are good opening texts, serving as an introduction to El Movimiento, the larger Chicano civil rights movement, in which women resisted stereotypes and marginalization through performance: groups that did so included Women in Teatro (a subsidiary of Teatro Campesino) and all female groups like Valentina Productions, El Teatro de la Esperanza (The Theater of Hope), and Las Cucarachas (which translates literally to The Cockroaches, although the phrase has several colloquial interpretations). Another excellent critical reading for students is Yvonne Yarbro-Bejarano's early essay "The Female Subject in Chicano Theatre: Sexuality, 'Race,' and Class" (1986).

Notably, Cherríe Moraga's play *Giving Up the Ghost* led the way for lesbian representation in theater. This and other early plays by Chicana authors reconfigure narrative history and engage in critical meaning making that challenges the status quo. A study of one of Moraga's plays in that collection can be helpful to students, as can the study by Elizabeth Jacobs, "*Shadow of a Man*: A Chicana/Latina Drama as Embodied Feminist Practice," which argues that Moraga "radically restages the Chicana body through an exploration of the sexual and gendered politics of the family" (49). It is interesting to note that because the second edition of *The Panza Monologues* includes a wealth of information that bridges the concerns of theater, performance, pedagogy, and activism, it participates in the creation of a veritable "theory in the flesh" (Moraga and Anzaldúa 21), an idea originally conceptualized in a groundbreaking anthology for Chicana feminist studies edited by Moraga and Gloria Anzaldúa, *This Bridge Called My Back: Writings by Radical Women of Color*. This book is another excellent resource for helping students contextualize the literary contributions of Chicanas who write in conversation with other women of color who were writing and publishing in the 1980s.

The Panza Monologues was born, then, from the efforts of a generation of Chicana playwrights who challenged erasure, patriarchal representations, impossible beauty standards, and colonial violence. Josefina López's play *Real Women Have Curves*, for example, sets the tone for Mexican American women to bare their bodies in an act of resistance to constricting gender roles, a political protest against anti-immigrant sentiment and policy, defiance against exploitative labor practices, and a show of solidarity with other women. Actors baring their bodies onstage stand as a powerful symbol of the connections between performance and social transformation, contextualized within the policing of women's bodies through heteropatriarchal norms. Audiences of *Real Women Have Curves* employ what Tiffany Ana López calls "the dynamics of 'critical witnessing' [that] position the audience in relationship to social change, with the work designed to provoke questions about agency and subjectivity in a way that causes audience members to leave with a sense of responsibility for either participating in the problem or creating a path for changing it" (301). This kind of audience response extends to *The Panza Monologues*, where the solo performer uses her body and exposes her panza in both celebration and demonstration. Students can grasp the ideas behind the project by reading T. Jackie Cuevas's article "Power to the Panza: Stomaching Oppression in Virginia Grise and Irma Mayorga's *The Panza Monologues*," which argues that the play "demonstrates how an intersectional analysis is crucial for leveling a gutsy critique of the historical structures of oppression that have continued to denigrate brown women's bodies" (1).

Other assigned readings might include the introduction to *Puro Teatro*, an anthology of Latina drama that establishes an important framework for understanding the critical interventions that Latina playwrights have contributed to contemporary performance, and that is an accessible entryway into the material for undergraduates (Sandoval-Sánchez xi–xiv). Instructors could also assign the introduction to *Performing the US Latina and Latino Borderlands*, so that students become aware of the contemporary conversation around borderlands performance studies as a growing field that looks to theater as a form of social protest, and even to the concept of culture as performance (Aldama et al. 1–27). Several of the essays in that book would enhance the students' understandings of Latinx performance, particularly for graduate students. The popular blog *HowlRound Theatre Commons* is also an accessible resource for instructors and students who want to learn more about the state of contemporary Latinx theater. Marci McMahon's "Pedagogy Notebook: Latin@ Theatre for Social Action in the Time of Donald Trump," for example, addresses many of these questions. *The Panza Monologues Blog* even has its own "Pedagogy of the Panza" section in which scholars, including me, discuss how they have implemented analysis and performance of the monologues in their courses (Santos).

Teaching and staging *The Panza Monologues* can be an invaluable experience. Instructors can enhance the learning of students by having them perform *The Panza Monologues* themselves. What follows are some examples of how instructors might approach staging monologues with students, to improve their comfort and experience with the dramatic arts, and suggestions for institutional funding and resources to support such an endeavor. Instructors may consider coaching students to stage the monologues and to recruit students who are not in the class to help. Working in groups of about ten, students can then prepare a fifteen-minute production. Each group divides up responsibilities such as directing, acting, public relations, music, costumes, props, and so on. By following the useful checklists in the second edition of *The Panza Monologues*, instructors can guide students in their production plans, allotting time to prepare and rehearse both in and outside of class. For instructors teaching outside of drama programs, helpful tactics can be found in Augusto Boal's *Theatre of the Oppressed*, and theoretical approaches can be found in Diana Taylor's *Performance*. Often students have not seen a live play before, and participating in the production of *The Panza Monologues* will instill in them interest in viewing other performances at universities or in local communities.

Grise and Mayorga's "DIY Production Manual," a guidebook for Chicanas (and other women of color) who aspire to be cultural producers, teachers, and students—which the authors insist is simply a jumping off point—is actually quite extensive (Grise and Mayorga 157–202). "Guidelines, Advice, and Good Wishes for Staging a Production" includes examples of form letters for obtaining permission to stage the play and for negotiating royalties, promotional materials from past productions of the play, notes for staging a production, a planning checklist, event planning notes, and more. The manual includes advice from instructors about seeking departmental support and university resources, and ideas for collaborating with community theater professionals. Faculty in drama and performance studies, or directors from local theaters, can be invited to provide workshops. Grise herself travels throughout the country to work with students, actors, and community organizers and could be available for a workshop.

In Grise and Mayorga's "Panza Pilón: A Manifesto for Panza Positive Chicana Cultural Production," the playwrights make incisive suggestions about the future direction of Chicana/o and women's theater (Grise and

Mayorga 223–232). They assess the mixed successes of social justice organizations and cultural spaces to foster productive relations with women and artists of color and to produce their creative endeavors. Especially important are the discussions of artistic labor and the value of women's work, conversations that will continue to grow as women's theater is recognized and performed in public spaces. Therefore, instructors who reach out to theater professionals should interact with them ethically, remembering that they are professionals who should be paid for their labor.

Importantly, students should also do background research for the play, including on its historical context, its critical reception, controversies it may have sparked, and general audience response. To help understand the recollections of the speaker in the monologue "A Hunger for Justice," they can conduct research on the Levi's jeans plant closing in the early 1990s, when more than a thousand women lost their jobs overnight, and on the collective effort by hundreds of laid-off workers to sue the company for severance packages. Notably, the former employees created a successful nonprofit called Fuerza Unida that effected positive change in their community for more than two decades. Significantly, Grise and Mayorga stress the importance of self-care alongside social justice work, concluding that "[i]f our body breaks down, then how are we going to do all this work?" (57).

Another approach to the material involves examining issues of reproductive justice. Women's health matters are particularly prevalent in the play and resonate with students because of the personal nature of the monologue format. Texas has one of the highest maternal mortality rates in the country (MacDorman et al. 172). Budget cuts to women's health clinics make the material even more pressing for classroom discussion, which can address access to prenatal care, cancer screenings, and other health-care resources for women, especially low-income women, and how restrictions on public health-care options often affect women of color disproportionately. Responding to comments in the media about San Antonio's high obesity rate, the playwrights ponder, "So, if obesity is a disease of capitalism, why is it that San Antonio is one of the largest cities in the nation and at the same time one of the poorest?" (Grise and Mayorga 77). This link between socioeconomics and structural oppression is crucial to analyzing the monologues. Research prior to reading and preparing portions of the play can help students understand the impact of what is dramatized and place these accounts within the larger context of women and society.

> If we asked how the *panza* was for all the citizens of a given society, we might not have hunger for our children or our elders. If we asked how the *panza* was for a woman with child, we might have quality prenatal care for all expectant mothers. If we asked, how is the *panza*? Is it fed, is it warm? Is it nourished? Was this *panza* living next to an electrical plant? A lead site? A cancer cluster? Will it get the medicine needed for a healthy *panza*? (81)

By completing critical readings on race, gender, sexuality, and historical context, students begin to understand the significance of the dramatic monologues and their major themes, recognizing specific sociopolitical, generational, and linguistic distinctions and the literary histories of Chicana/o/x communities.

The opportunity to recreate and interpret the material itself conceivably engages students more fully with the content. They take ownership of their education. Working in collaboration holds them accountable to their peers and fosters a sense of community that is reflective of the nature of theater. By embodying the characters of these monologues, they experience firsthand the powerful potential of performance as a tool of social justice. Toward the end of the course, students need to complete an individual self-reflection on the experience of performing the material, an exercise that provides an important final step in the process of reading, witnessing, and staging *The Panza Monologues*. Exposing students to this living history of San Antonio will leave a lasting impression. *The Panza Monologues*, framed within the geographic space of a south Texas city in the borderlands, can help shape future generations of theater makers and civically engaged community members. Contemplating and understanding women's and queer narratives help students better understand issues of equity and social justice in the context of intersectional oppression. And the critical eye that students will have cultivated through study and participatory dramatizations will advance their understandings of themselves and their society.

Note

1. *Chicano* is the masculine and *Chicana* the feminine form of the word. It is often written with the endings *a/o*, *o/a*, or @ to make women visible, whose contributions within the Chicano Movement have been erased, ignored, or collapsed into movement history. *Chicano* can refer to the community as a whole, to men specifically, or to the Chicano Movement. *Latina/o* is meant as an umbrella term to include communities of Latin American and Spanish origin. Similarly, *Hispanic* was previously meant to refer to those of Spanish-speaking heritage (and is still

used in the South and the Southwest of the United States). Finally, *Latinx* and *Chicanx* have recently been employed in critical race and gender scholarship because these terms are inclusive of sexual and gender diversity. I also use *Chicana/o/x* to reflect the variants.

Works Cited

Aldama, Arturo J., et al., editors. *Performing the US Latina and Latino Borderlands.* Indiana UP, 2012.

Boal, Augusto. *Theatre of The Oppressed.* Pluto Press, 2008.

Cuevas, T. Jackie. "Power to the Panza: Stomaching Oppression in Virginia Grise and Irma Mayorga's *The Panza Monologues.*" *Praxis*, vol. 23, no. 1, 2011, pp. 1–10.

García, Laura E., et al. *Teatro Chicana: A Collective Memoir and Selected Plays.* U of Texas P, 2008.

Grise, Virginia, and Irma Mayorga. *The Panza Monologues.* 2nd ed., U of Texas P, 2014.

Herrera, Patricia. "Power to the Panza! Feminist Body Politics in *The Panza Monologues* (Video Performance Review)." *Chicana/Latina Studies*, vol. 10, no. 2, 2011, pp. 206–11.

Jacobs, Elizabeth. "*Shadow of a Man*: A Chicana/Latina Drama as Embodied Feminist Practice." *New Theatre Quarterly*, vol. 31, no. 1, 2015, pp. 49–58.

López, Tiffany Ana. "Suturing Las Ramblas to East LA: Transnational Performances of Josefina López's *Real Women Have Curves.*" *Performing the US Latina and Latino Borderlands*, edited by Arturo J. Aldama et al., Indiana UP, 2012, pp. 296–308.

MacDorman, M. F., et al. "Trends in Texas Maternal Mortality by Maternal Age, Race/Ethnicity, and Cause of Death, 2006–2015." *Birth*, vol. 45, no. 2, June 2018, pp. 169–77.

McMahon, Marci "Pedagogy Notebook: Latin@ Theatre for Social Action in the Time of Donald Trump." *HowlRound*, 26 Aug. 2016, howlround.com/pedagogy-notebook-latin-theatre-for-social-action-in-the-time-of-donald-trump.

Moraga, Cherríe, and Gloria Anzaldúa, editors. *This Bridge Called My Back: Writings by Radical Women of Color.* State U of New York P, 1981.

Sandoval-Sánchez, Alberto, and Nancy Saporta Sternbach, editors. *Puro Teatro: A Latina Anthology.* U of Arizona P, 2000.

Santos, Adrianna M. "Pedagogy of the Panza." *The Panza Monologues Blog*, 22 Apr. 2017, panzamonologues.blogspot.com/2017/04/pedagogy-of-panza-featuring-adrianna-m.html.

Taylor, Diana. *Performance.* Duke University Press, 2016.

Valdez, Luis. *Luis Valdez—Early Works: Actos,* Bernabé *and "Pensamiento Serpentino."* Arte Público Press, 1990.

Yarbro-Bejarano, Yvonne. "The Female Subject in Chicano Theatre: Sexuality, 'Race,' and Class." *Theatre Journal*, vol. 38, no. 4, 1986, pp. 389–407.

Norma A. Valenzuela

Evolution of a Transnational Imaginary in the Drama of Josefina Niggli, Josefina López, and Yareli Arizmendi

When contextualized sociohistorically, dramatic texts can help us examine lives lived, and Chicana cultural production is amenable to this praxis. Through such a process of contextualization, I propose teaching patterns of an evolving transnational imaginary and the methods that plays by Chicanas use to deconstruct hegemonic discourses. The three plays discussed here, *Soldadera: A Play of the Mexican Revolution*, by Josefina Niggli; *Simply Maria; or, The American Dream*, by Josefina López; and *Nostalgia Maldita: 1-900-Mexico: A StairMaster Piece*, by Yareli Arizmendi, offer opportunities to evaluate themes of racism, classism, loss, displacement, violence, activism, education, solidarity, and identity.

To prepare students to read these plays, I first provide them with short critical readings on Sonia Saldívar-Hull's notion of intersectionality of gender and politics (27–58) and on concepts of border identity and subjectivity. I teach Sonia Saldívar-Hull's work with Emma Pérez's explanation of the decolonial imaginary (3–30) and with Gloria Anzaldúa's discussion of mestiza consciousness (99–113) to help students understand how these concepts can reflect the changing ways in which the contemporary world is imagined, and to help them consider that "key actors of transnationalism are international migrants who are assumed to create new transnational spaces beyond the national borders" (Maasilta 83). Applying a transnationalist approach to the discussion of these plays enhances students' understanding of how dramatic texts help make visible perspectives outside of national ideologies. Undergraduate students may already recognize recurring themes of identity formation and of cultural renegotiation and resignification; however, I expand on a discussion of those themes in my course to let students discover how playwrights subvert the traditional roles imposed on women by patriarchal constraints through the creation of transformational central characters.

Focusing class discussion on the early twentieth century, a time when male playwrights were more prominently recognized than female playwrights, brings into greater relief Chicana dramatists and their processes of expressing and articulating Chicana identities, through which they center their female characters. I use the genealogy of Chicana/o dramatists' work to facilitate a final discussion in which students are asked to communicate their understanding of the evolution of a transnational imaginary in Chicana drama.

Josefina Niggli and the *Soldadera*

To contextualize the historical setting for Niggli's play, I begin with a brief overview of the 1910 Mexican Revolution. We discuss the revolution's impact on the migration of many Mexicans to the United States, the invisibility of women in this history, and the general lack of knowledge in the United States about Mexican culture. Here I underscore Niggli's desire to educate Americans about Mexico and her unique, early-twentieth-century role as an artist in Mexican culture. Niggli's insider point of view sets the stage for readers to examine more closely the levels of complexity represented in *Soldadera*. Although the play can be misinterpreted as problematizing reckless women and men, the narrative actually disrupts traditional roles ascribed to working-class Mexican women. In *Soldadera* the site for exploration is a battleground. Niggli takes readers on a tour of the women and men on that battleground. Her social commentary counters Anglocentric views of Mexicans as she reclaims the figure of the *soldadera* ("woman soldier"). The one-act play serves as a precursor to works by Chicana playwrights in the late twentieth century such as Josefina López and Yareli Arizmendi. Alongside class discussions of this significant historical period and of Niggli's play, I assign readings from the critical biography on Niggli by Elizabeth Coonrod Martínez (1–39).

We then engage in discussions about language use, particularly the reasons bilingual Chicana writers prefer to work in one language over the other. Students discover that Niggli faced criticism because she wrote in English and, most important, that she was one of the earliest Mexican writers to document "creative works in English, [about] the changes brought by the Mexican Revolution, from feminist ideals to the rise of the mestizo (person of mixed blood) in Mexican society" (Martínez 2). We discuss how Niggli's perspective as an insider who grew up in northern Mexico gave her direct knowledge of the realities of life during the Mexican Revolution. Thus students recognize Niggli's need to tell stories based on her lived experiences while growing up in the borderlands. I emphasize Martínez's assertion that "Niggli is the first writer to bring the 'Adelita' [or *soldadera*] image—a symbol of struggle and freedom for the U.S. Chicana—to English language literature" (5), to encourage students to examine the center stage role that the *soldadera* figure played in the revolution.

Guided class discussion centers on the impact of war on marginalized communities and specifically the trauma that war inflicts on women's bodies and psyches. As students delve into the reading, they recognize the transformation that the young protagonist, Adelita, is undergoing. She becomes conscious of the battles taking place around her and the manner in which her life and the lives of the other *soldaderas* are directly affected by the revolution; she comments on the death of children, husbands, lovers, relatives, and friends. Reading the play out loud helps students understand and embody this *soldadera*'s pent-up sadness, devastation, hatred, and rancor and helps them connect with the other characters. Allowing the students to "become" the characters is powerful. But before they read the play out loud, I invite students to explore tensions in the characters that result from frustrated aspirations or from goals that have been achieved by unacceptable means. This exercise helps students grasp Niggli's critique of the Mexican upper class, who misjudged the lower class, which participated collectively to overthrow those in power, who had neglected much of the Mexican population: "Although he possesses no name, he is called THE RICH ONE, by the women, since he represents the hated upperclass which has held them in subjection for so long" (Niggli 160). When reading this scene, students are able to empathize with the *soldaderas* because by now they understand the reasons for their participation in the revolution.

In another scene, the powerful images that Niggli uses to describe the women's feelings further students' understanding of the consequences of war for women of all ages: "THE OLD ONE shambles in. . . . She is a very old woman who has seen too much of death, but still she clings to life with the hope burning in her . . . the same hope that burns in all these women . . . that this time the Revolution must succeed" (162). Guiding students in reading the scenes foments understanding of the perseverance, strength, and courage of the women, embodied in the *soldadera* Adelita. As we begin to interpret her death, students see that Adelita exercises her agency when she willingly gives her life for the revolution. Niggli's creative work retells history with substantial details. In fact, the abundance of details and descriptions gives students a thorough female perspective on this history, which can be understood through Pérez's decolonial imaginary, a concept that views women as central to Mexican and Chicano social movements. Students understand through Niggli's play that *soldaderas* took center stage in the 1910 Revolution. We end our conversation of this play by discussing the ability of Niggli to move historical female figures into creative work as she participates in setting the frames for contemporary Chicana drama.

Reimagining the American Dream in *Simply Maria*

The 1980s and 1990s were an era of increased Mexican immigration to the United States in which entire families were crossing the border in pursuit of *el sueño americano* ("the American dream"), which for migrant parents meant an education for their children. In one of her early plays, *Simply Maria,* López reimagines the American dream by foreshadowing future events and internal conflicts in a nightmare that the young protagonist has. To prepare students for the reading, I have them brainstorm in small groups what they believe the American dream is and why one would sacrifice one's life to move to another country to chase such a dream. Many of the themes that students discuss transfer into our examination of the play, which is set in a dream state. In it, Maria is forced to confront her predicament: follow her aspirations and pursue an education or assume the traditional role for Chicana and Mexicana women. In a preliminary activity, I invite students to explore the tensions that arise from conflicting expectations in their own lives—such as their personal goals and those imposed on them by their parents or society. This activity helps students relate to Maria and her challenges.

In the next prereading exercise, students in small groups answer the question "Who am I?" considering their own racial, economic, ethnic, gender, and other social positioning within society in the United States. This exercise helps students begin to grasp the themes manifested in *Simply Maria*. Some students might relate to a young Mexican girl who is a first-generation immigrant trying to make sense of her family's conservative values and her new life in the United States. López foreshadows Maria's conundrum in scene 3, where the Statue of Liberty proclaims: "I give you life, liberty, and the pursuit of happiness, for the price of your heritage, your roots, your history, your family, your language. . . . Conform, adapt, give up what is yours, and I will give you the opportunity to have what is mine" (15). The protagonist is then thrown into a whirlwind of self-questioning and doubt.

Students make sense of Maria's self-questioning by exploring their own doubts, frustrations, and insecurities—first by jotting down personal, professional, or academic issues they've confronted. Then in small groups they share with other students the feelings they experienced when confronting those issues. This activity engages students with the text as they begin to connect the characters' circumstances with their own lived experiences. These activities help students focus on issues that strike their interest; through a guided reading, they begin to perceive how López enacts the tensions between traditional family values of the home country and those of the host country. Becoming acquainted with these issues assists students in examining the beliefs and stereotypes of their own society. López's play captures students' feelings by inspiring sympathy, anxiety, and stress in readers or an audience. Students who have confronted their own parents about something may especially relate to the play.

In one scene, Maria recalls that her father always told her that he brought the family to the United States for a better life. And yet, when Maria wants to pursue higher education, neither parent supports her decision. Maria's turmoil manifests itself in a nightmare that serves as a catharsis for the character and that assists readers in seeing themselves reflected in the text. To understand such turmoil, students embody the play by acting it out. To prepare students for the activity, I ask them to think of an instance in which they were extremely stressed and actually had a nightmare. This activity creates anticipation and tension among the students and later helps them understand Maria's transformation into an empowered young girl. In the play, when Maria wakes up from the dream, she discovers she has agency. A close reading of this scene paired with a discussion of the students' tensions guides them in recognizing Maria's realization that she can make her own future. They can then revel in Maria's newly discovered agency, which allows her to examine the role she does not want to play in her conservative family. López stages the impact of the struggle in Maria, who in a dream state confronts her father, mother, husband, and judge. She is gradually transformed by the experience. By "waking up" from the nightmare, the students and Maria dismantle taboos about gender and sexuality and break their silence by becoming speaking subjects.

When reading *Simply Maria*, students discover new ways to consider the tension that young immigrants experience between their role within a traditional Mexican family and their search for the American dream. The portrayals of Maria, her conservative Mexican family, and societal values in the United States—embodied through different characters—can elicit for the students an identification with their own experience, which may encourage them to articulate for themselves the forces that structure oppressive realities. This exercise sometimes prompts students to begin sharing their own everyday hardships and to understand the courage it takes to find their own voice. Our discussion of the play reveals how López subverts the American dream and how she develops a young Chicana character who has agency and who recognizes that she must and can live in two worlds:

GIRL 1. Mexico is in my blood . . .
GIRL 3. . . . and America is in my heart. (53)

In a guided discussion that complements this in-class conversation, students explore Saldívar-Hull's theories about intersectionality of gender and politics. I pose the following questions: "Would it be different if Maria were a boy? What do politics have to do with gender?" Student discussions almost always generate insightful analyses of gender politics.

Popular Culture as Subversive Performance in *Nostalgia Maldita*

Arizmendi's play *Nostalgia Maldita*, written in the 1990s, is saturated with references to the consumerism of that era in the United States and lays the groundwork for students to deepen their understanding of popular culture. To prepare students in their reading of the solo piece, I ask them to brainstorm what they think American culture is. The occasional student might respond with "Americans have no culture," so we then define culture and explore what defines popular culture. I also pose the following question:

"What is the first thing that comes to your mind when I say 'America'?" This question tends to elicit numerous responses and comments that we utilize to dive into the text.

In a guided reading, students discover that the playwright proposes that the mainstream media perpetuates the myth that immigrants reach the American dream once they can saturate themselves with artificial sweeteners, call 1-900 phone numbers, consume Diet Coke, enjoy the music of Donny Osmond, become actors and actresses, and always watch their fat and calorie intake. Arizmendi proposes that nostalgic Mexicans call the phone number 1-900-Mexico because doing so is a catharsis in which they can vent, think about old times, and romanticize Mexico. I point out that in the United States of the 1990s salsa became more popular than ketchup, Latino buying power tripled, and the Latino media exploded. To help students understand the references to the 1990s, I have them do a brief *YouTube* search on popular culture of the era. This exercise allows them to see the images and understand the era's health fads and then recognize the richness of the play. Especially important is the staging of the play—Arizmendi performs it on a StairMaster to underscore the '90s health fads.

By embodying multiple characters in her solo piece, Arizmendi criticizes the cultures of Mexico and the United States and the realities faced by immigrants who make the United States their home. A guided discussion on how playwrights utilize language to influence audiences is a clever technique to criticize aspects of society. Understanding language use allows students to appreciate Arizmendi's solo performance as funny, poignant, and political. I find it useful for students to brainstorm possible reasons a dramatist would include subversive acts of contestation, persistence, resistance, and negotiation.

Students begin to see that the play uses nostalgia to provide a critique of the assimilation route that immigrants take in order to succeed in the United States. The scene where the character Actress embraces her "gringa self, the dream and turns off the culturally correct alarm clock" (Arizmendi 232) helps students see that American stereotypes are constructed by Hollywood and marketed globally. Actress asks the audience questions that exemplify commonly held values and priorities in the United States, and she jokingly criticizes Americans for always doing what the new fad tells them to do. At this point in the text, I ask students to skim the words and phrases that highlight social criticism. They see that Actress, in her preaching attitude, criticizes society's material wealth and values.

Arizmendi's social criticism about the corporation that owns Diet Coke being the benefactor in "a country with rampant homelessness, violence and despair everywhere" serves to highlight the hypocrisy of societal values in the United States. Arizmendi also tackles the identity crisis that many Latino immigrants face. Actress has a mini-meltdown—"is she or is she not Mexican?" (234). Arizmendi also does not fail to make a political statement about the constant need of Latino immigrants to be on the lookout for government officials: in one scene Actress asks, "Are you one of Pete's boys?" referring to the California governor Pete Wilson, and makes an aside about how the name "Pete" could be changed to that of any other xenophobic government official (234). A guided conversation on the theme of police brutality, racism, prejudice, and scapegoating can expand students' notions of racial and ethnic inequities.

At the end of the performance, the students, like Actress, recognize that immigrants choose to remain in the United States despite the presence of people like Pete Wilson. Actress embraces both her heritage and her adopted country. Arizmendi poignantly concludes the play with an "Amexican" anthem and flag (238).

These plays by Niggli, López, and Arizmendi help students discern the development of a transnational imaginary in which the characters focus their attention on remaking their lives, in Niggli's play, and making the United States their home, in the two more recent plays. The dramatists create an empowering discourse that represents their own transnational identities. The characters in the plays figure out ways of making sense of society and their place in it as they become active participants in social, political, and economic movements. They empower themselves through their activities and reflections. Students can thus evaluate how plays use discursive tools to explore and represent the effects of assimilation, race and ethnicity, gender identity, sexuality, family relations, and community. Through close attention to group work and exercises, students begin to map strategies for critical thinking about theater and deeper conversations about the role of Latina playwrights.

Works Cited

Anzaldúa, Gloria. *Borderlands / La frontera: The New Mestiza*. Spinsters / Aunt Lute, 1987.

Arizmendi, Yareli. *Nostalgia Maldita: 1-900-Mexico: A StairMaster Piece*. *Puro Teatro: A Latina Anthology*, edited by Alberto Sandoval-Sánchez and Nancy Saporta Sternbach, U of Arizona P, 2000, pp. 229–38.

López, Josefina. *Simply Maria; or, the American Dream*. Dramatic Publications, 1996.

Maasilta, Mari. *African Carmen: Transnational Cinema as an Arena for Cultural Contradictions*. 2007. U of Tampere, Finland, PhD dissertation.

Martínez, Elizabeth Coonrod. *Josefina Niggli, Mexican American Writer: A Critical Biography*. U of New Mexico P, 2007.

Niggli, Josefina. *Soldadera: A Play of the Mexican Revolution. The Plays of Josefina Niggli: Recovered Landmarks of Latino Literature*, edited by Willliam Orchard and Yolanda Padilla, U of Wisconsin P, 2007, pp. 157–92.

Pérez, Emma. *The Decolonial Imaginary: Writing Chicanas into History*. Indiana UP, 1999.

Saldívar-Hull, Sonia. *Feminism on the Border: Chicana Gender Politics and Literature*. U of California P, 2000.

Susan C. Méndez

Confronting Gender and Sexual Identity in Cherríe Moraga's *Shadow of a Man*

The Chicana feminist playwright, essayist, poet, and activist Cherríe Moraga is a central figure in the literatures of women of color, including Chicana literature, and her plays have been performed regularly since the late twentieth century. This essay discusses the use of her play *Shadow of a Man* in a freshman-level English course with a focus on gender and sexuality and in a senior seminar in English; both courses involve thematic analysis of ghosts, shadows, and theories of homosocial bonding. Of course, students read other creative works in these courses to further develop the topics of gender and sexuality and the analysis of ghosts. In the freshman class, three other plays, two novels, and several short stories are assigned; meanwhile in the senior seminar, one other play and four other novels (all by Chicana and other Latina authors) are required reading. However, what makes this play so applicable to both courses is its concrete cultural and historical setting in a Chicano family home in Los Angeles, in 1969, and its abstract contemplation of the ideas of ghosts and shadows and their relation to the male characters of the play.

This setting permits readers of the play to imagine what ideas about sexuality and gender were commonplace at the time, while the figurative use of shadows and ghosts raises questions about what conflicts and issues involving gender and sexuality will arise for these characters and haunt them until they understand the meaning of the figurative entities. In both the freshman and senior courses, the instructor must lay some groundwork before addressing the play. This work consists of defining and discussing some foundational concepts: Who are Chicanas/os, and what is their experience? What is meant by use of the word "Aztlán" in the play? For general background on Latino history in the United States, I have used brief excerpts from Himilce Novas's *Everything You Need to Know about Latino History* (45–123) and Juan Gonzalez's *Harvest of Empire: A History of Latinos in America* (96–107) to define central concepts before the class moves on to the play. Another point of consideration for the instructor is how the overall theme of each course (social justice for the freshman course and haunting in literature for the senior course) permits different learning outcomes.

Literature and Social Justice

In the freshman course, Literature and Social Justice, the play is discussed in five class sessions. The final three sessions are devoted to analysis of the short play. In the first two class sessions, to put certain concepts in motion for the play, students present critical readings about queer identity and community and about gender and sexual identity being on a continuum. For these first two sessions, I assign a chapter in Moraga's book of essays, *The Last Generation* (145–74), and then two chapters in Julia Serano's *Whipping Girl: A Transsexual Woman on Sexism and the Scapegoating of Feminism* (23–34, 77–93). Having completed these readings, students open discussion by defining terminology and ascertaining relevant historical and cultural details, all of which are necessary to understand the plot and characters' actions in *Shadow of a Man*. For example, Moraga's chapter provides the useful definition of "queer Aztlán" as "a nation strong enough to embrace a range of racial diversities, human sexualities, and expressions of gender. . . . In a 'queer' Aztlán, there would be no freaks, no 'others' to point one's fingers at" (*Last Generation* 164).

Students will need to recognize and apply this concept in discussion of the Rodríguez family in the play: Hortensia, Manuel, and their children—Rigo, Leticia, and Lupe—and a family friend, Conrado. Serrano's text provides a more nuanced and contemporary understanding of gender and sexual identity as being on a continuum, an understanding that extends beyond queer identity. Serrano uses the terms transsexuality, cisgenderism, subconscious sex, and gender entitlement. Such terms come into use during class discussions, significantly those about the play's end; given the class's focus on social justice, expansive understandings of gender and sexual identity are critical.

Although there are other social justice issues in this play, such as gender equality (e.g., how the eldest daughter, Leticia, rails against her mother's double standards and gendered behavior expectations regarding her, her sister, and her brother), these moments buttress the evolution of the larger issue of gender and sexual identity, especially as it concerns the male characters. To help students understand the meaning and importance of Manuel and Conrado's relationship, I assign roles to students, and they act out scene 8 of act 1, where Hortensia and Manuel discuss a shared secret, something that makes Hortensia feel dirty and Manuel resentful. However, Manuel and Hortensia's marriage becomes secondary in importance to Manuel's idealized relationship with his best friend, Conrado. It appears that no one is more important to Manuel than Conrado except Manuel's children, and primarily his son, Rigo. Rigo is mentioned at certain times in the play, during the preparations for his marriage and the birth of his son, Rigo Jr., but Rigo never appears on stage: he is another shadow in this play, like Conrado, who is much talked about but does not come on stage until the very end of the play.

The history between Manuel and Conrado is telling because Manuel can never seem to forget Conrado. He appears to idolize his friend. Manuel recalls how Conrado left for Arizona to become a successful businessman and, for much of the play, appears to greatly miss Conrado and to want to be him. It is only late in the play that readers learn that Manuel even offered his wife, Hortensia, to Conrado to make him stay, and that despite Conrado's acceptance of this offer, he did not stay, and this one-night encounter is the root of the permanent tension between Manuel and Hortensia (especially since Conrado, the play suggests, may be Lupe's biological father). Manuel's fascination with Conrado appears to move beyond financial or personal envy, or even sexual jealousy for his tryst with Manuel's wife.

Near the end of the play, Manuel confesses his conflicted state when thinking of that night, "I floated into that room with him. In my mind, I was him. And then, I was her too. In my mind, I imagined their pleasure and I turned into nothing" (Moraga 71). When this point of the play is reached in discussion, I again assign roles, and the students read out scene 6 of act 2, which is the final confrontation between Hortensia, Manuel, and

Conrado: they argue over the past and the present. Manuel rejects both his wife and his friend and soon after overdoses on his heart medication. Questions can be posed here such as: What drives Manuel to take his life? Why can he not forgive Hortensia and Conrado, considering the role he played in what happened between them? What is the true cause of his anger and depression, and how does it link back to his own memory and commentary about the night between Hortensia and Conrado? Students can be assigned to small groups to work on finding lines of argument that answer these questions, thereby leading up to and confirming Manuel's suspected homosexuality.

As the students deliberate on Manuel's daydreams about what it would be like if Conrado returned for a visit, how Manuel furtively carries a photo of Conrado in his wallet, and the final descriptive scene of Conrado and Hortensia's lovemaking, they have much to discuss. Perhaps Manuel's unarticulated and prohibited love for Conrado is why Manuel could not forgive either his wife or his friend and could not live with himself anymore. Perplexing for students is Manuel's fixation on Lupe (who could be Conrado's daughter), and his statement to her, "You're different from the rest. You got a heart that was made to love. Don't ever leave me, baby" (52). Is he speaking directly to her, or channeling his possible desire for Conrado?

Once the topic of Lupe and Manuel's relationship is raised, students again work in small groups to try to find lines that describe Lupe and her struggles outside her relationship with Manuel. At the beginning of the play, students note that Lupe has secrets regarding her own sexuality that she is afraid of making known. After a church confession, Lupe wonders what it means that she thinks of what Sister Genevieve must look like naked under her uniform and that she cannot confess it: "I try. I really do try. But no matter how many times I make confession, no matter how many times I try to tell the priest what I hold insida me, I know I'm still lying. Sinning. Keeping secrets" (42). Later on, Lupe tells her sister that when she looks at her own eyes in the mirror, she can confirm that there are two versions of herself: "Two little faces, one in each eye. It's like you got other people living inside you. Maybe you're not really you. Maybe they're the real you and the big you is just a dream you" (53).

After brief sessions of group work, students begin to connect the development of Lupe's character to that of Manuel's: each struggles with issues of sexual identity in a time and space that are not accepting of such struggles. The characters sometimes suggest that they are both in need of a queer Aztlán, a nation that accepts them. Lupe finally discusses her crush on her friend Frankie in her closing lines: "If I could, I'd like to jus' unzip her chest and climb right inside there, next to her heart, to feel everything she's feeling and I could forget about me" (84). Students discuss similarities in each character's search for sexual identity and acknowledgment.

Latina Feminist Literature

I also assign Moraga's *Shadow of a Man* in my senior seminar for English majors, Latina Feminist Literature: Ghosts, Letters, and Damaged/ Damaging Bodies as Messages/Messengers across Generations. Here class discussions are crucial, as is ensuring that students understand and can utilize foundational literary concepts, themes, and definitions. Thus, before students analyze any literature, I assign key excerpts from Mary Eagleton's *Feminist Literary Criticism* (1–23) and Frederick Luis Aldama's *The Routledge Concise History of Latino/a Literature* (15–39), though other sources could be equally fitting. In addition to these excerpts, students read the first chapter of Avery Gordon's *Ghostly Matters: Haunting and the Sociological Imagination* for a more nuanced understanding of the ghost figure and the use of haunting in literature (3–28). Gordon explains, "The ghost is not simply a dead or missing person, but a social figure, and investigating it can lead to that dense site where history and subjectivity make social life. . . . The way of the ghost is haunting and haunting is a very particular way of knowing what has happened or is happening" (8).

Gordon specifically describes why a new lens, such as that of haunting, is needed: "To study social life one must confront the ghostly aspects of it. This confrontation requires (or produces) a fundamental change in the way we know and make knowledge, in our mode of production" (7). One of my goals for this course is to get students to think about how we know what we know and to question this process. The epistemological urge fuels this course and forces students to reorient their framework of knowledge by considering what cannot be seen or is insubstantial to the eye, hence the focus on ghosts and shadows in Moraga's play.

Thus, one of the first discussion questions is, Who are the ghosts and shadows here? Again, students are assigned to work in small groups. The occasional mention of Rigo, despite his absence on stage, and the consistent mention of Conrado, despite his absence until the play's conclusion, each fall under the category of "shadow." Manuel seems unfulfilled and unhappy throughout the play, as when he declares that he was turned into nothing when he gave Hortensia to Conrado. Manuel refers to himself as a "ghost" at the end of that confession (71). Oriented to focus on shadows and ghosts, students begin to consider what is wrong in this household and society.

A reading of the first chapter in Eve Kosofsky Sedgwick's *Epistemology of the Closet* is also helpful here (67–90). Students working in groups develop discussion questions that use Sedgwick's main argument to further their understanding of the play. Sedgwick's chapter considers how society lacks an understanding and acceptance of homosociality and homosocial bonding, such as in the development of a love triangle between two men and a woman, which can illustrate a sublimated attraction (not necessarily sexual) between the two men. The presence of such intense male-male relationships is still not easily understood and provides excellent discussion potential for this play. While a superficial reading could indicate jealousy of Conrado and love for Hortensia as reasons for Manuel's unhappiness, further critical study and theoretically informed reading can help students consider other facets.

Students may also discuss the character of Hortensia and how women are often conduits through which intense male bonds are expressed. A reading focused on the possible homosexuality of Manuel (and Lupe) and the homophobia of society (much like the analysis by students in the freshman-level class) can focus more generally on society or social systems and not enough on individuals and their potential relationships and struggles with reality. The application of theory can mitigate this tendency among students. Then, if a reading of the individual characters proceeds quickly, further consideration can be directed to how the individual character functions in a community. Perhaps this dual reading of both the individual character and the community is the best way to approach a complex text such as this play. Finally, by prioritizing the analysis of Manuel and Conrado's relationship in ways suggested by Gordon and Sedgwick, the students can recognize other perspectives and other ways to comprehend male-male relationships that are nonsexual.

For the final class session on this play, I ask students to present on one of the articles or book chapters about this play from a list that I compiled. Last time I taught this course, students selected Julia de Foor Jay's essay "(Re)Claiming the Race of the Mother: Cherríe Moraga's *Shadow of a Man*, *Giving Up the Ghost*, and *Heroes and Saints*." Such presentations help students consider their own critical points of view alongside those that have been published, an empowering activity for their future studies. These presentations are also an opportunity for students to assess other character dynamics, for example, the relationships between Hortensia and her daughters Leticia and Lupe, in terms of gender equality and sexual identity.

After students have completed their presentations, read aloud scenes from the play, and done their group work, they must write an essay. For the freshman course, I place the following on the essay prompt sheet:

> In *Shadow of a Man*, by Cherríe Moraga, how does the character Manuel suffer? What is he struggling with in his life? What seems to be the cause of his unhappiness, and does he realize what it is? How does his unhappiness resolve itself? Does he achieve a sense of social justice in his life? Is there hope for any other character in the play who may be struggling with the same issue as he is?

In the senior seminar, I ask the following:

> Ghosts and shadows are used in figurative ways in *Giving Up the Ghost* and *Shadow of a Man*, as opposed to the literal way in which Avery Gordon discusses ghosts in her text. However, in both cases, figurative and literal, the ghost or shadow can be seen as illuminating the wrongs that are taking place in society (e.g., the abuse of power). Who are the ghosts and shadows of these two plays? Why are they ghosts and shadows? What forms of social oppression might they be manifesting?

I find that an essay prompt about Moraga's *Shadow of a Man* works well in either course when it asks students to make a specific argument in response to focused questions, so that learning outcomes can be achieved. The learning outcomes are, in both courses, to identify ways in which literary works expose markers of gender and sexual difference that are situated in societal frameworks; in the freshman course, to recognize how these markers are then used in fomenting or discovering practices of social injustice; and in the senior seminar, to achieve more complex understandings of knowledge, self, community, and the interconnections between the last two concepts.

Note

For similar approaches to analyzing *Shadow of a Man*, see Elizabeth Jacobs's article "*Shadow of a Man*" and Yvonne Yarbro-Bejarano's book *The Wounded Heart*. Jacobs argues that Moraga expresses embodied Chicana feminist practice in the characters, sounds, and images in her plays. Through contextualization of the play within Chicano theater history and archival analysis of earlier drafts and performances, Jacobs asserts that the female characters of this play reclaim the role of the speaking subject in ways that disrupt narrative patterns of representation for

Chicanas, namely as La Malinche, who is considered in modern Mexicano and Chicano culture to be a traitor to indigenous peoples because she was the indigenous mistress of the Spanish conquistador Hernán Cortés. In this repossession, the female characters' bodies function as locales for Manuel's repressed and displaced homosexual desires. Jacobs furthers her argument with discussion of homosocial bonding. Yarbro-Bejarano explains how homosocial and homosexual relationships are intertwined, as Chicano culture permits homosociality but prohibits homosexuality, and this dynamic is shown through the history and the relationship between Manuel and Conrado in Moraga's play.

Works Cited

Aldama, Frederick Luis. *The Routledge Concise History of Latino/a Literature.* Routledge, 2013.

Eagleton, Mary, editor. *Feminist Literary Criticism.* Longman, 1991.

Gonzalez, Juan. *Harvest of Empire: A History of Latinos in America.* Penguin Books, 2000.

Gordon, Avery. *Ghostly Matters: Haunting and the Sociological Imagination.* U of Minnesota P, 1997.

Jacobs, Elizabeth. "*Shadow of a Man*: A Chicana/Latina Drama as Embodied Feminist Practice." *New Theatre Quarterly*, vol. 31, no. 1, 2015, pp. 49–58.

Jay, Julia de Foor. "(Re)Claiming the Race of the Mother: Cherríe Moraga's *Shadow of a Man*, *Giving Up the Ghost*, and *Heroes and Saints*." *Women of Color: Mother-Daughter Relationships in Twentieth-Century Literature*, edited by Elizabeth Brown-Guillory, U of Texas P, 1996, pp. 95–116.

Moraga, Cherríe. *The Last Generation: Prose and Poetry.* South End Press, 1993.

———. *Shadow of a Man.* Heroes and Saints *and Other Plays*, by Moraga, West End Press, 1994, pp. 37–84.

Novas, Himilce. *Everything You Need to Know about Latino History.* Plume, 2003.

Sedgwick, Eve Kosofsky. *Epistemology of the Closet.* U of California P, 1990.

Serano, Julia. *Whipping Girl: A Transsexual Woman on Sexism and the Scapegoating of Femininity.* Seal Press, 2007.

Yarbro-Bejarano, Yvonne. *The Wounded Heart: Writing on Cherríe Moraga.* U of Texas P, 2015.

William R. Stark

Mapping and Performing Indigenous Mexicana Identities: Violeta Luna and the Woman of Maize

I recently taught an undergraduate Spanish conversation class that was designed to develop students' speaking skills through readings, discussions, and presentations on cultural topics, and that centered on Chicana and Mexicana identity. Composed of juniors and sophomores, the class met for seventy-five minutes twice weekly. Teaching strategies included video, printed and virtual texts, and the use of the *Blackboard* online learning management system. In addition to in-class written work, students posted weekly online journal entries, responding to questions based on classroom activities, discussions, and reading materials.

I structured the class such that students worked in groups and individually to lead discussions of assigned readings. Multiple formats, such as roundtable discussions, reaction papers, and presentations, fostered student engagement. Students were encouraged to identify diverse representations of Latina identity in readings, music, videos, and performances. I used selected critical readings from Gloria Anzaldúa, Cherríe Moraga, Coco Fusco, Diana Taylor, and Doris Sommer, among other texts that touch on history, cultural studies, sociology, and Latina imaginaries and that are geared toward identifying issues that ground history and culture in the United States and Mexico.[1] I wanted students to grapple with the ways in which class, gender, sexuality, race, and national origin affect and mediate Chicana and Mexicana experiences.

The overall objective was for students to deconstruct binary thinking and reductive narratives through reflective analytical inquiry, while also learning to critically understand performance art. Classroom and online discussions focused on questions of whether culturally marked individuals can occupy space in the center or periphery of hegemonic discourse, whether the body can be decolonized, whether there are political and ethical limits to art, what the role of academic instruction is in a time of intensifying global censorship and crisis, and whether the artistic, political, racial, and sexual borders crossed by artists bleed into the social sphere. Such considerations, I hoped, would contribute to full-throated discussions about history, society, and culture.

To achieve the course objective, I chose a somewhat unconventional approach. In addition to the text-based materials, students were introduced to a handful of performance exercises I adapted from a performance pedagogy workshop that I attended in Santa Fe, New Mexico, organized by La Pocha Nostra. Performance exercises took five to ten minutes of each class. Exercises challenged students to introduce themselves creatively with either a 280-character tweet or a haiku. Other exercises included basic warm-ups, in which students moved around the room, and stretching and breathing exercises borrowed from dance, theater, and yoga. One effective exercise was "The Gaze," in which students held prolonged eye contact with one another. Another exercise was a poetic extension of the Surrealist game the exquisite corpse: as students stood in a circle, I used previously assigned vocabulary to form the beginnings of sentences that students would then finish. This was a fast-paced exercise that allowed me to assess students' grasp of the vocabulary in a dynamic and engaging way. Following Vicki Galloway's approach (9), I made no effort to discourage views expressed by students. This activity was a favorite; students loosened up and became energized for later discussions.

Prior to class meetings, I assigned readings with specific vocabulary and on specific themes to facilitate discussions in class. For one such discussion, the assigned vocabulary centered on borders—particularly ethnic, gender-based, geopolitical, and racial border crossings—to accompany a reading from Anzaldúa that invokes the image of the border between Mexico and the United States as "*una herida abierta* ["an open wound"] where the Third World grates against the first and bleeds" (25). Students worked together in groups to discuss ways in which the notion of borders is elaborated conceptually, metaphorically, and symbolically. To extend this discussion, I introduced students to Violeta Luna and her performance art piece *NK603: Action for Performer and E-corn*, a critical reflection on the devastating consequences of genetically modified corn and a work that provides a unique lens for exploring Anzaldúa's influential book *Borderlands / La frontera*.[2] The following is a brief summary of Luna's work and background.

Luna is a self-described actor and activist whose aesthetic projects engage ethnographic representations and hybrid entities whose cultural, political, aesthetic, and sexual identities are informed by their mixed race and their multilingual and multicontextual lives. She is a Creative Capital and National Association of Latino Arts and Cultures grant recipient and a member of the Magdalena Project: International Network of Women in Contemporary Theater. She earned graduate degrees in acting from the Centro Universitario de Teatro (University Theater Center) in 1995 and from Casa del Teatro (Theater House) in 1998, both in Mexico. She is cofounder and associate artist of the performance collaborative Seco y Mojado (Dry and Wet)—along with Víctor Cartagena, David Molina, and her husband, Roberto Gutiérrez Varea—and was previously associate director of El Teatro Jornalero sin Fronteras (Day Labor Theater without Borders). Luna has performed with the Mexican artists and directors José Caballero, Raúl Zermeño, José Ramón Enríquez, Alicia Martínez Álvarez, and Estela Leñero Franco.[3] She has performed in and directed performance workshops in Africa, Canada, Europe, Japan, Latin America, New Zealand, and the United States, and yet her solo work remains relatively unknown outside an intimate cohort of performance artists and academics.

Within this circle of collaborators and critics, she is perhaps best known for her work with the performance artist Guillermo Gómez-Peña and the performance collective La Pocha Nostra.[4] Her most noteworthy works include *Requiem for a Lost Land*, an artistic intervention in which she explores the representation of violence in terms of the human body; *Frida*, a spectacle that centers the Mexican icon and painter Frida Kahlo as the embodiment of women who challenge normative cultural values and affirm identity beyond politically and societally imposed gender boundaries; *Apuntes sobre la frontera* (*Notes on the Border*), a performance in which Luna incorporates a collage of corporeal actions and images to tell the story of an immigrant leaving her country to find better living conditions; and *NK603*.

Lured to performance art from the theater, Luna uses the human body, space, and time in ways distinct from traditional forms of dramatic discourse. According to Luna, her performance projects afford her greater autonomy, permitting her to be the action and the locus of enunciation. She operates as a free agent, able to articulate aesthetic concepts politically, even biographically. Her performances are in themselves horizontal spaces—liberated zones where she generates every aspect of the action, which, in theater, is delimited according to hierarchical roles. For Luna, performance requires thinking in terms of praxis—not only as a creator, but also as an activist. In this regard, her approach to performance moves beyond traditional relations of power that mark the actor as a tool of the director. As an actor, she sees herself as a dynamic and integral part of the dramatic process and theatrical architecture—not merely a tool in the box of a predominantly male pool of directors.

Luna identifies with hybridity on a personal and physical level; her cultural and stylistic hybridizations move beyond geopolitically reinforced markers associated with national identity and border crossings. Her works problematize notions such as ethnic and lingual purity. She believes it is her responsibility to speak out about sociopolitical issues. In this respect, there is a visceral connection between Luna's formation as an activist and the way she began to access the world of performance art. This in turn relates to her family's connections with the art world in Mexico City, and to her six sisters' influence on her work. There has always been a strong female presence in Luna's work, and that is the normative space from which she works.

Luna's performances "function as vital acts of transfer, transmitting social knowledge, memory and a sense of identity" (Taylor 2), wherein the bodily subjectivity of the performer is an end in itself, and "the site for a . . . text's genesis, appearance, and reception" (Allatson 254). Robert Neustadt observes that performance art may be read as a text, where it "is a collection of *signs* that articulates meaning through internal and intertextual juxtapositions" (xvi). Neustadt goes on to say that writers "structure texts from a myriad of linguistic, visual and political signs" (xvii), a notion that dovetails conveniently with Luna's view that performance art employs gestures and movements as a kind of language with which the performer may create meaning without a text.

Luna's intention in this piece was to mobilize public opinion against transnational corporate projects that have "nothing to do with the interests of the Mexican people, and much to do with the implementation of policies designed to grab from them land and natural resources" (Luna, *NK603* [*E-maiz*] 4). Luna notes that the groups most affected by these projects are the Mexican Native people, particularly the Raramuri, Huastecos, Cora, Huichol, Nahuatl, Purépecha, Maya, Tzotlzil, Zapotec, and Mixtec peoples.

The performance begins when Luna appears on a dimly lit dais wearing a corn-husk skirt, Zapatista bandana, serape, and straw hat. An ear of corn is emblazoned on her back. Machete in hand, she cleaves the air between herself and the spectators. Her movements are deliberate and represent the ceremonies and rituals of traditional indigenous festivals and celebrations around the sowing, growing, and harvesting of Mesoamerican corn. Also evident in Luna's portrayal is the "strength of . . . indigenous women, keepers of the corn" (Luna, *NK603* [*E-maiz*] 5). While her corn-husk skirt speaks to a symbolic female and racialized identity, her hat and machete speak to ongoing indigenous presence.

NK603 emerges from two historical markers: the North American Free Trade Agreement, signed in 1994, and the Zapatista movement. Luna uses images that expose the dangers of genetic engineering and that feature Monsanto seeds, and—in collaboration with composer David Molina—sound recordings from various social movements, including the Zapatistas, juxtaposed with recordings of scientific discourse in favor of and against the transgenic modification of corn. The soundtrack performs a textual drama that works with the other elements in the performance. In *NK603*, Luna delimits three imaginary spaces that correspond temporally to a mythical Mexican past that revolves around corn, community, and tradition, and two settings in a technologically advanced, futuristic bioengineering laboratory that belongs to a transnational corporation. These sites are distinct loci of enunciation where spatiotemporal and racial and gender relations take shape between performer, audience, and multimedia technology.

To frame the ideas introduced by *NK603*, I asked students to engage the following passage in Anzaldúa's *Borderlands*:

> Indigenous like corn, like corn, the mestiza is a product of crossbreeding, designed for preservation under a variety of conditions. Like an ear of corn—a female seed-bearing organ—the mestiza is tenacious, tightly wrapped in the husks of her culture. Like kernels she clings to the cob; with thick stalks and strong brace roots, she holds tight to the earth—she will survive the crossroads. (103)

Other critical readings included selected passages from *Reading Chican@ Like a Queer: The De-mastery of Desire* (65–69), in which Sandra K. Soto observes that in Anzaldúa's description, the mestiza is "genetically engineered corn . . . a biological hybrid" (61). After viewing Luna's performance, students explored ways in which Luna approaches corn and identity. I challenged students to explain Luna's description of *NK603*, in the synopsis accompanying the video, as a "reflection on genetically-engineered corn," where she links *maíz*, the native corn of the Americas, with a new, genetically modified identity (Luna, *NK603* [*E-corn*]). I then asked students to identify ways in which Luna's performance represents a twenty-first-century version of Anzaldúa's new mestiza—an updated border crosser, and an embodiment of what Donna Haraway calls a "hybrid of machine and organism, a creature of social reality as well as a creature of fiction" (191). Students discussed ways in which Luna's body becomes a "battleground / where enemies are kin to each other" (Anzaldúa 216) and considered how this subjective internalization of geography, and the mapping of contested cultural terrain, makes Luna's body a site from which notions of gender and *mestizaje* ("racial mixing") are reimagined and rearticulated with inclusive parameters, only to be disrupted and denatured, while their dominant cultural formations are dismantled.

Students ascertained Luna's political intentions and formed questions regarding her aesthetic articulation of indigenous iconography, wherein "black and purple corn represents the heart; white corn, the bones. Red corn represents the blood, and yellow the flesh-skin" (Luna, *NK603* [*E-maiz*] 1). They were asked to elaborate on Luna's body, painted purple as a representation of the heart of corn. I also asked them to compare Luna's imagery with Anzaldúa's descriptions of the relation between the mestiza and nature: She is "[i]ndigenous like corn," she is a "product of crossbreeding," she is like an "ear of corn," she is "tightly wrapped in the husks of her culture," and, "with thick stalks and strong brace roots, she holds tight to the earth" (Anzaldúa 103). I noted Luna's observation that for "Mexicans, and many other Latin American people, corn is not a 'thing.' It is a symbol of our origin, what gives us *existence*" (*NK603* [*E-maiz*] 1). I then asked students to consider Soto's claim that the aptitude of Anzaldúa's mestiza "originates not just from experiential knowledge but from a more innate connection to the natural" (67). I encouraged them to entertain the idea that Luna's performance calls attention to ceremonies, rituals, and organic processes as ways of knowing that inform dialogue between humans and nature.

An interesting discussion regarding the juxtaposition of native Mesoamerican corn with a new, genetically modified variety of corn led to a more prolonged conversation about the perilous relation between technology and humans. Students examined Luna's development of a hybrid identity that intersects biology, technology, the human organism, selfhood, and gender. They also debated the possible meanings of identity in light of the importance of corn, community, and traditions for a people who consider themselves "Women and Men of Maize" (*NK603* [*E-maiz*] 1). There were a lot of biology majors in the class, and the scientific knowledge they brought to the table shaped the conversation and established its tone. Some students were critical of Luna's depiction of the perils of transnational agricultural corporations in Mexico.

I asked students to consider Luna's use of the body as a conceptual map, where Luna locates memory, culture, and capitalist intervention. Bearing in mind her personal cartography, and the metaphorical space she creates, students discussed how Luna's body serves as both object and subject—signified and signifier, a site of representation and a liberated zone. This discussion extended to ways in which *NK603* incorporates Mexican iconography as it articulates concepts such as *mexicanidad* ("Mexicanness") to problematize binary constructs such as male and female, Catholic and Protestant, north and south, Anglo and indigenous, center and periphery, and interior and exterior. I asked students to correlate Luna's performance with Anzaldúa's description of the borderlands of the United States and Mexico as an open wound from which "the lifeblood of two worlds [merges] to form a third country—a border culture" (25). Students identified in Luna's work alternative, multidimensional views. They said that these views corresponded to the notion of a "third country," Luna's locus of enunciation being the aesthetic and conceptual borders that Luna crosses. Her body becomes a site of interrogation of political and social phenomena, and a site of focus on community engagement, political action, and theater.

The strategies used for the undergraduate Spanish conversation class described here would work equally well in an undergraduate English course or in a high school setting. While students' reactions varied, many students expressed appreciation for material that was taught through a different medium and for a more rounded learning experience. They were respectful of each other's views and brought diverse perspectives to topics that they described as interesting and relevant. Most students had never heard of performance art before. The integration of performance with text-based materials and group discussions that were conducted in Spanish opened their eyes to other forms of sociopolitical critique.

My approach to this class was based primarily on the notion that culture is not a material substance, a blueprint, or a finite body of knowledge; rather, culture "is made by people interacting, and at the same time determining further interaction" (Trompenaars and Hampden-Turner 24). To this end, the course did not merely teach language and culture; it got students to physically engage language *as* culture.

Notes

1. The readings assigned to students are as follows: Anzaldúa 23–35, 99–113; Moraga 79–96; Fusco; Taylor 16–52; and Sommer.

2. All biographical information about Violeta Luna used in this essay comes from two interviews I conducted with her in June 2016. See Luna, *NK603 [E-corn]* for an online video of the performance piece. The approximately thirty-three-minute video documents Luna's performance in the gallery of the Museo de Arte de la Universidad Nacional de Colombia (Art Museum of the National University of Colombia), Bogotá, on 28 August 2009, as part of the seventh *encuentro* ("meeting") of the Hemispheric Institute of Performance and Politics.

3. José Teodoro Caballero Betanzo received the Medalla de Bellas Artes in Mexico City 23 October 2017, in recognition of his distinguished forty-five-year career as one of the most recognized actors, directors, and dramaturgs of the Mexican theater. Rául Zermeño Saucedo, one of the most essential figures of Mexican theater, was an actor, docent, and director at the Compañía Nacional de Teatro de México (National Theater Company of Mexico), the Compañía Universitaria de Teatro (University Theater Company), and the Centro Universitario de Teatro. José Ramón Enríquez received the Medalla de Bellas Artes in Mexico City in 2016. For more than fifty years he has written and directed works such as *Héctor y Aquiles* (*Hector and Achilles*); *El fuego:* Ciudad sin sueño, Orestes parte *y* El fuego (*The Fire:* City without Sleep, Orestes Leaves, *and* The Fire); *Lamentaciones: Loa para la ciudad que espera* (*Lamentations: Loa for the City You Expect*); *Madre Juana* (*Mother Juana*); and *La cueva de Montesinos* (*The Cave of Montesinos*). Alicia Martínez Álvarez, founder of the center for actor training and theatre company Tablas y Diablas (Tables and Devils), graduated from the Centro Universitario de Teatro in 1987 and attended the Conservatoire Supérieur National d'Art Dramatique (National Conservatory of Dramatic Art) in Paris. She is currently the director and pedagogue of Laboratorio de la Máscara (Mask Laboratory). Estela Leñero Franco is a Mexicana director, playwright, and theater analyst whose works center Mexican women and women in general.

4. The Mexican-born interdisciplinary and multimedia performance artist and author Guillermo Gómez-Peña is an important voice in debates on identity formation, multiculturalism, and globalization. His performance art transgresses national, linguistic, and ethnographic frontiers—real and imagined—as he problematizes virtual and conceptual spaces for identity formation. He has founded several collaborative performance groups, including Poyesis Genética, The Border Arts Workshop, and La Pocha Nostra, the last of which he formed with Ro-

berto Sifuentes in 1991. That year Gómez-Peña received a MacArthur fellowship for his performance works and texts. An international performance troupe, La Pocha Nostra also includes collaborating artists Michéle Ceballos, Saul Lopez Garcia, Gabriela Salgado, Emma Tramposch, Dani D'Emilia, and Erica Mott, in addition to Violeta Luna. For more information, see www.guillermogomezpena.com/la-pocha-nostra/.

Works Cited

Allatson, Paul. *Latino Dreams: Transcultural Traffic and the U.S. National Imaginary*. Rodopi, 2002.

Anzaldúa, Gloria. *Borderlands / La frontera: The New Mestiza*. 3rd ed., Aunt Lute Books, 2007.

Fusco, Coco. "La historia del performance intercultural." *Estudios avanzados de performance*, edited by Diana Taylor and Marcela Fuentes, Fondo de Cultura Económica, 2011, pp. 305–42.

Galloway, Vicki. "Giving Dimension to *Mappaemundi*: The Matter of Perspective." *Teaching Cultures of the Hispanic World: Products and Practices of Perspective*, edited by Galloway, Cengage Learning, 2001, pp. 3–64.

Haraway, Donna. "A Manifesto for Cyborgs: Science, Technology, and Socialist Feminism in the 1980s." *Feminism/Postmodernism*, edited by Linda J. Nicholson, Routledge, 1990, pp. 190–233.

Luna, Violeta. *NK603: Action for Performance and E-corn*. 28 Aug. 2009. Hemispheric Institute Digital Video Library, hidvl.nyu.edu/video/003678529.html.

———. *NK603: Action for Performance and E-maiz*. 2015, California State University, Los Angeles. Transcript.

Moraga, Cherríe. *Indígena as Scribe: The (W)Rite to Remember*. Duke UP, 2005.

Neustadt, Robert. *(Con)Fusing Signs and Postmodern Positions*. Routledge, 1999.

Sommer, Doris. "Slaps and Embraces: A Rhetoric of Particularism." *Latin American Subaltern Studies Reader*, edited by Ileana Rodríguez, Duke UP, 2001, pp. 175–90.

Soto, Sandra K. *Reading Chican@ Like a Queer: The De-mastery of Desire*. U of Texas P, 2010.

Taylor, Diana. *The Archive and the Repertoire: Performing Cultural Memory in the Americas*. Duke UP, 2003.

Trompenaars, Fons, and Charles Hampden-Turner. *Riding the Waves of Culture: Understanding Diversity in Global Business*. 2nd ed., McGraw Hill, 1998.

Notes on Contributors

Carolina E. Alonso is assistant professor of borders and languages and gender and sexuality studies at Fort Lewis College in Durango, Colorado. She holds a PhD from the University of Houston and an MA and a BA from the University of Texas, Rio Grande Valley. Her research interests include Latinx literature in the United States and Latin American literature, gender and sexuality studies, and queer theory. Her publications include the forthcoming book chapters "The Coming-of-Age Experience in Chicanx Queer Novels" (2020) and "Teaching Gloria Anzaldúa: Decolonizing, Writing, and Healing in the Classroom" (2021). She is a border native from Reynosa in Tamaulipas, Mexico, and from the Rio Grande Valley region in Texas.

Laura P. Alonso-Gallo is professor of English at Barry University. She earned her BA, MA, and PhD degrees at the Universidad Complutense de Madrid, Spain. She has lectured on Spanish and Latin American literature and literature in the United States both in Spain and in the United States. Her scholarly work concentrates on Latino/a literature and comparative literature. She has contributed articles and chapters to books in the field of Chicano/a, Cuban American, and Dominican American fiction and has edited or coedited several critical volumes on contemporary American literature, her most recent edited collection being *Postnacionalismo e identidad en la cultura cubana* (2019).

Marcel Brousseau is visiting assistant professor of English and an affiliate of the Indigenous, Race, and Ethnic Studies Department at the University of Oregon. From 2015 to 2017 he served as Carlos E. Castañeda Postdoctoral Fellow in the Center for Mexican American Studies at the University of Texas, Austin. He earned his PhD in comparative literature at the University of California, Santa Barbara. He has published articles on Gloria Anzaldúa and the poetics of the border wall between the United States and Mexico, the symbolism of bridges and tunnels on the border, and Kiowa literary and digital mapping, and he is working on the book *Cultural Techniques of the Trans-American Borderlands*, which is under contract.

Jessica Burke earned a doctorate in Spanish from Princeton University in 2005 and is currently associate professor of Hispanic studies at Hamilton College. Her research and teaching interests include Latin American literatures and cultures, and she is especially interested in Mexico, gender studies, and the twentieth-century novel. Burke has published articles on the works of Carmen Boullosa, José Donoso, Elena Garro, Manuel Puig, and Pedro Almodóvar.

Margaret Cantú-Sánchez teaches composition and literature courses with a focus on Latinx theory and literature at St. Mary's University. Her PhD in English, with a specialization in Latino/a literature, is from the University of Texas, San Antonio. Her research focuses on the identity conflict imposed on Latinx students by Anglocentric institutions of learning. As an instructor at a Hispanic-serving institution, she strives to include multicultural texts in the courses that she teaches there, especially courses in the core curriculum. She writes about the teaching of Latinx literature and theory and is the lead coeditor of *Teaching Gloria E. Anzaldúa: Pedagogy and Practice for Our Classrooms and Communities* (2020).

Sheila Marie Contreras is associate professor in the Department of English and was previously director of Chicano/Latino studies at Michigan State University. Her research and teaching interests include Chicanx and Latinx literature in the United States, comparative indigeneities, and women's studies. Contreras's book *Blood Lines: Myth, Indigenism, and Chicana/o Literature* (2008) examines indigenism in Chicanx literary and cultural discourse. Her current research agenda includes a comparatist literary exploration of indigeneity and the relation to land in Chicanx literature and activism, and an interdisciplinary project on Latinx undergraduate success. Contreras entered higher education as a first-generation student and began her journey to the PhD in the community college system of south Texas.

David S. Dalton is assistant professor of Spanish at the University of North Carolina, Charlotte. He is the author of *Mestizo Modernity: Race, Technology, and the Body in Postrevolutionary Mexico* (2018) and a coeditor of *Ibero-American Zombies: Undead Colonialism*, a special issue of *Alambique: Revista Académica de Ciencia Ficción y Fantasía* (2018). His research focuses primarily on the intersections of science, race, and technology in Mexico. He has published numerous articles, is currently coediting two volumes, and is working on his next book, "Neoliberalism: Markets of Death and Cyborg Resistance in Post-NAFTA Mexico."

Elena Díaz Björkquist is the author of *Suffer Smoke* and *Water from the Moon* and coeditor of *Sowing the Seeds, una Cosecha de Recuerdos* and *Our Spirit, Our Reality: Celebrating Our Stories.* She is a Southwest Institute for Research on Women scholar at the University of Arizona. For eighteen years as an Arizona Humanities Road Scholar, she performed in a living history presentation as Teresa Urrea, a *curandera* ("woman healer"), not only in Arizona but also at the University of California, Davis; the University of New Mexico, Albuquerque and Las Cruces; and the University of Texas, El Paso and San Antonio. In 2012 Arizona Humanities presented her with the Dan Schilling Public Humanities Scholar Award in recognition of her research and presentations of Teresa Urrea.

Emron Esplin is associate professor of English at Brigham Young University, where he teaches courses in literature of the United States and inter-American literary studies. He is the editor, with Margarida Vale de Gato, of *Translated Poe* (2014) and *Anthologizing Poe: Editions, Translations, and (Trans)National Canons* (2020), and he edits the journal *Poe Studies: History, Theory, Interpretation*. His monograph, *Borges's Poe: The Influence and Reinvention of Edgar Allan Poe in Spanish America*, was published by the University of Georgia Press in the New Southern Studies series in 2016. He has also published articles on Katherine Anne Porter, Nellie Campobello, Pancho Villa, William Faulkner, Julio Cortázar, and Nathaniel Hawthorne.

Oswaldo Estrada is professor of Latin American literature at the University of North Carolina, Chapel Hill. He is the author of *La imaginación novelesca: Bernal Díaz entre géneros y épocas* (2009), *Ser mujer y estar presente: Disidencias de género en la literatura mexicana contemporánea* (2014), and *Troubled Memories: Iconic Mexican Women and the Traps of Representation* (2018). He has edited *Cristina Rivera Garza: Ningún crítico cuenta esto . . .* (2010), *Colonial Itineraries of Contemporary Mexico: Literary and Cultural Inquiries* (with Anna M. Nogar; 2014), *Senderos de violencia: Latinoamérica y sus narrativas armadas* (2015), *McCrack: McOndo, el Crack y los destinos de la literatura latinoamericana* (with Pablo Brescia; 2018), and *Literatura y globalización: Latinoamérica en el nuevo milenio* (with Eva Valero Juan; 2019).

Shelley García earned her PhD in English at the University of California, Riverside, and teaches in Southern California at Biola University. Her research and publications focus on innovative writings by Latinx authors. She utilizes the lens of genre studies to explain the work of groundbreaking authors in terms of both deep literary history and current disciplinary approaches. Her teaching demonstrates similar breadth, covering studies in genre, American literature, gender studies, and composition.

Pedro García-Caro is associate professor of Spanish at the University of Oregon and directs the Latin American studies program. His recent work has been on the cultural history of mining (literature, film, and photography) in the Western hemisphere during the nineteenth and twentieth centuries. His publications include *Transatlantic Studies: Latin America, Iberia, Africa* (coedited; 2019); *After the Nation: Postnational Satire in the Works of Carlos Fuentes and Thomas Pynchon* (2014); a critical edition of the first secular play performed in California in the late eighteenth century, *Astucias por heredar un sobrino a un tío*, by Fermín de Reygadas (2018); and a Spanish translation of Wallace Shawn's *The Fever*, with Rafael Spregelburd (2012).

Nathanial Gardner is a tenured academic at the University of Glasgow, where he researches on text and image in Latin America and collaborates with the Stirling Maxwell Centre for the Study of Text and Image. He is a member of the research network University of California Mexicanists and the research unit on text, image, media, and translation at the Universidad de Salamanca, Spain, where he has been a visiting Erasmus professor. He has recently completed a book on Latin American photography for the University of New Mexico Press.

Rabi'a Hakima is assistant professor of English at East Georgia State College in Augusta. She earned her PhD in English from Auburn University with concentrations in feminist theory, nineteenth-century literature of the United States, and women's poetry. She has taught college composition, world literature, and multicultural literature of the United States since 2003. She is working on a lyric narrative as well as her first novel.

Emily Hind is associate professor at the University of Florida, where she received a University Term Professorship for distinguished scholarship, 2016–19, and was voted Professor of the Year, 2016–17, by graduate students in the Hispanic literature program. She was a Fulbright scholar in 2015. Her latest book is *Dude Lit: Mexican Men Writing and Performing Competence, 1955–2012* (2019). In 2020, Peter Lang will publish her third book of interviews with Mexican writers, this one focusing on children's and YA literature.

Mary Jane Hurst is professor emeritus of English at Texas Tech University, where she taught for more than thirty years; she also served for six years as associate dean of the College of Arts and Sciences, and for three years as special assistant to the president. Recipient of the President's Book Award, the Faculty Distinguished Service Award, and the President's Excellence in Teaching Award, she publishes on linguistics, literature, and professional issues. Her primary research area is language in literature.

Leigh C. Johnson is associate professor of English at Marymount University in Arlington, Virginia. She directs the small but active gender and society minor and teaches American literature, ethnic literary traditions, and composition to (mostly) nonmajors. Her research is on the intersections of race, gender, ethnicity, and motherwork. She has published in *Meridians*, *Rejoinder*, and *American Literary Naturalism.*

Beth E. Jörgensen is professor emerita of Spanish at the University of Rochester. Her research and teaching areas include Mexican women writers, the genre of the chronicle, theory of nonfiction, and literary representations of disability. Her publications include *The Writing of Elena Poniatowska: Engaging Dialogues* (1994), *Documents in Crisis: Nonfiction Literatures in Twentieth-Century Mexico* (2011), and the edited volumes *The Contemporary Mexican Chronicle: Theoretical Perspectives on the Liminal Genre* (2002), with Ignacio Corona; and *Libre Acceso: Latin American Literature and Film* *through Disability Studies* (2016), with Susan Antebi. She translated *Los de abajo*, by Mariano Azuela, as *The Underdogs* (2002), and she has written articles on Rosario Castellanos, Benita Galeana, Margo Glantz, Lina Meruane, Carlos Monsiváis, Elena Poniatowska, María Luisa Puga, and Juan Villoro.

Magdalena Maíz-Peña is the William H. Williamson Professor of Hispanic Studies at Davidson College. She specializes in contemporary Latin American women writers, life writing, gender, and the politics of representation. Her teaching interests include Latin American human rights, the Latin American or Latino city, and twenty-first-century Latin American short narratives. She edited a book with Nora Erro-Peralta, *La palabra contra el silencio: Elena Poniatowska ante la crítica* (2013), and a special issue of *Diálogo* with Elizabeth C. Martinez, *Teaching the Works of Elena Poniatowska in Twenty-First-Century Frames* (Spring 2014). She has served on the boards of the North Carolina Humanities Council, the Charlotte Mecklenburg Library, The Levine Museum of the New South, and E2D: Eliminate the Digital Divide.

Elizabeth Coonrod Martínez is professor of Latin American and Latino studies at DePaul University, where she served as director of the Center for Latino Research and editor of *Diálogo: An Interdisciplinary Studies Journal*, published with U of Texas P, between 2010 and 2019. In 2015 the journal received the Council of Editors of Learned Journals' Phoenix Award for outstanding revitalization and transformation of a journal over a three-year period. She has published articles on contemporary Latin American and Latino literature and culture; her books include a critical study of the 1920s Latin American vanguard novel, a critical biography on the playwright and novelist Josefina Niggli, and a translated collection of Elena Poniatowska's stories. Martínez previously held a professorship at Sonoma State University in California, where in 2006 she received the President's Teaching Excellence Award.

Mark J. Mascia received his PhD at Columbia University and is associate professor of Spanish at Sacred Heart University. His publications include articles on golden-age Spanish literature, twentieth-century Latin American poetry, and the twentieth-century Spanish novel. Within the golden age, his principal interests are metapoetry and the *conceptismo-culteranismo* debate, and Lope de Vega's lyric poetry. From 2012 to 2020, he was secretary-treasurer of the Society for Renaissance and Baroque Hispanic Poetry. He has developed courses for his department's undergraduate program on the *Siglo de oro*, notably the Society of Golden Age Spain, among numerous other advanced courses.

Anne M. McGee is associate professor of Spanish at Arkansas State University, Jonesboro. She teaches courses in Latin American literature and culture and specializes in Mexican literature. Her current research centers on questions of border and regional identities in the literature and cultural production of northern Mexico and the borderlands of the United States and Mexico. She has published articles on the works of Luis Humberto Crosthwaite, Arturo Pérez Reverte, Nellie Campobello, Sandra Cisneros, and Gloria Anzaldúa.

Manuel F. Medina is professor in the Department of Classical and Modern Languages at the University of Louisville. He received his doctorate in Spanish from the University of Kansas. He has published extensively and read papers at professional meetings on topics related to his areas of interest in the narrative, film, and theater of Latin America and of Latinos in the United States. His book *Archivo y discurso en la nueva novela histórica mexicana* (2012) is a cultural studies analysis of Mexican fiction in the 1980s. He serves as the current president of the Asociación de Ecuatorianistas.

Susan C. Méndez earned her doctorate at the University of California, Riverside. She is professor in the English and Theatre Department and the Department of Latin American and Women's Studies at the University of Scranton. Her courses address multiethnic American literature and are cross-listed with the university's peace and justice studies program. Her research primarily addresses Latina/o literary texts, namely novels, and her articles have appeared in *Centro: Journal of the Center for Puerto Rican Studies*, *Chicana/Latina Studies*, *Afro-Hispanic Review*, *Label Me Latina/o*, and *Latin American Literary Review*.

Carol E. Pearson is professor emerita of Spanish and Latin American literature and culture and former chair in the Modern Languages Department at North Dakota State University. Her publications, including articles in *Hispania*, *Confluencia*, and *Interdisciplinary Literary Studies*, have focused on resistance and gender in works by contemporary Central American, Mexican, and Chicana women authors.

Liliana Pedroza, author and researcher, holds a PhD in Hispanoamerican literature from the Universidad Complutense de Madrid in Spain and is a specialist in contemporary Mexican short stories. She is a member of Seminario de Estudios de Narrativa Latinoamericana Contemporánea in the Universidad Nacional Autónoma de México. Her publications include a book of essays, *Andamos huyendo, Elena*, on works by Elena Garro, and the book *Historia secreta del cuento mexicano, 1910–2017*, a historiographic catalog of short stories by more than five hundred Mexican women writers.

Luis H. Peña is professor in the Department of Hispanic Studies and Latin American Studies at Davidson College. He received his doctorate from Arizona State University. His books include *La metamorfosis del deseo: Una aproximación a la narrativa mexicana contemporánea, 1958–1970* and *Mo-*

dalidades de representación del sujeto auto/biográfico femenino. He has published extensively and read papers at professional meetings on topics related to his areas of interest in twentieth- and twenty-first-century Latin American film, literature, and culture, Latin American literary and cultural theories since the 1960s, and images of the border between the United States and Mexico. Two of his recent essays are "Memoria, diálogo y escritura: *Hasta no verte Jesús mío*" and "Intersticios, cruzamientos e intersecciones: Desafíos pedagógicos en *La noche de Tlatelolco* de Elena Poniatowska."

Ashley Hope Pérez is assistant professor of world literatures in the Department of Comparative Studies at Ohio State University. Her research focuses on narrative ethics in twentieth-century Latin American and Latinx literatures. She is also the author of three novels, including *Out of Darkness*, which won the Américas Award and the Tomás Rivera Book Award.

Betsy A. Sandlin is associate dean for inclusion and faculty development and professor of Spanish at the University of the South in Sewanee, Tennessee, and serves as director of the annual Summer Teaching and Learning Workshop hosted by the Associated Colleges of the South, a consortium of sixteen liberal arts colleges. She teaches Spanish, from beginner language courses to upper-level seminars on Latinx and Latin American literature and culture. Her current research interests include faculty development, inclusive teaching practices, language pedagogy, and gender and sexuality in contemporary Latinx literature. She holds a PhD in Latin American literature from the University of North Carolina, Chapel Hill.

Adrianna M. Santos earned her BA in English from the University of Texas, Austin, and her MA and PhD in Chicana/o studies with an emphasis on feminist studies from the University of California, Santa Barbara. She teaches Chicanx and Latinx literature as assistant professor of English at Texas A&M University, San Antonio, where she is faculty advisor for the Mexican American Student Association. She was awarded membership in the National Women's Studies Association's Women of Color Leadership Project and has volunteered at the Santa Barbara Rape Crisis Center and Child Advocates of San Antonio. She has published on antiviolence advocacy in *El Mundo Zurdo* and *Aztlán* and has spoken on the subject at various conferences. She is working on a book manuscript, "Beyond Survival: Trauma Studies and Chicanx Poetics in the Literary Borderlands."

Peter Schmidt is the William R. Kenan Professor of English Literature at Swarthmore College. He specializes in literature of the twentieth and twenty-first centuries in the United States and lyric poetry from the Middle Ages to the present. His books are on William Carlos Williams, Eudora Welty, and southern fiction of the post–Civil War period that debates Reconstruction, Black education, civil rights, white supremacy, and the future of postslavery democracy. He edited (with Amritjit Singh) the anthology *Postcolonial Theory and the U.S.* Current projects include online lesson plans for high school and university American literature classes and a series of essays on how the portrayal of multiracial families in contemporary fiction in the United States revises our national narrative.

William R. Stark is lecturer in Spanish at the University of Rhode Island and was previously visiting assistant professor at Brown University. He earned his BA in French studies from Western Washington University, his MA in Hispanic studies from the University of Rhode Island, and his doctorate in Spanish studies from the University of Connecticut. His research and teaching interests include Latin American literatures and cultures and Chicano and Latino cultural production, with an emphasis on transcultural performance art in the United States since the 1980s. Cofounder of the online, peer-reviewed *The Quiet Corner Interdisciplinary Journal*, at the University of Connecticut, he is currently working on a monograph that examines the work of the performance artists Guillermo Gómez-Peña, Coco Fusco, Violeta Luna, and Roberto Sifuentes and the group La Pocha Nostra.

Ron Thomas is professor of American literature at Baylor University. He teaches survey courses and the contemporary novel, including the Chicano novel, to both undergraduate and graduate students. He has published on Ezra Pound, Robert Frost, and Henry David Thoreau, among others.

Norma A. Valenzuela is assistant professor of Spanish at New Mexico Highlands University. She earned her MA and PhD in Spanish cultural studies from Arizona State University. Her book *Lourdes Portillo: Luchas feministas barriales y transnacionales:* Después del terremoto, Las Madres *y* Señorita extraviada (2012) is the first monograph that positions Lourdes Portillo as a Chicana transnational filmmaker. Her essay "Mestiza Consciousness a la MeXicana in Ultima and Agueda Martínez: Bridging and Legitimizing Querencia in the Borderlands" will be published in the 2020 Querencia anthology.

Alberto Varon is assistant professor of English and Latino studies at Indiana University Bloomington. He is the author of *Before Chicano: Citizenship and the Making of Mexican American Manhood, 1848–1959* (2018).